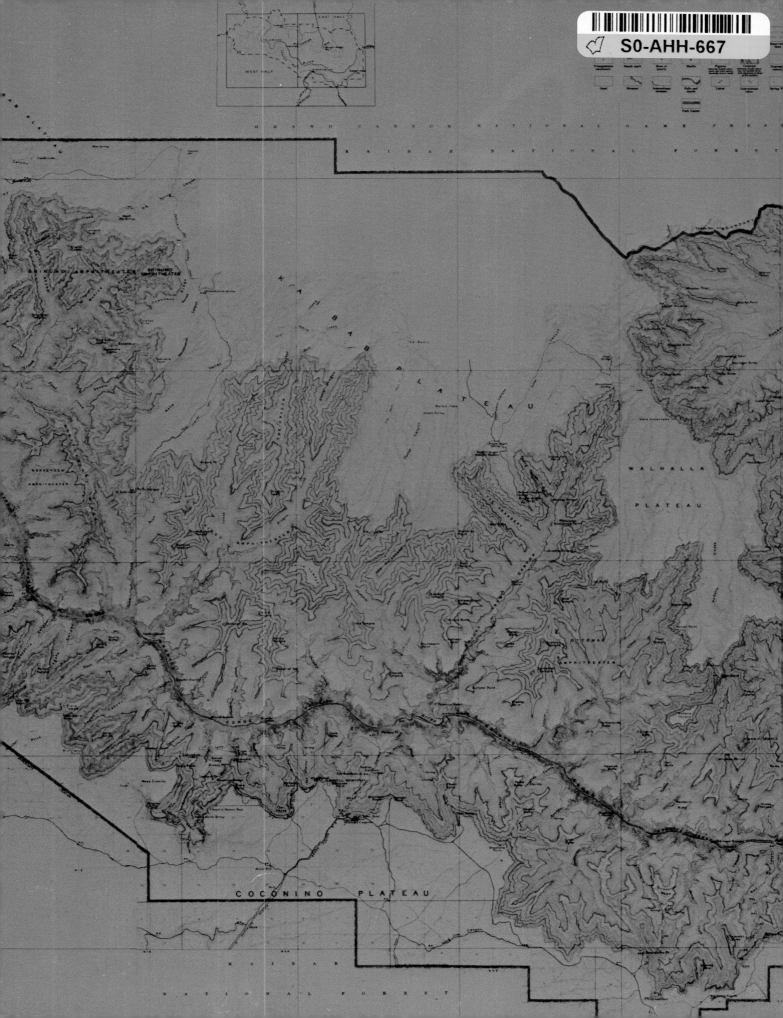

THE GRAND COLORADO

*The Story of a River
and its Canyons*

When men first looked
upon the river and its
canyons, they found in
them myths and dreams;
these briefly-glimpsed
chasms were beyond the
experience of European
civilization, too awesome
for comprehension, too
beautiful for belief...

Twenty-seven Miles Rapids, Marble Gorge, Grand Cañyon National Park

THE GRAND

COLORADO

Glen Cañyon bend above Klondike

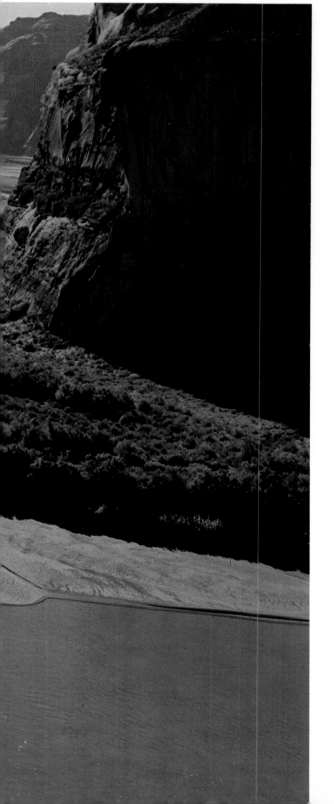

The Story of a River and its Canyons

By T. H. Watkins
and Contributors

William E. Brown, Jr.	Roger Olmsted
Robert C. Euler	Wallace Stegner
Helen Hosmer	Paul S. Taylor
Roderick Nash	Robert A. Weinstein

With a Foreword by Wallace Stegner

Color Photography by Philip Hyde

Published by American West Publishing Company

Granite Falls, Grand Cañyon National Park

Portions of this book first appeared in the following publications and are used here by permission: "The Diary of the Escalante Expedition," translated and edited by Herbert E. Bolton in the *Utah Historical Quarterly*, January-October, 1950; "The West of William H. Ashley, 1822 to 1838" (Fred A. Rosenstock, 1964), edited by Dale Morgan, 1954-1955; *Beyond the Hundredth Meridian* by Wallace Stegner (Houghton-Mifflin, 1954); *Desert Solitaire: A Season in the Wilderness* by Edward Abbey (McGraw-Hill, 1968); *Open Horizons* by Sigurd Olson (Alfred A. Knopf, 1969); *Grand Canyon: Today and All Its Yesterdays* by Joseph Wood Krutch (William Sloane Associates, 1957); *Through the Grand Canyon from Wyoming to Mexico* by Ellsworth Kolb (Macmillan, 1914).

Library of Congress Catalog Card Number 71-88204

CONTENTS

FOREWORD

IT IS OFTEN SAID that to stand on the rim of the Grand Canyon is to be made aware of our human littleness and transience, and it is assumed as a corollary that this experience is good for us. It brings us down to size. But I wonder. Transience, yes; littleness, not so certainly. Some observers may even feel a half-conscious satisfaction that simply by *looking* they are making that mighty gorge serve their human need.

A river traverses time as well as topography, it runs not only through country but through mankind. So far as I can see, there is no particular sanity, health, or satisfaction in being forced to an awareness of geological time. Imagining what the Colorado River may have been like ten million years ago is an abstract exercise like imagining a moonscape. But imagining that minute in the year 1540 when Cárdenas' men rode up to the Grand Canyon rim and looked unbelievingly into the chasm—that is something else. The human response is somehow important.

Magnificent as they are, the most instructive geological display and probably the greatest natural spectacle on earth, the canyons of the Colorado sometimes disappoint. They may oppress the observer instead of uplifting him. Sometimes an especially honest tourist, oversold on the clichés of grandeur, will admit to being bored, and many never stay long enough to adjust to this "great innovation in natural scenery."

That adjustment is necessary, as Dutton insists, and it is more than getting used to bizarre colors and unfamiliar forms. It involves scale as well—and I don't think we adjust ourselves to inhuman size and geological time. Quite the reverse. The viewer must reassert human scale and human time in the teeth of a spectacle where time and topography are dismayingly one, and too big to be readily grasped. The reactions of dogs and poets on the rim are suggestive. Dogs, having no way of reasserting their doggish scale, very often get the shakes. Poets begin at once to put the canyon into words, and thus make it behave in a way that poets can understand.

Incorrigibly anthropocentric as we are, we can only respond humanly. In the canyons I have seen people get so used to magnificent scenery that they quit noticing it, but I have never seen anyone who was not instantly galvanized by signs of human habitation down there, however small: a walled granary tucked into a cave above Nankoweap Rapid, a line of steps chiseled up the sandstone in Navajo Canyon, perhaps even a rare find such as a split-twig figurine put into a cave thousands of years ago by some stone-age hunter. A hunter who made such a figurine was trying by sympathetic magic to bend the forces of nature to his intense little human purpose: to make the rabbit run into the snare, to bring the bighorn within range. He was not so different from the rest of us; and the more impressive the natural force or object that we try to control, the greater the satisfaction if we seem to succeed. I used to have a schnauzer dog that adored chasing moose up in the Grand Teton country. I am sure that when she put a bull with a six-foot rack down the meadow she felt twice as big and important as when she only made a marmot dive down his hole.

In something like that fashion, I believe, the Colorado's canyons at first appall and oppress us with their inhuman scale and their message from inhuman geological time, but in the end reassure us. Even here, in this inhospitable rock desert, in this place where the earth is

Wallace Stegner

gashed open to the dark mile-deep bone, people have made marks, even homes. The chasm that dismays me was once some Indian's front yard.

IT IS THE ATTEMPT of this book to provide a profile of the Colorado River, not so much through topography and geological time as through human time, human history. The river matters to men only insofar as they have discovered and used it, and recorded what they knew. It is a surprisingly long record, considering how long the river was hidden in legend and guess, and how thin the population of the region, aboriginal or Spanish or American, has always been. For the first time within a single set of covers, it is possible to follow the process of discovery from the day when Cárdenas reached the rim, a year before De Soto discovered the Mississippi and less than fifty years after Columbus made landfall in the Indies, to the day in August, 1869, when Major Powell's party floated out the gateway of the Grand Wash Cliffs. It is further possible, in this same single volume, to trace the uses and abuses of the river by human agencies in the hundred years since Powell brought it into the known world. The Colorado's history may be thin, but it is longer than that of any major American river.

Long, thin, and intermittent; much of what was known faded out and had to be rediscovered. Almost all of it had been forgotten when Lieutenant Ives and later Powell attacked the river from opposite ends and made the legendary stream into a factual one. The earliest history, that which was recorded only by archaeological remains, had never been known; the beginning of knowledge in that line came when Powell found dwellings and granaries in Glen Canyon. What little we know of the prehistoric tribes of the Colorado basin has since been painstakingly put together by many hands, for human history is not a thing to be run and mapped like a canyon, but an artifact to be assembled, recorded, interpreted, and understood; it does not exist until it has been written.

It did not exist for Major Powell. When he pushed off from Green River, Wyoming, on May 24, 1869, he knew nothing of what the Spaniards had discovered, and practically nothing about the mountain men who had trapped the headwater streams (he did not know who Ashley was, for instance). He did know the reports of Lieutenant Ives, and he had read and discounted the newspaper reports of James White's raft journey. He also says that he carried with him a diary of Jacob Hamblin's covering the stretch from the Grand Wash Cliffs to Callville, but he must have carried that on his second expedition, since he had not yet met Hamblin when he made the first; and if he carried it on the second expedition he never got to make use of it, for he left the river at Kanab Wash.

What men had discovered and then forgotten or mislaid when Powell started through the canyons is all here in this book, most of it in the words of the men who did the discovering. Nothing less than their own words will do, for they were very different men, of different centuries and different civilizations, and no paraphrase could communicate so vividly their varieties of response: the dismay of the Cárdenas party as reported by Castañeda; the laconics of Father Escalante; the muscular matter-of-factness of Ives; the romantic nature-appreciation, enlightened by science, of Powell and Dutton.

Powell is basic to any book about the Colorado, the great Ancestor, the first man who ob-
served what he saw instead of what he wanted to see or what he persuaded himself he had seen.
As this book amply demonstrates, it was he and his assistants Dutton, Gilbert, Thompson, and
Holmes who made the Plateau Province a province of knowledge. Thus it is not inappropriate
that *The Grand Colorado* is published on the hundredth anniversary of Powell's exploration.
That trip tied headwaters to lower river and filled in the last great blank on the map of the
United States. Powell began the geological studies that Dutton and Gilbert carried on; he
founded the bureau through which later studies were largely made.

It was not only as an explorer and scientist that he was seminal. Through his lectures and
his *Report,* through the sketches and paintings of his artists Moran and Holmes, through the
stereopticon views taken by his photographers Beaman, Fennemore, and Hillers, he put the
hitherto unknown canyons of the Colorado into ten thousand parlors. It was his publicizing that
started the Grand Canyon toward becoming what it is—a symbol of natural majesty that has
totally displaced the shopworn Niagara Falls that satisfied the young republic.

In Powell begins the study of the native tribes, both historic and prehistoric, of the area.
Even the sport of river-running owes its origin to him, and in these years when many thousands
run the canyons every summer, there is hardly a cataract boat or neoprene raft without a copy
of Powell's *Report* stowed away somewhere in a waterproof bag; and hardly a river captain
passes the mouth of the Little Colorado without reading aloud—or intoning—Powell's ominous paragraphs that record his feelings at the inner brink of the unknown.

Powell's explorations and his continuing survey of the Plateau Province helped turn to
civilian purposes, to the opening of the unknown or half-known West, national energies that
had been blown up dangerously by the Civil War. What he had learned on the desert plateaus led him to resist methods of settlement, water laws, land laws, and even time-honored
methods of subdividing land into states and counties that he knew were inappropriate or
disastrous in a dry country. He was not naive enough to believe, with the promoters of
western homestead settlement, that rain follows the plow. He proposed that no western
agriculture land be patented unless it had with it an indissoluble water right. He suggested
modifying the sacred 160 acres of the homestead law downward in irrigated land, far upward
in range land. He thought the boundaries of states and counties should be laid out along
drainage divides.

If his advice had been followed in his time, we would have been spared much built-in
difficulty, much litigation and wrangling, including a lot of the wrangling over the water of
the Colorado. In the years since the western irrigation interests broke him and discontinued
his classification of the public lands, some of what he advocated has come laboriously and
imperfectly to pass. Regional planners now make a bible of his *Report on the Lands of the
Arid Region,* and the United States Geological Survey and the Bureau of Ethnology, which
he founded, have been from the beginning models of government science.

Though he was unaware of much of its human past, Powell gave the plateau country
a solid present, and he foresaw its future problems with remarkable prescience. He stands at

the end of the time of exploration and at the beginning of the time of human control. Having cleared away the myths about the physical river, he tried all the rest of his life to correct misconceptions about the arid West, to prevent monopoly of land through water control, to discourage the optimists who believed that you could ensure an adequate water supply by simply asserting it.

The continuing controversies between preservation and reclamation interests are also in this book; a profile of the Colorado that showed it only as adventure and scenery would be sadly incomplete. It is probable that Powell would have approved some of the dams on the Colorado—Hoover probably, two or three of the upper-tributary dams possibly. He would not likely have approved them all, for he could read cost-benefit ratios and appreciate grand scenery; and he would have deplored the way in which the reclamation law he favored and did much to bring about has often been perverted to the uses of monopolistic groups of precisely the sort he foresaw and resisted.

ALONG WITH THE story of the human time through which the Colorado runs, the pages of this book contain bundles of "images" that are the next best thing to standing on the rim or running the river. The whole river is literally here, as I think it has been in no single book heretofore, not to make propaganda for a specific conservationist or resource-development position, but to illustrate the complexity—and I insist it is a human complexity—of a great river.

If it is really consoling, there is the consolation of geological time for those who deplore, as I do, the engineering that would further tame and harness our greatest natural wonder and mutilate our greatest scenic (which is to say spiritual) resource. It is completely true that human engineering can modify the Colorado, and to some extent has; can tame it, and to some degree has; can diminish it, and to some degree has. But kill it we cannot. All we have to do is to shift into geological time, and we can smile at the dams and power plants. The river will cut through them, after a century or two, as it has cut through the lava dike at Lava Falls, or as it has split the Uinta Mountains. There, as the mountains rose across its course, the river simply dug in. In Powell's words, it cut through the uplift as a saw cuts through a log held against it.

He called it an "antecedent" stream, by which he meant it has the tools to overcome interruptions on its way to eternity, that gently rolling plain from which human engineering will be wiped away as the cliffs and towers and buttes of the Grand Canyon will be wiped away.

But that is not much of a consolation. We are on our way to eternity too, but by a shorter path, and it is no help to us to have the dams wiped out by a process that wipes out everything else. We couldn't wait for it if we wanted to. So we must take the Colorado on our human terms, and from among the purposes that it might serve, elect those that seem most lasting and most satisfying. Both the ages and man have been at work on that river and those canyons. Short of a visit, or many visits, this book is the best way I know for a citizen to find out which has been doing the better job.

PART ONE:

THE MYTH

15

INTRODUCTION

IT IS ONE of the great rivers of the West. It extends 1,700 miles from its source in the Laramie Range of southeastern Wyoming to its mouth in the Gulf of California. Together with its hundreds of tributaries and sub-tributaries—among them the Gunnison, the Green, the Dirty Devil, the San Juan, the Little Colorado, the Virgin, and the Gila—it is the dominant river system in the entire southwestern corner of America, draining an area one-twelfth the size of the continental United States, including parts of Wyoming, Colorado, Utah, Nevada, California, New Mexico, and almost all of Arizona. The land through which it travels and which it has helped to shape contains three distinct geographic provinces and some of the most varied and spectacular natural beauty on the face of the earth. Beginning in the high ranges and parklands of the Rocky Mountains, it courses southwest through the sheer canyons it has cut into the enormous plateaus of Utah and Arizona—the Kaiparowits, the Paria, the Kaibab, the Kanab, the Unkaret, the Coconino, and the Shivwits—and finally winds through the Mojave, Colorado, and Sonoran deserts on the final leg of its journey to the sea. And in that long journeying, it lays bare the face of time.

The Colorado is a young river, as the ages of rivers are measured, even though it was born in mists of time so distant they are beyond human scale or understanding. Twelve million years ago, give or take a few hundred thousand years, a trickle of water began to cut a channel in the top of an enormous plateau laid down by nearly two billion years of sedimentation. In time, in much time, the trickle became a stream and then a river that ultimately reached the sea. Slowly, using the grinding and cutting tools of rock, gravel, and sand, it began to slice its way down into the great plateau, tearing it down, carrying it grain by grain to the sea. For like all rivers, the Colorado had a job to do from youth to maturity: to erode its way down to the level of the sea, and in the process to carry the land with it, reducing all to the level of a plain. As it coursed deeper and deeper into the plateau, tributaries began to form, adding their own efforts to the enormous task, and the ancient layers of the plateau were exposed, one by one: the limestones, sandstones, and shales of the Permian Period, deposited more than two hundred million years ago; through the deeper rocks of the Mississippian, Devonian, and Cambrian periods, laid down as long ago as a billion years; and finally down to the very rocks from which the earth began, those of the Archeozoic Era.

The task began perhaps twelve million years ago, and the river has cut through nearly six thousand feet of the plateau; yet the job has only begun, for several million years ago the land mass began to rise, as it had many times before, slowly swelling and wrinkling, creating new mountain ranges and mesas, and presenting the river with another five thousand feet of the earth's crust to contend with. The land is still rising. So the river continues, slowed now by all the dams that have stoppered its flow, grinding its way further into the earth, never being able to do more than slice its bed deeper and deeper, never being able to reduce the surrounding land. In this way, the river formed —and continues to form—the wondrous maze of its canyons, carving them out of sedimentary rocks accumulated by all the millennia of geological evolution and exposing a nearly complete record of the earth's history from that dim moment in the unimaginable past when its molten skin began to cool and harden.

I T IS NO WONDER that when men first looked upon the river and its canyons, they found in them myths and dreams. The river was a mystery, its canyons too awesome for comprehension, too beautiful for belief. The Indians, who first came to the Colorado's canyons more than four thousand years ago, must have felt the magic that hovered in a land which spoke of the beginning of time itself. Secure in their serene relationship with the natural order of things, the Indians could accept the land; but the first Europeans, who did not come until the middle of the sixteenth century, could neither accept nor understand. The river was a symbol and embodiment of the vast mystery of a land the Spanish priests and soldiers who traversed it would never fully know; a river encountered but never realized; a river whose briefly glimpsed chasms were beyond the experience of European civilization, a ghastly affront, an outrage upon the earth, the representation of a mediaeval hell.

T HE ANGLO-SAXON EXPLORERS who came to the river in the nineteenth century were less susceptible to the impossible legends that had seduced the Spanish into the arid, tumbling-down country of the Colorado. Yet even they could not resist the temptation to see in the river and its canyons their own kind of legends and distortions—that the river harbored fortunes in gold, that it was the West's "natural thoroughfare" to the Pacific, that it could become the center of a new civilization. It would not be until Major John Wesley Powell and his men rode the wild river in 1869 that these myths would begin to fade, and for more than three centuries the Colorado would never be completely free of the dark trappings of fantasy and fable.

CHAPTER I

THE CANYON DWELLERS

Four Thousand Years of Human History in the Grand Canyon

Robert C. Euler

FOUR THOUSAND YEARS before Major Powell's men tumbled through the Grand Canyon in their wooden boats, before geologists and archaeologists investigated its lessons and records, before photographers adjusted their focus and tourists stood on the south rim in awe—four thousand years before all this, human beings had wandered the Canyon's depths.

These men were prehistoric American Indians, primitive hunters and gatherers who used isolated caves in the Canyon's bottom as religious shrines. In several limestone-solution caverns they deposited caches of ingenious split-willow figurines of animals. Many of these effigies were pierced, probably in ritualistic fashion, with tiny wooden sticks seemingly meant to represent spears, and archaeologists believe that this was some type of imitative hunting magic. If a miniature figure of the animal to be hunted were ritually killed, success would be more certain in the actual quest.

When such split-willow figurines were first discovered in the Canyon in 1933, their great antiquity was not realized. In the late 1950's some of the figurines were radiocarbon-dated at the University of Michigan and the University of Arizona. These analyses indicated an age of 1580 B.C. ± 300 years and 1150 B.C. ± 110 years, and led to the suggestion that the tiny figures may have been associated with the Desert Culture which was widespread over western North America from about 7000 to 2000 B.C. Recent archaeological investigations support the figurine dates and hypotheses. In 1963 additional split-twig figurines, recovered from a huge limestone cavern in Marble Canyon and examined at the University of California, revealed a radiocarbon date of 2145 B.C. ± 100 years, the earliest date yet recorded for such specimens. Other archaeologists have discovered similar figurines in portions of the Mojave Desert in eastern California and Nevada, and south of Grand Canyon near Flagstaff and the Verde Valley.

In the early spring of 1964, what may be an important clue to the identity of the makers of the figurines was discovered on the summit and slopes of Red Butte, a prominent sandstone- and lava-capped pinnacle a few miles south of Grand Canyon. Here archaeologists found projectile points and other chipped-stone tools affiliated with the Pinto Complex, a Desert Culture people first recognized in the Pinto Basin of the Mojave Desert. While the Pinto Complex is not yet fully understood or dated with incontrovertible accuracy, most archaeologists feel that an age of three to four thousand years would not be out of order. Thus, although split-twig figurines have not been found in absolutely certain association with Pinto Complex artifacts, the discovery of a Pinto site near caves containing the figurines in Grand Canyon supports the probability of some association.

THE SPLIT-TWIG animal figurines, then, give mute evidence for the beginnings of human history in Grand Canyon. It is not known how long these hunters and magicians continued to use its limestone caves, but they had probably disappeared long before the opening of the Christian era. Archaeologists have found no record of further human occupation of the Grand Canyon until about 700 A.D., when Indians who were culturally much different began tentative exploration of its depths. These were Pueblo peoples, most probably direct ancestors of the Hopi. For almost one hundred years, prehistorians have been studying the history of the Pueblo Indians,

This brother and sister, members of one of the many Paiute "tribelets" common to the country of the Colorado, were photographed by Jack Hillers in 1871.

THE MYTH

A group of Walapai, probably descendants of the ancient cerbat culture, drawn by a member of Lieutenant J. C. Ives's Colorado Exploring Expedition of 1857–58.

and we now have a relatively complete picture of how their culture developed.

It is quite probable that they, too, began as a Desert Culture people in the Great Basin. Some time around the year 1 A.D., or slightly earlier, they moved into the northern portions of the Southwest, near the Four Corners (where Arizona, Utah, Colorado, and New Mexico meet). Archaeologists refer to this period in their culture as that of the "Basketmaker," a name derived from their most common material attribute. These hunters and gatherers had added corn and squash to their economy by using rudimentary agricultural techniques acquired from Indians farther south. In fertile valleys they raised their crops, and in surrounding uplands they hunted deer, mountain sheep, and rabbits. They cultivated the soil with digging sticks and hunted game with spears, spear-throwers, and curved throwing sticks; rabbits were driven into nets stretched across defiles.

The early Basketmakers wove beautiful baskets, fine sandals, loincloths, and twined bags. Blankets woven of cords covered with rabbit fur kept them warm in winter. Fired pottery was not made at this time, but they produced crude clay vessels.

Caves or rock-shelters seem to have been preferred for dwellings, and into their floors the Indians dug storage chambers that later became burial cists. Occasionally they constructed saucer-shaped wooden houses in the protection of cliffs.

A ROUND 500 A.D. (the exact date varying with the section of the Southwest) the Basketmaker style of life changed in several ways. New varieties of corn were developed, and beans introduced. Caves became less popular than circular, open-pit houses, often grouped in a manner suggestive of the beginnings of village life. The weaving of sandals reached its highest development, and baskets were still widely made. Fired pottery was introduced—usually gray with simple designs painted in black—and the bow and arrow came into use to supplement the spear-thrower. This was an important era in the lives of these people. They enlarged their geographic range westerly to the lower Little Colorado River, almost to Grand Canyon, and laid a foundation for the later flowering of their culture.

With a stable economic base that combined hunting and gathering with corn, bean, and squash agriculture, the Pueblos turned to other matters. They refined their ceramic art, producing corrugated cooking ware, vessels with broad- and fine-lined black-on-white decoration, and some red pottery decorated with black paint. They added cotton to their agriculture, spinning and loom-weaving it into fabrics for clothing, and made good stone axes and hoes. Surface storage rooms, made first of mud and poles and later of masonry, became common. These ultimately developed into above-ground dwellings, the pit houses being reserved for religious and ceremonial functions.

By the middle of the eleventh century A.D., this development flowered into the classic traditions of Pueblo culture, apparently reaching a zenith first in the east, in the Chaco district of northwestern New Mexico, and later in northern Arizona. This period, continuing into historic times, saw the rise of great communal pueblos, up to five stories high and housing several hundreds of people. Subterranean religious structures (kivas) became specialized, with local variations in details. Exquisite pottery, black-on-white, black-on-red, and polychrome, abounded. Objects of personal adornment appeared—turquoise mosaics, beads, pendants, and shell bracelets. Communal living must have been highly organized, and if we can judge by the social, religious, and political structures of modern pueblos, authority probably centered in a theocratic hierarchy of priests.

DURING THESE CENTURIES other great changes were taking place. Precipitation patterns that may have affected the maturation of crops began to vary in certain parts of the Southwest by the middle of the twelfth century; more intensive drought conditions came a century later. About this time, too, seminomadic non-Pueblo peoples made their appearance from the northwestern horizon.

These ancestors of the Southern Paiute may have been responsible for what appears to have been an intercultural

relationship similar to a "cold war." Apparently, the strangers soon reached the northern rim of Grand Canyon. About this time the Pueblos consolidated their numbers along the more reliable water courses—the Little Colorado and the Rio Grande, and the usually infallible springs of the Hopi country. Here they were when the Spaniards found them in the summer of 1540.

Yet, even as the Pueblos were flourishing and, later, reconsolidating, other indigenous peoples of the Southwest were following different patterns of culture. In west central Arizona were the Cohonina people, whose presence on the plateau of northern Arizona has been recorded from about 700 to 1150 over a range that included the south rim of Grand Canyon.

The Cohonina adopted a veneer of Pueblo culture. They attempted to build pit houses and masonry pueblos. Their pottery, although of a different technique, was gray and decorated with black painted designs in imitation of that made by their eastern neighbors. Apparently unable to produce the red pottery of the Pueblos, they slipped some of it after firing with a fugitive red paint to give it the superficial appearance of true red ware. They farmed essentially the same crops but hunted to a lesser extent. Their social and religious life probably differed considerably from that of the Pueblos.

About 1150, or perhaps slightly later, the Cohonina disappear from the archaeological record. By then, and continuing until about 1300, the Cerbat, probably direct ancestors of the Walapai and Havasupai, moved from the deserts near the lower Colorado River Valley to the plateaus that had been the Cohonina homeland. These Indians were but incipient farmers, planting near permanent springs. Hunting and gathering was their economic mainstay. They lived in rock-shelters or impermanent brush wikiups. Their material culture was simple and their interest in ceramics confined to the production of brown, undecorated vessels. Yet they established a very stable way of life on the plateau, for it was here that the Spanish Franciscan, Father Garcés, first described them in 1776; and it was here they remained until forcibly removed to their present restricted reserves in the early 1880's.

It was these native peoples—the Pueblos and to a lesser extent the Cohonina, the Havasupai and Walapai, and the Southern Paiute—who made the indigenous history of the Grand Canyon.

There is no evidence that Pueblo Indians entered the

(Overleaf): City made of earth: A Moquis (Zuñi) Pueblo photographed by Timothy O'Sullivan of the Wheeler Expedition, 1871.

THE MYTH

Canyon before the opening of their Developmental Period (about 700 A.D.). Then, and for the next three centuries, there was halting exploration and limited seasonal occupation. The few Developmental sites that have been discovered are marked on the surface only by fine-lined black-on-white pottery fragments. These are mostly in the eastern reaches of the Canyon, but at least one such site has been recorded near Deer Creek, 136 miles down the Colorado River from Lees Ferry. In all probability, these and later Pueblo Indians approached the great gorge from the heartland of their territory to the east.

At about the same time, but probably coming from the opposite direction, small groups of Cohonina Indians made their appearance. One excavated site of this period, located on the south rim near the Tusayán Pueblo ruin in the eastern portion of Grand Canyon National Park, consists of a circular house, two storage rooms, and several storage pits, all dug into the shallow, limestone-studded soil of the area. Within the next three centuries, the Cohonina occupied many more sites along the south rim, but not in the Canyon itself. Their buildings were mostly surface masonry structures, a style evidently acquired from contact with the Pueblos.

By 1150 A.D., for reasons not yet fully understood, the Cohonina disappeared as a cultural group. Some archaeologists believe that they became the Havasupai, while others have presented evidence that both the Havasupai and the Walapai were descendants of the prehistoric Cerbat people.

MEANWHILE, ABOUT 1000 A.D., there began a much larger influx of Pueblo peoples into the Canyon, culminating a century later in a major occupation of hundreds of sites in its myriad recesses and on both rims. The overwhelming majority of prehistoric ruins in Grand Canyon consists of small, surface masonry pueblos with associated storage rooms, mescal pits, and occasional kivas. Frequently these were built on open, relatively flat terraces. Many Indians did take advantage of the towering cliffs and built against them at the tops of steep talus slopes, but true cliff dwellings are not often encountered.

The ruins are now visible as low remnants of masonry walls that mark room outlines. The ground around them usually is littered with broken pottery and stone tools, such as arrow points, scrapers, and milling stones. Storage rooms and the talus-top pueblos are usually found in a better state of preservation, and in a few instances the original wooden roofs are still intact. At one site in Shinumo Canyon, for example, the masonry walls of a room are spanned by cottonwood timbers, crossed at right angles with smaller poles, slabs of rock, and finally a layer of earth, as is typical of Pueblo architecture elsewhere. The storerooms, placed in protected niches or overhangs, ordinarily are well preserved, but except for an occasional corncob, their contents have long since been consumed by rodents. Mescal pits, where the roots and tender young shoots of the Agave plant were roasted, are marked by large circular depressions, some with diameters of 20 to 25 feet, ringed with masses of small, charred rocks.

TODAY, VISITORS VIEWING Grand Canyon only from the comfortable vantage of the rim may wonder how Indians could have survived down in the Canyon and, indeed, why they entered it in the first place. The answers to these questions can be found in the cultural adaptations the Pueblos made to their natural environment. One must remember that these Indians had a well-balanced economy based upon hunting, gathering of many wild edible plants, and agriculture. While deer-hunting undoubtedly was excellent on both north and south rims, such other game animals as mountain sheep and rabbits were to be found below the rims. Wild food plants grew in abundance on the rims, but only those ecologically adjusted to the high plateau elevations (7,000 to 8,000 feet). In the Canyon below, many other staples could be gathered: the tasty fruits of certain varieties of cactus, the edible beans of the mesquite, the catclaw, and the Agave. Furthermore, successful farming of beans, squash, corn, and cotton depends upon a rather long, frost-free growing season and sufficient water. Both were obtainable at Canyon elevations below 3,000 feet. While both rims are relatively devoid of dependable water sources, the recesses of the Canyon contain many springs and, particularly in the side canyons near the north rim, permanently flowing streams. While there undoubtedly have been some climatic changes in the several centuries since the Pueblo occupation was at its height, particularly changes in rainfall pattern, it is worthwhile to note that in some side canyons where there are permanent streams or springs today, there are ruins; where there is no water now, prehistoric sites are lacking.

Environmentally, then, the Canyon provided excellent resources to sustain Pueblo life, though in all probability

The "south forty" of one prehistoric Grand Canyon farmer was tucked into the circular creek delta shown in the photograph above.

occupation was in large part seasonal. While archaeologists will not be more certain until excavations are undertaken at selected ruins in the inner canyons, the lack of an extensive fuel supply for winter warmth would seem to suggest habitation of the lower reaches in the summer growing season and of the well-wooded plateaus back from the rims, particularly the south rim, in the winter. Indeed, this was the pattern of the Havasupai until they were restricted to their present village in the Canyon bottom around 1895.

But this is not to say that every spring saw mass migrations of Indians into the Canyon. Hundreds of ruins on both north and south rims indicate that many families remained on the plateau and farmed there during the summer months.

One of the most significant of the twelfth-century Pueblo agricultural communities was on the plateau near the Canyon's rim. (Its precise location is withheld to prevent vandalism.) Here, along a relatively shallow drainage

for a distance of some two and one-half miles, archaeologists recorded 44 small masonry pueblo ruins and, in the drainage itself, 77 agricultural check dams. Here, for perhaps a hundred years, a number of family groups, possibly interrelated, planted crops, hunted, and gathered wild plants in the Canyon below. On the Canyon walls nearby are remnants of precipitous trails, marked in one instance by a small masonry storeroom tucked into a recess in the cliff some two thousand feet below the rim; below that, only a few hundred feet above the Colorado River, is a prehistoric wooden bridge that spanned a crevice on a narrow ledge. From this trail it was possible to cross the river and climb out the other side.

Throughout many tributary canyons, especially in the eastern portions of Grand Canyon, are similar Pueblo masonry ruins in association with low check dams. At one site there is a long stone wall that was apparently built to divert sheet drainage from the hills above to agricultural fields. There is abundant evidence that these

25

THE MYTH

A cave in the sheer wall of Marble Canyon—occupied by man two thousand years before the birth of Christ.

Indians practiced erosional control and other conservation measures.

Studies have been made that indicate a strong correlation between the locations of prehistoric sites and routes of access into the Canyon where its sheer walls are broken down. In one such area there exists additional evidence that the Indians moved from plateau to Canyon and from rim to rim with relative ease. On a ledge, seemingly inaccessible from ruins in the Canyon below or from the rim above, is a small limestone cave that con-

tained corncobs and two pottery vessels. Presumably, this was a way station along a prehistoric trail to the rim, where travelers could find a cache of food and water. The ledge marks the only place within many miles where it is possible to climb out of the Canyon.

At another locale, in the eastern portion of the Canyon below Lipan Point, a one-room masonry structure with what appear to be loopholes in its walls may have been some type of look-out on a cross-Canyon trail. The structure commands an excellent view up the river and across to a large concentration of Pueblo ruins on the north side. And from this site it is possible to climb to the south rim near Desert View.

It should be noted that along the south rim from Desert View west to the Great Thumb peninsula, several masonry structures stand on small, and sometimes quite isolated, sections of cliff that project out from the main rim. Often massive limestone walls rim the edges of these "islands." To many observers, these Pueblo buildings seem to have been fort-like in character, but absolutely no evidence of actual hostility has ever been discovered in Grand Canyon. In fact, these south rim "forts" would have been virtually indefensible against attack from the "mainland," for they are *cul-de-sacs,* cut off from all food and water save that which might have been stockpiled before a siege.

Grand Canyon and its immediate environs to the north and south were almost completely abandoned by 1150 or 1200 A.D., not only by the Pueblos but by the Cohonina population on the south rim. Why did they leave? Present evidence would seem to point to climatic changes rather than the presence of hostile peoples. It is true that about 1150 A.D. the Cerbat Indians made their appearance on the plateaus along the south rim and the forerunners of the Southern Paiute penetrated the high, forested lands near the north rim, but there is nothing to indicate that either the Pai (as the combined Walapai and Havasupai once termed themselves) or the Southern Paiute forced the Pueblo abandonment.

In adjacent regions of the northern Southwest, however, studies of fossil pollen rains and annual tree-ring growth point to a shift from winter to summer precipitation at about this time. Since successful maize agriculture depends in large part upon soil storage of water from winter snows and rains, such a change could well have made farming impossible, or extremely marginal except near a few choice springs or streams.

The mystery of the exodus from the Canyon indicates a need for more detailed archaeological excavation (only two ruins on the south rim and none in the Canyon or on the north rim have been dug scientifically) and for more paleo-climatological studies based upon detailed examination of soil stratigraphy, pollen, and tree-ring growth.

Soon after 1150 A.D. the Pai spread over the southern plateau and penetrated much of the western and central part of the Canyon. By 1300 they had reached their maximum range and occupied all of the south portion of Grand Canyon and its plateau east to the Little Colorado River. Throughout this region they hunted, gathered, and carried on some farming near permanent springs and streams. The habitation sites discovered within the Canyon consist of rock-shelters, on the floors of which lie trash and cultural debris, including reddish-brown potsherds, flat-slab milling stones, and small, triangular, side-notched arrow points, all differing from those of the Cohonina or the Pueblos.

On the north rim uplands and in their tributary canyons, the Southern Paiute maintained a similar existence after the twelfth century. Their fingernail-incised brown pottery, milling stones, and arrow points were somewhat different from those of the Pai, but they also occupied rock-shelters and roasted Agave in stone-ringed pits. Now and then they camped in abandoned Pueblo ruins, for their pottery sometimes has been found mixed with that of the Pueblos around the masonry structures.

Both the Pai and the Paiute occupations were stable and long lived. From about 1150 until the latter part of the nineteenth century, they continued to use the natural resources of Grand Canyon.

There is some evidence that both groups maintained amicable trade relations with the Pueblos in the present Hopi country. By 1300 the Pueblos had ceased to make black-on-white and polychrome pottery, and had developed a yellow ware, exquisitely decorated with designs in brownish-black paint, similar to the Hopi ceramics of today. Fragments of this black-on-yellow pottery are found on many Havasupai, Walapai, and Southern Paiute ruins in Grand Canyon, probably the remains of vessels traded from the Hopi Pueblos in exchange for deer skins, red paint, and mescal.

Occasionally, too, from 1300 until relatively recently, the Hopi periodically returned to Grand Canyon to collect salt from a natural deposit near the confluence of the Little Colorado and Colorado rivers. They approached these salt mines either by way of the Little Colorado gorge or down what is now known as the Tanner Trail below Desert View. On both these routes are former camp sites of the Hopi, marked by the bright yellow potsherds.

The discovery, or rather rediscovery, of one such Hopi site near the mouth of the Little Colorado River involved some elementary archaeological detective work. In August of 1869, when Major Powell camped there on his first exploration down the Colorado, his men reported finding traces of an ancient Indian habitation. Eighty years later, when professional archaeologists first surveyed the river banks through Grand Canyon, they could not find this ruin. The only sign of human habitation by the blue lagoon at the mouth of the Little Colorado was a one-room stone cabin built by a prospector named Beamer about 1889. After two later visits, archaeologists noted some erosion in the bank at the front of the cabin. Protruding from this bank were fragments of Beamer's trash—broken bottles and rusted tins. Beneath them were aboriginal potsherds, first the post-1300 Hopi yellow wares and then, lower down, the earlier Pueblo black-on-white and gray types. Between the time of Major Powell's observations and that of modern archaeologists, Beamer apparently had modernized a prehistoric Pueblo structure!

Beamer was not the only Anglo-American to explore Grand Canyon in those decades after Major Powell's trips. Mormons investigated the north rim and visited the Southern Paiute. On the south side, after the United States had forcibly established peaceful relations with the Pai and placed them on separate reservations in the early 1880's, other Anglo prospectors tramped over former Indian trails and discovered copper, asbestos, lead, and other mineral deposits. They dug shafts, transported heavy mining equipment on the backs of mules, and even constructed cable crossings of the river. Intrepid boatmen left the wreckage of their craft and the graves of some of their men by the river. Early tourist accommodations, forerunners of modern hotels and motels, were built on the south rim. Today, even these structures are in ruins—if not obliterated. History and prehistory are absorbed by the contemporary scene, and hundreds of thousands of tourists who come to gaze in awe at the Canyon are unaware that this great natural wonder has formed the stage and the backdrop for four thousand years of human endeavor.

CHAPTER II

THE MANY-NAMED RIVER

*Conquistadores and Missionaries
—Two Centuries of Spanish Exploration*

Granted that they did not find the riches of which they had been told, they found a place in which to search for them, and the beginning of a good country to settle in, so as to go farther from there. Since they came back from the country which they conquered and abandoned, time has given them a chance to understand the direction and locality in which they were, and the borders of the good country they had in their hands, and their hearts weep for having lost so favorable an opportunity. . . .

Pedro de Castañeda, writing finish to the narrative of Coronado's 1540 expedition into the barren wilds of the American Southwest, articulated a theme that rings like a Vespers for the story of the Spanish experience in the lands of the Colorado. Driven by righteous greed and wading knee-deep in heathen blood, the *conquistadores* of New Spain thrust into the land of clear lights following a mirage whose vague conformations tantalized the court of Old Spain for more than two centuries. Following them, a ragged and unbelievably courageous army of soul-hungry priests made their own *entradas* into the wild land, attempting, like a corps of diplomats, to patch up relations shattered by the blood and conquest of soldiers, and to plant the seeds of settlement and empire for His Holy Catholic Majesty. Time gave both priest and *conquistador* nearly three hundred years to understand; they never did.

It took the *conquistadores* very little time to subjugate the Valley of Mexico. Less than thirty years after Columbus first sighted the green, humpbacked island mountains of San Salvador, Hernando Cortez had shattered the empire of the Aztecs, a civilization that had neither spirit nor technique to resist a war machine tempered by more than seven hundred years of intermittent con-

flict. Spain, freed of the internal agonies that had crippled her development since the Moorish Invasion of the eighth century, was beginning her first aggressive thrust into the arenas of world power, seeking empire and contesting the efforts of France and England on a score of fronts. She needed money, and the *conquistadores* of the New World—of whom Cortez was representative—were the tools with which she intended to extract the wealth necessary to finance her experiment in conquest. Cortez superbly justified the strategy by looting the treasures of the Aztecs in 1521, and when Francisco de Pizarro with even more astounding success pillaged the Inca empire of Peru in 1533, it seemed the New World was nothing less than a bottomless pit filled with gold.

After the loose gold and silver of the Aztecs had been exhausted, Cortez appropriated the mines from which the metals had come and set enslaved Indians to working them. The wealth remained incredible, but it was not enough, so Cortez began moving into the unknown lands west and north of the Valley of Mexico. Surely, across some ridge of mountains there must be yet another civilization where men adorned themselves with silver and ate from plates of gold; the imperative of *must be* became the theme of a narrative in which rumor carried the weight of documented fact and the following of myth became the pattern of exploration.

The myth that gave birth to the discovery of the Colorado River of the West had its roots in a legend that predated the days of Spain's glory by several centuries. When the Mohammedan Moors crossed the Strait of Gibraltar in the eighth century, the legend had it, seven Christian prelates with their followers escaped the heathen wrath of the Muslims by sailing west into the Atlantic. They found an island—which later took on the name

*"Granted that they did not find the riches of which they had been told, they found a place
in which to search for them . . ." (Twin Buttes, Arizona; photograph by Adam Clark Vroman, 1895).*

THE MYTH

Hernan Cortez, conqueror of Mexico, follower of myths.

gold; of a land called Gran Quivira, whose emperor slept under a tree hung with golden bells—but at the time of Cortez it already had begun to reappear in a form altered by time and geography. Nuño de Guzmán, who had raped and depopulated the lands of Mexico's west coast in 1535, had encountered stories of seven immensely rich cities lying beyond the northern mountains, and Cortez himself had known tales of seven rich tribes living in seven rich caves . . . somewhere. In 1536, four unfortunates stumbled out of the deserts of Sinaloa after spending eight years in and out of Indian captivity, wandering aimlessly and sometimes hopelessly across Texas, New Mexico, Arizona, and northwestern Mexico. One of them was Cabeza de Vaca, an agent of the king assigned to Pánfilo de Narváez's land expedition of 1527; another was named Esteban, a Negro slave of the same ill-fated expedition (which had disintegrated somewhere in the Florida panhandle). Both had stories to tell, tantalizing hints of great cities to the north and west.

In the spring of 1539 Don Antonio de Mendoza, vice-regal successor to Cortez, followed up on the story. He sent Esteban back up into the wild country with Fray Marcos, a priest whose devotion to God and Viceroy transcended truth, as it turned out. Posing as a black god —a role that had helped keep him alive on the immense trek with Cabeza de Vaca—Esteban traveled ahead of Fray Marcos through northern Sonora, a country, so he reported back to Fray Marcos, called Cíbola, and on up to the Zuñi pueblo of Hawikah, in southern Arizona. Here he died, apparently done in by his arrogance in the face of Indian reluctance to take his godhead seriously. But Fray Marcos followed his trail, until he, too, looked from a distance upon this pueblo city gilded by the summer sun, shimmering impressively in the bleak and angular land. The good father hurried back to Mendoza. He had seen one of the golden cities of Cíbola. There were six more. There *must be* six more.

Four months after Esteban and Fray Marcos had left for Cíbola, Mendoza dispatched Francisco de Ulloa in three ships up the west coast of Mexico to a point at which it might be possible to march overland to Cíbola. Ulloa sailed north up the Gulf of California until he came to a dead stop at tidal bores that frightened and astonished him: "We perceived the sea to run with so great a rage into the land that it was a thing much to be marvelled at; and with a like fury it returned back again with the ebb. . . . There were divers opinions amongst us, and some

Antillia—and there each prelate established a city. The Seven Cities of Antillia, as vague and intangible as the mists of dream, became part of the mental baggage carried over to the New World by the *conquistadores*. "Since they were cities beyond the horizon and of miracle," Bernard DeVoto has written, "the sands they stood on would be gold."

This shimmering myth had to contend with many others in the New World—stories of one-breasted Amazons; of El Dorado, the Gilded Man; of lakes and rivers of

Emperor and conquistador: Montezuma (seated on the left) and Cortez (on the right) meet in Tenochtitlan, the City of Mexico, in a contemporary Aztec drawing.

thought . . . that some great river might be the cause thereof.' In 1539, nearly seventy years before a group of sickened English settlers miserably stumbled ashore at the site of Jamestown in the East, the Colorado River of the West had entered the annals of Spanish exploration.

Ulloa's expedition had been notable for at least one reason: his encounter with the tidal bores of the Colorado indicated that the Sea of Cortez was not a sea at all and that California—still wallowing in its own sea of mystery —was not an island, but part of the northern mainland.

(The insistence of myth, however, was such that most cartographers managed to evade Ulloa's observations until the end of the seventeenth century.) Remarkable as its contribution was, Ulloa's expedition still had uncovered no Cíbola, and Viceroy Mendoza carefully organized a major land-sea operation for the spring and summer of 1540.

It was the most ambitious such undertaking in the history of New World exploration up to that time. Hernando de Alarcón, with two ships—the *San Pedro* and

THE MYTH

the *Santa Catalina*—was dispatched in late 1539 to San Miguel de Culiacán, on the west coast. His mission would be to pick up a third ship, the *San Gabriel,* then sail up the Sea of Cortez, eventually to make contact with the land expedition. The land force, under the general command of Francisco Vásquez de Coronado, young governor of New Galicia (no raging *conquistador,* but an able, relatively level-headed man), assembled in Culiacán early in 1540. It was an impressive gathering—230 *caballeros* recruited from the greedy nobility of New Spain, with numerous footmen, five friars to carry the word of God, a military escort under the command of Melchior Díaz, nearly a thousand Indian servants, and more than fifteen hundred horses, mules, and beef cattle. With the expedition was Pedro de Castañeda, a common—and uncommonly literate—soldier who became the expedition's official historian, setting down his narrative of events upon return to Spain.

I N FEBRUARY, after review in Compostela by Viceroy Mendoza, the grandiose expedition set out for the golden cities of Cíbola. Painfully straggling north through the tangled foothills of Mexico's west coast, then crossing over the Sierra Madre—the convoluted backbone of Mexico—near the site of Arizpe, the immense column moved slowly, so slowly that Coronado and a force of one hundred set out ahead of the main contingent. Half-starved and exhausted, the expedition did not reach the deserts of southern Arizona until June. From there, they could at least rationalize, it was a comparatively short, easy march to Cíbola; food, water, and incredible wealth lay just beyond the horizon, over the next range of hills.

Alarcón, in the meantime, had sailed into Culiacán, picked up the supply-laden *San Gabriel,* and headed north for his rendezvous with the land expedition. In late August, he reached the head of the gulf and near-disaster in a direct confrontation with the particularly dangerous tides of late summer. All three ships were driven upon sand bars: "Whereupon we were in such jeopardy that the deck of the Admiral was oftentimes under water; and if a great surge of the sea had not come and driven our ship right up and gave her leave, as it were, to breathe awhile, we had there been drowned." Most of Alarcón's men displayed a sudden eagerness to return, but Alarcón was firm, as he carefully pointed out in his report to Mendoza: "But because your Lordship commanded me that I should bring you the secret of that gulf, I resolved

that although I had known I should have lost the ships, I would not have ceased for anything to have seen the head thereof. . . .

"Now it pleased God upon the return of the flood that the ships came on float, and so we went forward. . . . And we passed forward with much ado, turning our sterns now this way, now that way, to seek and find the channel. And it pleased God that after this sort we came to the very bottom of the bay, where we found a very mighty river, which ran with so great fury of a storm, that we could hardly sail against it."

B UT SAIL AGAINST it they did, in a fashion, utilizing the uncommonly cheerful aid of the local Indians, the Cocopahs, in towing ship's boats to the mouth of the Gila. There, Alarcón met Indians who had heard of the black man, Esteban, killed at the Hawikah pueblo—news possibly carried over the ancient Indian trail that paralleled the Gila River through Arizona (and possibly, in part or whole, the trail still called today Camino del Diablo) — but no word of Coronado and the land expedition. Still determined, Alarcón continued up the turbid Colorado to a point nearly a hundred miles above the Gila, where he inquired again and attempted to persuade the local Indians to allow him to send a messenger east to Hawikah. They refused, so Alarcón made a small cache on the banks of the river, then headed back to his ships. At the end of the summer, giving up hope of ever meeting the land expedition, the three ships sailed out of the mouth of the Colorado.

They had named it *El Río de Buena Guia*—River of Good Guidance. It would be the first of many names.

On July 7, the legions of Coronado found the end of the Spanish rainbow: Hawikah, the adobe city-state of the Zuñi Indians. Here, after putting down a brief and useless flurry of resistance during which Coronado himself received a minor foot wound, the expedition found water and food—but no more. There were no rooms filled with gold and silver trinkets, nothing at all with which to justify the effort and expense of more than six months. Fray Marcos, Coronado reported bitterly to Mendoza, "has not told the truth in a single thing he said."

Frustrated almost beyond endurance yet still hopeful of finding the treasures of Cíbola, Coronado set about exploring the surrounding country for the next several weeks, sending bits and pieces of the expedition off on forays into the ragged land. In late September, he sent

Jan Mostaert's "An Episode of the Conquest of America" documented with more imagination than fact;
Coronado's conquest of "Cíbolo." The Spanish soldiers are outfitted correctly, and the
Indians did in fact throw rocks; the rest—including the landscape—is pure European fancy.

Melchior Díaz west with twenty-five men and instructions to make contact with Alarcón and the badly needed supplies. Following *El Camino del Diablo,* the much-traveled Indian trail that provided the only route with available water, Díaz arrived at the Colorado. The Indians in the region, Castañeda reported in his narrative, "carry a firebrand in the hand when they go from one place to another. . . . On this account the large river which is in that country was called Rio del Tison. It is a very great river and is more than two leagues wide at its mouth; here it is half a league across. Here the captain heard that there had been ships at a point three days down toward the sea. When he reached the place where the ships had been, which was more than fifteen leagues up the river from the mouth of the harbor, they found written on a tree: 'Alarcón reached this place; there are letters at the foot of this tree.' He dug up the letters and learned from them how long Alarcón had waited for news of the army and that he had gone back with the ships to New Spain, because he was unable to proceed farther, since this sea was

a bay, which was formed by the Isle of the Marquis [Cortez], which is called California, and it was explained that California was not an island, but a point of the mainland forming the other side of that gulf."

HAVING CHRISTENED THE Colorado with its second name in as many months and discovered corroboration of Ulloa's contentions regarding California (which most cartographers continued to ignore), the Díaz expedition then crossed the river on Indian-built rafts and may have continued as far west as the site of Volcano Lake (inundated when the river shifted course in 1910), thus completing the first overland journey to California. After some days of perfunctory exploration, they headed back to Cíbola. On the return trip, Díaz—who had otherwise displayed admirable competence—managed to impale himself on the butt of his own lance while attempting to spear a rabbit. His ludicrous death stands as fitting annotation to the entire star-crossed expedition.

Other forays were less disastrous, if no more fruitful,

33

THE MYTH

than that of Díaz, but two of the subsidiary expeditions into the unknown country led to Spain's third confrontation with the Colorado River—and to civilized man's first glimpse of the awesome gash of the Grand Canyon. Castañeda told the story:

Cíbola being at peace, the General Francisco Vazquez [Coronado] found out from the people of the province about the provinces that lay around it, and got them to tell their friends and neighbors that Christians had come into the country, whose only desire was to be their friends, and to find out about good lands to live in, and for them to come to see the strangers and talk with them. They did this, since they know how to communicate with one another in these regions, and they informed him about a province with seven villages of the same sort as theirs, although somewhat different. They had nothing to do with these people. This province is called Tusayán. It is twenty-five leagues from Cíbola. The villages are high and the people are warlike.

The general had sent Don Pedro de Tovar to these villages with seventeen horsemen and three or four foot-soldiers. Juan de Padilla, a Franciscan friar, who had been a fighting man in his youth, went with them. When they reached the region, they entered the country so quietly that nobody observed them, because there were no settlements or farms between one village and another and the people do not leave the villages except to go to their farms, especially at this time, when they had heard that Cíbola had been captured by very fierce people, who travelled on animals which ate people. This information was generally believed by those who had never seen horses, although it was so strange as to cause much wonder. Our men arrived after nightfall and were able to conceal themselves under the edge of the village, where they heard the natives talking in their houses. But in the morning they were discovered and drew up in regular order, while the natives came out to meet them, with bows, and shields, and wooden clubs, drawn up in lines without any confusion. The interpreter was given a chance to speak to them and give them due warning, for they were very intelligent people, but nevertheless they drew lines and insisted that our men should not go across these lines toward their village.

While they were talking, some men acted as if they would cross the lines, and one of the natives lost control of himself and struck a horse a blow on the cheek of the bridle with his club. Friar Juan, fretted by the time that was being wasted in talking with them, said to the captain: "To tell the truth, I do not know why we came here." When the men heard this, they gave the Santiago so suddenly that they ran down many of the Indians and the others fled to the town in confusion. Some indeed did not have a chance to do this, so quickly did the people in the village come out with presents, asking for peace. The captain ordered his force to collect, and, as the natives did not do any more harm, he and those who were with him found a place to establish their headquarters near the village. They had dismounted here when the natives came peacefully, saying that they had come to give in the submission of the whole province and that they wanted him to be friends with them and to accept the presents which they gave him. This was some cotton cloth, although not much, because they do not make it in that district. They also gave him some dressed skins and cornmeal, and pine nuts and corn and birds of the country. Afterward they presented some turquoises, but not many. The people of the whole district came together that day and submitted themselves, and they allowed him to enter their villages freely to visit, buy, sell, and barter with them.

It is governed like Cíbola, by an assembly of the oldest men. They have their governors and generals. This was where they obtained the information about a large river, and that several days down the river there were some people with very large bodies.

As Don Pedro de Tovar was not commissioned to go farther, he returned from there and gave this information to the general, who *dispatched* Don Garcia Lopez de Cardeñas with about twelve companions to go to see this river. He was well received when he reached *Tusayán* and was entertained by the natives who gave him guides for his journey. They started from here laden with provisions, for they had to go through a desert country before reaching the inhabited region, which the Indians said was more than 20 days' journey. After they had gone 20 days they came to the banks of the river. It seemed to be more than three or four leagues in an air line across to the other bank of the stream which flowed between them.

This country was elevated and full of low twisted pines, very cold, and lying open toward the north, so that, this being the warm season, no one could live there on account of the cold. They spent three days on this bank looking for a passage down to the river, which looked from above as if the water was six feet across, although the Indians said it was half a league wide. It was impossible to descend, for after these three days Captain Melgosa & one Juan Galeras and another companion, who were the three lightest and most agile men, made an attempt to go down at the least difficult place, and went down until those who were above were unable to keep sight of them. They returned about four o'clock in the afternoon, not having succeeded in reaching the bottom on account of the great difficulties which they found, because what seemed to be easy from above was not so, but instead very hard and difficult. They said that they had been down about a third of the way and that the river seemed very large from the place which they reached, and that from what they saw they thought the Indians had given the width correctly. Those who stayed above had estimated that some huge rocks on the sides of the cliffs seemed to be about as tall as a man, but those who went down swore that when they reached these rocks they were bigger than the great tower of Seville. They did not go farther up the river, because they could not get water.

Before this they had had to go a league or two inland every day late in the evening in order to find water, and the guides said that if they should go four days farther it would not be possible to go on, because there was no water within three or four days, for when they travel across this region themselves they take with them women laden with water in gourds, and bury the gourds of water along the way, to use when they return, & besides this, they travel in one day over what it takes us two days to accomplish.

This was the Tison (Firebrand) River, much nearer its source than where Melchior Díaz and his company crossed it. These were the same kind of Indians, judging from what was afterward learned. They came back from this point & the expedition did not have any other result. On the way they saw some water falling over a rock and learned from the guides that some bunches of crystals which were hanging there were salt. They went and gathered a quantity of this & brought it back to Cíbola, dividing it among those who were there. They gave the general a written account of what they had seen, because one Pedro de Sotomayor was able to do this and had gone with Don Garcia Lopez as chronicler for the army. The villages of that province remained peaceful, since they were never visited again, nor was any attempt made to find other peoples in that direction.

BY THE EARLY winter of 1540, the dreams of Cíbola had ended in unqualified failure; an immense territory had been explored, a river discovered, and many astounding sights reported—but there had been no gold, the only accomplishment likely to impress Viceroy Mendoza and the court of Old Spain. Coronado moved the entire expeditionary force east to the valley of the Río Grande (near the present site of Albuquerque), and there they wintered. By the following spring hope once again had been kindled by rumors of another place, a land called Gran Quivira to the far northeast, a land richer even than the legends of Cíbola, richer than the Aztec country of the Valley of Mexico, richer than the Inca country of Peru. Coronado and his band picked up and followed one more mirage, this one clear to the Kansas plains, where the dream of Golconda that had sustained them for two years and several thousand miles finally withered, then died, and the expedition straggled back to the Valley of Mexico in 1542.

The Colorado and its canyons had been discovered. They would now be ignored for sixty years.

BY THE END of the sixteenth century, Spain possessed a North American empire whose outlines she did not fully know, whose diminishing treasures she had already depleted, and whose native inhabitants—particularly on the edges of the northern frontier—continued to display a sulky disinclination to embrace the twin benefits of Cross and King. She had acquired a white elephant the size of a continent, but it would take more than another century before the truth became brutally and inescapably obvious. In the meantime, the government of New Spain—like all governments before and since—clung tenaciously to its myths. An empire was not an empire until it was settled and exploited. The frontier territories of New Spain were consequently carved into provinces and governors were assigned; from these governors results were expected —tangible, concrete evidence that the king's interests (as well as those of his New World officialdom) were being furthered by colonization, conversion, and profit.

It was an atmosphere in which such a governor might be inspired to extraordinary acts in order to retain his post. Such was the ambition of Juan de Oñate, governor of New Mexico, when he set out at the turn of the sixteenth century to blaze a route to the great South Sea and a fortune in pearls. Having more or less conquered

Hawikuh, the Zuñi pueblo where Coronado's dream of Cíbola came to a disappointing and violent end.

New Mexico's indigenous population and colonized the region of the Pueblos in the 1590's, Oñate led an expedition to Gran Quivira on the southern plains in 1601, hoping to establish the area as a jumping-off point for his mystic route to the Pacific. Indians drove them back, but in 1604, Oñate—beginning to feel the pinch of his government's impatience for something grand and profitable—organized another expedition and set out on a more westerly route. With thirty men and two priests, including Fray Francisco de Escobar, who narrated the events of the journey, the Oñate expedition followed Bill Williams Fork (which they named the San Andreas) to its juncture with the Colorado. Here, they gave the river its third name, as related by Escobar: "It was named Río de Buena Esperanza [River of Good Hope], because we reached it on the day of the expectation or hope of

Chapter II: The Many-Named River

an Indian population he estimated at more than thirty thousand, and as the expedition followed the banks of the Colorado down to the Gila, then beyond, many days were spent investigating and converting heathens into minions of the Lord. Finally, on January 23, 1605, they completed the first land journey to the mouth of the Colorado: "On the day of the Conversion of the Glorious Apostle Saint Paul, we arrived with great joy at the sea or Gulf of California, where we saw, according to the declaration of seamen, the finest bay, or port (for it is called by both names), which any of them had ever seen." Escobar did not report who the "seamen" were, or what their experience; we may be sure, however, that they had never attempted to sail the gelid, unpredictable currents of the Colorado's delta region.

Oñate had made it to at least an arm of the great South Sea, but—as might have been expected—discovered that his dream of a veritable empire of oyster pearls possessed approximately the substance of Coronado's quest for rooms filled with gold. The return trip was made via *El Camino del Diablo,* and passed the regions of the Zuñi pueblos. Here, they came upon a sheer sandstone cliff which has since become known as Inscription Rock. On its wall, Oñate carved the words that gave the place its name:

> PASSED BY HERE THE COMMANDER
> DON JUAN DE OÑATE FROM THE
> DISCOVERY OF THE SOUTH SEA
> ON THE 16TH OF APRIL, YEAR 1605.

The words have a brave ring to them, but the South Sea had not been discovered, and *"Pasó par aqui"* ("Passed by here") must stand as a poignant comment on the subsequent fate of even the colonization of New Mexico. Less than twenty years after Oñate's march, the Indians of New Mexico rebelled with such success that they drove the Spanish back to Old Mexico—leaving more than four hundred dead in the land. The Colorado would not again be encountered by civilized man for three-quarters of a century.

The seventeenth century was the age of the Black Robes, the Jesuit army of the Church Militant, who saw in the wilderness of New Spain (and of New France to the far north) a treasure trove far richer and more significant than the lunatic dreams of the *conquistadores* —a storehouse of souls. With the cheerful dedication of

the most happy parturition of the Virgin Mary, Our Lady. Where it joins the San Andreas it flows from northwest to southeast, and from here turns northeast-southwest to the sea or Gulf of California, bearing on either side high ranges, between which it forms a very wide river bottom, all densely populated by people on both sides of the river, clear to the sea. . . ."

Escobar's missionary heart reveled in the existence of

THE MYTH

prospective martyrs and the organizational skill of Vatican politicians, they invaded the wilderness valleys of Mexico from Acapulco to Pimería Alta, continental Mexico's northwestern bulge. "The Black Robe story is one of Homeric quality," Herbert Bolton wrote in *Rim of Christendom*. "The missionaries were the adventurers of the seventeenth and eighteenth centuries, successors to the conquistadores of an earlier day. They traveled vast distances, coped with rugged nature and the fickle savage, performed astounding physical feats, won amazing victories over mountains, rivers, hunger, cold, and thirst.... The missionary calling demanded the highest qualities of manhood—character, intelligence, courage, resourcefulness, health, and endurance. Missionaries were required to face dangers and hardships almost beyond belief." In the course of their dangerous, purposeful wanderings in the savage land, the Black Robes also laid great sweeps of unknown country open to the knowledge of man for the first time, performing a distinctly secular service while carrying the message of the Cross.

F EW OF THE three thousand or more Jesuits who served in New Spain from its discovery to their expulsion in 1767 were so effective as Fray Eusebio Francisco Kino, a transplanted Austrian who came to Mexico in 1681 at the age of thirty-six. His first mission was a colony on the bleak peninsula of Baja California. It failed, and in 1687 he was assigned to the northern country of the Pima Indians—Pimería Alta—a harsh, wild, windswept, and unyielding land that he would call home for the next twenty-four years. At the time of his arrival, the northernmost mission was on the banks of the Río San Miguel; by the time of his death, the cross of empire had been carried throughout the country, from Cucurpe on the San Miguel to the Río Magdalena and the Altar Valley, and as far north as the Gila River.

This was his country; he crossed and recrossed its desert and mountain wastes many times during his twenty-four years, mapping it repeatedly. It intrigued him, and like others who had come to the lands of the Colorado, he was stricken with a vision—but his was the vision of truth: that California was not an island and could, in fact, be reached by land passage from Pimería Alta. Both contentions had actually been proved by Melchior Díaz in 1540, but for a century and a half the weight of myth had been more than enough to stifle the truth of the matter. By 1701, Kino felt sure enough of his belief

in the land passage to California to attempt to establish a route himself: "At present I am equipping myself to enter, with divine favor, this October and November, very far into California, until I get sight of or until I reach the very South Sea," he reported in a letter. He left Dolores in northern Pimería Alta on November 3 with one companion and his Indian servants.

By November 16 he had reached San Dionysio, which he had founded some time earlier between the forks of the Gila and the Colorado. On November 18, he started southwest down the Colorado, accompanied by an army of hungry Indians hopeful that he would be able to barter for food with the more prosperous tribes to the south. They were met with abundance—"maize, beans, various kinds of pumpkins . . . things which in the six preceding days we had not been able to procure. So great was the affection of these natives that with these provisions they came more than two leagues to meet and welcome us."* The friendliness of the natives did not impress Kino's white companion, who deserted him. Kino went on. If he was daunted, he did not show it.

Accompanied by still more helpful Indians, Kino continued south to a river crossing at Old Colonia Lerdo. There, he became the first European to cross the Colorado River since Melchior Díaz. A raft was built, and a large basket placed on it for Kino: "I accepted the basket in which they wished me to cross, and placing it and fastening it upon the raft, I seated myself in it and crossed very comfortably and pleasantly, without the least risk, taking with me only my Breviary, some trifles, and a blanket in which to sleep, afterwards wrapping up some branches of broom weed in my bandana to serve me as a pillow." The poverty of his equipment is appalling, but Kino was resting easy in the comfort of God and his own surety.

Word of the Black Robe's journey spread, and as Kino walked westward into a village in "a veritable champaign of most fertile lands," he was visited by Cutgan Indians from the north, bringing gifts, "in particular many blue shells from . . . the other or South Sea, giving us very detailed information in regard to them, and saying that they were not more than eight or ten days' journey to the westward, and that the Sea of California

*From Kino's *Favores Celestiales,* as translated by Herbert E. Bolton in *Rim of Christendom* (N.Y., 1936). Unless otherwise specified, all the Kino quotations on the following pages are from this translation.

ended a day's journey further south." He had come as far as he needed to prove his point: "already this much disputed but now very certain land route to California had been discovered." He returned to Dolores in triumph and drew a map that would make him famous and stand as the authoritative depiction of the unknown lands for decades to follow; on that map he gave the river its final name: Colorado.

MOREOVER, THERE NOW were two Californias: "I, and others, are of the opinion that this California near the new land passage recently discovered might be called California Alta, just as the preceding region ... as far as 30° of north latitude, might be called California Baja," he wrote in a letter to his superior, and went on in an excess of enthusiasm: "For with the favor of Heaven, if your Reverence and his Majesty, Philip V, God spare him, will give us workers and missionaries, all in good time they must go forward until they reach perhaps as far as Gran China, and nearly to Japan.... And perhaps to the north of these our lands we may be able to find a shorter road to Europe, partly through these lands and partly by way of the North Sea."

The excess can be forgiven him.

The *entradas* of the Black Robes were successful in opening up much unknown country in the New World, but political and international dissension caused their expulsion from New Spain in 1767. Their chores were taken up by the Franciscans, less militantly organized but no less dedicated to the garnering of souls and the perpetuation of the Spanish Empire. By the 1770's Spain's fringe of settlement extended well up the coastal rim of Alta California, and Eusebio Kino's land passage had become a logistic essential if communications were to be maintained between the City of Mexico and the farthest colonies of empire. In 1774 Juan Bautista de Anza organized an expedition whose purpose was to establish such a route from Tubac in northern Sonora to Mission San Gabriel in the San Fernando Valley of southern California. On January 8, 1774, the expedition set out with 34 men, 140 horses, and 65 cattle. With the group was Fray Francisco Garcés, a Franciscan missionary with his own brand of wanderlust. Following the by now well-traveled trail west along the Gila to its juncture with the Colorado, the party crossed into California and reached San Gabriel only a little more than two months after its departure. The land bridge to California had been opened.

So successful had the expedition been that De Anza was able to organize a second, more ambitious one the following year—this one not only to traverse the land route to California a second time, but to continue north and colonize the spit of land that one day would become San Francisco. There were 235 persons in the expedition, together with several hundred head of livestock—and Francisco Garcés. The party left San Miguel de Horcasitas on October 23, 1775, and reached the mouth of the Gila by the end of the month. While the expedition went on from there to Mission San Gabriel (and ultimately to the site of San Francisco, arriving by the summer of 1776), Garcés remained behind to do some exploring on his own "and learn the disposition of the natives toward the Christians," as H. H. Bancroft described it. It was a journey of epic scope.

Garcés crossed the Mojave Desert to the San Bernardino Mountains, turned north through Cajon Pass, circled up to Lake Tulare and the Kern River, then down to the Mojave River. Setting off toward the east, he recrossed the Colorado and trudged into the southern reaches of the Colorado Plateau, skirting the rim of the Grand Canyon. By June of 1776, the footloose missionary was in the forests of the plateau and here heard that he was not far from the Colorado River again, as he recorded in his diary: "*June 16*: In the morning I went four leagues northeast and north, over highlands clothed with junipers [cedars] and pines; in the evening five north to a sierra of red earth [Aubrey Cliffs, bounding the Grand Canyon on the east]. The Indians who were accompanying me said that the Río Colorado was near, and already were visible cañons very profound which had the color of the Sierra."

Encountering a group of Havasupai Indians from "*rancherías* of the north" who wanted him to come to their villages with the word of God, he was willing: "I determined to go with them whithersoever they wished; the occasion being favorable to see yet other peoples and discover new regions.... I went five leagues east, two northeast, and three north, the last four of these over very bad ground through some cañons the most profound.... I arrived at a *ranchería* which is on the Río Jebusua, which I named de San Antonio [Cataract Creek]; and in order to reach this place I traversed a strait which ... extends about three-quarters [of a league]; on one side is a very lofty cliff, and on the other a horrible abyss. This difficult road passed, there presented itself another and a worse one, which obliged us to leave, I my mule and they their horses, in order that we might climb down a ladder of wood."*

Garcés remained with the Havasupai until June 26, 1776, when he left for the east and even more canyons: "I traveled four leagues southeast, and south, and turning to the east; and halted at the sight of the most profound cañons which ever onward continue; and within these flows the Río Colorado. There is seen a very great sierra [actually the walls of the Grand Canyon] which in the distance [looks] blue; and there runs from southeast to northwest a pass open to the very base, as if the sierra were cut artificially to give entrance to the Río Colorado into these lands.... I am astonished at the roughness of this country, and at the barrier which nature has fixed therein." With this note of awe, Garcés left the canyons of the Colorado. He had not quite understood them—what in his experience could have provided for understanding? —but he described them in an age in which the word "profound" must have stood as the ultimate expression of wonder. He had been the first European to see the canyons since 1540.

There would be but one more major Spanish exploration into the country of the Colorado. It is fitting, then, that the last *entrada* into the land of mystery should be touched with the same myth-seeking and futility that had marked the journeys of Coronado in the 1540's.

The land bridge that Kino had predicted and De Anza established had its disadvantages, not the least of which were the numerous waterless marches it entailed and the persistent danger of Indian harassment (the bridge would indeed be closed by the Yuma uprising of 1781). But the imperative of *must be* still had the power to sway decision —and there had to be another route to Monterey.

Silvestre Velez de Escalante, a Franciscan missionary, became convinced that he was destined to establish a northern land bridge to California. On July 29, 1776, he and nine others left Santa Fe well equipped with horses, mules, presents for Indians, and a small herd of beef. Their destination was vague; they knew only that Monterey lay somewhere to the north and west.

Following this misty course, they skirted the base of the San Juan Mountains, crossed the San Juan River,

then wandered north to the Grand. They turned in a westerly direction here, following a valley of the Uinta Mountains to the Green River, which Escalante christened the San Buenaventura, then crossed it at a point not far above the mouth of the White. They now were in virgin country, new country that continued to the ragged Wasatch Mountains. By September 21, they had crossed the Wasatch Range and entered the Great Basin and the fertile valley of Utah Lake.

Turning south and west, the expedition entered the Utah deserts. Completely lost, running short of food, with exhausted animals and flagging spirits, they decided to turn back for Santa Fe—but did not know precisely how they were going to get there. For weeks they marched vaguely south through an agonizing series of canyons and ridges, seeking the crossing of the Colorado that must at times have seemed as mythical as the Seven Cities of Cíbola. By the last days of October, the search took on the tones of desperation, as Escalante outlined it in his diary of the expedition (translated by Herbert E. Bolton in the *Utah Historical Quarterly,* January to October, 1950):

In the afternoon Don Juan Pedro Cisneros went to explore the northern corner of the valley to see if there was a pass and if he could find or get a glimpse of the river and its ford. He returned after midnight with the desired report that he had reached the river, but said that he did not know whether or not we would be able to cross some mesas and high crests which were on the other bank. Nevertheless, because he said the river appeared to him to be all right and to have a ford here we decided to go to it.

October 26. We set out from San Fructo* toward the north, traveled three and a half leagues, and reached the place where previously we thought the northern exit from the valley was. It is a bend completely surrounded by very high cliffs and crests of red earth of various formations; and since the intervening plain below is of the same color, it has an agreeably confused appearance. We continued in the same direction with excessive difficulty because the animals, breaking through the surface gravel, sank to their knees in the ground, and having traveled a league and a half we arrived at the Río Grande de los

---

*For a graphic account of this terrifying climb from the 6000-foot level of the plateau to the 4000-foot bed of Cataract Canyon, see the *Report* of Lieutenant J. C. Ives in Chapter III.

*Probably at Jacobs Pools.

Images of
the Colorado: I

The Cartography of Myth

As the *conquistadores* grimly followed one shimmering myth after another into the wild New World country of Mexico and the Southwest, information about the physical outlines of the empire they had found was slowly pieced together by European cartographers, who utilized every stray bit of information, including the wildest of rumors, to create an image of Spanish America in maps. The results frequently were grotesque, but at times the map makers could be startlingly correct. The map at the left, executed by the Portuguese cartographer Diego Homen in 1558, less than twenty years after Coronado's men discovered the Grand Canyon, is particularly remarkable for its rendition of the country of the Colorado. It is the first general map of Spanish America that shows California as a peninsula, not an island mistily detached from the rest of the continent, and the first to indicate the existence of the Colorado River itself, which would suggest that Homen had access to the notes and sketches of Ulloa's sea expedition of 1539, as well as those of Alarcón in 1540. As accurate as it is, a hint of the power of myth can be seen in the turreted, castle-like pueblo villages drawn at the top left portion of the map — Homen's concession to the Seven Golden Cities of Cíbola. California would continue to be rendered as an island in the work of most cartographers for the next century and a half. California and the Colorado River would disappear, not to be "discovered" again until Fray Eusebio Francisco Kino's maps at the end of the seventeenth century.

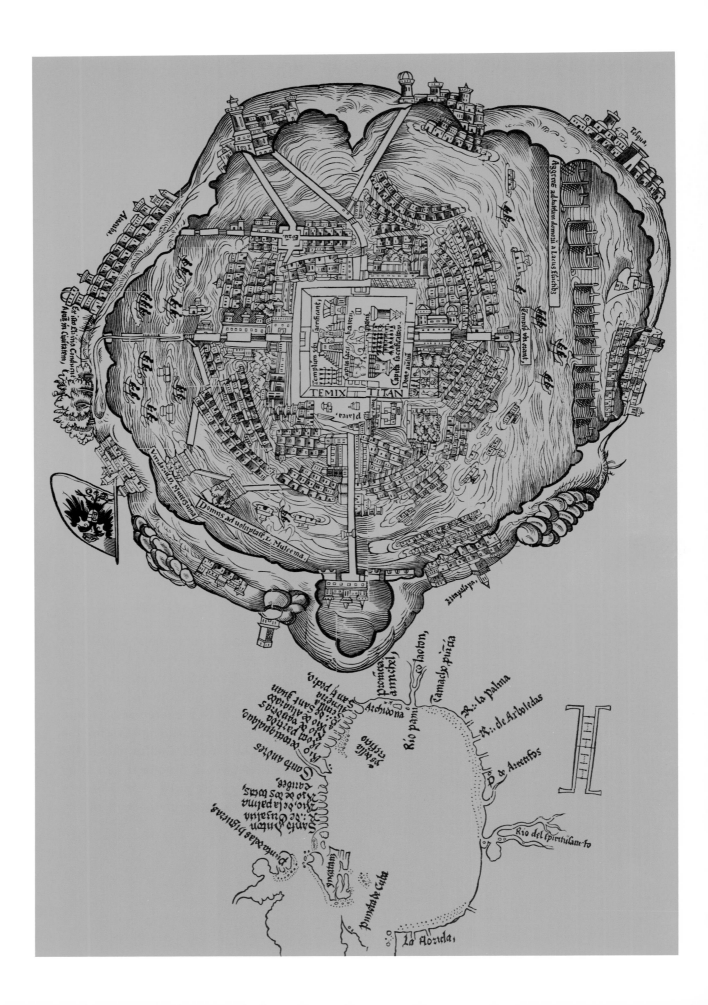

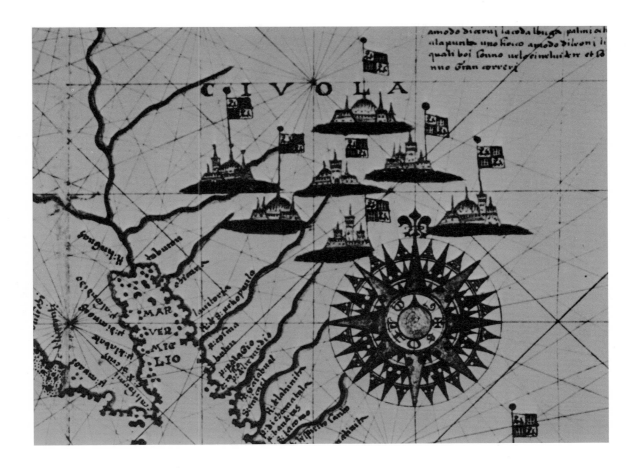

The profound effect of America and all its wonders on the European imagination is suggested by these two maps and by that on the overleaf. The one at the left, a stylistic rendering of Temixtitan (the City of Mexico) before the conquest of the Aztec empire, is identified as "Cortez's Map" and was drawn in 1524 from information said to have been supplied by Montezuma himself. The sketch at the bottom of the page is the Gulf of Mexico, with the Mississippi River ("Rio del Spiritu Sancto") at the right. Above, the Spanish cartographer Juan Martines gave the Seven Cities of Cíbola (spelled here with a "v") mystic form in a portion of a map of the west coast of Mexico, drawn in 1578. The Gulf of California is shown at the bottom left. On the following two pages an anonymous, undated (but probably shortly after 1600), and beautiful depiction of North and South America embodies any number of myths, including natives with faces in their torsos; "Cevola" (the tiny speck just above the Gulf of California in the left center of the map); Gran Quivira ("Quivira Regnu," near the top left corner), whose trees, legend had it, were hung with golden bells; and the Straits of Anian (top left corner), the mythical sea passage through the North American continent.

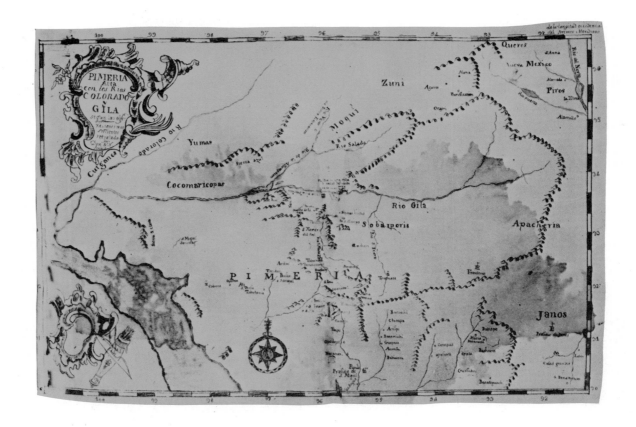

"California no es isla," Fray Eusebio Francisco Kino maintained, and this intrepid Jesuit, who had spent the bulk of his career serving the Indians in the desert wilderness of Pimería Alta (sketched below by Don N. N. Anbile in 1757), set out in 1698 to prove that a land passage to California was possible. He did not go all the way to the missions of Lower California, as he had planned to do, but he did travel far enough to prove to his own satisfaction that the province of California was divided into two parts and to gather enough information to put together the map reproduced at the right — the first truly accurate depiction of the lower Colorado and a major contribution to the cartography of Spanish America. Note the absence of any reference to "Gran Quivira" or the cities of Cíbola. Fray Kino dealt in realities, and in this country there was no treasure to be won but heathen souls.

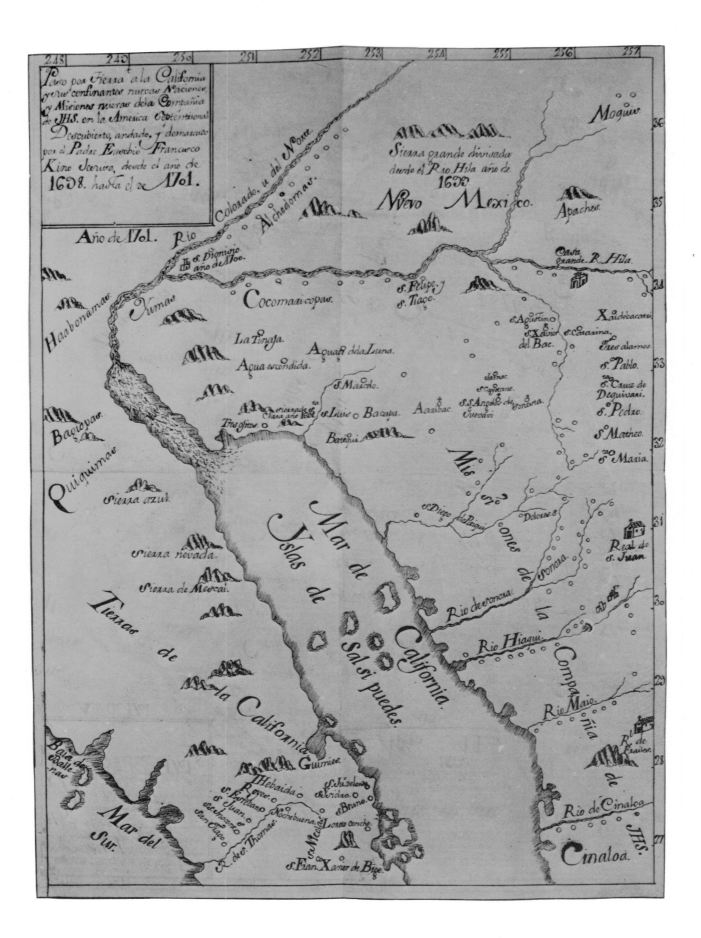

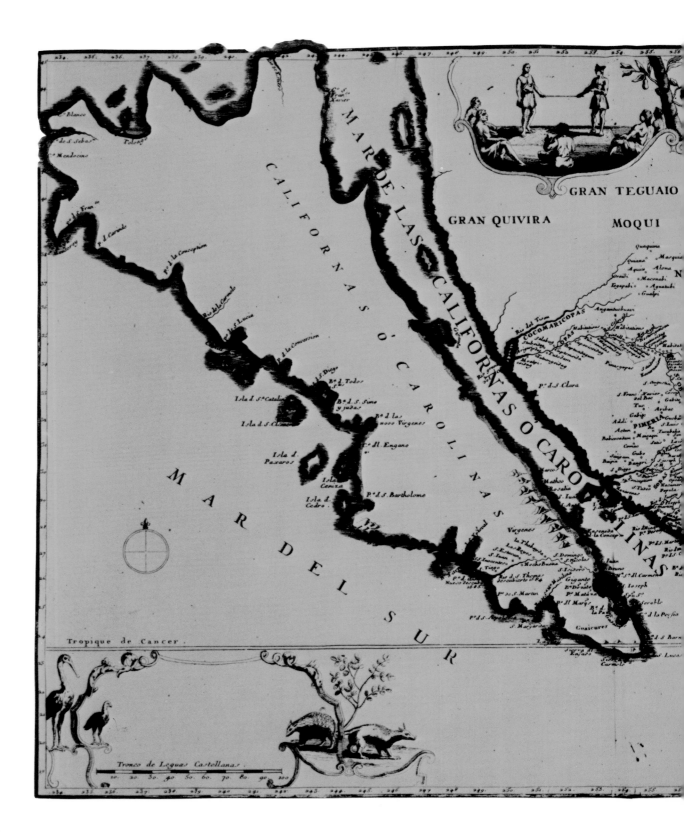

MAR DE LAS CALIFORNAS Ó CAROLINAS Ó CARO LINAS

GRAN TEGUAIO

GRAN QUIVIRA   MOQUI

CALIFORNAS Ó CAROLINAS

MAR DEL SUR

Tropique de Cancer.

Tronco de Leguas Castellanas.
10. 20. 30. 40. 50. 60. 70. 80. 90. 100.

Copies of Kino's maps of Pimería Alta spread quickly throughout Europe, but apparently not quickly enough to prevent this French version of California as an island, a map showing the areas of missionary activity by the Society of Jesus on the western coast of Mexico. Although published in 1720, it depicts a detached California and retains the Colorado's original name — "Rio del Tison" (the Firebrand River) — given to it by Cárdenas and his men in 1540. Other curiosities include "Gran Quivira" (near the center of the map), which had long before gone the way of legend, and a "bay" at the mouth of the Colorado that suggests a version of the Gulf of California.

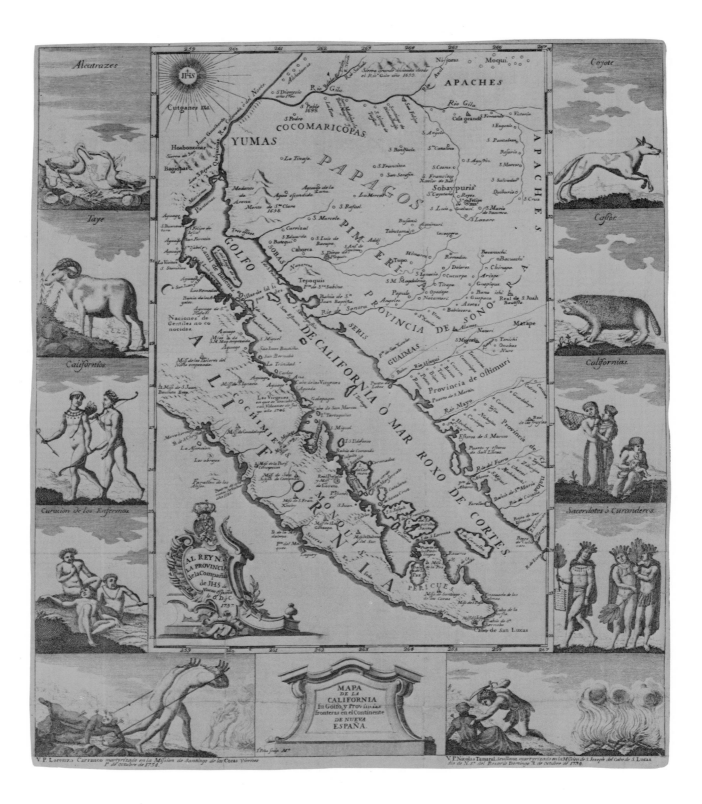

MAPA DE LA CALIFORNIA Su Golfo, y Provincias fronteras en el Continente DE NUEVA ESPAÑA.

By the middle of the eighteenth century, Kino's work had become the basis from which most cartographers fashioned maps of the country of the lower Colorado, as did Miguel Venegas in the 1757 version of California and northwestern Mexico reproduced at the left. A detail from one of the marginal drawings is shown below; if Kino had managed finally to dispel the cartographic myths of the lower Colorado, it is obvious that popular conceptions of the natives of the region still derived more from imaginative hearsay than from fact.

While the lower Colorado was comparatively well known by the latter half of the eighteenth century, the country of the upper Colorado was close to *terra incognita* and still capable of producing myths. One such was the theory of Fray Silvestre Velez de Escalante that it harbored an easy northern route from Santa Fe, New Mexico, to the newly established outpost of empire at Monterey, California. In July, 1776, Escalante with a party of nine set out to find that route; it was a journey from which they very nearly did not return. The map on the following two pages, drawn in 1778 by Don Bernardo de Miera y Pacheco, traces their wanderings in the brutal plateau wilderness of the upper Colorado with tiny circles topped by crosses, which run northwest from Santa Fe (in the lower right corner of the map) up to "Laguna de los Timpanogos" (Utah Lake), south from there to "Llanos del Nuestra Senora de la Luz" (center left), east across the Colorado to the Moqui (Zuñi) pueblos (center bottom), and finally back to Santa Fe.

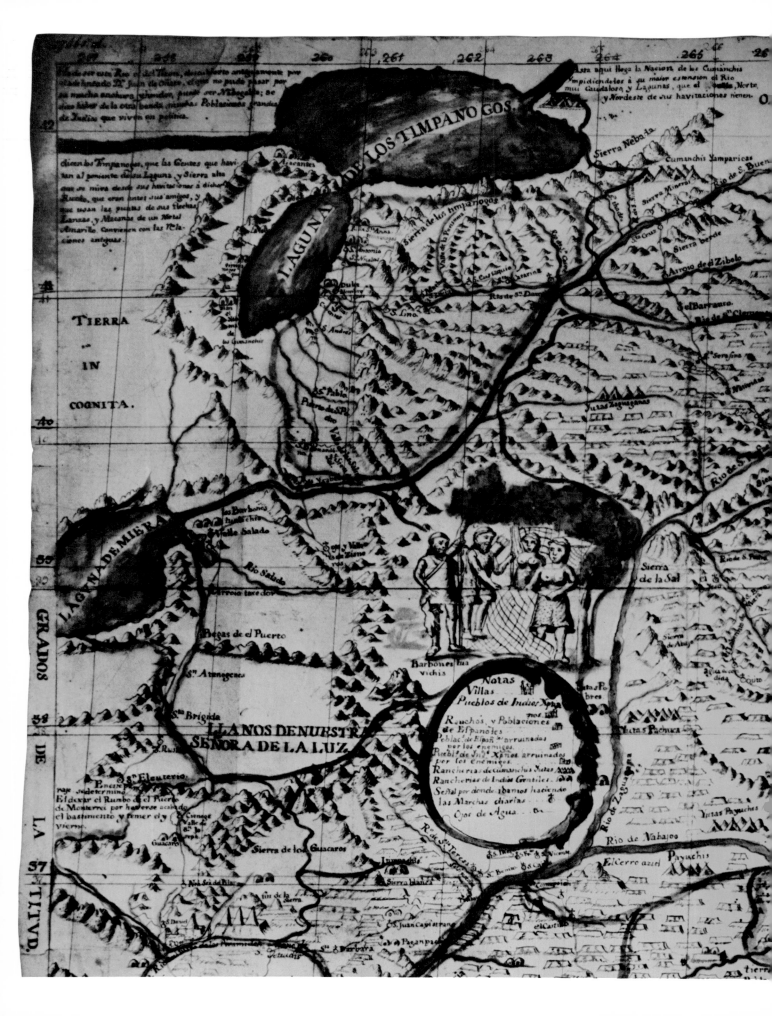

Fin de este Rio es el Thson, descubierto antiguamente por
el Adelantado D.n Juan de Oñate, el que no puede pasar por
su mucha anchura, y hondon, puede ser Navegable; se
tiene haber de la otra banda, muchas Poblaciones grandes
de Indios que viven en politica.

Dicen los Timpanois, que las Gentes que havi-
tan al poniente de su Laguna, y Sierra alta
que en mira desde sus havitaciones á dicho
Rumbo, que eran antes sus amigos, y
que usan las puntas de sus flechas
Lanzas y Mazanas de un Metal
Amarillo. Convienen con las Rela-
ciones antiguas.

Hasta aqui llega la Nacion de los Cumanchis
impidiendoles á su maior estension el Rio
mui Caudaloso, y Lagunas, que al Oeste, Norte,
y Nordeste de sus havitaciones tienen.   O.

LAGUNA DE LOS TIMPANOGOS.

Sierra Nevada.

Cumanchis Yamparicas

TIERRA

IN

COGNITA.

Sierra de los Timpanogos

Sierra Mineral

Rio de S. Buen

Sta Cruz

Sierra Verde

Arroyo de el Zibolo

el Barranco.

Rio de el Clemen

Yutas Zaguaganas

Rio de S.

LAGUNA DE MIERA

Sierra
de la Sal

Barbones ttas
Vichis

GRADOS

DE

LA

TITVD.

Vegas de el Puerto

Sn Atanagenes

Sta Brigida

LLANOS DE NUESTRA
SEÑORA DE LA LUZ.

Pn Eleuterio.

En este
paraje se determino
El dexar el Rumbo de el Puerto
de Monterrei por haverse acabado
el bastimento y temer el y.
Vierno.

Guacaro

Sierra de los Guacaros

Rio de Zaguagua

Yutas Pachuca

Yutas Payuchis

Rio de Nabajoo

El Cerro azul   Payuchis

Notas
Villas
Pueblos de Indios Xpia
nos.
Ranchos, y Poblaciones
de Españoles
Poblac. de Españ. arruinadas
por los enemigos.
Pueb. de Indios Xpnos arruinados
por los Enemigos.
Rancherias de cumanchis Yutas
Rancherias de Indios Gentiles.
Señal por donde ibamos haciendo
las Marchas diarias
Ojos de Agua.

LESTE.

Yamparicas

Cumanchis piviánes

Esta Nacion Cumanchi, hace pocos años... apareció primero a los Yutas, dicen salió por la banda de el Norte Rompiendo por entre barias Naciones, y ellos Yutas los trajeron à hacer Cambios con los Españoles, traian multitud de Perros, Cargados con sus Pieles y tiendas; se hicieron de Caballos y Armas de fierro, y se han ajilitado tanto, à el manejo de el Caballo, y à ellas que abentajaban à todas las Naciones en su agilidad y Animo, se han echo S. y dueños de todos Campos... los Zibolos, quitandoselos à la Nacion Apache, la... que era la mas dilatada que se ha conocido en la America, han destruido muchas Naciones della Y los que han quedado, los han arrinconado à las fronteras de las Provincias de Nro Rey. Causa porque se experimentà tanto daño, pues les fara su primer mantenimiento... Obliga la necesidad a mantenerse con Caballos, y Mulas.

Esta Sierra es el espinazo de esta America Septentrional, pues... Aguas que en muchos... que en los Nor... vierten en los Mares... res El Sur y Sertentrion se crian en las Gredas.

Plano Geographico, de la tierra descubierta, nueva mente, à los Rumbos Norte Noroeste y Oeste, del Nuevo Mexico. demarcada por mi Don Bernardo de Miera y Pacheco que entrò ahacer su descubrimiento, en compañia de los RRs PPs fr. Francisco Atanacio Doming.s y Fr. Silbestre Veles, segun consta en el Diario y Derrotero que se hizo y se remitio à S.M. por mano de su Virrei con Plano à la letra: El que dedica Al Sr. D. Teodoro de la Crois, del Insigne Orden Teutonica... Comandante General en Gefe de Linea y Provincias de esta America Setemptrional, por S.M. hecho en S.Ph el Real de Chiguagua. Año de 1778.

Cumanchis Jupis

Sierra del Almagre

Rio de Napeste.

Sierra mojada.

Rio de Aquinas

Sierra de la Plata

Sierra de las Grullas

Rio de Nabajoo

Rio del Norte

Cumanchis Cuchtas Marica

Rio de S. Joachin

Rio de los Pinos

Rio de las Animas

El Bosque

Rio de la Yara

Sierra blanca

Cerro de la Xi

origen del Rio Rojo

Cerro y Valle de S. Anto

Sierra de Taos

Piedra del Carne

Empieza la tierra de los Yutas

Las tres Mesas Laguna de la Trinidad

Rio de Moca

PROVINCIA
toda esta Provincia es mui escasa de Aguas, siembran con... Gentiles Maiz, y Legumbres de temporal, tienen Cria de... nado menor, y tejen de sus Lanas finas Mantas, y Cotones... que se visten con decencia, son mui inclinados al urto Es Nacion Apache tienen el mesmo Idioma que los Yutas con poca diferencia

NUEBO MEX

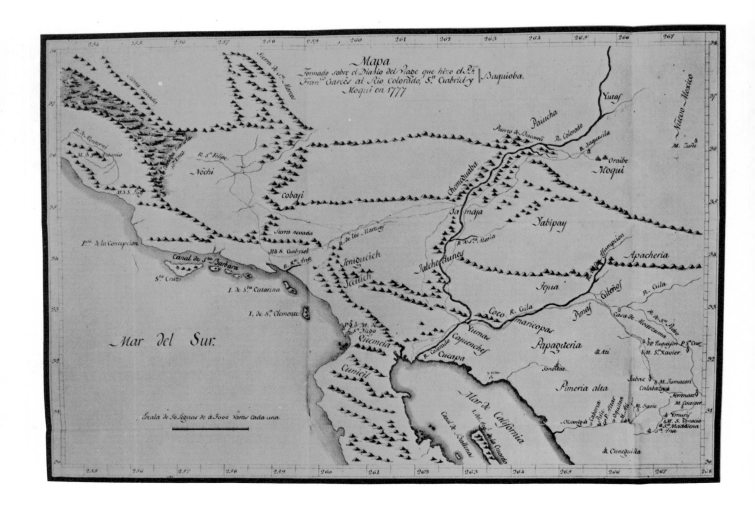

The journey of Fray Francisco Garcés from California to the Moqui pueblos of
Arizona in 1776–77 was no less astounding than that of Escalante across the
Colorado Plateaus. His travels are indicated on the map above (anonymous, but
possibly drawn by Pedro Font, Garcés' biographer, shortly after the trip). They
netted him a significant number of conversions and led him to the rims of the Grand
Canyon, which he was the first European to see since Cárdenas and his men had
discovered it in 1540. The canyons of the Colorado, Garcés noted in his diary, were
"the most profound. . . ."

Cosninas [The Colorado]. Here it is joined by another small river which we named Santa Teresa. We crossed this latter stream and camped on the banks of the Río Grande near a high gray rock. . . . All the terrain from San Fructo to here is very difficult and in places where a little moisture has been left from snow or rain it is entirely impassable. — Today five leagues north.

We decided to reconnoiter this afternoon to learn whether, having crossed the river, we might continue from here to the southeast or east. On all sides we were surrounded by mesas and inaccessible heights. Therefore, two men who knew how to swim well entered the river naked, carrying their clothing on their heads. It was so deep and wide that the swimmers, in spite of their prowess, were scarcely able to reach the opposite shore, and they lost their clothing in the middle of the river, never seeing it again. Since they arrived very tired, naked, and barefoot they were unable to walk the distance necessary for the reconnaissance and returned after having eaten something.

October 27. Don Juan Pedro Cisneros went up the bed of the Río de Santa Teresa to see whether by way of it he could find a pass by which to cross the eastern mesa and return to the Río Grande in more open country where, being wider, the river might be fordable or at least where it would be possible for the horses to cross without the danger, encountered here, of being drowned in its waters. He traveled all day and part of the night without finding a way out. He saw an acclivity very near here by which it would be possible to cross the mesa but it appeared to him to be very difficult. Others went to reconnoiter in different directions but found only insuperable obstacles in the way of reaching the ford without going back a long distance.

October 28. We returned to the same undertaking, but all in vain. In a short time a raft of logs was constructed and with it Father Fray Silvestre, accompanied by the servants, attempted to cross the river. But since the poles which served for propelling the raft, although they were five varas long, failed to touch the bottom a short distance from the shore, the waves caused by the contrary wind drove it back. So it returned three times to the shore it had left, but was unable to reach even the middle of the river. Aside from being so deep and so wide, the river here has on both banks such deep, miry places that in them we might lose all or the greater part of the animals. We had been assured by the Yubuincariri and Pagam-

pachi Indians that the river everywhere else was very deep, but not at the ford, for when they crossed it the water reached only a little above their waists. For this reason and on account of other landmarks which they gave us, we conjectured that the ford must be higher up, so we dispatched Andrés Muñiz and his brother Lucrecio with orders to travel until they found a place where we might cross the mesa mentioned above, and that, when they arrived at the river, they should seek a good ford, or at least some place where we could cross on the raft and the animals could swim without danger.

October 29. Not knowing when we might leave this place, and having consumed all the flesh of the first horse, and the piñon nuts and other things we had purchased, we ordered another horse killed.

October 30, and 31. We remained here awaiting the men who went to look for a pass and a ford.

November 1. They returned at one o'clock in the afternoon, saying that they had found a pass, although a difficult one, and a ford in the river. The pass over the mesa was the acclivity which Cisneros had seen, and since it was very high and rugged, we decided to approach it this afternoon. We set out from the bank of the Río de Santa Teresa, and having traveled a league northwest we camped on its bank. . . .

This night, from sunset until seven o'clock in the morning, we suffered greatly from the cold.

November 2. We set out from Río de Santa Teresa and climbed the acclivity, which we called Cuesta de las Ánimas and which must be half a league long. We spent more than three hours in climbing it because at the beginning it is very rugged and sandy and afterward has very difficult stretches and extremely perilous ledges of rock, and finally it becomes impassable. Having finished the ascent toward the east, we descended the other side through rocky gorges with extreme difficulty. Swinging north, and having gone a league, we turned northeast for half a league through a stretch of red sand which was very troublesome for the animals. We ascended a little elevation, and having traveled two and a half leagues also to the northeast, we descended to an arroyo which in places had running water which although saline was fit to drink. There was pasturage also, so we camped here, naming the place San Diego.* — Today four and a half leagues. . . .

*Apparently on Wahweap Creek some distance above the point where it enters the Colorado River.

THE MYTH

November 3. We set out from San Diego to the east-southeast, and having traveled two leagues we came a second time to the river, that is to say, at the edge of the canyon which here serves it as a bed, whose descent to the river is very long, high, rough and rocky, and has such bad ledges of rock that two pack animals which went down to the first one were unable to climb up it in return, even without the pack saddles. The men who had come here previously had not told us of this precipice, and we now learned that they had neither found the ford, nor in so many days even made the necessary reconnaissance of such a short stretch of country, because they spent the time seeking some of the Indians who live hereabouts, and accomplished nothing. The river was very deep here . . . for a long distance it was necessary for the animals to swim. The good thing about it was that they did not mire, either going in or getting out. The companions insisted that we should go down to the river, but on the other side there was no way to go forward after having crossed the river, except by a deep and narrow canyon of another little river which here joins it. And not having learned whether or not this could be traveled, we feared that (if we descended and crossed the river) we should find ourselves forced to go back, which on this cliff would be extremely difficult. In order not to expose ourselves to this predicament, we stopped above and sent the *genízaro,* Juan Domingo, to cross the river to see if that canyon had an outlet. But if this afternoon he should not find one, he was to return in order that we might continue upstream on this bank until we should find the ford and trail of the Indians. We sent Juan Domingo on foot. Thereupon Lucrecio Muñiz said that with our permission he would go also, on a horse, bareback, carrying equipment for making a fire, and if he found an exit he would send up smoke signals for us, in order that upon this advice we might try to descend so that the delay would be less. We told him to go, but informed him that whether or not he found the exit we would wait for him this afternoon. They did not return, so we spent the night here, not being able to water the animals although the river was so close by. We named the campsite El Vado de los Cosninas, or San Carlos.*— Today two leagues east-southeast.

November 4. Day broke without our getting news of the two we sent yesterday to make the reconnaissance.

We had used up the flesh of the second horse, and today we had not taken any nourishment whatsoever, so we broke our fast with toasted leaves of small cactus plants and a sauce made of a berry they brought from the banks of the river. This berry is by itself very pleasant to taste, but crushed and boiled in water as we ate it today it is very insipid. Since it was already late, and the two emissaries had not appeared, we ordered that an attempt should be made to get the animals down to the river, and that on its banks another horse should be killed. With great difficulty they got the animals down, some of them being injured because, losing their footing on the rocks, they rolled down long distances. Shortly before nightfall the *genízaro,* Juan Domingo, returned, declaring that he had not found an exit, and that the other emissary, leaving his horse in the middle of the canyon, had followed some fresh Indian tracks. Thereupon we decided to continue upstream until we should find a good ford and passable terrain on both banks.

November 5. We set out from San Carlos although Lucrecio had not returned. His brother Andrés remained with orders to await him only until afternoon, and to attempt to overtake us before morning. We traveled on this west bank over many ridges and gullies for a league and a half to the north, then descended to a dry arroyo and a very deep canyon, in which there was a great deal of copperas. In it we found a little-used trail, followed it, and by it left the canyon, passing a small bench of white rock, difficult but capable of being made passable. We continued on our way and having traveled a league and a quarter to the north-northeast, we found sufficient pasturage and some water, although not much, and since it was almost night we camped near a high mesa, naming the campsite Santa Francisca Romana.*—Today three short leagues.

Tonight it rained heavily here and in some places it snowed. At day break it was raining and continued to do so for several hours. About six o'clock in the morning Andrés Muñiz arrived, saying his brother had not appeared. This report caused us great anxiety, because by now he had traveled three days without provisions and with no more shelter than a shirt for he had not even worn trousers. Although he crossed the river on horseback the horse swam for a long stretch and where it faltered

---

*On the cliffs of Glen Canyon.

*At the foot of a high mesa near Warm Creek Canyon, across the Utah state line.

the water reached almost to its shoulders. And so the *genízaro* decided to go to look for him, following the trail from the place where he had last seen him, and we sent him off, giving him meat from our supply and instructing him that if the horse could not get out of the canyon he should leave it and follow on foot; that if he found Lucrecio on the other bank, from that side they should look for signs of us and follow us, and if on this side, they should try to overtake us as quickly as possible.

November 6. The rain having ceased we set out from Santa Francisca toward the northeast, and having traveled three leagues we were stopped for a long time by a heavy storm and a torrent of rain and large hail, with horrible thunder and lightning. We chanted the Litany of the Virgin in order that She might ask some relief for us and God was pleased that the storm should cease. We continued half a league toward the east and camped near the river* because it continued to rain and our way was blocked by some boulders. We named the campsite San Vicente Ferrer.—Today three and a half leagues.

Don Juan Pedro Cisneros went to see if the ford was in this vicinity, and returned with the report that he had seen that here the river was very wide, and judging from the current it did not appear to him to be deep, but that we would be able to reach it only through a nearby canyon. We sent two other persons to examine the canyon and ford the river, and they returned saying that it was very difficult. But we did not give much credence to their report and decided to examine everything ourselves next day in company with Don Juan Pedro Cisneros. Before nightfall the *genízaro* arrived with Lucrecio.

November 7. We went very early to inspect the canyon and the ford, taking along the two *genízaros* Felipe and Juan Domingo, so that they might ford the river on foot since they were good swimmers. In order to lead the animals down the side of the canyon mentioned it was necessary to cut steps in a rock with axes for the distance of three *varas* or a little less. The rest of the way the animals were able to get down, although without pack or rider. We went down to the canyon and having traveled a mile we descended to the river and went along it downstream about two musket shots, sometimes in the water, sometimes on the bank, until we reached the widest part of its current where the ford appeared to be. One of the

*On the cliffs above the Colorado River at the spot now known as the Crossing of the Fathers.

men waded in and found it good, not having to swim at any place. We followed him on horseback a little lower down, and when half way across, two horses which went ahead lost their footing and swam a short distance. We waited, although in some peril, until the first wader returned from the other side to guide us and then we crossed with ease, the horses on which we crossed not having to swim at all. We notified the rest of our companions, who had remained at San Vicente, that with lassoes and ropes they should let the pack saddles and other effects, down a not very high cliff to the bend of the ford, and that they should bring the animals by the route over which we had come. They did so and about five o'clock in the afternoon they finished crossing the river, praising God our Lord and firing off a few muskets as a sign of the great joy which we all felt at having overcome so great a difficulty and which had cost us so much labor and delay, although the principal cause of our having suffered so much . . . was our lack of someone to guide us through such bad terrain. For through lack of an experienced guide we went by a very round-about route, spent many days in such a small area, and suffered hunger and thirst. . . .

THE WORST of their travails were over; after a long march south from the Crossing of the Fathers, they reached the Hopi Indians, and from there made it back to Santa Fe. They had been the first Europeans to cross the Colorado River above the Grand Canyon, and the first to enter the stark wilds of the Great Basin. But they also were the last representatives of His Holy Catholic Majesty to enter the country of the Colorado. "Nothing came of this sunnily stupendous journey," Bernard DeVoto wrote. "Thirty-odd years later, traders out of Santa Fe and Taos took to using some of their route in Colorado, and on the way to California crossed their trace in the Parowan Country. . . . But no one followed Escalante into the Great Basin now, to baptize the Utes and Timpanogos whom he had promised salvation. The brilliant promise of the Spanish reawakening turned out to be a sunset color after all and it had already begun to fade. . . ."

But the river had a name—the Colorado. It had been at least partially explored and taken from the framework of fantasy; some of its outlines had been placed on paper, some of its secrets exposed. The rest would have to wait for the arrival of the Anglo—who would bring with him his own baggage of myth.

CHAPTER III

THE

PROFITLESS LOCALITY

Anglo Exploration, from Mountain Men to Government Scientists

THE SPANISH, from Coronado to Escalante, had come to the country of the river, driven by dreams of conquest. Coronado sought the conquest and pillage of Cíbola, presumed to be another kingdom whose riches would rival those of the Aztecs and the Incas. Fifty years of sanguine experience in the New World had demanded the continuing generation of such myths, and the dream of the *conquistadores* died hard. The *padres* had followed their own kind of dream, seeing in this land of clear lights the opportunity to garner souls like so many shocks of wheat, rescuing the land from heathen perdition and making it a fiefdom of the Lord. Both dreams had failed in the face of hard reality.

Yet the river continued to harbor myth. It had been encountered several times, even traveled upon, and its general course guessed at by the beginning of the nineteenth century, but beyond that was mystery; the river was still a blank, its canyons uncharted and almost unknown, its meaning lost and puzzling. The mystery would be a long time in being solved, but the first half of the nineteenth century saw at least the beginning of solution with the arrival of the Anglo-Saxon and his sometimes obsessive compulsion to *know,* as well as to exploit. Curiously, for all the fact that more pragmatism than romance marked the entrance of the Anglos, they were not always able to escape the magic the river held, and their dreams often became as myth-ridden and unrealistic as those of the *conquistadores* and the *padres.*

One of the first was William H. Ashley, trapper, trader, and trans-Mississippi entrepreneur in the age of the 'mountain man'. He had been born in Virginia in 1778,

and by 1805 had moved to Missouri, where he remained, serving in various political capacities and in the state militia during the second war with England. He also took his first flyer into business in these years, manufacturing gunpowder in Potosi, Washington County; the enterprise foundered after the war, and Ashley took himself to St. Louis. There he formed a fur trade partnership with Andrew Henry and in 1822 organized his first trapping expedition by boat up to the headwaters of the Missouri River. Ashley deposited his partner and a party of trappers at the mouth of the Yellowstone in October to put in the winter trapping and then returned to St. Louis to organize another run up the river in the following spring. The business suffered disaster almost immediately. Henry and his men were driven by Indians from their trapping operations on the upper Missouri, and Ashley's spring expedition was attacked by Arikaras and stopped cold. It was not until the late fall of 1824 that Ashley put together another expedition to the Rocky Mountains—this time by land.

Leaving Fort Atkinson early in November, 1824, the expedition proceeded up the Platte River to the Forks, then up the South Platte into the mountains, arriving on the Laramie Plains in February, 1825. The high wall of the Medicine Bow Range obstructed movement to the west, but Ashley followed the base of the mountains up to the North Platte, then crossed west through the Great Divide Basin, south of South Pass. By the third week of April, the group had reached the Green River (still called by its Indian name, "Seedskeedee"). Here, Ashley split the party into four parts—six men went to the source

Grand Canyon from Zuñi Point (photograph by Henry K. Peabody, 1900).

THE MYTH

of the Green, seven off to a distant mountain, and six south to make rendezvous with the men still out trapping with Andrew Henry. By this time, trapping all the way, they had accumulated a healthy supply of furs, and Ashley with the remaining six men prepared to descend the Green to cache the furs and to select and mark a point of general rendezvous where the sundry parties could meet early that summer. Two bullboats—crudely framed vessels covered with buffalo hide—were constructed, and on April 21 Ashley set off down the Green. The first cache of goods was made about fourteen miles above Henrys Fork, and by May 4, the party had reached a point above Flaming Gorge, where Ashley established a place of rendezvous.

Here they might have stopped, and probably should have. The Green at this point cuts into the Uinta Mountains, beginning the long chain of canyons and rapids that even the Indians saw filled with mystery and danger. It could not have presented a comforting sight to men accustomed to the broad and knowable—if nonetheless dangerous—eddies of the Missouri and Mississippi. But Ashley went on, perhaps pulled into the dark canyons and the narrow river by that seemingly insatiable need-to-know that for the next fifteen years would give to the wanderings of the mountain men the air of a great adventure. The story of this first assault upon the unknown canyons of the Green has been preserved in Ashley's own hand in a diary first edited by historian Dale L. Morgan and published in *The West of William H. Ashley* (Old West Publishing Co., 1964). All notes and bracketed information in the following excerpt have been compiled from Dr. Morgan's own annotations.

The canyon journey began on May 5, 1825:

We proceeded down the river which is closely confined between two verry high mountains, about ten miles the river is verry crooked its general course to day S S E, at 7 miles Entered a small creek [Sheep Creek] on the West side about thirty feet wide bg. E & W. rappid current bottoms were timbered with willow burch box Elders &c and from all appearances there are many beaver on its head— These mountains present a most gloomy scene They are Entire rock generally of a redish appearance, they rise to the hight of from 2 to 4000 feet out of their Crevices grows a Species of dwarf pine [piñon pine] & Ceder

[juniper] the only timber upon them, they are on the one side or other of the river perpendicular or projecting over —on the othur side so steep & rugged as to prevent the passage of a man over them—the rocks that fall in the river from the walls of the mountan make the passage in some places dangerous—windy unpleasant weather. . . .
May 6:
continu[e]d our voyge at ½ mile Enters a small creek on the W side the river becomes more confined by the Mountains and the obstructions by rocks in the passage so great as almost to prevent our passage down it—at ten miles there is a fall of 10 or 15 feet in the distance of 150 feet caused by the mountains given way and throughing rock from 20 to 40 feet in diameter Entirely across the river, it is not passable for boats of any description* here we performed a portage of 100 yards, reloaded our canoes and proceeded down the river about 2 miles farther & Encamped The afternoon was cold & stormy considerable snow during the night—
May 7:
Cold Stormy Snowy morning we decended the river to day about 25 miles its general course S E The mountain continued verry high & rugged untill the last five miles when they became much lower—the channel of the river is yet confined no low ground or timber—we passed several places where it was Extremely dangerous but recd. no Injury except shiping considerable quantities of water & wetting our baggage An Indian road passes along the north bank of the river—from the appearance of an Encampment we supposed a party of 100 or more has passed along the road about a month since
May 8:
3 miles Enters a verry small branch on the N side here the mountains withdraw to the distance of an half mile from the river and the bottoms Enlarge on which are small Willows—we decended the river about ten miles E S E & camped on the E Bank. . . .†

*They had now entered Red Canyon. The falls mentioned were named Ashley Falls by John Wesley Powell in 1869. Powell and his men found "Ashley, 1825" painted on a rock near the site, an inscription that remained nominally visible until well after the turn of the century. "It would be pleasant," Dale L. Morgan points out, "had Ashley recorded in his diary making this inscription on the canyon walls; and it would be interesting to know how he happened to have good quality paint with him."

†They now were in Browns Hole, where the river flows in a generally peaceful fashion for ten or fifteen miles before curving sharply to the southwest and entering the canyons of the Uinta Mountains—the first of which is Lodore Canyon.

May 9:

at 3 miles the river Enters a third [second] mountain [Lodore Canyon] the bottom above which is an Encampment where some thousands of Indians wintered. Their camps were principally in the thick willows & covered with the bark of cedar oposite & Just below the Encampment on the E side of the river above the mountain Enters a small creek [Vermilion Creek] 20 feet wide bg E & W: has on it willows and some large timber—did not examine it for Beaver—The Channel of the river is more confined by this than the mountain above the walls of the mountain are perpendicular on Each side of the river and from three to 4000 feet high of a reddish colour the channel of the river is much obstructed by rocks which make it exceedingly dangerous to decend in the distance of six miles from the Entrance I had to perform two portages one of 50 the other 250 yards—we Encamped after making about 12 miles S S W—Raw unpleasant weather

May 10:

mended our canoes which had recd considerable injury yesterday, and proceeded down the river—at the distance of 2 miles the river became so verry bad that we were unable to proceed with our canoes loaded we discharged them and performed a portage of half mile which in consequence of the roughness of the side of the mountain along which we were obliged to pass made it extremely difficult and tedious—these may be well called the Rocky mountains for there is nothing but mountains of rocks to be seen partially covered with a dwarf groth of cedar & pines—violent wind with snow & rain

May 11:

The portage of yesterday consumed the whole of that day a short distance below the passage is an other of a quarter of a mile the road for the porters is much more difficult than that of yesterday—we decended the river to day about 4 miles S W and have 5 portages to perform —at many of these places the river is not more than forty or 50 yards wide Roling over rocks with great violence some of my men are the most skilfull of watermen or I could not have proceeded at all Even with the Empty canoes we are now destitute of provisions and know not when we shall be able to get where we can supply ourselves—

May 12:

Our boats recd. considerable injury yesterday in passing over rocks, they had this morning to undergo some repares

which was completed by 11 Ock when we continued our voyge—we did not proceed more than a mile before we had to perform a portage of 150 yds. which were followed by two others in the distance of two miles the last was the most difficult we have had in the distance of about 300 yards the fall is at least 50 feet our boats as well as cargo had to be taken over the rocks out of the water about 100 yards then let down with ropes to the foot of the fall this portage had to be performed along the side of a mountain wher it was almost impossible for a man to pass without any burthen. This days progress 3 miles was S W—cool clear weather—

May 13:

We reloaded our canoes and descended the river about 8 miles where another River [The Yampa] Enters on the south side bg. E & W nearly or quite as large as The one of our decension we performed no portages to day but there are Several dangerous Rapids from our camp Junction of these rivers here is a remarkable bend in the river a point of the mountain runs for a mile not wider than 50 or 100 yds. bg N & S and the river runs immediately round it in the bend on the south side Enters a small creek bg N & S the mountain at this point changes Colour to a light sand or nankeen colour and gradually declines there are some small bottoms [Echo Park] and some sign of beaver —I call This the river Entering on The south side Marys River on which is some sign of beaver it no dout heads in the N. E and has many beaver on it—at the second bend to the left is a verry considerable fall The river is remarkably crooked rapid and dangerous general course from the Junction of the rivers S W—we made this day about 25 miles and Encamped on the N Bank. where the mountain with draws on that side from the river to the distance of an half mile, there are some Islands and Small bottoms well timbered with thrifty cotton wood of the *sweet* kind —here is the first fresh buffalloe sign we have seen for some days indeed since we Entered the 2d. mountain [Lodore Canyon] great abundance of Elk we saw last night about 100 Buffaloe but could not kill any, they having got the wind of us, we were so Exosted with the fatiegue of portages and the tediousness of our progress that we crossed many dangerous places This day without examining them previously and other when in the draft there was no possibility of landing—In passing of the most of them we shiped considerable water—but met with no serious injury—fine pleasant day—my men in fine spirits although nothing to Eat—

THE MYTH

May 14:

we proceeded Early for the purpose of getting something to Eat which we accomplished after going about 3 miles—I killed a Buffaloe at 4 miles mountains on Each side of the river and the river again confined to a verry narrow Channel here commences a consider[able] Fall which has continued about six miles where we Encamped general course of the River S W—after we had proceeded on these falls about four miles They became more dangerous, and we with difficulty Effected a landing for the purpose of examining them lower down—I with one man performed that duty as far as the mountain would permit—although The fall continued and the waves were verry high I concluded to proceed with the boats believing that should the river become impassable or more dangerous, that we could discover it, and land the boats—but after proceeding about one and an half mil[e]s we discovered at the distance of about 4 or 600 yards by the motion of the water &c a verry great & dangerous fall and attempt was immediately made to land the large boat (the small one being in the rear a considerable distance and had fortunate[ly] capsized which had detained here untill the information relative to this fall was communicated to the men) but we were already in the draft to land was imposible I discovered from the appearances of the rocks that our only way & that doubtfull to avoid immedeate destruction was to lay the boat straight with the current and pass in the middle of the river I directed the stearsman accordingly my orders were obeyed & the men performed their duty handsomely, but soon after Entering the heavy billows our boat filled with water but did not sink she was in that situation th[r]own against a rock at or near the foot of the falls, and near a large Eddy, to which by the rock she was inclined and Entered, two of the most active men then leaped in the water took the cables and towed her to land Just as from all appearance she was about making her exit and me with her for I cannot swim & my only hope was that the boat would not sink—the Cargo recd great injury some articles Entirely lost & others greatly damaged fortunately I had my powder so secured with bear skins that it was but little injured we were detained there drying the cargo untill the afternoon of Friday the 15th. when we again proceeded the falls continued but we had no alternative but to decend & without a knowledge of what was at any considerable distance before us for the walls of the mountain Extended to the edge of the water and them impassable in the distance of

three miles we passed several dangerous places where we shiped considerable water and at about 6 miles (where we Encamped for the night.*

May 16:

Embarked & proceeded Early the river rapid but not at all dangerous at 3 miles the mountains withdrew from Each side of the river and bottoms of considerable size Well timbered. the river is remarkable crooked general course S W we decended this day about ten miles and Encamped at the Entrance of a bold Stream [Ashleys Fork] on the N. Side bg N W & S E about 40 feet wide its bottoms are timbered with small willow and some large Cotton wood about 3 miles above this Creek Enters another—of about the same Size and appearance & on the oposite side about half way between thes two Enters anoth[e]r South side bg N W & S E.—high hills on the south and mountains covered with snow at the distance of 2 or 3 miles on the N—

May 17:

we remain at the Entrance of the Creek to day to procure meat having understood from two Frenchmen† who we met last night that the country below for a great distance is Entirely destitute of game, These men with 20 or 30 others crossed the Country from Toues 4 of whom decended the river in a canoe but finding it so verry dangerous and destitute of game returnd they give a lamentable account of their voyge—they had to live on the skins of beaver which they had caught in this neighbourhood. They also inform me that the Indians generally in this country are hostile desposed and have killed & robed 15 or 20 men who were from the neighbourhood of St Louis having procured sufficient meat we on Monday 18th. decended the river about 2 miles where we made a cache and deposited the greater part of my goods

about 2 miles below the 2nd little river Entering on the N Side after the 3rd mountain [*i.e.*, Ashleys Fork and Split Mountain Canyon] Just below say ½ mile of a large Island [still existing, about 3 miles below Ashleys Fork] on the left bank at the foot of a small bare [*i.e.*, bar?] a cotton wood tree 10 inches in diameter—Standing alone is about 50 yds above it and immedeately North of it near the bank of the river are two cluster of Bushes the cashe is about 60

---

*The camp was in Split Mountain Canyon, from which they emerged the next day.

†This was the party of Etienne Provost and (Francois?) Leclerc, based on Taos, in New Mexico, which penetrated to the Uinta Basin sometime in the late summer or early fall of 1824.

feet from the waters Edge N W of two little prickly bushes say 4 feet

Cash No. 2

2½ Kegs Tobacco	150 lbs
14 dozen Knives	
2 peaces scarlett Cloth	
2 ditto Blue Stroud	
3 Bags coffee	200 lbs.
Bale & Bag Sugar	130 lbs.
3 packs beaver	50 skins
pack of beads assorted	
& vermillion	
assortment of Indian trinkett, mockerson alls do.	
2 Bags gun powder	150 lbs.
3 Bars lead	120 lbs
Bag flints	1000
Bag salt	10 lbs
pack cloths—	
pack conta[in]ing a variety of Indian trinketts—	
Ribbons Binding &c	
axes hoes &c	

—from The cash we decended the river on the 19th about ten miles to the entrance of a small river on the N. bank thirty feet wide bg. N W & S E, great appearance of Buffaloe & Elk—pleasant weather general course of the river to day West but verry crooked one bend of six miles around is not more than 200 yd. across—*

May 20:
We descended the river to day about 12 miles general course S W but verry crooked—The bottoms have become large as well as The river, and are Well timbered with Sweet cotton wood The mountains are at the distan[c]e of about 5 miles on Each side the river to which there is a high broken country. The Cotton wood trees are in these bottoms sufficiently large for canoes, or perogues great appearance of game but none of consequence immediately on the river—This river over flows its bottoms from the place of my Embarcation to this—pleasant weather—

May 21:
proceeded about 4 miles to the Entrance of a River [The Duchesne] about 30 yds wide on the north side the Indian name of this River is Tewinty, Bg. N & S—about

*Horeshoe Bend. The diary markedly understates the distance around it.

two miles farther to the wintering place of Mess. Provo &c there found a paper directing his hunters who were in the mountains trapping to decend the river 6 miles where they would find Mr. La clare with articles for them. I consequently decended to that place but unfortunately found that they had left their camp—in pursuit of game as there is none in this neighbourhood—having reason to believe that they would not return sooner than 6 or 8 days, I cached the cargo of my Canoes and get 12 miles—

May 22:
proceeded down the river in a wood canoe* with three of my men & sent the other 3 to procure game by our return—my object is to find Indians of whom I can procure horses and ascertain the true situation of the country described as so verry mountanous and barren— notwithstanding the unfavourable account given of the Country we had to Enter it without provisions warm day ——S. W. 6 miles

May 23:
last Evening one of the men killed a goose which boiled gave us a good supper we decended to day about 12 miles find the Country a barren heap of rocky mountains— could not kill any thing to Eat found a fresh Indian trail and appearance as if they had Camped & hunted in this Neighbourhood for some days

May 24:
followed some of the Indian roads on which they had Just passed and ascertained that a party were ascending the river I directed the men to return with the Canoe as expediceously as possible—and I followed the hillier road, but finding it to pass over such rugged ground was compeled to leave it and select the best way to travel to the place where I had appointed to meet the 3 men sent in persuit of game—every diligence were used by all to procure game without success. we were again this day without any thing to eat

May 25:
left camp Early with a view of reaching our rendavoze to day two men by land and two by water, determin[ed] to shoot beasts or birds of any kind for food if in our power to do so with all our Exertions nothing was killed —late in the afternoon discovered The trail of foot and

*"Ashley's 'canoe' was probably a cottonwood dugout; this was a more solid craft than the bullboats he had been using, but his reason for abandoning the latter may have been the immediately expedient one that the prolonged immersion in water was disintegrating the buffalo skins of which the bullboats were constructed."

THE MYTH

horsemen who had but a few hours passed and from all appearances had been in serch of me. followed the trail till night without finding the people. next morning [May 26] about 10ck met with one of the party of Snake [Ute] Indian he met me with great familiarity and Ease as much so as if he had been accustomed to being with white men all his life calling aloud American, I answered in the affirmative he then advanced and extended his hand, and by signs asked many questions to wit how many men were with me. where they were and the object of our persuit in this country all of which I gave him to understand by signs—after passing about an hour with me during which I made Enquiries relative to The Country Westwardly, his knowledge of any white men in the Country &c &c he departed with a view notifying a band of his nation to which he belonged and who were not more than a days march from my camp of my situation, and to Endeavour to induce them to bring and sell me 7 horses of which I informed him I was in want

May 27:

I arrived at the place appointed to meet the men sent to kill Buffaloe [Willow Creek] as well as The band of Indians & late in the afternoon two Indians arrived to inform me that in consequence of the mountanous situation of the Country that the Lodges would not arrive sooner than three days; and requested that I would wait their arrival that they would supply me with 6 horses, I consented to wait....

The river journey ended here, near the mouth of Minnie Maud Creek at a point just north of Desolation Canyon, where the river thunders into another set of canyons whose dangers would not be tested for another forty years. Ashley purchased several horses from the Indians and on May 30 headed west up the Uinta and an eventual meeting with Henry's men. By October, he was back in St. Louis with some nine thousand pounds of beaver pelts—more than enough to clear up the backlog of debts that had nearly foundered the business the previous two years. Ashley went on to further business and political success, and died in 1838 a comfortably rich man. Remaining a major force in the affairs of the West until his death, Ashley left his mark on the land in many ways—but never more compellingly than when he painted his name—if indeed it was he who painted it—on a wall in the canyons of the Green.

LITTLE MORE THAN a year after Ashley had tumbled down the Green, exploring for the first time the far northern reaches of the river system, a young British lieutenant in His Majesty's Royal Navy was pushing a twenty-five-ton schooner against the thick current of the Colorado's mouth. Lt. Robert W. H. Hardy, who had entered the service as a boy in 1806, had been sent to the west coast of Mexico by the General Pearl and Coral Fishery Association of England to scout out the existence of profitable oyster beds in the Sea of Cortez. Following rumore with the kind of dogged enthusiasm that had been displayed by Coronado's men, Hardy determined in July of 1826 to go to the mouth of the Colorado, where rich fisheries were said to abound. Leaving his original ship *Wolf* at the island of Tiburon, Hardy boarded the smaller, lighter *Bruja* and set out for the north, accompanied by a motley group, as he reported in his *Travels in the Interior of Mexico* in 1829:

Our crew was composed of the most wretched set of people, in the shape of men and sailors, that ever set foot on the deck of a vessel. The captain was an Englishman. Two seamen whom I had taken from the Wolf ... were also Englishmen. Two were Italians; my Mexican servant; one California Yuma Indian, our diver; and two Indians from the Manillas, one of whom was the cook.... These were all the living souls, except flies, fleas, bugs, etc., on board the *Bruja*. The maneuvers were conducted sometimes in the English, and sometimes in the Spanish language; but neither in one or the other did work go on with activity. The captain used never to hurry himself; the two Englishmen had been old man-of-war's men, and would not hurry themselves; the two Italians were forever talking ...; my servant, although an indefatigable worker on shore, did not know how to employ his strength and activity on board; the cook was always playing with the fire ... and the other Indian was generally a looker-on, except at meal times, when he played a "good stick."

I never in my life was disposed to play the tyrant until I joined this vessel, and here the apathy of the whole crew rendered harsh measures necessary, as the adoption of mild ones would probably have been productive of the loss of the vessel.... I had therefore been in almost one uninterrupted rage since we left the Gulf of Molexe. Example was of little avail, and I am convinced, "al-

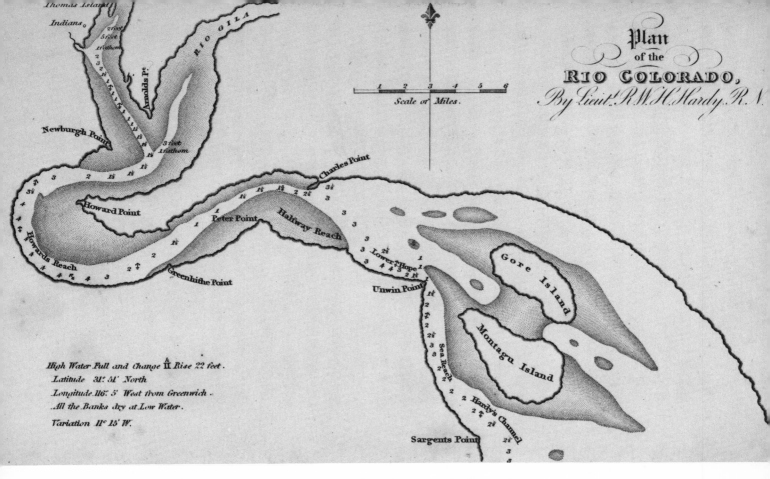

Labels on map:
Thomas Island
Indians
RIO GILA
Arnolds Pt.
Newburgh Point
Plan
of the
RIO COLORADO,
By Lieut. R.W.H. Hardy. R.N.
Scale of Miles.
Charles Point
Howard Point
Peter Point
Halfway Reach
Howards Reach
Greenhithe Point
Lower Hope
Unwin Point
Gore Island
Montagu Island
Sea Reach
Hardy's Channel
Sargents Point

High Water Full and Change Ⅱ Rise 22 feet.
Latitude 31° 51' North
Longitude 116° 5' West from Greenwich.
All the Banks dry at Low Water.
Variation 11° 15' W.

Hardy's 1829 map (published in his Travels in the Interior of Mexico) *was the first to chart accurately the mouth of the Colorado—and the river itself to its confluence with the Gila.*

though I say it," that I did more work than all the rest of the crew together.

Somehow, Hardy and his crew of incompetents muddled their way north, surviving even the gulf's perverse gales, which the good lieutenant described as well as anyone ever has: "The variable winds of the gulf raise each of them a short sea, and then comes a gale, which swallows up the 'gentle airs,' and roughly superseding their feeble efforts, puts the element beneath into such a state of chaotic wildness, that the vessel will sometimes be lifted on the top of three conflicting seas at once, which meet under her bows, and with their reflex leave a sort of deep vortex into which the vessel tumbles unresistingly...." Reaching the head of the gulf, the *Bruja* searched for the mouth of the Colorado, finally encountering it on July 20: "At two we saw an opening ahead, which appeared to be the mouth of the river.... At three, all doubts of the fact were removed from our minds. The river had clearly two, if not three months, and the land on either side was very low."

EARLY THAT EVENING, the *Bruja* anchored in the mouth in two fathoms of water, her commander believing the depth to represent the lowest possible tide. During the night, however, the thundering ripple of the river's incredible bore woke them all, and Hardy took a midnight sounding that revealed they were sitting in precisely a foot-and-a-half of water. While waiting for the high tide to lift the *Bruja,* Hardy spent the next day exploring upriver. He was impressed, if inaccurate: "I was now gazing at a vast extent of country visited only by the elements. It is probably in the same state that it was ages ago, and perhaps I am the first person, from creation up to the present time, whose eyes ever beheld it."

For three weeks Hardy explored and charted the Colorado from its mouth to nearly its junction with the Gila, fighting the river's antic currents ("There is *no such thing as slack water in the Colorado River*," he wrote in frustration), visiting the local Indians (the Cocopahs), taking meticulous soundings, and cheerfully giving English names to channels, islands, and shoals once provided with the names of His Holy Catholic Majesty's saints.

THE MYTH

Hardy and the *Bruja* departed the Colorado on the morning tide of August 15. He had discovered no rich oyster beds, but he had been the first man to navigate the Colorado River in nearly three hundred years.

While Ashley was exploring the Green and Lieutenant Hardy charting the mouth of the Colorado, an itinerant trapper by the name of James Ohio Pattie was making his own mark on the history of the river. Among the wanderings of the mountain men during the first forty years of the nineteenth century, few journeys approach the scope and mystery of that undertaken by this Missouri-born vagabond in 1825 and 1826. After a fur-trapping expedition on the Gila that ended in the loss of their beaver pelts to the Indians, James Ohio Pattie left his grandfather, Sylvester, and followed the Gila to the Colorado, turned north to the mouth of Bill Williams Fork (the San Andreas River of Oñate), crossed the country of the Mojaves, skirted the rim of the Grand Canyon, crossed the Continental Divide to the Platte, and ended his journey at the Yellowstone in May of 1826. James Ohio, again accompanied by his grandfather, returned to the Gila the following winter, trapped it to the Colorado, hacked out some cottonwood canoes to carry the furs, and started down the river to the mouth, where they expected to find a Spanish settlement. Camping on the banks of the river one night, they encountered the bore of the Colorado and disaster: "... the rush of the tide coming in from the sea, in conflict with the current of the river. At the point of conflict rose a high ridge of water, over which came the sea current combing down like the water over a milldam...." In a few minutes, their campsite was under three feet of water, and they had barely escaped with their lives and a few furs. Desperate, they set out on foot to the north and west, stumbling finally into San Diego, where they were arrested and thrown into jail. Sylvester died, but James Ohio eventually was released and made his way to the States.

THE YOUNG TRAPPER quite possibly had seen and experienced more of the Colorado than any of his predecessors; yet we will never know. *The Personal Narrative of James O. Pattie*, in which his adventures were set down in 1831, had the helping hand of Timothy Flint, the amanuensis who later would cheerfully abet the lying autobiography of mountain man James P. Beckwourth. As a result, history has lost a document whose value can only be guessed at; the *Narrative* as rendered by Timothy Flint abounds in colorful improbabilities and crosses vague topography that makes it impossible to determine precisely where Pattie was at any given time. James Ohio Pattie was no explorer; he was an illiterate trapper. Timothy Flint was no reporter; he was a storyteller. The combination was not the best for the uses of history. But Pattie had been there; he had seen.

During the next thirty years, great portions of the river system would become known. In 1847, Brigham Young laid the base of the Mormon empire at Deseret, on the shores of the Great Salt Lake, and from there in the 1850's he sent groups of obedient Saints to colonize the pockets and crannies of the arid plateau, until the land was pricked by more than a dozen tiny settlements with names like Lehi, Moab, Kanab, Bountiful, St. George, Callville, and Lees Ferry—on almost the very spot where Escalante and his desperate men had camped on the river in 1776. To service their needs and to keep peace with the Indians, Young appointed Jacob Hamblin, a strong, resolute, and thoroughly dedicated man, as head of the Southern Mission. Hamblin's wanderings in the name of New Jerusalem exceeded in scope even those of his Catholic counterpart of the previous century, Fray Garcés. Hamblin found new river crossings at the lower end of the Grand Canyon and at the mouth of the Paria, and he rediscovered the Crossing of the Fathers at the mouth of Padre Creek; he ran the waters of the lower Virgin River and those of the Colorado from Grand Wash to Callville; he crossed and recrossed fold upon fold of the corrugated wilderness of the plateau and saw and understood more of the land than any man before him.

Others entered the land on missions less spiritual but none the less compelling. In 1849, 1850, and 1851 thousands crossed the Colorado near the Gila, heading for the new Golconda of California, traveling west from Santa Fe across trails that may have been known by Coronado's men three centuries before, or north from Mexico on what would come to be called the El Dorado Trail. For their protection the army built Fort Yuma on a bluff overlooking the river—a nondescript adobe outpost that was the most ambitious manifestation of civilized man that the Colorado had yet experienced.

Gradually, then, the river took form in the minds of men. Yet it remained, at best, only half known. It could still give birth to myths.

The West needed a river badly enough to invent it if

necessary; but invention was not necessary. Here was the Colorado, a magnificent stream that drained a major portion of the western slopes of the Rockies and possessed an outlet on the Gulf of California. The West could not ask for a better thoroughfare, a veritable Mississippi simply waiting for the arrival of steamers and flatboats, for the construction of great ports where the riches of the West could be shipped to foreign and domestic markets. It was a grand and necessary dream; that it was also impossible was a long time in being recognized.

The first man to attempt to convert the turgid waters of the Colorado into an avenue of commerce was George A. Johnson, who constructed a little stern-wheel steamer called the *Yuma* in 1851, which sluggishly ran supplies for Fort Yuma up from the mouth of the river. In 1852, he added the *Uncle Sam*, which hit a snag and sank. Still another attempt, the *General Jessup*, blew up; but the fourth vessel, the *Colorado*, stayed on the river for many years. Until after the Civil War Johnson's laborious enterprise continued to function, one way or another, possessing a final total of eight vessels and sporting the impressive title of the Colorado Steam Navigation Company. In time, it simply vanished, as stubborn a dream as was ever shot down by reality.

In the meantime, the War Department fell in love with the same dream. It, too, needed a river—to keep its western forts supplied and to provide a reliable line of communication between them. So in 1857, under the leadership of Jefferson Davis, the department ordered the construction of a fifty-eight-foot steel-hulled steamboat in Philadelphia. Calling it the *Explorer*, they then dismantled it and sent it around the horn to San Francisco, and from there down to the mouth of the river, where it was to be reassembled. Lt. Joseph Christmas Ives was assigned as her commander: his mission was to open up the Colorado River and explore the blank spots of her canyons. He did his best.

After nearly a month of backbreaking effort, the reconstructed *Explorer* slid from her ways at the mouth of the river and steamed up to Fort Yuma, arriving on January 5, 1858. Final preparations were made there for the assault upon the upper portions of the river, and on the morning of January 11, the *Explorer* and her complement of twenty-four men (including topographer-engraver F. W. Egloffstein and artist Edward Mollhausen, whose sketches imbue Ives' *Report* with a distinct air of nightmare) set off for points north. Almost immediately,

the *Explorer* ran aground. Everyone debarked, and after four hours of painful manipulation, the boat was pushed into deeper water and the trip continued.

Navigation of the Colorado above Fort Yuma continued to reveal problems, including sandbars, disappearing channels, hidden rocks, and the vagaries of the current itself, which several times stopped the *Explorer* cold and forced the crew to get off and tow. On February 9, after almost a month of travel, they had reached only to the head of Mojave Canyon, some one hundred and fifty miles north of Fort Yuma. Here they spent some time trading with the Mojave Indians and picking up a pair of guides—one of whom, Ireteba, would be especially helpful to Ives for the rest of the trip. On February 24 they left Mojave Canyon for the last leg of a trip whose difficulties, as outlined in Ives' 1861 *Report upon the Colorado River of the West*, had only begun:

Camp 50, foot of Cottonwood valley, February 24.— An imposing mountain stands near the west bank of the Colorado at the head of the Mojave valley. It is the highest peak in sight, and is regarded with reverence by the Indians, who believe it to be the abode of their departed spirits. Ireteba informed me, with awe in his countenance, that should any one dare to visit it he would be instantly struck dead. This is the first time I have been able to extract any allusion to the religious belief of the Mojaves, and Ireteba was reluctant to speak upon the subject.

From the Dead mountain a range extends to the northwest and a spur crosses the river and connects with the Black mountains. This spur forms the northern limit of the Mojave valley. For several miles our course lay through the foot hills, when the river narrowed and entered a cañon through a gate, one side of which looked like the head of a bull. The scenery in this cañon was picturesque and beautiful, but nevertheless seemed tame in comparison with the grand and startling effects presented in the cañons through the Monument and Mojave mountains.

Near the upper end a rapid occurred upon a pebbly shoal, and the Explorer received some hard knocks, to which she has become lately quite accustomed. After traversing the Pyramid cañon—so called from a natural pyramid, of symmetrical proportions, twenty or thirty feet high, standing near the rapid just mentioned—rapids were encountered in quick succession, and have been met with, at short intervals, up to camp, which is twenty miles from the head of the Mojave valley. Most of them have been ascended without difficulty. At one (Deep rapid) there was sufficient depth and a channel unobstructed by rocks, but the rush of water was very strong. When we first heard its roar and saw the surging and foaming torrent we were startled, and a little apprehensive that we might have reached the head of navigation. There was less difficulty in making the ascent than had been anticipated. Not knowing what depth of water would be found, Captain Robinson had the boat lightened and Mr. Carroll put on a head of steam that made the stern wheel spin around like a top, and a line being taken out ahead, the summit of the rapid was quickly attained.

Abreast of the last camp was a rapid that occasioned more trouble, although the flow was less violent. The river was divided by an island into two channels, and in neither was there more than two feet of water. The shoal extended for some distance and the bottom was covered with rocks. A long line had to be taken ahead, in order to reach a place where there was good holding ground. The boat was lightened and, after several hours of hard labor, had been brought to the crest of the rapid, when the line broke and the Explorer drifted down, bumping upon the rocks, and was in imminent danger of having her hull stove. The day's work was undone in an instant, and we were very glad that it was no worse. When she finally brought up, it was upon some rocks, where she was wedged so fast that it occupied half of the next day to extricate her. The remainder of the day was spent in a second and more successful attempt, and at dark we had the satisfaction of seeing our steamer safely anchored above. That same night the fiercest norther sprang up that has yet been experienced, and continued throughout the following day. We ate, drank, breathed, and saw little but sand for twenty-four hours, and the gale was so violent that the Explorer was dragged from her anchorage and driven upon the rocks. At night the wind subsided, but recommenced the next day, though with diminished force, and we got the steamboat, by evening, into deep water. To-day we had made one or two miles when the wind once more sprang up and blew with such fury that we were but too happy to find a cove where the boat could lie in safety. We have spent the day sitting on a bank, blinded and choked by masses of sand that have been beating upon us without an instant's cessation.

The timbers fastened to the Explorer's hull are a greater hindrance to her progress in this part of the river than below. They become wedged in the rocks, and render it difficult to extricate the boat, besides increasing the draught by the amount of their thickness, which is four or five inches. As has been the case at places in the lower portions of the Colorado, the bar that has here detained us three days would not have stopped a boat of six inches less draught, with a smooth bottom, as many hours. It is probable that there is not one season in ten when even the Explorer would encounter one-fourth of the difficulty that she has during the present unprecedentedly low stage of water. . . .

The late detentions have afforded Dr. Newberry and Mr. Egloffstein excellent opportunities to pursue their respective avocations. The doctor has had leisure to make a very full and perfect mineralogical collection, and become thoroughly conversant with the geological characteristics of the region. Mr. Egloffstein has taken panoramic views of the river and the adjacent country, and has now completed a set that extends from Fort Yuma to the present camp. The ascent of a prominent peak on the opposite side of the river (Mount Newberry) has given him a view of the whole of the Black mountain range. . . .

An occasional lull in the blast has permitted the partial subsidence of the sand clouds, and afforded glimpses of a valley immediately above camp. Groves of cottonwood trees, of a larger growth than any seen before, indicate that there is some alluvial land, but the valley does not appear to be of great extent.

Camp 53, Round island, March 1. — The Cottonwood valley was found to be only five or six miles in length and completely hemmed in by wild-looking mountains. The belt of bottom land is narrow, and dotted with graceful clusters of stately cottonwood in full and brilliant leaf. The river flows sometimes through green meadows, bordered with purple and gold rushes, and then between high banks, where rich masses of foliage overhang the stream, and afford a cool and inviting shade. From the edges of this garden-like precinct sterile slopes extend to the bases of the surrounding mountain chains. . . .

We have now entered a region that has never, as far as any records show, been visited by whites, and are approaching a locality where it is supposed that the famous "Big Cañon" of the Colorado commences; every point of the view is scanned with eager interest. We can

The St. Vallier, *a stern-wheel steamer of George A. Johnson's Colorado Steam Navigation Company.*

The Yuma, *the first of Johnson's Colorado River vessels, steams through the railroad drawbridge at Fort Yuma.*

distinctly see to the north the steep wall of one side of the gorge where the Colorado breaks through the Black mountains. Whether this is the "Big Cañon" or not it is certainly of far grander proportions than any which we have thus far traversed.

At the head of the Cottonwood valley we threaded a cañon formed by the passage of the river through a spur that connects the Black and Dead mountain ranges. It was only two or three miles in extent, and the sides were of moderate height, but the gorgeous contrast and intensity of color exhibited upon the rocks exceeded in beauty anything that had been witnessed of a similar character. Various and vivid tints of blue, brown, white, purple, and crimson, were blended with exquisite shading upon the gateways and inner walls, producing effects so novel and surprising as to make the cañon, in some respects, the most picturesque and striking of any of these wonderful mountain passes. . . .

A few scattered Mojave families inhabit the Cottonwood valley. We saw no fields under cultivation, and the residents brought neither corn nor beans to trade. One of them agreed to take a letter for me to Lieutenant Tipton, and to guide the pack-train from the Mojave valley until it should overtake us. This may be at no great distance ahead, for Ireteba, while admitting that we may reach the mouth of the Black cañon, still maintains that we can never get the steamboat through it. Since leaving the Cottonwood valley he has appeared uneasy, and has given me constant warnings to exercise precaution, for that the "bad Pai-utes" are prowling about. He says that great numbers of them live near the Mormon road, from which we are not far distant; that there are many white

men among them, and that some Pai-utes who lately visited the Mojaves told them that they intended to destroy our party as soon as it should enter their territory. He thinks that we are too few in number, and looks dubiously at us and then at the bank, when we come to places where the river is narrow and the formation of the gravel hills is favorable for an ambuscade. There is seldom difficulty in selecting a spot for camp that would be impregnable against almost any number of Indians armed only with bows and clubs; and as full moon is approaching the nights do not invite attack. . . .

Camp 57, mouth of Black cañon, March 8. — The twenty miles of distance between Round island and the present camp required five days to accomplish. A dozen or more rapids, of all descriptions, had to be passed; some were violent and deep, others shallow. At a few the bed of the stream was sandy; but generally it was composed of gravel and pebbles. Below the crest of one rapid the current forked, forming two eddies. Several attempts were made to ascend; but the bow was not pointed exactly towards the centre of the fork, and, being thrown off by the eddy, the boat would go down stream, whirling around like a teetotum. After four or five unsuccessful trials, Captain Robinson struck the right point, and we got through without further trouble. The worst places encountered have been where the banks were low and destitute of vegetation, and the rocky bed of the river afforded no holding ground near by for an anchor. The lines have become almost worn out by hard service; the skiff is badly battered, and scarcely able to float, and all the oars are broken. The last seventy miles will, perhaps, be the best part of the Colorado to navigate when the

The Explorer, *after running aground once, finally gets under way from Fort Yuma for the mysterious unknown of the Colorado's canyons on January 11, 1858.*

water is not at so exceedingly low a stage. The rapids will be less violent, and the bottom being gravelly no new bars will be formed as the river rises.

Between Mount Davis and the Black mountains the river flows between gravel bluffs and the foot-hills of the latter chain. The view in all directions was intercepted, and before we were conscious of its neighborhood a sudden turn around the base of a conical peak disclosed the southern portal of the Black cañon directly in front. The Black mountains were piled overhead in grand confusion, and through a narrow gateway flanked by walls many hundreds of feet in height, rising perpendicularly out of the water, the Colorado emerged from the bowels of the range.

A rapid, a hundred yards below the mouth of the cañon, created a short detention, and a strong head of steam was put on to make the ascent. After passing the crest the current became slack, the soundings were unusually favorable, and we were shooting swiftly past the entrance, eagerly gazing into the mysterious depths beyond, when the Explorer, with a stunning crash, brought up abruptly and instantaneously against a sunken rock. For a second the impression was that the cañon had fallen in. The concussion was so violent that the men near the bow were thrown overboard; the doctor, Mr. Mollhausen, and myself, having been seated in front of the upper deck, were precipitated head foremost into the bottom of the boat; the fireman, who was pitching a log into the fire, went half-way in with it; the boiler was thrown out of place;

the steam pipe doubled up; the wheel-house torn away; and it was expected that the boat would fill and sink instantly by all, but Mr. Carroll, who was looking for an explosion from the injured steam pipes. Finding, after a few moments had passed, that she still floated, Captain Robinson had a line taken into the skiff, and the steamer was towed alongside of a gravelly spit a little below; it was then ascertained that the stem of the boat, where the iron flanges of the two bow sections were joined, had struck fair upon the rock, and that, although the flanges were torn away, no hole had been made, and the hull was uninjured. The other damages were such as a day or two of labor could repair. . . .

Nearly three days have elapsed since the accident, and everything is restored to its former condition. I have thought it would be imprudent, after this experience of sunken rocks, to attempt the passage of the cañon without making a preliminary reconnaissance in the skiff. A second escape of the boat, in the event of a similar encounter with a rock, would be too much to hope for; and should she be sunk in the cañon, and there be nothing to swim to but perpendicular walls five hundred or a thousand feet high, the individuals on board would be likely to share the fate of the steamer. The carpenter has been working at the skiff, to put it in a more serviceable condition, and two or three oars have been mended; to-morrow the captain, the mate, and myself, are going to make an attempt to ascend the cañon. . . .

Camp 59, head of Black cañon, March 10.—The skiff

72

Colorado Country: A place of "grand confusion," in the words of Lieutenant J. C. Ives (In The Maze, Canyonlands National Park).

By January 15, 1858, Lieutenant Ives and the twenty-four crew members of the Explorer *had reached Canebrake Canyon, about fifteen miles above Fort Yuma. Here, Ives said, the Colorado was a river "deserving of the name".*

having been put in tolerable order, a bucket full of corn and beans, three pairs of blankets, a compass, and a sextant and chronometer were stowed away in it, and a little before sunrise the captain, mate, and myself commenced the exploration of the cañon. My companions each pulled a pair of sculls, and with considerable vigor; but as the current has a flow of three miles an hour we could not make rapid progress. We had proceeded a quarter of a mile, and had just rounded the first bend, when one of the sculls snapped, reducing by half our motive power. There was, fortunately, a current of air drawing in the right direction through the narrow gorge, and, with the odd scull and a blanket, an apology for a sail was rigged, which, at intervals, rendered great assistance.

In a few minutes, having passed what may be called the outworks of the range, we fairly entered its gigantic precincts, and commenced to thread the mazes of a cañon, far exceeding in vastness any that had been yet traversed. The walls were perpendicular, and more than double the height of those in the Mojave mountains, rising, in many places, sheer from the water, for over a thousand feet. The naked rocks presented, in lieu of the brilliant tints that had illuminated the sides of the lower passes, a uniform sombre hue, that added much to the solemn and impressive sublimity of the place. The river was narrow and devious, and each turn disclosed new combinations of colossal and fantastic forms, dimly seen in the dizzy heights overhead, or through the sunless depths

of the vista beyond. With every mile the view became more picturesque and imposing, exhibiting the same romantic effects and varied transformations that were displayed in the Mojave cañon, but on an enlarged and grander scale.

Rapids were of frequent occurrence, and at every one we were obliged to get out of the skiff, and haul it over. Eight miles from the mouth of the cañon, a loud sullen roaring betokened that something unusual was ahead, and a rapid appeared which was undoubtedly the same that had been described by Ireteba. Masses of rock filled up the sides of the channel. In the centre, at the foot of the rapid, and rising four or five feet above the surface of the water, was a pyramidal rock, against which the billows dashed as they plunged down from above, and glanced upwards, like a water spout.

The torrent was swifter than at any place below, but a steamboat, entirely emptied of its cargo, which could be deposited upon the rocks alongside of the rapid, could, if provided with long and stout lines, be hauled up. During a higher stage of the river the difficulty of the place would be much diminished. With our nearly worn out ropes it would be very hazardous to attempt the ascent.

Several rapids followed, at short distances, all of which would be troublesome to pass at the present depth of water. The constant getting out of the boat, and the labor of dragging it through these difficult places, made our progress for some miles exceedingly tedious and fatiguing. As sunset was approaching we came to a nook

Colorado Country: "The river was narrow and devious," Ives reported, "and each turn disclosed new combinations of colossal and fantastic forms" (Colorado River near Shafer Trail).

in the side of the cañon, four miles above the Roaring rapid, where a patch of gravel and a few pieces of drift-wood, lodged upon the rocks, offered a tolerable camping place, and we hauled the skiff upon the shingle, and stopped for the night. There was no need of keeping a watch, with two grim lines of sentinels, a thousand feet high, guarding the camp. Even though we could have been seen from the verge of the cliff above, our position was totally inaccessible. . . .

This morning, as soon as the light permitted, we were again upon the way. The ascent of the river was attended with as much labor as it had been the day before; for though none of the rapids were of so violent a character, they were of constant occurrence. The wind still held to the south, and the blanket sail was again set to great advantage.

The cañon continued increasing in size and magnificence. No description can convey an idea of the varied and majestic grandeur of this peerless water-way. Wherever the river makes a turn the entire panorama changes, and one startling novelty after another appears and disappears with bewildering rapidity. Stately façades, august cathedrals, amphitheatres, rotundas, castellated walls, and rows of time-stained ruins, surmounted by every form of tower, minaret, dome, and spire, have been moulded from the cyclopean masses of rock that form the mighty defile. The solitude, the stillness, the subdued light, and the vastness of every surrounding object, produce an impression of awe that ultimately becomes almost painful. As hour after hour passed we began to look anxiously ahead for some sign of an outlet from the range, but the declining day brought only fresh piles of mountains, higher, apparently, than any before seen. We had made up our minds to pass another night in the cañon, and were searching for a spot large enough to serve as a resting-place, when we came into a narrow passage, between two mammoth peaks, that seemed to be nodding to each other across the stream, and unexpectedly found, at the upper end, the termination of the Black cañon.

Low hills of gravel intercepted the view, and prevented us from seeing far into the unknown region beyond. A mile above the cañon the river swept the base of a high hill, with salient angles, like the bastions of a fort. At the base was a little ravine, which offered a camping place that would be sheltred from observation, and we drew the skiff out of the water, determining not to proceed any further till to-morrow. Leaving the mate to take charge of the boat, the captain and myself ascended the hill, which is over a thousand feet high. A scene of barren and desolate confusion was spread before us. We seemed to have reached the focus or culminating point of the volcanic disturbances that have left their traces over the whole region south. In almost every direction were hills and mountains heaped together without any apparent system or order. A small open area intervened between camp and a range to the north, and we could trace the course of the river as it wound towards the east, forming the Great Bend. In the direction of the Mormon road to Utah, which is but twenty miles distant, the country looked less broken, and it was evident that there would be no difficulty in opening a wagon communication between the road and the river. We tried to discover the valley of the Virgen, but could see no indication of any stream coming in from the northwest. The view in that direction was partially obstructed by another summit of Fortification rock.

Not a trace of vegetation could be discovered, but the glaring monotony of the rocks was somewhat relieved by grotesque and fanciful varieties of coloring. The great towers that formed the northern gateway of the cañon were striped with crimson and yellow bands; the gravel bluffs bordering the river exhibited brilliant alternations of the same hues, and not far to the east, mingled with the gray summits, were two or three hills, altogether of a blood-red color, that imparted a peculiarly ghastly air to the scene.

The approach of darkness stopped further observations, and we descended to camp, having first taken a good look, in every direction, for the smoke of Indian camp-fires, but without discovering any. In making the sixteen miles from last night's bivouac, we have had to labor hard for thirteen hours, stemming the strong current, and crossing the numerous rapids, and being thoroughly exhausted, depend for security to-night more upon our concealed position than upon any vigilance that is likely to be exhibited.

Camp 57, foot of Black cañon, March 12.—Skirting the base of Fortification rock, we ascended the river a couple of miles, and came to the mouth of a stream about the size of Bill Williams's Fork, as the latter was when we passed it. We disembarked, and followed for some distance along its border. The appearance of the bed and the banks indicated the existence, during some seasons, of a wide and deep river. It was now but a few inches deep. The water was clear, and had a strong brackish taste. This fact, and its position, led me to suppose that we were at the mouth of the Virgen, but I could scarcely believe that that river could ever present so insignificant an appearance.

I now determined not to try to ascend the Colorado any further. The water above the Black cañon had been shoal, and the current swift. Rapids had occurred in such quick succession as to make navigation almost impossible, and there would be no object in proceeding beyond the Great Bend. The difficulties encountered in the cañon were of a character to prevent a steamboat from attempting to traverse it at low water, and we had seen driftwood lodged in clefts fifty feet above the river, betokening a condition of things during the summer freshet that would render navigation more hazardous at that season than now. It appeared, therefore, that the foot of the Black cañon should be considered the practical head of navigation, and I concluded to have a reconnaissance made to connect that point with the Mormon road, and to let this finish the exploration of the navigable portion of the Colorado.

The *Explorer's* return trip as far as Mojave Canyon was accomplished almost without incident, but at Cottonwood Valley, where the expedition arrived on March 16, they encountered rumors of a possible Indian uprising— one allegedly fomented by local Mormons. The scuttlebutt proved to be precisely that, but it did give the expedition an added fillip of danger for the next week. Upon the arrival of a relief pack train under the command of Lieutenant Tipton of the Topographical Engineers, Ives divided his force, half of the expedition to return to Fort Yuma on the *Explorer*, the other half to complete the exploring mission by land under his command. On the morning of March 24, they set off north and east on the first leg of a journey that would take them across the Cerbat Range and the Colorado Plateau to the Grand Canyon. By evening they halted in Sitgreave's Pass "and, for the first time during the expedition, pitched camp out of sight of the Colorado."

Camp 61, Meadow creek, March 25.—The grazing at the camp in Sitgreaves's Pass was poor, and the mules were ill prepared for the rough road before them. A few miles brought us to the base of a steep and difficult ascent that led to the summit of the Black mountains. The path was narrow and devious, and attended with hazard to the weak and heavily-loaded beasts. All of the party had to clamber up on foot, leading their riding animals; and as the ascent was accomplished under a burning sun, it was a matter of some congratulation when the top of the pass was attained. A wide and beautiful valley divided the Black mountains from a high snow-capped chain called by Lieutenant Whipple, who had seen it from the east, the Cerbat range. A rapid descent led through a ravine to the eastern base of the range we were crossing. When nearly down the hill the head of a creek was encountered, and half a mile from the valley the ravine spread out for a few hundred yards, forming a snug meadow carpeted with good grass, and fringed on one side by a growth of willows that bordered the stream. The half-starved animals would hardly allow the saddles to be removed in their impatience to enjoy the unaccustomed plenty. They ate greedily for the rest of the day, and nearly all night, and this morning still seemed so ravenous that I have remained in camp to let them appease their appetites. The delay has permittted me to set up a transit and get some observations on moon culminations for longitude.

Ireteba informed me after breakfast that there were a few Hualpais living at no great distance, and that he would hunt them up, and endeavor to engage one to accompany us beyond the point where he himself would be compelled to go back. He has not yet returned from his mission. He has told me that in a few days we shall strike the Colorado and come to a large settlement of Hualpais Indians; that it would be unsafe for himself and companions to proceed further, and that we must secure Hualpais guides to conduct us to another tribe that reside upon a tributary of the Colorado, a long distance above. Between the two villages he says the river is inaccessible and the country sterile, with few watering places, and those difficult to find. . . .

Camp 64, spur from Cerbat range, March 29.—Leaving Meadow creek and its abundant pasturage, we descended to the valley, which is of immense extent, and runs in a northwest and southeast direction, extending either way beyond the limit of vision. Toward the south, below the Black mountains, it unites with the Mojave valley, and from the base of the Cerbat range the eye could follow the gentle slope for over forty miles till it

THE MYTH

Ireteba, the expedition's trusty Mojave guide, is seen at the left in this H. B. Mollhausen drawing from Ives's Report.

terminated near the head of the Mojave cañon.

The pass by which we were to cross the Cerbat mountains was apparent as soon as we left the Black range, and Ireteba, who had joined us early in the morning, headed directly for it. The pure atmosphere made it seem close by, and it was disappointing to plod through the hot sand hour after hour, and find it appearing as far off as ever. When the base of the mountains was at last reached, it was found that the ascent was scarcely perceptible. A place more like a cañon than an ordinary mountain pass presented itself, and we penetrated the range for a few miles through the windings of a nearly level avenue. In a pretty ravine, hemmed in by picturesque bluffs, our guide pointed out a good spring of water, with grass enough near by to afford a tolerable camping place.

The next day, after proceeding one or two miles along the pass, which we called Railroad Pass, we emerged from the Cerbat range, and came into what was at first supposed to be a broad valley, but which turned out to be a basin formed by the chain we had passed, and spurs extending from it. . . .

Instead of crossing the basin, Ireteba took us north, for ten or fifteen miles along the eastern base of the Cerbat range, to an excellent grazing camp, but where there was only a small spring of sulphurous water. This he told me was the last water we should have for two days. The mules had become so much weakened that I found it again necessary to remain a day in camp to permit them to graze. A violent hail-storm, followed by a raw and piercing sleet that kept them huddled all day with bent backs, shivering in the blast, counterbalanced the good effects that might have otherwise resulted from the delay.

A weary twenty miles of travel through a soft yielding soil have brought us to the northeastern rim of the basin, where we have camped without water. For two or three days we have been passing through a good grazing country. In the valleys and mountain slopes the blue grama and pin grass, both highly nutritive, grow luxuriantly. The want of water renders the region valueless.

Each successive valley crossed has been twelve or fifteen hundred feet higher than the preceding, and we have attained now an elevation of nearly four thousand feet above the level of the sea. Thus far the scenery has been monotonous and rather uninteresting; the valleys and ranges possess the same general character, and all appear to head somewhere about the mouth of the Virgen. The appearance of the country just passed over, and what I saw from the top of Fortification rock, have led me to suppose that at the Great Bend of the Colorado there may be a focus from which quite a number of mountain chains radiate; but the observations have been too limited to warrant a decided opinion. . . .

Camp 65, Peacock's spring, March 31.—Leaving the Cerbat basin, the course lay towards a low point in the extension of Aquarius mountains—another chain almost parallel to the Black and Cerbat ranges. The gap much resembles the Railroad Pass. After entering it the trail took a sudden turn to the north, in which direction it continued. The sun was very hot, and the mules, not having had a plentiful drink of water for four days, showed marks of distress. Ten or twelve miles from camp, Mr. Peacock, who was riding in advance, discovered a large spring of clear, sweet water in a ravine near the road. There were no signs of the place having been used as a camp, and even Ireteba did not appear to have known previously of its existence. A Mexican subsequently found a running stream a mile or two further on, where the Indians passing this way had been in the habit of stopping.

Ireteba, at my request, again went in search of some Hualpais tractable enough to enlist for a few days in our service. After an absence of several hours he came back and reported that he had discovered two who were willing to go. In a little while, from the top of a neighboring hill, a discordant screaming was heard, proceeding from two Indians who were suspiciously surveying camp. It was some time before our Mojaves could persuade them to approach, and when they did they looked like men who had screwed up their courage to face a mortal peril. They were squalid, wretched-looking creatures, with splay feet, large joints, and diminutive figures, but had bright eyes

and cunning faces, and resembled a little the Chemehuevis. Taking them into the tent occupied by Lieutenant Tipton and myself, with many misgivings as to how many varieties of animal life were being introduced there, I brought out some pipes and tobacco and told Ireteba to proceed with the negotiations. These were not soon arranged. The sentiousness belonging to Mr. Cooper's and other story-book Indians is not a gift of the tribes that one encounters in travelling. Our old guides and the two new candidates talked all at once, and with amazing volubility; they seemed to be recounting their personal histories from birth to the present date. The conclusion arrived at was that they knew nothing about the country —neither a good road nor the localities of grass and water; that they were out hunting and had lost their way, and had no idea of the direction even of their own villages. This very probable statement I correctly supposed to be a hint that they were not to be approached empty-handed; for when Ireteba had been authorized to make a distinct offer of beads and blankets, one of them recollected where he was, and also that there were watering places ahead to which he could guide us. It was thought advisable to again lie over for a day; and they went away, agreeing to be in camp on the day but one following. . . .

Camp 67, Big cañon of the Colorado, April 3.—The two Hualpais preserved the credit of the Indian employés by being punctual to their engagement, and led off in company with the Mojaves as we ascended the ravine from Peacock's spring. It was a cool lovely morning, and a favorable day for travel. After proceeding a mile or two we issued from the hills and entered a region totally different from any that had been seen during the expedition. A broad table-land, unbroken by the volcanic hills that had overspread the country since leaving Fort Yuma, extended before us, rising in a gradual swell towards the north. The road became hard and smooth, and the plain was covered with excellent grass. Herds of antelope and deer were seen bounding over the slopes. Groves of cedar occurred, and with every mile became more frequent and of larger size. At the end of ten miles the ridge of the swell was attained, and a splendid panorama burst suddenly into view. In the foreground were low table-hills, intersected by numberless ravines; beyond these a lofty line of bluffs marked the edge of an immense cañon; a wide gap was directly ahead, and through it were beheld, to the extreme limit of vision, vast plateaus, towering one above the other thousands of feet in the air, the long horizontal bands broken at intervals by wide and profound abysses, and extending a hundred miles to the north, till the deep azure blue faded into a light cerulean tint that blended with the dome of the heavens. The famous "Big cañon" was before us; and for a long time we paused in wondering delight, surveying that stupendous formation through which the Colorado and its tributaries break their way.

OUR GUIDES, becoming impatient of the detention, plunged into a narrow and precipitous ravine that opened at our feet, and we followed as well as we could, stumbling along a rough and rocky pathway. The Hualpais were now of great assistance, for the ravines crossed and forked in intricate confusion; even Ireteba, who had hitherto led the train, became at a loss how to proceed, and had to put the little Hualpais in front. The latter, being perfectly at home, conducted us rapidly down the declivity. The descent was great and the trail blind and circuitous. A few miles of difficult travelling brought us into a narrow valley flanked by steep and high slopes; a sparkling stream crossed its centre, and a gurgling in some tall grass near by announced the presence of a spring. The water was delicious. The grass in the neighborhood was sparse, but of good quality.

This morning we left the valley and followed the course of a creek down a ravine, in the bed of which the water at intervals sank and rose for two or three miles, when it altogether disappeared. The ravine soon attained the proportions of a cañon. The bottom was rocky and irregular, and there were some jump-offs over which it was hard to make the pack animals pass. The vegetation began to disappear, leaving only a few stunted cedars projecting from the sides of the rugged bluffs. The place grew wilder and grander. The sides of the tortuous cañon became loftier, and before long we were hemmed in by walls two thousand feet high. The scenery much resembled that in the Black cañon, excepting that the rapid descent, the increasing magnitude of the collossal piles that blocked the end of the vista, and the corresponding depth and gloom of the gaping chasms into which we were plunging, imparted an unearthly character to a way that might have resembled the portals of the infernal regions. Harsh screams issuing from aerial recesses in the cañon sides and apparitions of goblin-like figures perched in the rifts and hollows of the impending cliffs,

gave an odd reality to this impression. At short distances other avenues of equally magnificent proportions came in from one side or the other; and no trail being left on the rocky pathway, the idea suggested itself that were the guides to desert us our experience might further resemble that of the dwellers in the unblest abodes—in the difficulty of getting out. . . .

Camp 69, Cedar Forest, April 5.—A short walk down the bed of Diamond river, on the morning after we had reached it, verified the statement of Ireteba, and disclosed the famous Colorado cañon. The view from the ridge, beyond the creek to which the Hualpais had first conducted us, had shown that the plateaus further north and east were several thousand feet higher than that through which the Colorado cuts at this point, and the cañons proportionally deeper; but the scene was sufficiently grand to well repay for the labor of the descent. The cañon was similar in character to others that have been mentioned, but on a larger scale, and thus far unrivalled in grandeur. Mr. Mollhausen has taken a sketch, which gives a better idea of it than any description. The course of the river could be traced for only a few hundred yards, above or below, but what had been seen from the table-land showed that we were at the apex of a great southern bend. The walls, on either side, rose directly out of the water. The river was about fifty yards wide. The channel was studded with rocks, and the torrent rushed through like a mill-race.

The day was spent in an examination of the localities. Dr. Newberry has had opportunities for observation seldom afforded to the geologist. This plateau formation has been undisturbed by volcanic action, and the sides of the cañons exhibit all of the series that compose the tablelands of New Mexico, presenting, perhaps, the most splendid exposure of stratified rocks that there is in the world.

A few of the Hualpais paid us a visit, but their intelligence is of so low an order that it is impossible to glean information from them, and besides that their filthiness makes them objectionable. Our new guides seemed to think we should have great difficulty in ascending to the portion of the plateau which they traverse on the way to higher points upon the river. The route they ordinarily pursue follows the cañon of Diabond creek, but this they pronounced impracticable for mules, and said that we must retrace our course for several miles in order to strike a more circuitous, but easier trail, that ascended one of the branch cañons.

At camp on the Colorado Plateau, April, 1858.

Following their advice and guidance, yesterday morning we toiled up the rough road by which we had come, for six miles, when they struck off into a side ravine that led towards the southeast. Half a mile from the mouth, the Hualpais told Ireteba that our camping place was just ahead, and scrambling over the summit of a hill, in a minute were both out of sight. For a mile we kept on, every few moments coming to a fork, where the selection of the right road was left to chance. There was a network of cañons, and the probabilities were that nine out of ten would lead to an impassable precipice. The ascent became so rough that it was already almost impracticable for the mules, and at last the Mojaves stopped, declaring that they had lost their way, and had no idea how to find the camping place or the water, and that the Hualpais were a very bad set. This opinion no one was inclined just then to dispute. I however asked one of the Indians to go back and endeavor to find the deserters or some other member of their tribe. We waited

impatiently half an hour, and then the order was given to countermarch, for I intended to search for the route by which we had come; but before going far, the little Hualpais came back. He seemed amused that we should not have been able to find the water, and again took his place at the head of the column. He conducted us for two miles through a difficult and intricate maze of ravines, and then climbed a side hill, and in a most unexpected place pointed out a little spring. There was a sufficiency of water, and tolerable grass near by. The second Hualpais came back during the evening, and seemed also to be astonished that we should have had trouble in finding what to him was so familiar. They both professed a determination to accompany the train, and Ireteba told me that it was time for himself and companions to return. . . .

Camp 71, Pine forest, April 10.—Four miles from the camp, in the Cedar forest, were some large pools of water in a rocky ravine. There was no spring. The supply had been derived from melting snows, and the place would

A superbly romanticized view of Upper Cataract Creek, "near Big Cañon" (from the Ives Report).

be dry a little later in the season. The Hualpais seated themselves upon the ground as though they had made up their minds to camp. I questioned them as well as I could about the marches ahead, and they assured me that no more water would be found for three days. This did not agree with a former statement, but they adhered positively to it, and it was possible that it might be true. We thought it better, therefore, to go no further. The next morning both the Hualpais were missing. They had run away during the night, taking with them a little flour and a pair of blankets. It was expected that many of the mules would be missing. They were at once counted, but the number was found to be correct. What had frightened the guides off we could not imagine. . . .

We had now entered the region of pines. The growth was thicker, and trees of considerable size began to be mingled with the low cedars. The ascent from the Hualpais spring, though gradual, had been rapid, and the barometer indicated an altitude of about six thousand feet. The increase of elevation was felt very sensibly in the changed temperature, which had become wintry and raw.

FOR THE FIRST TIME black-tailed deer were seen, and some of the soldiers took advantage of the early arrival at camp to go out hunting. One of them had not returned at dark, and two days passed before he was found. Signal fires by night and smokes by day were kept up, and searching parties scoured the country in every direction. A light snow storm, that occurred the night after the man's disappearance, had covered up his footprints and made it impossible to follow him. During the storm he wandered to a great distance from camp, and when the snow melted there was a break in the trail which it was difficult for our most experienced trailers, the Mexicans, to connect. They at last got upon the track, at a time when the man was completely bewildered, and by mere accident was travelling in the right course. He had given himself up for lost, and was wandering in a state of desperation bordering on insanity, when he happened to see one of the signal smokes, and followed its direction to camp, which the Mexicans reached an hour afterwards, having traced him over the whole line he had pursued since his departure.

The next day an early start was made. We had to select our own way through the forest, being for the first time without the guidance of those who were familiar with the country, and what was more important, in this arid region, with the whereabouts of watering places. It was an unfortunate morning for the experiment. Dark clouds covered the sky, and masses of mist were drifting through the glades of the forest, enveloping the landscape in obscurity. We held a course a little east of north. The pine trees became larger and the forest more dense as we proceeded. A heavy gale roared among the branches overhead, and about noon it commenced snowing. For some time we kept at the bottom of a ravine that afforded a partial shelter from the blast, but the surface of the ground was rough, and the snow fell so thick and fast that it was impossible to select the way.

Ascending to the table-land, we happened upon an open portion of the forest and encountered the full violence of the storm. The fall of snow was accompanied with thunder and lightning, an unusual phenomenon at such a time. The flashes were vivid, and the reverberations loud and frequent. The scene would have been beautiful had it not been so thoroughly uncomfortable. The storm at last became so vehement that we were unable to proceed. Men and mules huddled together under such trees as afforded the best shelter, and waited as resignedly as possible till the fury of the tempest had somewhat abated. The day was nearly spent; the packs were therefore taken off, camp made, fires kindled, and the mules driven into a ravine. About sunset it promised to clear off, but the clouds reassembled, the wind and sleet again drove past, and the night was bleak and raw. The unfortunate mules, benumbed with cold, stood shuddering about the fires that were made in the ravine. The sudden change from hot summer weather was a severe test of endurance, and there was danger that in their weak condition they would not be able to stand it. The snow and the gale continued nearly all of the next day. The grass was entirely covered. The animals had to fast for twenty-four hours longer, and I thought that last night would have finished the majority of them, but singularly enough not one has died. . . .

Our altitude is very great. During the last march the ascent was continuous, and the barometer shows an elevation of nearly seven thousand feet. A still higher plateau rises towards the north. The Colorado is not far distant, and we must be opposite to the most stupendous part of the "Big Cañon." The bluffs are in view, but the intervening country is cut up by side cañons and cross ravines, and no place has yet been seen that presents a favorable approach to the gigantic chasm.

Camp 73, Colorado plateau, April 12 — Two miles beyond the snow camp some lagoons were discovered — one of them large enough to be called a pond. I recognized the place as having been described by the Hualpais to Ireteba, but of the position I had not been able to form a correct idea. As we advanced towards the northeast, long undulating swells followed each other and intercepted the view. The snow storm had extended over but a limited area, and the road, at first heavy, in the course of an hour

or two became dry and good. The pines disappeared, and the cedars gradually diminished. To our regret the patches of grass also were less frequently met with, and the little seen was of poor quality. Each slope surmounted disclosed a new summit similar to that just passed, till the end of ten miles, when the highest part of the plateau was attained, and a sublime spectacle lay spread before us.

Towards the north was the field of plateaus and cañons, already seen and described, and shooting out from these a line of magnificent bluffs, extending eastward an enormous distance, marked the course of the cañon of the Little Colorado. Further south, eighty miles distant, towered the vast pile of the San Francisco mountain, its conical summit covered with snow, and sharply defined against the sky. Several other peaks were visible a little to the right, and half way between us and this cluster of venerable and mightly volcanos was the "Red Butte," described by Lieutenant Whipple, standing in isolated prominence upon the level plain. On the north side of the Colorado appeared a short range of mountains, close to the cañon, which had been previously hidden by the intervening plateaus.

A march of twenty miles having been made, and no sign of water appearing, we had to put up with a dry camp. The grass was miserable, and altogether the mules fared badly. During the night the herders were negligent, and at daybreak nearly a hundred of the animals were missing. They had taken the back trail for the lagoons, but having started late and travelled leisurely were overtaken not many miles from camp. The trip did not render them better fitted for the day's journey, which had to be delayed until they were brought back.

The sun was oppressively warm, and every place whose appearance gave promise of water was carefully searched, but without success. Ten miles conducted to the head of a ravine, down which was a well-beaten Indian trail. There was every prospect therefore that we were approaching a settlement similar to that of the Hualpais, on Diamond river. The descent was more rapid than the former had been, and in the course of a few miles we had gone down into the plateau one or two thousand feet, and the bluffs on either side had assumed stupendous proportions. Still no signs of habitations were visible. The worn-out and thirsty beasts had begun to flag, when we were brought to a stand still by a fall a hundred feet deep in the bottom of the cañon. At the brink of the precipice was an overhanging ledge of rocks, from which we could look down as into a well upon the continuation of the gorge far below. The break reached completely across the ravine, and the side walls were nearly perpendicular. There was no egress in that direction, and it seemed a marvel that a trail should be found leading to a place where there was nothing to do but to return. A closer inspection showed that the trail still continued along the cañon, traversing horizontally the face of the right hand bluff. A short distance off it seemed as though a mountain goat could scarcely keep its footing upon the slight indentation that appeared like a thread attached to the rocky wall, but a trial proved that the path, though narrow and dizzy, had been cut with some care into the surface of the cliff, and afforded a foothold level and broad enough both for men and animals. I rode upon it first, and the rest of the party and the train followed—one by one—looking very much like a row of insects crawling upon the side of a building. We proceeded for nearly a mile along this singular pathway, which preserved its horizontal direction. The bottom of the cañon meanwhile had been rapidly descending, and there were two or three falls where it dropped a hundred feet at a time, thus greatly increasing the depth of the chasm. The change had taken place so gradually that I was not sensible of it, till glancing down the side of my mule I found that he was walking within three inches of the brink of a sheer gulf a thousand feet deep; on the other side, nearly touching my knee, was an almost vertical wall rising to an enormous altitude. The sight made my head swim, and I dismounted and got ahead of the mule, a difficult and delicate operation, which I was thankful to have safely performed. A part of the men became so giddy that they were obliged to creep upon their hands and knees, being unable to walk or stand. In some places there was barely room to walk, and a slight deviation in a step would have precipitated one into the frightful abyss. I was a good deal alarmed lest some obstacle should be encountered that would make it impossible to go ahead, for it was certainly impracticable to return. After an interval of uncomfortable suspense the face of the rock made an angle, and just beyond the turn was a projection from the main wall with a surface fifteen or twenty yards square that would afford a foothold. The continuation of the wall was perfectly vertical, so that the trail could no longer follow it, and we found that the path descended the steep face of the cliff to the bottom of the cañon. It was a desperate road to traverse, but located with a good deal of skill—zigzagging

down the precipice, and taking advantage of every crevice and fissure that could afford a foothold. It did not take long to discover that no mule could accomplish this descent, and nothing remained but to turn back. We were glad to have even this privilege in our power. The jaded brutes were collected upon the little summit where they could be turned around, and then commenced to re-perform the hazardous journey. The sun shone directly into the cañon, and the glare reflected from the walls made the heat intolerable. The disappointed beasts, now two days without water, with glassy eyes and protruding tongues, plodded slowly along, uttering the most melancholy cries. The nearest water, of which we had knowledge, was almost thirty miles distant. There was but one chance of saving the train, and after reaching an open portion of the ravine the packs and the saddles were removed, and two or three Mexicans started for the lagoons mounted upon the least exhausted animals, and driving the others loose before them. It was somewhat dangerous to detach them thus far from the main party, but there was no help for it. Some of the mules will doubtless give out before the night march is over, but the knowledge that they are on their way to water will enable most of them to reach it in spite of their weariness and the length of the way. . . .

Camp 73, Colorado plateau, April 14.—Lieutenant Tipton, Mr. Egloffstein, Mr. Peacock, and myself, with a dozen men, formed the party to explore the cañon. It was about five miles to the precipice. The descent of the latter was accomplished without serious trouble. In one or two places the path traversed smooth inclined ledges, where the insecure footing made the crossing dangerous. The bottom of the cañon, which from the summit looked smooth, was covered with hills, thirty or forty feet high. Along the centre we were surprised to find an inner cañon, a kind of under cellar, with low walls at the starting point, which were soon converted into lofty precipices, as the base of the ravine sank deeper and deeper into the earth. Along the bottom of this gorge we followed the trail, distinctly seen when the surface was not covered with rocks. Every few moments, low falls and ledges, which we had to jump or slide down, were met with, till there had accumulated a formidable number of obstacles to be encountered in returning. Like other cañons, it was circuitous, and at each turn we were impatient to find something novel or interesting. We were deeper in the bowels of the earth than we had ever been before, and surrounded by walls and towers of such imposing dimensions that it would be useless to attempt describing them; but the effects of magnitude had begun to pall, and the walk from the foot of the precipice was monotonously dull; no sign of life could be discerned above or below. At the end of thirteen miles from the precipice an obstacle presented itself that there seemed to be no possibility of overcoming. A stone slab, reaching from one side of the cañon to the other, terminated the plane which we were descending. Looking over the edge it appeared that the next level was forty feet below. This time there was no trail along the side bluffs, for these were smooth and perpendicular. A spring of water rose from the bed of the cañon not far above, and trickled over the ledge, forming a pretty cascade. It was supposed that the Indians must have come to this point merely to procure water, but this theory was not altogether satisfactory, and we sat down upon the rocks to discuss the matter.

Mr. Egloffstein lay down by the side of the creek, and projecting his head over the ledge to watch the cascade, discovered a solution of the mystery. Below the shelving rock, and hidden by it and the fall, stood a crazy looking ladder,* made of rough sticks bound together with thongs of bark. It was almost perpendicular, and rested upon a bed of angular stones. The rounds had become rotten from the incessant flow of water. Mr. Egloffstein, anxious to have the first view of what was below, scrambled over the ledge and got his feet upon the upper round. Being a solid weight, he was too much for the insecure fabric, which commenced giving way. One side fortunately stood firm, and holding on to this with a tight grip, he made a precipitate descent. The other side and all the rounds broke loose and accompanied him to the bottom in a general crash, effectually cutting off the communication. Leaving us to devise means of getting him back he ran to the bend to explore. The bottom of the cañon had been reached. He found that he was at the edge of a stream, ten or fifteen yards wide, fringed with cottonwoods and willows. The walls of the cañon spread out for a short distance, leaving room for a narrow belt of bottom land, on which were fields of corn and a few scattered huts.

A place was found near the ledge where one could clamber a little way up the wall, and we thus got a view of the valley. The river was nearly as large as the Gila at low water, and, with the exception of that stream, the

*It was at the same place, if not by the same ladder, that Garces had descended the canyon in 1776 (see Chapter II).

most important tributary of the Colorado between its mouth and our position. The cañon Mr. Egloffstein saw could not be followed far; there were cascades just below. He perceived, however, that he was very near to its mouth, though perhaps a thousand feet greater altitude, and an Indian pointed out the exact spot where it united with the cañon of the Rio Colorado. . . .

Having looked at all that was to be seen, it now remained to get Mr. Egloffstein back. The slings upon the soldiers' muskets were taken off and knotted together, and a line thus made which reached to the bottom. Whether it would support his weight was a matter of experiment. The general impression was that it would not, but of the two evils—breaking his neck or remaining among the Yampais—he preferred the former, and fastened the strap around his shoulders. It was a hard straight lift. The ladder pole was left, and rendered great assistance both to us and the rope, and the ascent was safely accomplished. We invited the Indian to follow Mr. Egloffstein's example, but this he energetically declined. The examination being finished, it was time to return. On leaving camp we had expected to be back before night, and had brought along neither provisions nor overcoats. An hour or two earlier, finding that the day was rapidly slipping by, two of the party were directed to go back and tell those who had remained that we might be detained till the next day, and in that case to forward in the morning something to eat. We walked as fast as possible, in order to get out of the cañon before dark, but the ascent was laborious, and the trail, made in coming down over the rocks, difficult to follow. Numerous branch cañons, all looking alike, would have rendered it easy to become lost had the trail been once departed from. Night came before the foot of the precipice where the train had stopped was reached. It was impossible to distinguish the way in the dark, and we had to halt. A few minutes previously the tracks of the two men that had been sent ahead had been noticed diverging from the proper course, and it was concluded that they were wandering astray somewhere in the labyrinth. After nightfall, as is always the case in these regions, it became bleak and cold. Some of the party, attired for a walk under a hot sun, had not even their coats. The cañon was as dark as a dungeon. The surface of the ground being covered with rocks, a recumbent position was uncomfortable, and the rocks being interspersed with prickly pear and some other varieties of cactaceæ it would have been unwise to walk about.

THE MYTH

The choice, therefore, lay between sitting down and standing still, which two recreations we essayed alternately for twelve hours that might have been, from the sensations of the party, twelve days. As soon as it was light enough to see the way we put our stiffened limbs in motion. Climbing the precipice was severe work. The summit once attained, it was but five miles to camp, but the violent exercise of the ascent, coming after a twenty-four hours' abstinence from food and rest, and a walk of more than thirty miles over a difficult road, proved so exhausting that, during the last stretch, two or three of the men broke down, and had to have coffee and food sent back to them before they could proceed. . . .

The region east of camp has been examined to-day. The extent and magnitude of the system of cañons in that direction is astounding. The plateau is cut into shreds by these gigantic chasms, and resembles a vast ruin. Belts of country miles in width have been swept away, leaving only isolated mountains standing in the gap. Fissures so profound that the eye cannot penetrate their depths are separated by walls whose thickness one can almost span, and slender spires that seem tottering upon their bases shoot up thousands of feet from the vaults below.

Towards the southeast, also, for a great distance, the surface is furrowed by these abysses. They appear to extend nearly to the San Francisco mountains, and bar all progress eastward. Northward we can proceed no further, and the only course is to go back to the nearest water as a starting point, and from thence strike south, and, heading these formidable barriers, cross Flax river, and again travel north upon the opposite side of that stream.

The mules were brought back this evening; only two were lost; the others reached the Lagoon. To-morrow morning we shall return to that place, and after making an examination of the cañons northwest of the trail proceed to follow the remaining route now open to us.

Camp 74, Forest lagoons, April 18.—Midway between the last camp and the lagoons, a trail was encountered leading towards another point of the Big cañon. With a small detachment I left the main party and followed its course. It headed directly for the north side mountains—the peaks already spoken of as seen upon the opposite bank of the Colorado. We travelled till dark; the trail ended near some deserted huts that resembled those seen at the Yampais village; they were in the midst of a pine grove; there was no water in the neighborhood, and the Yampais, who doubtless make this place their summer

resort, must be compelled to send to the bottom of the cañon for their supply.

The country became rough and so much cut up by ravines that it was impossible to approach very closely to the main river. A good view was obtained of the walls of the Flax river cañon, and its mouth approximately located. The junction was below the mouth of Cascade creek, showing that that stream is not, as had been supposed, a tributary of the Colorado, but of its smaller affluent.

We had to camp without water, and it being the second day that the animals had had nothing to drink, a great part of them broke from the herders as soon as their saddles were removed, and made a stampede for the lagoons. Barely enough were left to pack the few articles that had been brought.

Another reconnaissance has since been made on foot from the lagoons westward. A line thirty miles in extent was traversed, with results similar to those previously obtained. An excellent view was had of the Big cañon. The barometric observations upon the surface of the plateau, and at the mouths of Diamond and Cataract rivers, showed that the walls of this portion of the cañon were over a mile high. The formation of the ground was such that the eye could not follow them the whole distance to the bottom, but as far down as they could be traced they appeared almost vertical. A sketch taken upon the spot by Mr. Egloffstein does better justice than any description can do to the marvellous scene.

Our reconnoitering parties have now been out in all directions, and everywhere have been headed off by impassable obstacles. The positions of the main watercourses have been determined with considerable accuracy. The region last explored is, of course, altogether valueless. It can be approached only from the south, and after entering it there is nothing to do but to leave. Ours has been the first, and will doubtless be the last, party of whites to visit this profitless locality. It seems intended by nature that the Colorado river, along the greater portion of its lonely and majestic way, shall be forever unvisited and undisturbed. The handful of Indians that inhabit the sequestered retreats where we discovered them have probably remained in the same condition, and of the same number, for centuries. The country could not support a large population, and by some provision of nature they have ceased to multiply. The deer, the antelope, the birds, even the smaller reptiles, all of which frequent the adjacent territory, have deserted this uninhabitable district. Excepting when the melting snows send their annual torrents through the avenues to the Colorado, conveying with them sound and motion, these dismal abysses, and the arid table-lands that enclose them, are left, as they have been for ages, in unbroken solitude and silence. The lagoons by the side of which we are encamped furnish, as far as we have been able to discover, the only accessible watering place west of the mouth of Diamond river. During the summer it is probable they are dry, and that no water exists upon the whole of the Colorado plateau. We start for the south with some anxiety, not knowing how long it may be before water will be again met with.

Struggling eastward across the reaches of the Colorado Plateau, the expedition escaped the convoluted wilderness of the Grand Canyon, traversing the thick cedar stands of the San Francisco Forest and stopping off for a while in the Moquis [Hopi] pueblos just east of the Painted Desert. By May 23, 1858, it had reached Fort Defiance, Arizona Territory, and civilization.

"Ours has been the first, and will doubtless be the last, party of whites to visit this profitless locality. It seems intended by nature that the Colorado river, along the greater portion of its lonely and majestic way, shall be forever unvisited and undisturbed." Strong, realistic words, those, written by a man who had been there and knew.

But the West needed a river; the Colorado was not yet to be freed of its myths.

ALMOST TEN YEARS after Ives had passed judgment on the utility of the Colorado, Samuel Adams, a con man with the messianic zeal of the true believer, announced in a personal report to Congress, "The Colorado must be, emphatically, to the Pacific Coast what the Mississippi is to the Atlantic." This sanguine dogma grew out of a stern-wheeler trip undertaken by Adams in 1865 from the mouth of the Colorado to the head of Boulder Canyon. The journey, he said, satisfied him that there were "none of those dangerous obstructions which have been represented by those who may have viewed them at a distance, and whose imaginary cañons and rapids below had almost disappeared at the approach of the steamer."

Lieutenant Ives would have been surprised; James

White—an Indian-harried trapper who had boarded a handmade raft at some point on the Colorado in September of 1867 and weeks later was fished out at the Mormon settlement of Callville, half dead and on the verge of insanity—would have been astounded. Congress was neither surprised nor astounded. Congress knew what a river was. Couldn't its members walk down from the capitol building and watch the placid eddies of the Potomac? Responding to the lure of Adams' *must be,* the House of Representatives quickly passed a commendatory resolution, thanking Adams for "opening up the navigation of the Colorado River, the great natural thoroughfare of Arizona and Utah Territories."

The House of Representatives then promptly forgot about Adams and the great natural thoroughfare of Arizona and Utah Territories. Adams did not forget. In 1869, after an unsuccessful attempt to thrust himself into the exploring expedition of John Wesley Powell, Adams determined to organize his own expedition to prove the navigability of the river system from the Blue to the Gulf of California. Feeding his plan to a group of starry-eyed enthusiasts in Breckenridge, Colorado, Adams obtained financing for the project and a volunteer crew of ten. On July 12, 1869, the jaunt to the Gulf of California got under way. Within ten days five of the crew had abandoned the undertaking, and in another two weeks all four of the boats had disappeared in the rapids of the Grand. Adams's five remaining companions, for reasons lost to history, agreed to build a raft and continue. Two of them departed the following day, and on August 10 the raft hit a rock and dumped the major portion of their remaining rations into the river. Not even vision and the peculiar courage of the true believer could carry them further. The remaining four members tramped back to Breckenridge. Adams was sobered, but not discouraged. "I am fully satisfied that we had come over the worst part of our route," he wrote in his diary; everything indicated to him "that a prosperous passage was ahead of us had we been in a position to have gone on." He had not even reached the Colorado. Fortunately.

Still bemused with his visions, Adams was quick to render an unauthorized bill to Congress for his "services," together with a report to the Secretary of War. Both entered obscurity. So did Sam Adams, in time, although he hovered on the edges of history long enough to cast a nasty remark or two in the direction of the man who was the first to fill in all the blank spots in the Colorado's story.

CHAPTER IV

INTO THE GREAT UNKNOWN

The Colorado Exploring Expedition

of John Wesley Powell—With Commentary by Wallace Stegner

B Y THE CLOSE of the Civil War, more than three centuries after Coronado's men had gaped at the river from the south rim of the Grand Canyon and nearly twenty years after the United States had claimed it as her own, the Colorado River system remained unknown along most of its course from the headwaters of the Green to the Gulf of California. James Ohio Pattie may have seen the Grand Canyon, and William Ashley had tumbled down the Green nearly to Desolation Canyon; Lieutenant Ives had rammed his steamer up to Black Canyon and later led a land expedition to the mouth of Diamond Creek; and an itinerant trapper by the name of James White had found himself inadvertently running at least some portion of the Colorado. Yet the accumulated information from three centuries of exploration—deliberate and accidental—had illuminated but a fraction of the river. It still was a riddle, walled in mystery and susceptible to curiously insistent myths—not the least of which was the "certainty," as those like Samuel Adams would have it, that the Colorado was the productive West's natural thoroughfare to the Pacific.

The man who shattered this particular myth—together with a number of others during his career—was a one-armed major by the name of John Wesley Powell. Field scientist (largely self-educated), soldier, explorer, public servant in the first great age of public service, and a seer whose visions transcended the probabilities of his time, Powell's paramount determination in life was to *know*—and, having learned, to pass along his knowledge to a not always receptive audience. He contemplated the myths of the West with a cold scrutiny that marked him as one of the few realists of his time, yet he pursued what he saw as truth with a devotion that was almost romantic in its intensity. It was a devotion that sent him into a variety of wildernesses in his early years, searching, collecting, learning; a devotion that compelled him later to take the measure of the entire Colorado Plateau; a devotion that would not admit of the impossible and gave him the strength for thirty years to pit the validity of his knowledge against the blind stubbornness of tradition; a devotion that led him into the savagely beautiful river of the Colorado canyons to make the unknown the known.

Powell came by his westering naturally. Shortly after his birth in 1834 on a farm near Mount Morris, New York, the Powell family picked up and began a series of wanderings that led them west to Wisconsin, then to Ohio, and finally to Illinois—where they settled long enough for Powell to grow up before moving on again to Kansas. His father, a part-time farmer and Methodist circuit-rider, was a vocal abolitionist at a time when such

89

John Wesley Powell's river boat, the Emma Dean, *during his second Colorado trip, 1871—72. The well-secured "deck chair" enabled Powell to survey ahead of time what the river might have in store.*

THE MYTH

"The Major" with an Indian friend sometime in 1872.

1850 and 1861 was remarkable. Among the many excursions he took in these years was a hike across the state of Michigan, collecting specimens as he went, and long river journeys down the Ohio, the Illinois, the Des Moines, and even the Mississippi from St. Paul to New Orleans. By the time of the Civil War, he was recognized as one of the region's leading explorers and collectors; had become secretary of the Illinois Natural History Society; had made the lyceum circuit in Tennessee, Kentucky, and Mississippi; and been named principal of the public schools in Hennepin, Illinois. He was twenty-seven years old.

Typically, Powell was among the first to enlist in the volunteer army of the north in 1861. To his job as a soldier he brought all the vigor that had marked his civilian life, rising quickly from the rank of private to that of major and brevet lieutenant colonel—this after losing his right arm at the Battle of Shiloh. His will to make a way in the world was abetted by an equally tough intelligence not above making useful contacts even in the midst of war—contacts that included, among others, Gen. Ulysses S. Grant. After the war, Powell took a post as a professor of natural history, first at Illinois Wesleyan College, then at Illinois Normal University. The position was only a first step, however, in a long-range program. He next proceeded to persuade Illinois Normal, Wesleyan, and the Illinois Natural History Society to back the establishment of a natural history museum at Bloomington—of which he then became curator with an authorization of $500 for the collection of specimens from the Rocky Mountain region. His next step was characteristic: by dint of persuasion and persistence, he extracted further financial support from Illinois Industrial University; the Chicago Academy of Sciences; the Union Pacific Railroad; the Chicago, Alton, and St. Louis Railroad; the Pittsburgh, Fort Wayne, and Chicago Railroad; and the Chicago and Rock Island Railroad. Further, he went to Washington and enlisted the support of General Grant, which took the form of an authorization to draw rations at cost from western army posts and the assistance of an army escort out of Fort Laramie.

The expedition—composed of students, amateur naturalists, teachers, and even a few relatives, including Powell's wife—set off from Council Bluffs, Iowa, on June 1, 1867. After three months of work—which included a climbing expedition up Pike's Peak, the party returned a solid success. Powell himself returned with the beginning

sentiments were not held in general esteem; Powell learned to fight for an unpopular opinion at an early age. He learned other things while growing to maturity in a Midwest not far removed from the frontier conditions that had shaped such men as Abraham Lincoln: he learned how to manage a family farm often crippled by the long circuit-riding absences of his father; he learned to pick up his education where and how he could; above all, he acquired an abiding love of practical natural science. His formal training was scattered and incomplete, but his self-generated experience in the field between

Colorado Country: Powell's men faithfully expected that such sand bars as this would yield a small fortune (Conquistador Aisle, Colorado River).

of a vision: to explore the Grand River to its junction with the Colorado. A second, more ambitious and lengthy Rocky Mountain expedition the next year not only fortified his intent, but expanded it. He now wanted to know the entire river system from the canyons of the Green to the end of the Colorado canyons.

WITH TYPICAL VIGOR Powell immediately set about organizing his newest project, again obtaining ration authorization from the army, funds from Illinois Normal, the Chicago Academy, Illinois Industrial University, and the Union Pacific and Burlington railroads. As with his other expeditions, however, the bulk of funding came from his own resources. Boats were constructed to his specifications—designed according to what he had learned of the Green and the Colorado and from his wide experience on the rivers of the Midwest. The crew that assembled at Green River City, Wyoming, in May of 1869 was a curiously amateurish collection. With the exception of Powell himself, there were no scientists and few "professional" explorers. Walter Powell, the brother of the leader, was only partially recovered from the mind-destroying experience of a southern prisoner-of-war camp; Jack Sumner, Oramel and Seneca Howland, Bill Dunn, and Billy Rhodes Hawkins were all veterans of Powell's 1868 Rocky Mountain expedition and generally competent in the techniques of survival; George Bradley, an introspective complainer, was a New England boat expert and an army misfit whom Powell appropriated from Fort Bridger with the aid of President Grant; Andy Hall was a young wanderer in search of one adventure or another; and Frank Goodman was an Englishman caught up—like so many of his countrymen—in the grand excitement of the West. All were volunteers, and only those who expected to hunt could count on wages of any kind. There was some hope that the sandbars of the Green and the Colorado would release enough pan gold to make the trip worthwhile, and that there would be time and energy for such pursuits.

On the morning of May 11, the four boats and ten men pushed off into the Green. Only three boats and six men would make it all the way to the Grand Wash Cliffs—more than one hundred days and fifteen hundred miles removed. Three would die, and Goodman, the adventurous Englishman, would grow more and more thoughtful as the trip progressed, finally leaving the party at the mouth of Uinta Creek. The six survivors would emerge

from the unknown in deserved triumph, concluding one of the great exploring adventures in American history and laying open for the first time the geologic pages of the Grand Canyon. This is the story that follows, compiled from Powell's *Exploration of the Colorado River of the West and Its Tributaries,* published in 1875, and accompanied here by descriptive exerpts (these portions italicized) from Wallace Stegner's biography of Powell, *Beyond the Hundredth Meridian.** It is a story of courage and endurance; but more, it is the story of John Wesley Powell's first great contribution to the knowledge of the West and the end of the Colorado as a maker of myths.

May 24, 1869.—The good people of Green River City turn out to see us start. We raise our little flag, push the boats from shore, and the swift current carries us down.

Our boats are four in number. Three are built of oak; stanch and firm; doubled-ribbed, with double stem and stern posts, and further strengthened by bulkheads, dividing each into three compartments.

Two of these, the fore and aft, are decked, forming water-tight cabins. It is expected these will buoy the boats should the waves roll over them in rough water. The little vessels are twenty-one feet long, and, taking out the cargoes, can be carried by four men.

The fourth boat is made of pine, very light, but sixteen feet in length, with a sharp cut-water, and every way built for fast rowing, and divided into compartments as the others.

We take with us rations deemed sufficient to last ten months; for we expect, when winter comes on and the river is filled with ice, to lie over at some point until spring arrives; so we take with us abundant supplies of clothing. We have also a large quantity of ammunition and two or three dozen traps. For the purpose of building cabins, repairing boats, and meeting other exigencies, we are supplied with axes, hammers, saws, augers, and other tools, and a quantity of nails and screws. For scientific work, we have two sextants, four chronometers, a number of barometers, thermometers, compasses, and other instruments.

The flour is divided into three equal parts; the meat and all other articles of our rations in the same way.

Colorado Country: Amid the river's desert splendor, the Powell party discovered Eden-like regions of incredible verdancy (Vasey's Paradise, Colorado River).

THE MYTH

Starting at Green River City, Wyoming, on the second river expedition, 1871. It was at this same point that Powell and his crew had set off in May, 1869, for history's first navigation of the Colorado River—but unhappily, no photographer accompanied the first expedition. Thomas Moran's sketches, which illustrated Powell's Exploration of the Colorado River of the West, *were based on written observation and photographs taken during 1871 and 1872.*

Each of the larger boats has an ax, hammer, saw, auger, and other tools, so that all are loaded alike. We distribute the cargoes in this way, that we may not be entirely destitute of some important article should any one of the boats be lost. In the small boat, we pack a part of the scientific instruments, three guns, and three small bundles of clothing only. In this, I proceed in advance, to explore the channel.

J. C. Sumner and William II. Dunn are my boatmen in the "Emma Dean"; then follows "Kitty Clyde's Sister," manned by W. H. Powell and G. Y. Bradley; next, the "No Name," with O. G. Howland, Seneca Howland, and Frank Goodman; and last comes the "Maid of the Cañon," with W. R. Hawkins and Andrew Hall.

Our boats are heavily loaded, and only with the utmost of care is it even possible to float in the river, rough as it is, without shipping water.

A mile or two below town, we run on a sand-bar. The men jump into the stream, and thus lighten the vessels, so that they drift over; and on we go. In trying to avoid a rock, an oar is broken on one of the boats, and, thus crippled, she strikes. The current is swift, and she is sent reeling and rocking into the eddy. In the confusion, two others are lost overboard and the men seem quite discomfited, much to the amusement of the other members of the party.

Catching the oars and starting again, the boats are once more borne down the stream until we land at a small cottonwood grove on the bank, and camp for noon.

During the afternoon, we run down to a point where the river sweeps the foot of an overhanging cliff, and here we camp for the night. The sun is yet two hours high, so I climb the cliffs, and walk back among the strangely carved rocks of the Green River bad-lands. These are sandstones and shales, gray and buff, red and brown, blue and black strata in many alternations, lying nearly horizontal, and almost without soil and vegetation. They are very friable, and the rain and streams have carved them into quaint shapes. Barren desolation is stretched before me; and yet there is a beauty in the scene. The fantastic carving, imitating architectural forms, and suggesting rude but weird statuary with the bright and varied colors of the rocks, conspire to make a scene such as the dweller in verdure-clad hills can scarcely appreciate. . . .

May 25.—We start early this morning, and run along at a good rate until about nine o'clock, when we are brought up on a gravelly bar. All jump out, and help the boats over by main strength. Then a rain comes on, and river and clouds conspire to give us a thorough drenching. Wet, chilled, and tired to exhaustion, we stop at a cotton-wood grove on the bank, build a huge fire, make a cup of coffee, and are soon refreshed and quite merry. When the clouds "get out of our sunshine," we start again. A few miles farther down, a flock of mountain-sheep are seen on a cliff to the right. The boats are quietly tied up, and three or four men go after them. In the course of two or three hours, they return. The cook has been successful in bringing down a fat lamb. The unsuccessful hunters taunt him with finding it dead; but it is soon dressed, cooked, and eaten, making a fine four o'clock dinner. . . .

May 26.—To-day, we pass several curiously-shaped buttes, standing between the west bank of the river and the high bluffs beyond. These buttes are outliers of the same beds of rocks exposed on the faces of the bluffs; thinly laminated shales and sandstones of many colors, standing above in vertical cliffs, and buttressed below with a water-carved talus; some of them attain an altitude of nearly a thousand feet above the level of the river.

We glide quietly down the placid stream past the carved cliffs of the *mauvaises terres*, now and then obtaining glimpses of distant mountains. Occasionally, deer are started from the glades among the willows; and several wild geese, after a chase through the water, are shot.

After dinner, we pass through a short, narrow cañon into a broad valley; from this, long, lateral valleys stretch back on either side as far as the eye can reach.

Two or three miles below, Henry's Fork enters from the right. We land a short distance above the junction, where a *cache* of instruments and rations was made sev-eral months ago, in a cave at the foot of the cliff, a distance back from the river. Here it was safe from the elements and wild beasts, but not from man. Some anxiety is felt, as we have learned that a party of Indians have been camped near it for several weeks. Our fears are soon allayed, for we find it all right. Our chronometer wheels are not taken for hair ornaments; our barometer tubes, for beads; nor the sextant thrown into the river as "bad medicine," as had been predicted.

Taking up our *cache*, we pass down to the foot of the Uinta Mountains, and, in a cold storm, go into camp.

The river is running to the south; the mountains have an easterly and westerly trend directly athwart its course, yet it glides on in a quiet way as if it thought a mountain range no formidable obstruction to its course. It enters the range by a flaring, brilliant, red gorge, that may be seen from the north a score of miles away. We name it Flaming Gorge. . . .

---

*L*uckily *for the Powell Expedition's unpracticed boat-men, the Green for sixty miles south of Green River is a relatively mild stream, flowing through broken bad-lands. Though there are low bluffs, there are no real can-yons, and though the current is insistent and swift, there is nothing that can be called a rapid. In those sixty miles they had a chance to discover how their boats handled. . . . They learned too what every man who has ever han-dled a boat on Green or Colorado or San Juan learns: how trivial a mistake can lead to trouble. The rivers are not "treacherous." They are only forever dangerous. One who has not tried it finds it hard to believe the instant and terrible force that such a current exerts on a broadside boat out of control on a sandbar or rock. . . . On any of the rivers a spilled boatman, an upset boat, is swept off downstream as if by an avalanche. Powell's men, running aground, breaking an oar, spinning in eddies, learned respect for the river before it got dangerous. . . .*

Because they were an exploring party and not merely a group of thrill-hunters, they did not plunge directly in [to Flaming Gorge]. For three days they sat outside the gate, mending barometers, measuring the height of the cliffs (1,200 feet), climbing to the walls to look around. The peaks of the Wasatch notched the west, the barren Wyoming plateau northward swelled up toward South Pass and the snowy Wind River Mountains. . . . For a while the river flirts with the great mountain table rising east and west across its course. It cuts in through Flaming Gorge [now inundated by the lake behind Flaming Gorge Dam], emerges into a little park where today there are three or four remote ranches, and then wheels left into the mountain. But it does not cut through. The red walls turn it in a half circle, forcing it through a complete U out into the valley again, barely a half mile from where it entered. Powell named this stretch Horseshoe Canyon. In the part of it now called Hideout Canyon there is a footbridge across the Green to accommodate pack trains and deer hunters and sheep bands headed for the back country. This canyon gave the expedition its first real thrill—a curving rapid where the water plunged down among rocks. They ran it, at first scared and then exhilarated.

The walls widened out to make another little valley, pinched in to make another canyon. The river was broad and quiet here, and kingfishers playing along a tributary stream gave valley and canyon and stream a name. Just beyond their May 30 camp came a great domed point eroded into thousands of holes where swallows nested. They called it Beehive Point and followed the river around it, changing course from south to east as the river, having cut in close to the heart of the range, turned and ran along it lengthwise.

By now the walls were close to a half mile high, stepping backward in terraces, clean cliff and wooded slope and clean cliff again, to remote rims. Red Canyon they called it; it is one of the spectacular chasms of the Green. Today a tourist can look down into it from several spots on the rim, notably from Green Lake. But the tourist from that height sees only a thread of river, green in the low water, reddish in high. He will not see the rapids that for the first time gave Powell and his men a touch of danger and exhausting work, and he will not hear what is perhaps the most nerve-wearing accompaniment of any voyage in these canyons: the incessant, thundering, express-engine roar of the water. In many parts of the canyons it never ceases, day or night. It speeds the heartbeat and deafens the ears and shakes the ground underfoot. It comes from every side, echoed and multiplied by the walls. A man's voice is lost, shouting in it.

June 1.—To-day we have an exciting ride. The river rolls down the cañon at a wonderful rate, and, with no rocks in the way, we make almost railroad speed. Here and there the water rushes into a narrow gorge; the rocks on the side roll it into the center in great waves, and the boats go leaping and bounding over these like things of life. They remind me of scenes witnessed in Middle Park; herds of startled deer bounding through forests beset with fallen timber. I mention the resemblance to some of the hunters, and so striking is it that it comes to be a common expression, "See the black-tails jumping the logs." At times the waves break and roll over the boats, which necessitates much bailing, and obliges us to stop occasionally for that purpose. At one time, we run twelve miles in an hour, stoppages included.

Last spring, I had a conversation with an old Indian named Pá-ri-ats, who told me about one of his tribe attempting to run this cañon. "The rocks," he said, holding his hands above his head, his arms vertical, and looking between them to the heavens, "the rocks h-e-a-p, h-e-a-p high; the water go h-oo-woogh, h-oo-woogh; water-pony (boat) h-e-a-p buck; water catch 'em; no see 'em Injun any more! no see 'em squaw any more! no see 'em pappoose any more!"

Those who have seen these wild Indian ponies rearing alternately before and behind, or "bucking," as it is called in the vernacular, will appreciate his description.

At last we come to calm water, and a threatening roar is heard in the distance. Slowly approaching the point whence the sound issues, we come near to falls, and tie up just above them on the left. Here we will be compelled to make a portage; so we unload the boats, and fasten a long line to the bow, and another to the stern, of the smaller one, and moor her close to the brink of the fall. Then the bow-line is taken below, and made fast; the stern line is held by five or six men, and the boat let down as long as they can hold her against the rushing waters; then, letting go one end of the line, it runs through the ring; the boat leaps over the fall, and is caught by the lower rope.

Now we rest for the night.

June 2.—This morning we make a trail among the rocks, transport the cargoes to a point below the falls, let the remaining boats over, and are ready to start before noon.

On a high rock by which the trail passes we find the inscription: "Ashley 18-5." The third figure is obscure—some of the party reading it 1835, some 1855.

James Baker, an old time mountaineer, once told me about a party of men starting down the river, and Ashley was named as one. The story runs that the boat was swamped, and some of the party drowned in one of the cañons below. The word "Ashley" is a warning to us, and we resolve on great caution.

Ashley Falls is the name we give to the cataract.

They had thought they were the first into these red rock gorges, but at Ashley Falls, as they would do several times, they crossed the path of history. . . . Powell did not know who Ashley was, for Ashley's narrative was not printed until 1918. . . . He was not yet opening new country, but he was collecting data as he went, climbing the cliffs at every opportunity to measure altitudes and take geological sections, and most of all to fill his eye with the view and let the sweep of the Uintas take their place in the map that was forming in his mind. Climbing out to the rim from Red Canyon he looked down the narrowing wedge of forested mountain between the Uinta crest and the gorge of the river, and came close to history again. On the same piney uplands beyond the rims of Red Canyon, Henry Adams would be camping in a little more than a year, formulating in campfire discussions with Arnold Hague and S. F. Emmons some of the ideas that would mold a fascinating and cryptic career, and measuring his education against a primeval wilderness. And from the cliffs above Brown's Hole, where Powell climbed two days later, he could look eastward up the valley of the Vermillion through which Frémont had found his way to the parks of Colorado in 1844. . . .

Powell was not thinking of history as he camped in Brown's Hole, resting after the canyons, restoring the ears of his party with silence and birdsong, measuring the country he could reach or see. . . . For him this was the real beginning. Up to here he had been anticipated by trappers and prospectors. Brown's Hole itself was a vast cattle ranch, there were cabins and herds, and the place had been known years back by trappers on the Seedskeedee. But from here on was something else. Two thousand feet above the Hole, hanging his feet over the cliff, Powell sat and wrote a letter, dated June 7, 1869. . . .

While I write, I am sitting on the same rock where I sat last spring, with Mrs. Powell, looking down into this canon. When I came down at noon, the sun shone in splendor on its vermilion walls shaded into green and gray when the rocks are lichened over. The river

Entering the Canyon of Lodore (from Exploration of the Colorado River of the West, *1875).*

fills the channel from wall to wall. The canon opened like a beautiful portal to a region of glory. Now, as I write, the sun is going down, and the shadows are settling in the canon. The vermilion gleams and the rosy hues, the green and gray tints, are changing to sombre brown above, and black shadows below. Now 'tis a black portal to a region of gloom.

And that is the gateway through which we enter [on] our voyage of exploration tomorrow—and what shall we find?

June 8.—We enter the cañon, and, until noon, find a succession of rapids, over which our boats have to be taken.

Here I must explain our method of proceeding at such places. The "Emma Dean" goes in advance; the other boats follow, in obedience to signals. When we approach a rapid, or what, on other rivers, would often be called a fall, I stand on deck to examine it, while the oarsmen

THE MYTH

back water, and we drift on as slowly as possible. If I can see a clear chute between the rocks, away we go; but if the channel is beset entirely across, we signal the other boats, pull to land, and I walk along the shore for closer examination. If this reveals no clear channel, hard work begins. We drop the boats to the very head of the dangerous place, and let them over by lines, or make a portage, frequently carrying both boats and cargoes over the rocks, or, perhaps, only the cargoes, if it is safe to let the boats down.

The waves caused by such falls in a river differ much from the waves of the sea. The water of an ocean wave merely rises and falls; the form only passes on, and form chases form unceasingly. A body floating on such waves merely rises and sinks—does not progress unless impelled by wind or some other power. But here, the water of the wave passes on, while the form remains. The waters plunge down ten or twenty feet, to the foot of a fall; spring up again in a great wave; then down and up, in a series of billows, that gradually disappear in the more quiet waters below; but these waves are always there, and you can stand above and count them.

A boat riding such, leaps and plunges along with great velocity. Now, the difficulty in riding over these falls, when the rocks are out of the way, is in the first wave at the foot. This will sometimes gather for a moment, heaping up higher and higher, until it breaks back. If the boat strikes it the instant after it breaks, she cuts through, and the mad breaker dashes its spray over the boat, and would wash us overboard did we not cling tight. If the boat, in going over the falls, chances to get caught in some side current, and is turned from its course, so as to strike the wave "broadside on," and the wave breaks at the same instant, the boat is capsized. Still, we must cling to her, for, the water tight compartments acting as buoys, she cannot sink; and so we go, dragged through the waves, until still waters are reached. We then right the boat, and climb aboard. We have [had] several such experiences to day. . . .

June 9.—One of the party suggests that we call this the Cañon of Lodore, and the name is adopted. Very slowly we make our way, often climbing on the rocks at the edge of the water for a few hundred yards, to examine the channel before running it.

During the afternoon, we come to a place where it is necessary to make a portage. The little boat [is] landed, and the others are signaled to come up.

When these rapids or broken falls occur, usually the channel is suddenly narrowed by rocks which have been tumbled from the cliffs or have been washed in by lateral streams. Immediately above the narrow, rocky channel, on one or both sides, there is often a bay of quiet water, in which we can land with ease. Sometimes the water descends with a smooth, unruffled surface, from the broad, quiet spread above, into the narrow, angry channel below, by a semicircular sag. Great care must be taken not to pass over the brink into this deceptive pit, but above it we can row with safety. I walk along the bank to examine the ground, leaving one of my men with a flag to guide the other boats to the landing-place. I soon see one of the boats make shore all right and feel no more concern; but a minute after, I hear a shout, and looking around, see one of the boats shooting down the center of the sag. It is the "No Name," with Captain Howland, his brother, and Goodman. I feel that its going over is inevitable, and run to save the third boat. A minute more, and she turns the point and heads for the shore. Then I turn down stream again, and scramble along to look for the boat that has gone over. The first fall is not great, only ten or twelve feet, and we often run such; but below, the river tumbles down again for forty or fifty feet, in a channel filled with dangerous rocks that break the waves into whirlpools and beat them into foam. I pass around a great crag just in time to see the boat strike a rock, and, rebounding from the shock, careen and fill the open compartment with water. Two of the men lose their oars; she swings around, and is carried down at a rapid rate, broadside on, for a few yards, and strikes amidships on another rock with great force, is broken quite in two, and the men are thrown into the river; the larger part of the boat floating buoyantly, they soon seize it, and down the river they drift, past the rocks for a few hundred yards to a second rapid, filled with huge boulders, where the boat strikes again, and is dashed to pieces, and the men and fragments are soon carried beyond my sight. Running along, I turn a bend, and see a man's head above the water, washed about in a whirlpool below a great rock.

It is Frank Goodman, clinging to it with a grip upon which life depends. Coming opposite, I see Howland trying to go to his aid from an island on which he has been washed. Soon, he comes near enough to reach Frank with a pole, which he extends toward him. The latter lets go the rock, grasps the pole, and is pulled ashore. Seneca Howland is washed farther down the island, and is caught by some rocks, and, though somewhat bruised, manages to get ashore safely. . . .

And now the three men are on an island, with a swift, dangerous river on either side, and a fall below. The "Emma Dean" is soon brought down, and Sumner, starting above as far as possible, pushes out. Right skillfully he plies the oars, and a few strokes set him on the island at the proper point. Then they all pull the boat up stream, as far as they are able, until they stand in water up to their necks. One sits on a rock, and holds the boat until the others are ready to pull, then gives the boat a push, clings to it with his hands, and climbs in as they pull for mainland, which they reach in safety. We are as glad to shake hands with them as though they had been on a voyage around the world, and wrecked on a distant coast.

Down the river half a mile we find that the after cabin of the wrecked boat, with a part of the bottom, ragged and splintered, has floated against a rock, and stranded. There are valuable articles in the cabin; but, on examination, we determine that life should not be risked to save them. Of course, the cargo of rations, instruments, and clothing is gone.

We return to the boats, and make camp for the night. No sleep comes to me in all those dark hours. The rations, instruments, and clothing have been divided among the boats, anticipating such an accident as this; and we started with duplicates of everything that was deemed necessary to success. But, in the distribution, there was one exception to this precaution, and the barometers were all placed in one boat, and they are lost. There is a possibility that they are in the cabin lodged against the rock, for that is where they were kept. But, then, how to reach them! The river is rising. Will they be there to-morrow?

---

*P*owell lay awake that night, half inclined to try making his way out to Salt Lake to order new barometers from the east. But in the morning they saw that the wreck of the No Name had washed fifty yards further downstream. Her stern half had lodged where it might possibly be reached, and there was a chance that something remained in its compartment. Sumner and Hall volunteered to reach her, and did so. From their rummaging in the smashed after cabin they rose up to wave their arms and

The Canyon of Lodore in 1871
(E. O. Beaman photograph).

yell something across the roar of water, and in a few minutes they came back in triumph. No clothes and no rations were among their prizes, but they had found the whole package of thermometers, plus what had inspired their cheers: a keg of whiskey smuggled aboard at Green River without Powell's knowledge. . . . Powell good-naturedly admitted that the river was cold, and accepted the keg as medicine.

Presumably it served its medicinal function. They were days getting past this portage, nearly a mile long, and letting the boats down successive rapids. At the bottom they lay over two more days to dry their spoiling rations, which had now become a worry. The wreck had sobered their exuberance, which in the fast water above had left them feeling, as Sumner said, "like sparking a black-eyed girl—just dangerous enough to be exciting." Now they encountered evidence of another wreck before their own

THE MYTH

The wreck at Disaster Falls, June 9, 1869 (from Exploration of the Colorado River of the West).

—a broken boat, the lid of a bake oven, an old tin plate. Powell thought this might be Ashley's boat. Nobody has ever determined whose in fact it was. But it helped emphasize the prudence that Powell had emphasized from the beginning. It did not take sucks or Niagaras to wreck a boat or drown a man.

June 17.—We run down to the mouth of Yampa River. This has been a chapter of disasters and toils, notwithstanding which the cañon of Lodore was not devoid of scenic interest, even beyond the power of pen to tell. The roar of its waters was heard unceasingly from the hour we entered it until we landed here. No quiet in all that time. But its walls and cliffs, its peaks and crags, its

amphitheaters and alcoves, tell a story of beauty and grandeur that I hear yet—and shall hear. . . .

The Yampa enters the Green from the east. At a point opposite its mouth, the Green runs to the south, at the foot of a rock, about seven hundred feet high and a mile long, and then turns sharply around it to the right, and runs back in a northerly course, parallel to its former direction, for nearly another mile, thus having the opposite sides of a long, narrow rock for its bank. The tongue of rock so formed is a peninsular precipice, with a mural escarpment along its whole course on the east, but broken down at places on the west. . . .

Great hollow domes are seen in the eastern side of the rock, against which the Green sweeps; willows border the river; clumps of box-elder are seen; and a few cottonwoods stand at the lower end. Standing opposite the rock, our words are repeated with startling clearness, but in a soft, mellow tone, that transforms them into magical music. Scarcely can you believe it is the echo of your own voice. In some places two or three echoes come back; in other places they repeat themselves, passing back and forth across the river between this rock and the eastern wall. . . .

June 18.—We have named the long peninsular rock . . . Echo Rock. Desiring to climb it, Bradley and I take the little boat and pull up stream as far as possible, for it cannot be climbed directly opposite. We land on a talus of rocks at the upper end, to reach a place where it seems practicable to make the ascent; but we must go still farther up the river. So we scramble along, until we reach a place where the river sweeps against the wall. Here we find a shelf, along which we can pass, and now are ready for the climb.

We start up a gulch; then pass to the left, on a bench, along the wall; then up again, over broken rocks; then we reach more benches, along which we walk, until we find more broken rocks and crevices, by which we climb, still up, until we have ascended six or eight hundred feet; then we are met by a sheer precipice.

Looking about, we find a place where it seems possible to climb. I go ahead; Bradley hands the barometer to me, and follows. So we proceed, stage by stage, until we are nearly to the summit. Here, by making a spring, I gain a foothold in a little crevice, and grasp an angle of the rock overhead. I find I can get up no farther, and cannot step back, for I dare not let go with my hand, and cannot reach foot-hold below without. I call to Bradley for help. He finds a way by which he can get to the top of the rock over my head, but cannot reach me. Then he looks around for some stick or limb of a tree, but finds none. Then he suggests that he had better help me with the barometer case; but I fear I cannot hold on to it. The moment is critical. Standing on my toes, my muscles begin to tremble. It is sixty or eighty feet to the foot of the precipice. If I lose my hold I shall fall to the bottom, and then perhaps roll over the bench, and tumble still farther down the cliff. At this instant it occurs to Bradley to take off his drawers, which he does, and swings them down to me. I hug close to the rock, let go with my hand, seize the dangling legs, and, with his assistance, I am enabled to gain the top.

Then we walk out on a peninsular rock, make the necessary observations for determining its altitude above camp, and return, finding an easy way down. . . .

June 21.—We float around the long rock, and enter another cañon. The walls are high and vertical; the cañon is narrow; and the river fills the whole space below, so that there is no landing-place at the foot of the cliff. The Green is greatly increased by the Yampa, and we now have a much larger river. All this volume of water, confined, as it is, in a narrow channel, and rushing with great velocity, is set eddying and spinning in whirlpools by projecting rocks and short curves, and the waters waltz their way through the cañon, making their own rippling, rushing, roaring music. The cañon is much narrower than any we have seen. With difficulty we manage our boats. They spin about from side to side, and we know not where we are going, and find it impossible to keep them headed down the stream. At first, this causes us great alarm, but we soon find there is but little danger, and that there is a general movement of progression down the river, to which this whirling is but an adjunct; and it is the merry mood of the river to dance through this deep, dark gorge; and right gaily do we join in the sport.

Soon our revel is interrupted by a cataract; its roaring command is heeded by all our power at the oars, and we pull against the whirling current. The "Emma Dean" is brought up against a cliff, about fifty feet above the brink of the fall. By vigorously plying the oars on the side opposite the wall, as if to pull up stream, we can hold her against the rock. The boats behind are signaled to land where they can. The "Maid of the Cañon" is pulled to the left wall, and, by constant rowing, they can hold her

also. The "Sister" is run into an alcove on the right, where an eddy is in a dance, and in this she joins. Now my little boat is held against the wall only by the utmost exertion, and it is impossible to make headway against the current. On examination, I find a horizontal crevice in the rock, about ten feet above the water, and a boat's length below us, so we let her down to that point. One of the men clambers into the crevice, in which he can just crawl; we toss him the line, which he makes fast in the rocks, and now our boat is tied up. Then I follow into the crevice, and we crawl along a distance of fifty feet, or more, up stream, and find a broken place, where we can climb about fifty feet higher. Here we stand on a shelf, that passes along down stream to a point above the falls, where it is broken down, and a pile of rocks, over which we can descend to the river, is lying against the foot of the cliff.

It has been mentioned that one of the boats is on the other side. I signal for the men to pull her up alongside of the wall, but it cannot be done; then to cross. This they do, gaining the wall on our side just above where the "Emma Dean" is tied.

The third boat is out of sight, whirling in the eddy of a recess. Looking about, I find another horizontal crevice, along which I crawl to a point just over the water, where this boat is lying, and, calling loud and long, I finally succeed in making the crew understand that I want them to bring the boat down, hugging the wall. This they accomplish, by taking advantage of every crevice and knob on the face of the cliff, so that we have the three boats together at a point a few yards above the falls. Now, by passing a line up on the shelf, the boats can be let down to the broken rocks below. This we do, and, making a short portage, our troubles here are over. . . .

June 22.—Still making short portages and letting down with lines. While we are waiting for dinner to-day, I climb a point that gives me a good view of the river for two or three miles below, and I think we can make a long run. After dinner, we start; the large boats are to follow in fifteen minutes, and look out for the signal to land. Into the middle of the stream we row, and down the rapid river we glide, only making strokes enough with the oars to guide the boat. What a headlong ride it is! shooting past rocks and islands! I am soon filled with exhilaration only experienced before in riding a fleet horse over the outstretched prairie. One, two, three, four miles we go, rearing and plunging with the waves, until

THE MYTH

we wheel to the right into a beautiful park, and land on an island, where we go into camp.

---

*Q*uiet water had its drawbacks. If they wanted to make time, they had to row. Even so, they dragged their log for sixty-three miles down the Green's meanders on June 27, fought mosquitoes all night, and in the morning made the mouth of the Uinta, the site of the present town of Ouray, Utah.... This was the only opportunity along the whole course of the river for communication. From here letters could go out, and at the Uinta Agency, thirty miles up this creek, there might be mail waiting.

Powell sent his brother and Andy Hall on foot to the Agency for mail, setting out after them two days later with Goodman and Hawkins. The ones left behind rather mournfully celebrated the Fourth by chasing ducks on the Uinta. When the Major, Hawkins, Hall, Walter and two Indian packers returned, Frank Goodman was not with them. His appetite for border experiences had been satisfied....

They were all impatient. Nevertheless, for a mixed group, they had so far managed to remain remarkably harmonious. The river equivalent of cabin fever, which comes on fast and in virulent forms, had hardly touched them. Goodman, the near-pariah, was gone. Bradley, the loner, might herd by himself but he was a good boatman and a cool head ... and he had their respect. Walter Powell, though moody and increasingly disliked, was insulated by his relationship to the leader, and accepted for the quality of his singing and his great physical strength. As for the Major himself, in spite of his science they had to admire him. One-armed, he was as agile on the cliffs as any of them. He had nerve, and he had a variety of interests that excited him, and he participated fully in camp life. Actually, he was a commander more likely than most to hold so centrifugal a crew in hand. All they really objected to in him was his caution and his "waiting around." ...

On July 6, to their universal relief, they pushed off on the second leg of the journey, this time into the incontrovertible Unknown. As if to document their wanderlust and their unfitness for civilization, a squatter's garden encountered at the mouth of the White poisoned them all so thoroughly that they floated through the lower end of Uinta Valley vomiting over the side and cursing Andy Hall, who had suggested that potato tops made good

greens. By evening, almost imperceptibly, the valley closed in, the walls began to rise, the barren rock poured through, and they were in another canyon.

July 7.—We find quiet water to day, the river sweeping in great and beautiful curves, the cañon walls steadily increasing in altitude. The escarpment formed by the cut edges of the rock are often vertical, sometimes terraced, and in some places the treads of the terraces are sloping. In these quiet curves vast amphitheaters are formed, now in vertical rocks, now in steps.

The salient point of rock within the curve is usually broken down in a steep slope, and we stop occasionally to climb up, at such a place, where, on looking down, we can see the river sweeping the foot of the opposite cliff, in a great, easy curve, with a perpendicular or terraced wall rising from the water's edge many hundreds of feet. One of these we find very symmetrical, and name it Sumner's Amphitheater. The cliffs are rarely broken by the entrance of side cañons, and we sweep around curve after curve, with almost continuous walls, for several miles.

Late in the afternoon, we find the river much rougher, and come upon rapids, not dangerous, but still demanding close attention.

We camp at night on the right bank, having made to day twenty six miles.

July 8.—This morning, Bradley and I go out to climb, and gain an altitude of more than two thousand feet above the river, but still do not reach the summit of the wall.

After dinner, we pass through a region of the wildest desolation. The cañon is very tortuous, the river very rapid, and many lateral cañons enter on either side. These usually have their branches, so that the region is cut into a wilderness of gray and brown cliffs. In several places, these lateral cañons are only separated from each other by narrow walls, often hundreds of feet high, but so narrow in places that where softer rocks are found below, they have crumbled away, and left holes in the wall, forming passages from one cañon into another. These we often call natural bridges; but they were never intended to span streams. They had better, perhaps, be called side doors between cañon chambers.

Piles of broken rock lie against these walls; crags and tower shaped peaks are seen everywhere; and away above them, long lines of broken cliffs, and above and beyond the cliffs are pine forests, of which we obtain occasional glimpses, as we look up through a vista of rocks.

The walls are almost without vegetation; a few dwarf bushes are seen here and there, clinging to the rocks, and cedars grow from the crevices—not like the cedars of a land refreshed with rains, great cones bedecked with spray, but ugly clumps, like war clubs, beset with spines. We are minded to call this the Cañon of Desolation.

The wind annoys us much to day. The water, rough by reason of the rapids, is made more so by head gales. Wherever a great face of rock has a southern exposure, the rarified air rises, and the wind rushes in below, either up or down the cañon, or both, causing local currents.

Just at sunset, we run a bad rapid, and camp at its foot....

July 11.—A short distance below camp we run a rapid, and, in doing so, break an oar, and then lose another, both belonging to the "Emma Dean." So the pioneer boat has but two oars....

We soon approach another rapid. Standing on deck, I think it can be run, and on we go. Coming nearer, I see that at the foot it has a short turn to the left, where the waters pile up against the cliff. Here we try to land, but quickly discover that, being in swift water, above the fall, we cannot reach shore, crippled, as we are, by the loss of two oars; so the bow of the boat is turned down stream. We shoot by a big rock; a reflex wave rolls over our little boat and fills her. I see the place is dangerous, and quickly signal to the other boats to land where they can. This is scarcely completed when another wave rolls our boat over, and I am thrown some distance into the water. I soon find that swimming is very easy, and I cannot sink. It is only necessary to ply strokes sufficient to keep my head out of the water, though now and then, when a breaker rolls over me, I close my mouth, and am carried through it. The boat is drifting ahead of me twenty or thirty feet, and, when the great waves are passed, I overtake it, and find Sumner and Dunn clinging to her. As soon as we reach quiet water, we all swim to one side and turn her over. In doing this, Dunn loses his hold and goes under; when he comes up, he is caught by Sumner and pulled to the boat. In the mean time we have drifted down stream some distance, and see another rapid below. How bad it may be we cannot tell, so we swim toward shore, pulling our boat with us, with all the vigor possible, but are carried down much faster than

distance toward shore is gained. At last we reach a huge pile of drift wood. Our rolls of blankets, two guns, and a barometer were in the open compartment of the boat, and, when it went over, these were thrown out. The guns and barometer are lost, but I succeeded in catching one of the rolls of blankets, as it drifted by, when we were swimming to shore; the other two are lost, and sometimes hereafter we may sleep cold.

A huge fire is built on the bank, our clothing is spread to dry, and then from the drift logs we select one from which we think oars can be made, and the remainder of the day is spent in sawing them out.

July 12.—This morning, the new oars are finished, and we start once more. We pass several bad rapids, making a short portage at one, and before noon we come to a long, bad fall, where the channel is filled with rocks on the left, turning the waters to the right, where they pass under an overhanging rock. On examination, we determine to run it, keeping as close to the left hand rocks as safety will permit, in order to avoid the overhanging cliff. The little boat runs over all right; another follows, but the men are not able to keep her near enough to the left bank, and she is carried, by a swift chute, into great waves to the right, where she is tossed about, and Bradley is knocked over the side, but his foot catching under the seat, he is dragged along in the water, with his head down; making great exertion, he seizes the gunwale with his left hand, and can lift his head above water now and then. To us who are below, it seems impossible to keep the boat from going under the overhanging cliff; but Powell, for the moment, heedless of Bradley's mishap, pulls with all his power for half a dozen strokes, when the danger is past; then he seizes Bradley, and pulls him in. The men in the boat above, seeing this, land, and she is let down by lines.

Just here we emerge from the Cañon of Desolation, as we have named it, into a more open country, which extends for a distance of nearly a mile, when we enter another cañon, cut through gray sandstone.

About three o'clock in the afternoon we meet with a new difficulty. The river fills the entire channel; the walls are vertical on either side, from the water's edge, and a bad rapid is beset with rocks. We come to the head of it, and land on a rock in the stream; the little boat is let down to another rock below, the men of the larger boat holding to the line; the second boat is let down in the same way, and the line of the third boat is brought

Desolation Canyon in 1871. Its walls, Powell wrote in July, 1869, were "ugly clumps, like war clubs, beset with spines. We are minded to call this the Cañon of Desolation."

with them. Now, the third boat pushes out from the upper rock, and, as we have her line below, we pull in and catch her, as she is sweeping by at the foot of the rock on which we stand. Again the first boat is let down stream the full length of her line, and the second boat is passed down by the first to the extent of her line, which is held by the men in the first boat; so she is two lines' length from where she started. Then the third boat is let down past the second, and still down, nearly to the length of her line, so that she is fast to the second boat, and swinging down three lines' lengths, with the other two boats intervening. Held in this way, the men are able to

pull her into a cove, in the left wall, where she is made fast. But this leaves a man on the rock above, holding to the line of the little boat. When all is ready, he springs from the rock, clinging to the line with one hand, and swimming with the other, and we pull him in as he goes by. As the two boats, thus loosened, drift down, the men in the cove pull us all in, as we come opposite; then we pass around to a point of rock below the cove, close to the wall, land, and make a short portage over the worst places in the rapid, and start again.

At night we camp on a sand beach; the wind blows a hurricane; the drifting sand almost blinds us; and nowhere can we find shelter. The wind continues to blow all night; the sand sifts through our blankets, and piles over us, until we are covered as in a snow-drift. We are glad when morning comes. . . .

July 14.—This morning, we pass some curious black bluffs on the right, then two or three short cañons, and then we discover the mouth of the San Rafael, a stream which comes down from the distant mountains in the west. Here we stop for an hour or two, and take a short walk up the valley, and find it is a frequent resort for Indians. Arrow heads are scattered about, many of them very beautiful. Flint chips are seen strewn over the ground in great profusion, and the trails are well worn.

Starting after dinner, we pass some beautiful buttes on the left, many of which are very symmetrical. They are chiefly composed of gypsum of many hues, from light gray to slate color; then pink, purple, and brown beds.

Now, we enter another cañon. Gradually the walls rise higher and higher as we proceed, and the summit of the cañon is formed of the same beds of orange colored sandstone. Back from the brink, the hollows of the plateau are filled with sands disintegrated from these orange beds. They are of rich cream color, shaded into maroon, everywhere destitute of vegetation, and drifted into long, wave like ridges.

The course of the river is tortuous, and it nearly doubles upon itself many times. . . .

We camp at night on the left bank.

July 15.—Our camp is in a great bend of the cañon. The perimeter of the curve is to the west, and we are on the east side of the river. Just opposite, a little stream comes down through a narrow side cañon. We cross, and go up to explore it. Just at its mouth, another lateral cañon enters, in the angle between the former and the main cañon above. Still another enters in the angle between the cañon below and the side cañon first mentioned, so that three side cañons enter at the same point. These cañons are very tortuous, almost closed in from view, and, seen from the opposite side of the river, they appear like three alcoves; and we name this Trin-Alcove Bend. . . .

About six miles below noon camp, we go around a great bend to the right, five miles in length, and come back to a point within a quarter of a mile of where we started. Then we sweep around another great bend to the left, making a circuit of nine miles, and come back to a point within six hundred yards of the beginning of the bend. In the two circuits, we describe almost the figure 8. The men call it a bow-knot of river; so we name it Bow-knot Bend. The line of the figure is fourteen miles in length.

There is an exquisite charm in our ride to-day down this beautiful cañon. It gradually grows deeper with every mile of travel; the walls are symmetrically curved, and grandly arched; of a beautiful color, and reflected in the quiet waters in many places, so as to almost deceive the eye, and suggest the thought, to the beholder, that he is looking into profound depths. We are all in fine spirits, feel very gay, and the badinage of the men is echoed from wall to wall. Now and then we whistle, or shout, or discharge a pistol, to listen to the reverberations among the cliffs.

At night we camp on the south side of the great Bow-knot, and, as we eat our supper, which is spread on the beach, we name this Labyrinth Cañon. . . .

July 17.—The line which separates Labyrinth Cañon from the one below is but a line, and at once, this morning, we enter another cañon. The water fills the entire channel, so that nowhere is there room to land. The walls are low, but vertical, and, as we proceed, they gradually increase in altitude. Running a couple of miles, the river changes its course many degrees, toward the east. Just here, a little stream comes in on the right, and the wall is broken down; so we land, and go out to take a view of the surrounding country. We are now down among the buttes, and in a region, the surface of which is naked, solid rock—a beautiful red sandstone, forming a smooth, undulating pavement. The Indians call this the *"Toom'-pin Tu-weap'*,*"* or *"*Rock Land,*"* and sometimes the *Toom'-pin wu-near' Tu-weap'*,*"* or *"*Land of Standing Rock.*"*

Off to the south we see a butte, in the form of a fallen cross. It is several miles away, still it presents no inconspicuous figure on the landscape, and must be many hundreds of feet high, probably more than two thousand. We note its position on our map, and name it "The Butte of the Cross."

We continue our journey. In many places the walls, which rise from the water's edge, are overhanging on either side. The stream is still quiet, and we glide along, through a strange, weird, grand region. The landscape everywhere, away from the river, is of rock—cliffs of rock; tables of rock; plateaus of rock; terraces of rock; crags of rock—ten thousand strangely carved forms.

THE MYTH

Rocks everywhere, and no vegetation; no soil; no sand. In long, gentle curves, the river winds about these rocks.

When speaking of these rocks, we must not conceive of piles of boulders, or heaps of fragments, but a whole land of naked rock, with giant forms carved on it: cathedral shaped buttes, towering hundreds or thousands of feet; cliffs that cannot be scaled, and cañon walls that shrink the river into insignificance, with vast, hollow domes, and tall pinnacles, and shafts set on the verge overhead, and all highly colored—buff, gray, red, brown, and chocolate; never lichened; never moss-covered; but bare, and often polished. . . .

Late in the afternoon, the water becomes swift, and our boats make great speed. An hour of this rapid running brings us to the junction of the Grand and Green, the foot of Stillwater Cañon, as we have named it.

Those streams unite in solemn depths, more than one thousand two hundred feet below the general surface of the country. The walls of the lower end of Stillwater Cañon are very beautifully curved, as the river sweeps in its meandering course. The lower end of the cañon through which the Grand comes down, is also regular, but much more direct, and we look up this stream, and out into the country beyond, and obtain glimpses of snow clad peaks, the summits of a group of mountains known as the Sierra La Sal. Down the Colorado, the cañon walls are much broken.

We row around into the Grand, and camp on its northwest bank; and here we propose to stay several days, for the purpose of determining the latitude and longitude, and the altitude of the walls. Much of the night is spent in making observations with the sextant.

By the time they reached the junction of the Green and Grand the Powell party had been out almost two months, and in that time seen no man white or red except at the Uinta Agency. The ten-month supply of food with which they had started was diminished alarmingly by consumption, spoilage, and the loss of the No Name. When they sifted their musty flour through mosquito netting and checked over the rations that remained, they found themselves with a frugal two-month supply—if they didn't lose any more to the river. Their barometers were battered and their clothes considerably used up; the Howlands had only hand-me-downs to clothe their shanks. Nevertheless their camp at the junction was a satisfying one, and they made the most of the opportunity for exploration back from the canyons. . . .

It was July 21 before they pushed off into the real Colorado, the old man himself, an awesome river wide and deep and the color of cocoa.

July 21.—We start this morning on the Colorado. The river is rough, and bad rapids, in close succession, are found. Two very hard portages are made during the forenoon. After dinner, in running a rapid, the "Emma Dean" is swamped, and we are thrown into the river, we cling to her, and in the first quiet water below she is righted and bailed out; but three oars are lost in this mishap. The larger boats land above the dangerous place, and we make a portage, that occupies all the afternoon. We camp at night, on the rocks on the left bank, and can scarcely find room to lie down.

July 22.—This morning, we continue our journey, though short of oars. There is no timber growing on the walls within our reach, and no drift wood along the banks, so we are compelled to go on until something suitable can be found. A mile and three quarters below, we find a huge pile of drift wood, among which are some cottonwood logs. From these we select one which we think the best, and the men are set at work sawing oars. Our boats are leaking again, from the strains received in the bad rapids yesterday, so, after dinner, they are turned over, and some of the men are engaged in calking them. . . .

July 23.—On starting, we come at once to difficult rapids and falls, that, in many places, are more abrupt than in any of the cañons through which we have passed, and we decide to name this Cataract Cañon.

From morning until noon, the course of the river is to the west; the scenery is grand, with rapids and falls below, and walls above, beset with crags and pinnacles. Just at noon we wheel again to the south, and go into camp for dinner. . . .

Our way, after dinner, is through a gorge, grand beyond description. The walls are nearly vertical; the river broad and swift, but free from rocks and falls. From the edge of the water to the brink of the cliffs it is one thousand six hundred to one thousand eight hundred feet. At this great depth, the river rolls in solemn majesty. The cliffs are reflected from the more quiet river, and we seem to be in depths of the earth, and yet can look down into waters that reflect a bottomless abyss. We arrive, early in the afternoon, at the head of more rapids and falls, but, wearied with past work, we determine to rest, so go into camp, and the afternoon and evening are spent by the men in discussing the probabilities of successfully navigating the river below. . . .

July 24.—We examine the rapids below. Large rocks have fallen from the walls—great, angular blocks, which have rolled down the talus, and are strewn along the channel. We are compelled to make three portages in succession, the distance being less than three fourths of a mile, with a fall of seventy five feet. Among these rocks, in chutes, whirlpools, and great waves, with rushing breakers and foam, the water finds its way, still tumbling down. We stop for the night, only three fourths of a mile below the last camp. A very hard day's work has been done, and at evening I sit on a rock by the edge of the river, to look at the water, and listen to its roar. Hours ago, deep shadows had settled into the cañon as the sun passed behind the cliffs. Now, doubtless, the sun has gone down, for we can see no glint of light on the crags above. Darkness is coming on. The waves are rolling, with crests of foam so white they seem almost to give a light of their own. Near by, a chute of water strikes the foot of a great block of limestone, fifty feet high, and the waters pile up against it, and roll back. Where there are sunken rocks, the water heaps up in mounds, or even in cones. At a point where rocks come very near the surface, the water forms a chute above, strikes, and is shot up ten or fifteen feet, and piles back in gentle curves, as in a fountain; and on the river tumbles and rolls. . . .

July 26.—We run a short distance this morning, and go into camp, to make oars and repair boats and barometers. The walls of the cañon have been steadily increasing in altitude to this point, and now they are more than two thousand feet high. In many places, they are vertical from the water's edge; in others, there is a talus between the river and the foot of the cliffs, and they are often broken down by side cañons. It is probable that the river is nearly as low now as it is ever found. High water mark can be observed forty, fifty, sixty, or a hundred feet above its present stage. Sometimes logs and drift wood are seen wedged into the crevice overhead, where floods have carried them. . . .

July 27.—We have more rapids and falls until noon; then we come to a narrow place in the cañon, with vertical walls for several hundred feet, above which are steep

Running the rapids of Cataract Canyon in 1869.
"The river is rough," Powell noted.

steps and sloping rocks back to the summits. The river is very narrow, and we make our way with great care and much anxiety, hugging the wall on the left, and carefully examining the way before us.

Late in the afternoon, we pass to the left, around a sharp point, which is somewhat broken down near the foot, and discover a flock of mountain sheep on the rocks, more than a hundred feet above us. We quickly land in a cove out of sight, and away go all the hunters with their guns, for the sheep have not discovered us. Soon, we hear firing, and those of us who have remained in the boats climb up to see what success the hunters have had. One sheep has been killed, and two of the men are still pursuing them. In a few minutes, we hear firing again, and the next moment down come the flock, clattering over the rocks, within twenty yards of us. One of the hunters seizes his gun, and brings a second sheep down, and the next minute the remainder of the flock is lost

THE MYTH

behind the rocks. We all give chase; but it is impossible to follow their tracks over the naked rock, and we see them no more. Where they went out of this rock walled cañon is a mystery, for we can see no way of escape. Doubtless, if we could spare the time for the search, we could find some gulch up which they ran.

We lash our prizes to the deck of one of the boats, and go on for a short distance; but fresh meat is too tempting for us, and we stop early to have a feast. And a feast it is! Two fine, young sheep. We care not for bread, or beans, or dried apples to night; coffee and mutton is all we ask.

July 28.—We make two portages this morning, one of them very long. During the afternoon we run a chute, more than half a mile in length, narrow and rapid. This chute has a floor of marble; the rocks dip in the direction in which we are going, and the fall of the stream conforms to the inclination of the beds; so we float on water that is gliding down an inclined plane. At the foot of the chute, the river turns sharply to the right, and the water rolls up against a rock which, from above, seems to stand directly athwart its course. As we approach it, we pull with all our power to the right, but it seems impossible to avoid being carried headlong against the cliff, and we are carried up high on the waves—not against the rocks, for the rebounding water strikes us, and we are beaten back, and pass on with safety, except that we get a good drenching.

After this, the walls suddenly close in, so that the cañon is narrower than we have ever known it. The water fills it from wall to wall, giving us no landing place at the foot of the cliff; the river is very swift, the cañon is very tortuous, so that we can see but a few hundred yards ahead; the walls tower over us, often overhanging so as to almost shut out the light. I stand on deck, watching with intense anxiety, lest this may lead us into some danger; but we glide along, with no obstruction, no falls, no rocks, and, in a mile and a half, emerge from the narrow gorge into a more open and broken portion of the cañon. Now that it is past, it seems a very simple thing indeed to run through such a place, but the fear of what might be ahead made a deep impression on us.

At three o'clock we arrive at the foot of Cataract Cañon. Here a long cañon valley comes down from the east, and the river turns sharply to the west in a continuation of the line of the lateral valley. In the bend on the right, vast numbers of crags, and pinnacles, and tower shaped rocks are seen. We call it Mille Crag Bend.

And now we wheel into another cañon, on swift water, unobstructed by rocks. This new cañon is very narrow and very straight, with walls vertical below and terraced above. The brink of the cliff is 1,300 feet above the water, where we enter it, but the rocks dip to the west, and, as the course of the cañon is in that direction, the walls are seen to slowly decrease in altitude. Floating down this narrow channel, and looking out through the cañon crevice away in the distance, the river is seen to turn again to the left, and beyond this point, away many miles, a great mountain is seen. Still floating down, we see other mountains, now to the right, now on the left, until a great mountain range is unfolded to view. We name this Narrow Cañon, and it terminates at the bend of the river below.

As we go down to this point, we discover the mouth of a stream, which enters from the right. Into this our little boat is turned. One of the men in the boat following, seeing what we have done, shouts to Dunn, asking if it is a trout-stream. Dunn replies, much disgusted, that it is "a dirty devil," and by this name the river is to be known hereafter. The water is exceedingly muddy, and has an unpleasant odor. . . .

July 29.—We enter a cañon to-day, with low, red walls. A short distance below its head we discover the ruins of an old building, on the left wall. There is a narrow plain between the river and the wall just here, and on the brink of a rock two hundred feet high stands this old house. Its walls are of stone, laid in mortar, with much regularity. It was probably built three stories high; the lower story is yet almost intact; the second is much broken down, and scarcely anything is left of the third. Great quantities of flint chips are found on the rocks near by, and many arrow heads, some perfect, others broken; and fragments of pottery are strewn about in great profusion. On the face of the cliff, under the building, and along down the river, for two or three hundred yards, there are many etchings. Two hours are given to the examination of these interesting ruins, then we run down fifteen miles farther, and discover another group. The principal building was situated on the summit of the hill. A part of the walls are standing, to the height of eight or ten feet, and the mortar yet remains, in some places. The house was in the shape of an L, with five rooms on the ground floor, one in the angle, and two in each extension. In the space in the angle, there is a deep excavation. From what we know of the people in the province of Tusayan, who are, doubtless,

Images of
the Colorado: II

Art, Reality, and
the Colorado Canyons

The outlandish geography of the Colorado's canyon country was so far outside civilized experience that it seemed to violate the natural order of things. In the 1880's, Clarence E. Dutton called it a "great innovation," but in the eyes of most who preceded him, it was seen as nothing less than an aberration, a distortion of landscape that defied artistic expression. Baron von Egloffstein, artist and topographer for Lt. J. C. Ives's 1857-58 expedition, was the first man to give the canyons visual form, and his drawings for the expedition's *Report* are the representations of an outraged imagination that could not reconcile itself to the canyon country's spectacular realities. The first picture ever made of the Grand Canyon, Egloffstein's "Big Cañon" (seen at the left), ignores reality in splendid fashion, rendering the Canyon as it was *supposed* to be, not as it was. Above is his similarly distorted view of the plateau country near Upper Cataract Creek.

In most of his drawings, Egloffstein exaggerated verticality, ignored stratification, and superbly overemphasized the dark mysteries of the canyon country. The prime example of this is his view of Black Canyon, seen at the left, whose surrealistic qualities resemble nothing so much as what Gustave Doré might have worked up to illustrate the "profound abyss" of Dante's *Inferno*. One of Doré's famous *Inferno* drawings is reproduced above; the emotional similarity of Egloffstein is unmistakable.

Thomas Moran, who joined the Powell Survey of the Plateau Province in 1873, was the second man to illustrate the Grand Canyon proper. Although less susceptible to the fervid romanticism characterized by Egloffstein (his imagination had been tempered somewhat by working in such other spectacular landscapes as the Canyon of the Yellowstone and the Rocky Mountains), Moran was also capable of altering nature to suit his purposes — which, as he defined them, were to present a "true impression" of "pictorial nature." "I place no value on literal transcripts from nature," he said. "The Transept," reproduced on the following two pages, reflects his attitude. Compared to the nightmarish visions of Egloffstein, it is a realistic view of the Grand Canyon — but this is a realism arranged to emphasize carefully chosen details and the mists of space.

William Henry Holmes, whose drawings accompanied Moran's "The Transept" in the *Atlas* to Clarence E. Dutton's *Tertiary History of the Grand Canyon District* (1882), approached the canyon country in a manner diametrically opposed to that of Moran. He possessed a genius for detail, and his panoramic scenes were designed to give a literal rendition of geologic scope and variety. There was a certain amount of distortion in this approach, too, of course; the Holmes drawings encompass far more detail (much of it heightened for scientific, if not artistic, purposes) than the human eye could be expected to take in. Yet the impact of his drawings is overwhelming. "To open the *Tertiary History* atlas to any of its double-page panoramas," Wallace Stegner has written, "is to step to the edge of forty miles of outdoors."

The view above, titled "The Temples of the Virgen," was described by Clarence E. Dutton in his *Tertiary History*: "From right to left across the further foreground of the picture stretches the inner cañon of the Virgen, about 700 feet in depth, and here of considerable width.... Across the cañon, and rather more than a mile and a half beyond it, stands the central and commanding object of the picture, the western temple, rising 4,000 feet above the river.... It is only the central object of a mighty throng of structures wrought up in the same exalted style, and filling up the entire panorama.... There is an eloquence to their forms which stirs the imagination with a singular power, and kindles in the mind of the dullest observer a glowing response."

"Looking Up the Toroweap from Vulcan's Throne." The two pictures here form a continuous panorama, beginning from left to right in the top picture and continuing from left to right in the bottom. "The western wall of the Toroweap," Dutton wrote, "is here lower than the eastern, but still is more than a thousand feet high. . . . Above and beyond the western escarpment is the platform of the Uinkaret Plateau. Upon its summit is a throng of large basaltic cones in perfect preservation. Streams of lava

larger than any hitherto seen have poured from their vents, flooding many a square mile of mesa land, and in the wide alcoves they have reached the brink of the wall and cascaded over it. Still pouring down the long taluses they have reached the valley bottom below and spread out in wide fields.... The appearance of these old lava cascades, a mile or more wide, a thousand feet high, and black as Erebus, is striking in the extreme."

"The Grand Canyon at the Foot of the Toroweap — Looking East." Here Holmes has depicted, presumably for purposes of scale, a group of explorers approaching the canyon's edge at the bottom of the picture, an approach whose drama was described by Dutton: "In less than a minute after we have recognized the crest of the farther wall of this abyss we crane over its terrible brink and gaze upon the water of the river full 3,000 feet below. The scene before us is a type of the Grand Canon throughout

120

those portions which extend through the Kanab, Uinkaret, and Sheavwits Plateaus
. . . a broad upper chasm from five to six miles in width with walls varying in altitude
but little from 2,000 feet. Between these escarpments is a rocky plain, rough indeed,
but in the overpowering presence of such walls seeming relatively smooth and uniform. In this floor is cut the inner chasm 3,000 feet deep and from 3,500 to 4,000
feet wide from crest to crest.''

"Panorama from Point Sublime — Looking South." This view is one section of a three-part panorama that is the most spectacular of all of Holmes's drawings of the Grand Canyon. "The space under immediate view from our standpoint, 50 miles long and 10 to 12 wide," Dutton wrote, "is thronged with a great multitude of objects so vast in size, so bold yet majestic in form, so infinite in their details, that as the

truth gradually reveals itself to the perceptions it arouses the strongest emotions. Unquestionably the great, the overruling feature is the wall on the opposite side of the gulf. . . . If the wall were simple in its character, if it were only blank and sheer, some rest might be found in contemplating it; but it is full of diversity and eloquent with grand suggestions."

The Grand Canyon schemas that Holmes drew for the *Tertiary History* atlas are among the finest productions in the annals of scientific art. They are remarkable *as* art simply because Holmes abandoned popular notions of how landscapes should be rendered; he saw the canyon country as an incredible collection of intricacies, each one of which had to be placed on paper as precisely as humanly possible. The contrast between what he achieved by ignoring traditional concepts of art and what he produced when he attempted to be "artistic" is documented by the painting reproduced above, a view of Smithsonian Butte in the Valley of the Virgen — a pedestrian effort that served as the frontispiece for Dutton's *Tertiary History*.

of the same race as the former inhabitants of these ruins, we conclude that this was a "kiva," or underground chamber, in which their religious ceremonies were performed.

Through most of its course the canyoned Green and Colorado, though impressive beyond description, awesome and colorful and bizarre, is scenically disturbing, a trouble to the mind. It works on the nerves, there is no repose in it, nothing that is soft. The water roar emphasizes what the walls begin: a restlessness and excitement and irritability. But Glen Canyon*, into which they now floated and which they first called Monument Canyon from the domes and "baldheads" crowning its low walls, [was] completely different.... The first white men to see it except possibly James Ohio Pattie, and just possibly James White, they felt ...the stillness, the remoteness, the lovely withdrawn quiet of that 149-mile river groove. This country seemed kindlier to human intrusions....

Yet idyllic as Glen Canyon was, they could not relax and enjoy it. Their bacon was down to fifteen rancid pounds; they were short of everything but flour, coffee, and dried apples. After two cyclopean feasts, the mutton had spoiled in the heat, and though they saw other bighorn they were unable to bring any down....

Past the mouth of the Escalante they went without even noticing the river; it is not very noticeable, and perhaps they were all watching the east wall for the San Juan's mouth. Then in the afternoon of the last day of July they floated down toward a massive awning-striped wall that turned the river in a sharp right-hand bend. Just before the bend the San Juan came in through a trench-like gorge from the left, a swift, muddy stream as large as White River.

Now the whole enormous drainage basin of the river was floating them, melted snow from the high Wind River peaks, and from the Wasatch, and from the Uintas with their hundred cold streams, Black's Fork, Henry's Fork, Ham's Fork, Kingfisher Creek, Brush Creek, the Uinta; the western slopes of the Colorado Rockies whose creeks poured into the Yampa and the White; the waters all the way from Grand Lake under the shadow of Long's Peak, and the tributary springs and creeks and runoff gulches that fed the Grand all the way to modern Grand Junction and Moab; and finally the San Juan, muddy from recent

*Now drowned under Lake Powell.

rains, its headwaters tangled with those of the Rio Grande in the Five Rivers country of southwest Colorado, its gathering waters coming down from the San Juan Mountains through New Mexico and what would sometime be Arizona and across the southeastern corner of Utah through the country of the Navajo. It was a big river by now, a tremendous surge of muddy water.

August 4.—To-day the walls grow higher, and the cañon much narrower. Monuments are still seen on either side; beautiful glens, and alcoves, and gorges, and side cañons are yet found. After dinner, we find the river making a sudden turn to the northwest, and the whole character of the cañon changed. The walls are many hundreds of feet higher, and the rocks are chiefly variegated shales of beautiful colors—creamy orange above, then bright vermilion, and below, purple and chocolate beds, with green and yellow sands. We run four miles through this, in a direction a little to the west of north; wheel again to the west, and pass into a portion of the cañon where the characteristics are more like those above the bend. At night we stop at the mouth of a creek coming in from the right, and suppose it to be the Paria, which was described to me last year by a Mormon missionary.

Here the cañon terminates abruptly in a line of cliffs, which stretches from either side across the river.

August 5.—With some feeling of anxiety, we enter a new cañon this morning. We have learned to closely observe the texture of the rock. In softer strata, we have a quiet river; in harder, we find rapids and falls. Below us are the limestones and hard sandstones, which we found in Cataract Cañon. This bodes toil and danger. Besides the texture of the rocks, there is another condition which affects the character of the channel, as we have found by experience. Where the strata are horizontal, the river is often quiet; but, even though it may be very swift in places, no great obstacles are found. Where the rocks incline in the direction traveled, the river usually sweeps with great velocity, but still we have few rapids and falls. But where the rocks dip up stream, and the river cuts obliquely across the upturned formations, harder strata above, and softer below, we have rapids and falls. Into hard rocks, and into rocks dipping up stream, we pass this morning, and start on a long, rocky, mad rapid. On the left there is a vertical rock, and down by this cliff and around to the left we glide, just tossed enough by the waves to appreciate the rate at which we are traveling.

The cañon is narrow, with vertical walls, which gradually grow higher. More rapids and falls are found. We come to one with a drop of sixteen feet, around which we make a portage, and then stop for dinner.

Then a run of two miles, and another portage, long and difficult; then we camp for the night, on a bank of sand.

August 6. — Cañon walls, still higher and higher, as we go down through strata. There is a steep talus at the foot of the cliff, and, in some places, the upper parts of the walls are terraced.

About ten o'clock we come to a place where the river occupies the entire channel, and the walls are vertical from the water's edge. We see a fall below, and row up against the cliff. There is a little shelf, or rather a horizontal crevice, a few feet over our heads. One man stands on the deck of the boat, another climbs on his shoulders, and then into the crevice. Then we pass him a line, and two or three others, with myself, follow; then we pass along the crevice until it becomes a shelf, as the upper part, or roof, is broken off. On this we walk for a short distance, slowly climbing all the way, until we reach a point where the shelf is broken off, and we can pass no farther. Then we go back to the boat, cross the stream, and get some logs that have lodged in the rocks, bring them to our side, pass them along the crevice and shelf, and bridge over the broken place. Then we go on to a point over the falls, but do not obtain a satisfactory view. Then we climb out to the top of the wall, and walk along to find a point below the fall, from which it can be seen. From this point it seems possible to let down our boats, with lines, to the head of the rapids, and then make a portage; so we return, row down by the side of the cliff, as far as we dare, and fasten one of the boats to a rock. Then we let down another boat to the end of its line beyond the first, and the third boat to the end of its line below the second, which brings it to the head of the fall, and under an overhanging rock. Then the upper boat, in obedience to a signal, lets go; we pull in the line, and catch the nearest boat as it comes, and then the last. Then we make a portage, and go on.

We go into camp early this afternoon, at a place where it seems possible to climb out, and the evening is spent in "making observations for time."

August 7. — The almanac tells us that we are to have an eclipse of the sun to day, so Captain Powell and myself start early, taking our instruments with us, for the purpose of making observations on the eclipse, to determine our longitude. Arriving at the summit, after four hours' hard climbing, to attain 2,300 feet in height, we hurriedly build a platform of rocks, on which to place our instruments, and quietly wait for the eclipse; but clouds come on, and rain falls, and sun and moon are obscured.

Much disappointed, we start on our return to camp, but it is late, and the clouds make the night very dark. Still we feel our way down among the rocks with great care, for two or three hours, though making slow progress indeed. At last we lose our way, and dare proceed no farther. The rain comes down in torrents, and we can find no shelter. We can neither climb up nor go down, and in the darkness dare not move about, but sit and "weather out" the night.

August 8. — Daylight comes, after a long, oh! how long a night, and we soon reach camp.

After breakfast we start again, and make two portages during the forenoon.

The limestone of this cañon is often polished, and makes a beautiful marble. Sometimes the rocks are of many colors — white, gray, pink, and purple, with saffron tints. It is with very great labor that we make progress, meeting with many obstructions, running rapids, letting down our boats with lines, from rock to rock, and sometimes carrying boats and cargoes around bad places. We camp at night, just after a hard portage, under an overhanging wall, glad to find shelter from the rain. We have to search for some time to find a few sticks of driftwood, just sufficient to boil a cup of coffee.

The water sweeps rapidly in this elbow of river, and has cut its way under the rock, excavating a vast half circular chamber, which, if utilized for a theater, would give sitting to fifty thousand people. Objections might be raised against it, from the fact that, at high water, the floor is covered with a raging flood.

August 9. — And now, the scenery is on a grand scale. The walls of the cañon, 2,500 feet high, are of marble, of many beautiful colors, and often polished below by the waves, or far up the sides, where showers have washed the sands over the cliffs.

At one place I have a walk, for more than a mile, on a marble pavement, all polished and fretted with strange devices, and embossed in a thousand fantastic patterns.

Through a cleft in the wall the sun shines on this pavement, which gleams in iridescent beauty. . . .

It rains again this afternoon. Scarcely do the first drops fall, when little rills run down the walls. As the storm comes on, the little rills increase in size, until great streams are formed. Although the walls of the cañon are chiefly limestone, the adjacent country is of red sandstone; and now the waters, loaded with these sands, come down in rivers of bright red mud, leaping over the walls in innumerable cascades. It is plain now how these walls are polished in many places.

At last, the storm ceases, and we go on. We have cut through the sandstones and limestones met in the upper part of the cañon, and through one great bed of marble a thousand feet in thickness. In this, great numbers of caves are hollowed out, and carvings are seen, which suggest architectural forms, though on a scale so grand that architectural terms belittle them. As this great bed forms a distinctive feature of the cañon, we call it Marble Cañon.

At the lower end of Marble Canyon, 1872. "And now," Powell wrote of this canyon in 1869, "the scenery is on a grand scale" (J. K. Hillers photograph, 1872).

All across the great barren Marble Canyon Platform which stretches north of the river from the monoclinal eastern flank of the Kaibab to the angle of the Vermillion Cliffs, abrupt gorges come in, cut by runoff waters from the higher country. Badger Creek and Soap Creek and other lesser watercourses come in by canyons as deep as the river's own, and every junction is piled with the boulders of flash floods. Every junction is a rapid; the prevailing strike of the beds is upstream, a condition which is a maker of rapids as surely as hard rock and lateral gorges are. And the Colorado now is a great stream, but squeezed into a narrow frothing channel that reflects every summer shower by sharp rises. Between high and low water in parts of the canyon there is a vertical difference of a hundred feet. At low water the rocks are deadly, at high water the waves toss a boat like a chip. . . .

As they went on the walls grew higher, and still higher, and great buttresses thrust out into the channel to block the river into coves and twist it in whirlpools. But here the channel was wider, the river less swift, so that they could take a more leisurely look at the marble chambers and alcoves and caves. Through the gates of flaring canyons that came in from the right, draining the lofty table of the Kaibab westward, they saw the piney back

of that noble plateau. Finally they reached another landmark, one that Lieutenant Ives had tried for but failed to reach in 1858—the mouth of the River of Flax, the Colorado Chiquito of the Spaniards. . . .

Below the Colorado Chiquito lay the chasm, Ives' "Big Canyon," that had been a report on men's tongues for a good deal more than two hundred years without ever becoming known. Much more than the frowning gate of Lodore it seemed to [Powell] ominous, and for cause.

August 13.—We are now ready to start on our way down the Great Unknown. Our boats, tied to a common stake, are chafing each other, as they are tossed by the fretful river. They ride high and buoyant, for their loads are lighter than we could desire. We have but a month's rations remaining. The flour has been resifted through the mosquito net sieve; the spoiled bacon has been dried, and the worst of it boiled; the few pounds of dried apples have been spread in the sun, and reshrunken to their normal bulk; the sugar has all melted, and gone on its way down the river; but we have a large sack of coffee. The lightening of the boats has this advantage: they will ride the waves better, and we shall have but little to carry when we make a portage.

We are three quarters of a mile in the depths of the earth, and the great river shrinks into insignificance, as it dashes its angry waves against the walls and cliffs, that rise to the world above; they are but puny ripples, and we but pigmies, running up and down the sands, or lost among the boulders.

We have an unknown distance yet to run; an unknown river yet to explore. What falls there are, we know not; What rocks beset the channel, we know not; what walls rise over the river, we know not. Ah, well! we may conjecture many things. The men talk as cheerfully as ever; jests are bandied about freely this morning; but to me the cheer is somber and the jests are ghastly.

With some eagerness, and some anxiety, and some misgiving, we enter the cañon below, and are carried along by the swift water through walls which rise from its very edge. They have the same structure as we noticed yesterday—tiers of irregular shelves below, and, above these, steep slopes to the foot of marble cliffs. We run six miles in a little more than half an hour, and emerge into a more open portion of the cañon, where high hills and ledges of rock intervene between the river and the distant walls. Just at the head of this open place the river runs across a dike; that is, a fissure in the rocks, open to depths below, has been filled with eruptive matter, and this, on cooling, was harder than the rocks through which the crevice was made, and, when these were washed away, the harder volcanic matter remained as a wall, and the river has cut a gate-way through it several hundred feet high, and as many wide. As it crosses the wall, there is a fall below, and a bad rapid, filled with boulders of trap; so we stop to make a portage. Then on we go, gliding by hills and ledges, with distant walls in view; sweeping past sharp angles of rock; stopping at a few points to examine rapids, which we find can be run, until

we have made another five miles, when we land for dinner. . . .

August 14.—At daybreak we walk down the bank of the river, on a little sandy beach, to take a view of a new feature in the cañon. Heretofore, hard rocks have given us bad river; soft rocks, smooth water; and a series of rocks harder than any we have experienced sets in. The river enters the granite!

We can see but a little way into the granite gorge, but it looks threatening.

After breakfast we enter on the waves. At the very introduction, it inspires awe. The cañon is narrower than we have ever before seen it; the water is swifter; there are but few broken rocks in the channel; but the walls are set, on either side, with pinnacles and crags; and sharp, angular buttresses, bristling with wind and wave polished spires, extend far out into the river.

Ledges of rocks jut into the stream, their tops sometimes just below the surface, sometimes rising few or many feet above; and island ledges, and island pinnacles, and island towers break the swift course of the stream into chutes, and eddies, and whirlpools. We soon reach a place where a creek comes in from the left, and just below, the channel is choked with boulders, which have washed down this lateral cañon and formed a dam, over which there is a fall of thirty or forty feet; but on the boulders we can get foothold, and we make a portage. . . .

About eleven o'clock we hear a great roar ahead, and approach it very cautiously. The sound grows louder and louder as we run, and at last we find ourselves above a long, broken fall, with ledges and pinnacles of rock obstructing the river. There is a descent of, perhaps, seventy five or eighty feet in a third of a mile, and the rushing waters break into great waves on the rocks, and lash themselves into a mad, white foam. We can land just above, but there is no foot-hold on either side by which we can make a portage. It is nearly a thousand feet to the top of the granite, so it will be impossible to carry our boats around, though we can climb to the summit up a side gulch, and, passing along a mile or two, can descend to the river. This we find on examination; but such a portage would be impracticable for us, and we must run the rapid, or abandon the river. There is no hesitation. We step into our boats, push off and away we go, first on smooth but swift water, then we strike a glassy wave, and ride to its top, down again into the trough, up again on a higher wave, and down and up on waves higher and still higher, until we strike one just as it curls back, and a breaker rolls over our little boat. Still, on we speed, shooting past projecting rocks, till the little boat is caught in a whirlpool, and spun around several times. At last we pull out again into the stream, and now the other boats have passed us. The open compartment of the "Emma Dean" is filled with water, and every breaker rolls over us. Hurled back from a rock, now on this side, now on that, we are carried into an eddy, in which we struggle for a few minutes, and are then out again, the breakers still rolling over us. Our boat is unmanageable, but she cannot sink, and we drift down another hundred yards, through breakers; how, we scarcely know. We find the other boats have turned into an eddy at the foot of the fall, and are waiting to catch us as we come, for the men have seen that our boat is swamped. They push out as we come near, and pull us in against the wall. We bail our boat, and on we go again.

The walls, now, are more than a mile in height—a vertical distance difficult to appreciate. Stand on the south steps of the Treasury building, in Washington, and look down Pennsylvania Avenue to the Capitol Park, and measure this distance overhead, and imagine cliffs to extend to that altitude, and you will understand what I mean; or, stand at Canal street, in New York, and look up Broadway to Grace Church, and you have about the distance; or, stand at Lake street bridge, in Chicago, and look down to the Central Depot, and you have it again.

A thousand feet of this is up through granite crags, then steep slopes and perpendicular cliffs rise, one above another, to the summit. The gorge is black and narrow below, red and gray and flaring above, with crags and angular projections on the walls, which, cut in many places by side cañons, seem to be a vast wilderness of rocks. Down in these grand, gloomy depths we glide, ever listening, for the mad waters keep up their roar; ever watching, ever peering ahead, for the narrow cañon is winding, and the river is closed in so that we can see but a few hundred yards, and what there may be below we know not; but we listen for falls, and watch for rocks, or stop now and then, in the bay of a recess, to admire the gigantic scenery. And ever, as we go, there is some new pinnacle or tower, some crag or peak, some distant view of the upper plateau, some strange shaped rock, or some deep, narrow side cañon. Then we come to another broken fall, which appears more difficult than the one we ran this morning.

A small creek comes in on the right, and the first fall of the water is over boulders, which have been carried down by this lateral stream. We land at its mouth, and stop for an hour or two to examine the fall. It seems possible to let down with lines, at least a part of the way, from point to point, along the right hand wall. So we make a portage over the first rocks, and find footing on some boulders below. Then we let down one of the boats to the end of her line, when she reaches a corner of the projecting rock, to which one of the men clings, and steadies her, while I examine an eddy below. I think we can pass the other boats down by us, and catch them in the eddy. This is soon done and the men in the boats in the eddy pull us to their side. On the shore of this little eddy there is about two feet of gravel beach above the water. Standing on this beach, some of the men take the line of the little boat and let it drift down against another projecting angle. Here is a little shelf, on which a man from my boat climbs, and a shorter line is passed to him, and he fastens the boat to the side of the cliff. Then the second one is let down, bringing the line of the third. When the second boat is tied up, the two men standing on the beach above spring into the last boat, which is pulled up alongside of ours. Then we let down the boats, for twenty five or thirty yards, by walking along the shelf, landing them again in the mouth of a side cañon. Just below this there is another pile of boulders, over which we make another portage. From the foot of these rocks we can climb to another shelf, forty or fifty feet above the water.

On this bench we camp for the night. We find a few sticks, which have lodged in the rocks. It is raining hard, and we have no shelter, but kindle a fire and have our supper. We sit on the rocks all night, wrapped in our ponchos, getting what sleep we can.

August 15.—This morning we find we can let down for three or four hundred yards, and it is managed in this way: We pass along the wall, by climbing from projecting point to point, sometimes near the water's edge, at other places fifty or sixty feet above, and hold the boat with a line, while two men remain aboard, and prevent her from being dashed against the rocks, and keep the line from getting caught on the wall. In two hours we have brought them all down, as far as it is possible, in this way. A few yards below, the river strikes with great violence against a projecting rock, and our boats are pulled up in a little bay above. We must now manage to pull out of this, and clear the point below. The little boat is held by the bow obliquely up the stream. We jump in, and pull out only a few strokes, and sweep clear of the dangerous rock. The other boats follow in the same manner, and the rapid is passed. . . .

And now we go on through this solemn, mysterious way. The river is very deep, the cañon very narrow, and still obstructed, so that there is no steady flow of the stream; but the waters wheel, and roll, and boil, and we are scarcely able to determine where we can go. Now, the boat is carried to the right, perhaps close to the wall; again, she is shot into the stream, and perhaps is dragged over to the other side, where, caught in a whirlpool, she spins about. We can neither land nor run as we please. The boats are entirely unmanageable; no order in their running can be preserved; now one, now another, is ahead, each crew laboring for its own preservation. In such a place we come to another rapid. Two of the boats run it perforce. One succeeds in landing, but there is no foot-hold by which to make a portage, and she is pushed out again into the stream. The next minute a great reflex wave fills the open compartment; she is water-logged, and drifts unmanageable. Breaker after breaker rolls over her, and one capsizes her. The men are thrown out; but they cling to the boat, and she drifts down some distance, alongside of us, and we are able to catch her. She is soon bailed out, and the men are aboard once more; but the oars are lost, so a pair from the "Emma Dean" is spared. Then for two miles we find smooth water. . . .

August 16.—We must dry our rations again to day, and make oars.

The Colorado is never a clear stream,* but for the past three or four days it has been raining much of the time, and the floods, which are poured over the walls, have brought down great quantities of mud, making it exceedingly turbid now. The little affluent, which we have discovered here, is a clear, beautiful creek, or river, as it would be termed in this western country, where streams are not abundant. We have named one stream, away above, in honor of the great chief of the "Bad Angels," and, as this is in beautiful contrast to that, we conclude to name it "Bright Angel."

Early in the morning, the whole party starts up to explore the Bright Angel River, with the special purpose of seeking timber, from which to make oars. A couple of miles above, we find a large pine log, which has been floated down from the plateau, probably from an altitude of more than six thousand feet, but not many miles back. On its way, it must have passed over many cataracts and falls, for it bears scars in evidence of the rough usage which it has received. The men roll it on skids, and the work of sawing oars is commenced. . . .

August 17.—Our rations are still spoiling; the bacon is so badly injured that we are compelled to throw it away. By an accident, this morning, the saleratus is lost overboard. We have now only musty flour sufficient for ten days, a few dried apples, but plenty of coffee. We must make all haste possible. If we meet with difficulties, as we have done in the cañon above, we may be compelled to give up the expedition, and try to reach the Mormon settlements to the north. Our hopes are that the worst places are passed, but our barometers are all so much injured as to be useless, so we have lost our reckoning in altitude, and know not how much descent the river has yet to make.

The stream is still wild and rapid, and rolls through a narrow channel. We make but slow progress, often landing against a wall, and climbing around some point, where we can see the river below. Although very anxious to advance, we are determined to run with great caution, lest, by another accident, we lose all our supplies. How precious that little flour has become! We divide it among the boats, and carefully store it away, so that it can be lost only by the loss of the boat itself.

We make ten miles and a half, and camp among the rocks, on the right. We have had rain, from time to time, all day, and have been thoroughly drenched and chilled; but between showers the sun shines with great power, and the mercury in our thermometers stands at 115°, so that we have rapid changes from great extremes, which are very disagreeable. It is especially cold in the rain to-night. The little canvas we have is rotten and useless; the rubber ponchos, with which we started from Green River City, have all been lost; more than half the party is without hats,* and not one of us has an entire suit of clothes, and we have not a blanket apiece. So we gather drift wood,

*Now, since it is all released from several hundred feet down in Glen Canyon Dam, it runs crystal as far as the Little Colorado and reasonably clear all the way to Lake Mead.

*A simple statement, but to anyone who has boated down this river, an eloquent, even an appalling one.

and build a fire; but after supper the rain, coming down in torrents, extinguishes it, and we sit up all night, on the rocks, shivering, and are more exhausted by the night's discomfort than by the day's toil. . . .

August 20. — The characteristics of the cañon change this morning. The river is broader, the walls more sloping, and composed of black slates, that stand on edge. These nearly vertical slates are washed out in places — that is, the softer beds are washed out between the harder, which are left standing. In this way, curious little alcoves are formed, in which are quiet bays of water, but on a much smaller scale than the great bays and buttresses of Marble Cañon.

The river is still rapid, and we stop to let down with lines several times, but make greater progress as we run ten miles. . . .

August 21. — We start early this morning, cheered by the prospect of a fine day, and encouraged, also, by the good run made yesterday. A quarter of a mile below camp the river turns abruptly to the left, and between camp and that point is very swift, running down in a long, broken chute, and piling up against the foot of the cliff, where it turns to the left. We try to pull across, so as to go down on the other side, but the waters are swift, and it seems impossible for us to escape the rock below; but, in pulling across, the bow of the boat is turned to the farther shore, so that we are swept broadside down, and are prevented, by the rebounding waters, from striking against the wall. There we toss about for a few seconds in these billows, and are carried past the danger. Below, the river turns again to the right, the cañon is very narrow, and we see in advance but a short distance. The water, too, is very swift, and there is no landing place. From around this curve there comes a mad roar, and down we are carried, with a dizzying velocity, to the head of another rapid. On either side, high over our heads, there are overhanging granite walls, and the sharp bends cut off our view, so that a few minutes will carry us into unknown waters. Away we go, on one long, winding chute. I stand on deck, supporting myself with a strap, fastened on either side to the gunwale, and the boat glides rapidly, where the water is smooth, or, striking a wave, she leaps and bounds like a thing of life, and we have a wild, exhilarating ride for ten miles, which we make in less than an hour. The excitement is so great that we forget the danger, until we hear the roar of a great fall below; then we back on our oars, and are

Climbing Bright Angel Canyon, August 16, 1869 (Exploration of the Colorado River of the West).

carried slowly toward its head, and succeed in landing just above, and find that we have to make another portage. At this we are engaged until some time after dinner. . . .

August 22.—We come to rapids again, this morning, and are occupied several hours in passing them, letting the boats down, from rock to rock, with lines, for nearly half a mile, and then have to make a long portage. While the men are engaged in this, I climb the wall on the northeast, to a height of about two thousand five hundred feet, where I can obtain a good view of a long stretch of cañon below. Its course is to the southwest. The walls seem to rise very abruptly, for two thousand five hundred or three thousand feet, and then there is a gently sloping terrace, on each side, for two or three miles, and again we find cliffs, one thousand five hundred or two thousand feet high. From the brink of these the plateau stretches back to the north and south, for a long distance. Away down the cañon, on the right wall, I can see a group of mountains, some of which appear to stand on the brink of the cañon. The effect of the terrace is to give the appearance of a narrow winding valley, with high walls on either side, and a deep, dark, meandering gorge down its middle. It is impossible, from this point of view, to determine whether we have granite at the bottom, or not; but, from geological considerations, I conclude that we shall have marble walls below. . . .

August 23.—Our way to day is again through marble walls. Now and then we pass, for a short distance, through patches of granite, like hills thrust up into the limestone. At one of these places we have to make another portage, and, taking advantage of the delay, I go up a little stream, to the north, wading it all the way, sometimes having to plunge in to my neck; in other places being compelled to swim across little basins that have been excavated at the foot of the falls. Along its course are many cascades and springs gushing out from the rocks on either side. Sometimes a cottonwood tree grows over the water. I come to one beautiful fall, of more than a hundred and fifty feet, and climb around it to the right, on the broken rocks. Still going up, I find the cañon narrowing very much, being but fifteen or twenty feet wide; yet the walls rise on either side many hundreds of feet, perhaps thousands; I can hardly tell. . . .

Just after dinner we pass a stream on the right, which leaps into the Colorado by a direct fall of more than a hundred feet, forming a beautiful cascade. There is a bed

of very hard rock above, thirty or forty feet in thickness, and much softer beds below. The hard beds above project many yards beyond the softer, which are washed out, forming a deep cave behind the fall, and the stream pours through a narrow crevice above into a deep pool below. Around on the rocks, in the cave like chamber, are set beautiful ferns, with delicate fronds and enameled stalks. The little frondlets have their points turned down, to form spore cases. It has very much the appearance of the Maiden's Hair fern, but is much larger. This delicate foliage covers the rocks all about the fountain, and gives the chamber great beauty. But we have little time to spend in admiration, so on we go. . . .

August 27.—This morning the river takes a more southerly direction. The dip of the rocks is to the north, and we are rapidly running into lower formations. Unless our course changes, we shall very soon run again into the granite. This gives us some anxiety. Now and then the river turns to the west, and excites hopes that are soon destroyed by another turn to the south. About nine o'clock we come to the dreaded rock. It is with no little misgiving that we see the river enter these black, hard walls. At its very entrance we have to make a portage; then we have to let down with lines past some ugly rocks. Then we run a mile or two farther, and then the rapids below can be seen.

About eleven o'clock we come to a place in the river where it seems much worse than any we have yet met in all its course. A little creek comes down from the left. We land first on the right, and clamber up over the granite pinnacles for a mile or two, but can see no way by which we can let down, and to run it would be sure destruction. After dinner we cross to examine it on the left. . . .

Still another hour is spent in examining the river from this side, but no good view of it is obtained, so now we return to the side that was first examined, and the afternoon is spent in clambering among the crags and pinnacles, and carefully scanning the river again. We find that the lateral streams have washed boulders into the river, so as to form a dam, over which the water makes a broken fall of eighteen or twenty feet; then there is a rapid, beset with rocks, for two or three hundred yards, while, on the other side, points of the wall project into the river. Then there is a second fall below; how great, we cannot tell. Then there is a rapid, filled with huge rocks, for one or two hundred yards. At the bottom of

Laying over for repairs at Granite Falls, Grand Canyon, in 1872. On the first trip Powell reported that his boat leaped and bounded "like a thing alive" through the rapids (J. K. Hillers photograph).

it, from the right wall, a great rock projects quite half way across the river. It has a sloping surface extending up stream, and the water, coming down with all the momentum gained in the falls and rapids above, rolls up this inclined plane many feet, and tumbles over to the left. I decide that it is possible to let down over the first fall, then run near the right cliff to a point just above the second, where we can pull out into a little chute, and, having run over that in safety, we must pull with all our power across the stream, to avoid the great rock below. On my return to the boat, I announce to the men that we are to run it in the morning. Then we cross the river, and go into camp for the night on some rocks, in the mouth of the little side cañon.

After supper Captain Howland asks to have a talk with me. We walk up the little creek a short distance, and I soon find that his object is to remonstrate against my determination to proceed. He thinks that we had better abandon the river here. Talking with him, I learn that his brother, William Dunn, and himself have determined to go no farther in the boats. So we return to camp. Nothing is said to the other men.

For the last two days, our course has not been plotted. I sit down and do this now, for the purpose of finding where we are by dead reckoning. It is a clear night, and I take out the sextant to make observation for latitude, and find that the astronomic determination agrees very nearly with that of the plot—quite as closely as might be expected, from a meridian observation on a planet. In a direct line, we must be about forty five miles from the mouth of the Rio Virgen. If we can reach that point, we know that there are settlements up that river about twenty miles. This forty five miles, in a direct line, will probably be eighty or ninety in the meandering line of the river. But then we know that there is comparatively open country for many miles above the mouth of the Virgen, which is our point of destination.

As soon as I determine all this, I spread my plot on the sand, and wake Howland, who is sleeping down by the river, and show him where I suppose we are, and where several Mormon settlements are situated.

We have another short talk about the morrow, and he lies down again; but for me there is no sleep. All night long, I pace up and down a little path, on a few yards of sand beach, along by the river. Is it wise to go on? I go to the boats again, to look at our rations. I feel satisfied that we can get over the danger imme-

diately before us; what there may be below I know not. . . .

I wake my brother, and tell him of Howland's determination, and he promises to stay with me; then I call up Hawkins, the cook, and he makes a like promise; then Sumner, and Bradley, and Hall, and they all agree to go on.

August 28.—At last daylight comes, and we have breakfast, without a word being said about the future. The meal is as solemn as a funeral. After breakfast, I ask the three men if they still think it best to leave us. The elder Howland thinks it is, and Dunn agrees with him. The younger Howland tries to persuade them to go on with the party, failing in which, he decides to go with his brother.

Then we cross the river. The small boat is very much disabled, and unseaworthy. With the loss of hands, consequent on the departure of the three men, we shall not be able to run all of the boats, so I decide to leave my "Emma Dean."

Two rifles and a shot gun are given to the men who are going out. I ask them to help themselves to the rations, and take what they think to be a fair share. This they refuse to do, saying they have no fear but that they can get something to eat; but Billy, the cook, has a pan of biscuits prepared for dinner, and these he leaves on a rock.

Before starting, we take our barometers, fossils, the minerals, and some ammunition from the boat, and leave them on the rocks. We are going over this place as light as possible. The three men help us lift our boats over a rock twenty five or thirty feet high, and let them down again over the first fall, and now we are all ready to start. The last thing before leaving, I write a letter to my wife, and give it to Howland. Sumner gives him his watch, directing that it be sent to his sister, should he not be heard from again. The records of the expedition have been kept in duplicate. One set of these is given to Howland, and now we are ready. For the last time, they entreat us not to go on, and tell us that it is madness to set out in this place; that we can never get safely through it; and, further, that the river turns again to the south into the granite, and a few miles of such rapids and falls will exhaust our entire stock of rations, and then it will be too late to climb out. Some tears are shed; it is rather a solemn parting; each party thinks the other is taking the dangerous course.

My old boat left, I go on board of the "Maid of the

Cañon." The three men climb a crag, that overhangs the river, to watch us off. The "Maid of the Cañon" pushes out. We glide rapidly along the foot of the wall, just grazing one great rock, then pull out a little into the chute of the second fall, and plunge over it. The open compartment is filled when we strike the first wave below, but we cut through it, and then the men pull with all their power toward the left wall, and swing clear of the dangerous rock below all right. We are scarcely a minute in running it, and find that, although it looked bad from above, we have passed many places that were worse.

The other boat follows without more difficulty. We land at the first practicable point below and fire our guns, as a signal to the men above that we have come over in safety. Here we remain a couple of hours, hoping that they will take the smaller boat and follow us. We are behind a curve in the cañon, and cannot see up to where we left them, and so we wait until their coming seems hopeless, and push on.

And now we have a succession of rapids and falls until noon, all of which we run in safety. Just after dinner we come to another bad place. A little stream comes in from the left, and below there is a fall, and still below another fall. Above, the river tumbles down, over and among the rocks, in whirlpools and great waves, and the waters are lashed into mad, white foam. We run along the left, above this, and soon see that we cannot get down on this side, but it seems possible to let down on the other. We pull up stream again, for two or three hundred yards, and cross. Now there is a bed of basalt on this northern side of the cañon, with a bold escarpment, that seems to be a hundred feet high. We can climb it, and walk along its summit to a point where we are just at the head of the fall. Here the basalt is broken down again, so it seems to us, and I direct the men to take a line to the top of the cliff, and let the boats down along the wall. One man remains in the boat, to keep her clear of the rocks, and prevent her line from being caught on the projecting angles. I climb the cliff, and pass along to a point just over the fall, and descend by broken rocks, and find that the break of the fall is above the break of the wall, so that we cannot land; and that still below the river is very bad, and that there is no possibility of a portage. Without waiting further to examine and determine what shall be done, I hasten back to the top of the cliff, to stop the boats from coming

down. When I arrive, I find the men have let one of them down to the head of the fall. She is in swift water, and they are not able to pull her back; nor are they able to go on with the line, as it is not long enough to reach the higher part of the cliff, which is just before them; so they take a bight around a crag. I send two men back for the other line. The boat is in very swift water, and Bradley is standing in the open compartment, holding out his oar to prevent her from striking against the foot of the cliff. Now she shoots out into the stream, and up as far as the line will permit, and then, wheeling, drives headlong against the rock, then out and back again, now straining on the line, now striking against the rock. As soon as the second line is brought, we pass it down to him; but his attention is all taken up with his own situation, and he does not see that we are passing the line to him. I stand on a projecting rock, waving my hat to gain his attention, for my voice is drowned by the roaring of the falls. Just at this moment, I see him take his knife from its sheath, and step forward to cut the line. He has evidently decided that it is better to go over with the boat as it is, than to wait for her to be broken to pieces. As he leans over, the boat sheers again into the stream, the stem-post breaks away, and she is loose. With perfect composure Bradley seizes the great scull oar, places it in the stern rowlock, and pulls with all his power (and he is an athlete) to turn the bow of the boat down stream, for he wishes to go bow down, rather than to drift broadside on. One, two strokes he makes, and a third just as she goes over, and the boat is fairly turned, and she goes down almost beyond our sight, though we are more than a hundred feet above the river. Then she comes up again, on a great wave, and down and up, then around behind some great rocks, and is lost in the mad, white foam below. We stand frozen with fear, for we see no boat. Bradley is gone, so it seems. But now, away below, we see something coming out of the waves. It is evidently a boat. A moment more, and we see Bradley standing on deck, swinging his hat to show that he is all right. But he is in a whirlpool. We have the stem-post of his boat attached to the line. How badly she may be disabled we know not. I direct Sumner and Powell to pass along the cliff, and see if they can reach him from below. Rhodes, Hall, and myself run to the other boat, jump aboard, push out, and away we go over the falls. A wave rolls over us, and our boat is unmanageable. Another great wave strikes us, the boat rolls over, and tumbles and tosses, I know not how. All I know is that Bradley is picking us up. We soon have all right again, and row to the cliff, and wait until Sumner and Powell can come. After a difficult climb they reach us. We run two or three miles farther, and turn again to the northwest, continuing until night, when we have run out of the granite once more.

August 29.—We start very early this morning. The river still continues swift, but we have no serious difficulty, and at twelve o'clock emerge from the Grand Cañon of the Colorado.

We are in a valley now, and low mountains are seen in the distance, coming to the river below. We recognize this as the Grand Wash.

A few years ago, a party of Mormons set out from St. George, Utah, taking with them a boat, and came down to the mouth of the Grand Wash, where they divided, a portion of the party crossing the river to explore the San Francisco Mountains. Three men—Hamblin, Miller, and Crosby—taking the boat, went on down the river to Callville, landing a few miles below the mouth of the Rio Virgen. We have their manuscript journal with us, and so the stream is comparatively well known.

To night we camp on the left bank, in a *mesquite* thicket.

The relief from danger, and the joy of success, are great. When he who has been chained by wounds to a hospital cot, until his canvas tent seems like a dungeon cell, until the groans of those who lie about, tortured with probe and knife, are piled up, a weight of horror on his ears that he cannot throw off, cannot forget, and until the stench of festering wounds and anæsthetic drugs has filled the air with its loathsome burthen, at last goes out into the open field, what a world he sees! How beautiful the sky; how bright the sunshine; what "floods of delirious music" pour from the throats of birds; how sweet the fragrance of earth, and tree, and blossom! The first hour of convalescent freedom seems rich recompense for all—pain, gloom, terror.

Something like this are the feelings we experience to night. Ever before us has been an unknown danger, heavier than immediate peril. Every waking hour passed in the Grand Cañon has been one of toil. We have watched with deep solicitude the steady disappearance of our scant supply of rations, and from time to time have seen the river snatch a portion of the little left, while we were ahungered. And danger and toil were endured in those gloomy depths, where ofttimes the clouds hid the sky by day, and but a narrow zone of stars could be seen at night. Only during the few hours of deep sleep, consequent on hard labor, has the roar of the waters been hushed. Now the danger is over; now the toil has ceased; now the gloom has disappeared; now the firmament is bounded only by the horizon; and what a vast expanse of constellations can be seen!

Powell divided among his ragged volunteers the little money he had to spare, and gave them the two boats to continue on down. Of the four, Bradley and Sumner would leave the river at Yuma, and only Hawkins and Hall would run the Colorado's whole length to tidewater. For Powell's purposes, there was no use in going farther. Ives had surveyed up this far; steamboats had charted the full length of the lower river. As exploration, the expedition had ended at the Grand Wash Cliffs. Only the loyalty of five men and Powell's own resolution had kept it from ending in failure on the very brink of success, at Separation Rapid. What had been a tight and even tense organization, a desperate comradeship, a true expedition, had begun to crumble with the departure of the Howlands and Dunn. Now with the bond of danger gone, it suddenly dissolved. Almost lamely, Powell and his brother shook hands with the other four and turned north with their Mormon hosts to St. Thomas and on over the Beaver Dam Mountains to St. George, the capital of Brigham Young's southern province. As they went, they inquired of everyone they met for word of the three who had elected to fight their way out overland.

At St. Thomas there was no word, at Santa Clara no word, at St. George, well into the edge of civilization and linked to Salt Lake by a carriage road and the Deseret Telegraph, still nothing. The church authorities sent out riders to outlying ranches and to the Paiutes of the plateaus, but they disappeared into that silence from which the Powells had themselves only just emerged. They waited, though they were wild to get home, and the Deseret Telegraph had sent out ahead of them messages that assured them a hero's welcome. Perhaps then more than any time earlier they felt the implacable emptiness through which they had labored for a hundred days. Other western explorations had met Indians, buffalo and antelope and elk, grizzlies; they had passed alertly through a wilderness that teemed with life. Their own had passed through a wasteland naked even of game, sometimes even of vegetation, and its trademark was the ancient and terrible stillness which was all they heard now, waiting in St. George. That stillness had not been broken a day later when they had to leave.

They were only two days on their way, somewhere up along the Mormon Trail that followed the abrupt eastern edge of the Great Basin, when word of Dunn and the Howlands caught up with them from St. George. The three had climbed the wall and made it to the forested top of the plateau. They had made it no farther. They lay out there now somewhere beside a waterpocket, stripped and filled with Shivwits arrows, victims of an Indian misunderstanding and of their own miscalculation of the algebra of chance.

The voyage of 1869 had been a stupendous adventure, but Powell was not satisfied with adventure alone. He returned to civilization determined to give the Colorado Plateau the same kind of intense, lengthy, and comprehensive topographical exploration that had marked Clarence King's 40th Parallel Survey. Armed with a $10,000 appropriation from Congress and an exploring team whose scientific effectiveness would far outweigh the accomplishments of the 1869 expedition, Powell set off on the second exploration from Green River City in May of 1871. For the next eight years, with Powell himself departing and rejoining the expedition periodically, with personnel additions and changes, and with continuing financial support, the geographical and geological survey of the Plateau Province would map the canyons and rivers, outline the geologic history of the region, tramp across mountains and run rivers, delve into the ethnology of the native population, take hundreds of photographs, and produce a treasure trove of scientific information that would enable Powell to illuminate for the first time the complicated landforms in this immense region and to formulate many definitions and explanations whose scientific validity has remained unchallenged to this day.

Out of this near-decade of exploration came most of the theories that Powell promulgated tenaciously for nearly twenty-five years, chief among them the program outlined in his 1878 *Report on the Lands of the Arid Region of the United States*. This prescient treatise called for an end to the reasonless theories that envisioned the great West as a living garden. Much of the West, Powell pointed out, was simply unsuitable for settlement, certainly along the lines suggested by the Homestead Act of 1862. What the West demanded was a regional and environmental approach to settlement. Lands must be mapped and classified, and should be utilized according to the classifications—mineral lands, farming lands, pasturage lands, and timber lands. Moreover, land use in the West needed a sweeping revision of federal control, largely reflected in the proposed formation of irrigation districts and in a logical *regional* political framework rather than the purely arbitrary one of state boundaries. In essence, the report insisted that land must be utilized according to its best possibilities; that settlement must be planned, not extemporaneous; that simple logic and common sense should replace wishful thinking. Needless to say, Powell's twenty-five-year campaign for common sense met with a sometimes infuriated opposition; and while the Newlands Act, passed in 1902, the year of Powell's death, stood as a monument to his agitation, the full scope of his reform has yet to be implemented, and probably never will be.

Powell applied the same logic to proposed reform of Indian policy in the West, outlined in an 1874 report in collaboration with G. W. Ingalls. The concept of reservations, among other things, was wrong, "looked upon in the light of a pen where a horde of savages are to be fed with flour and beef, to be supplied with blankets from the Government bounty, and to be furnished with paint and gew-gaws by the greed of the traders. . . ." The true reservation, he said, "should be a school of industry and a home for these unfortunate people." While hampered by the "civilizing" methodology which dominated Indian reform for the next several decades, Powell's theories nevertheless attempted to establish some kind of logical bond between the cultural past and present of the Indian and the more complicated industrial world in which it was believed he must function to survive. Again, Powell's vision exceeded the probabilities of his time, but he put his theories to work as best he could through the Bureau of Ethnology, which he founded in 1879 and headed until his death.

IN AN AGE dominated by the self-seeking of the capitalist-politician whose most telling contribution to the future was the germination of agonizing problems we have not yet begun to solve, the career of John Wesley Powell is a kind of sardonic counterpoint; with an in-

THE MYTH

Frank M. Brown's ill-starred railway survey expedition in the Canyon of Lodore, 1889 (photograph by Franklin A. Nims).

tellectual vigor whose force was almost physical, with an integrity and a strength of purpose sometimes biblical in its intensity — Powell quite literally served the public for more than thirty years. He was not selfless, nor was he lacking in human deficiencies; he pursued his career with a singlemindedness that was sometimes brutal, and he was entirely capable of a protective jealousy in the tight, often deadly little bureaucratic jungle of nineteenth-century Washington. Yet his career, for all the attention he gave it, was not, in truth, his alone. A truly public career, it belonged to his age, and the sundry

legacies of that career have become part of America's cultural baggage.

In 1871, the year that Powell launched his massive exploration into the plateau wilderness, Lt. George Montague Wheeler of the Corps of Engineers made his own foray into the canyons of the Colorado. Wheeler, a young and immensely ambitious West Point man who would later head up the Army's Geographical Surveys of the Territories of the United States West of the 100th Meridian, promoted an 1871 assignment to explore and map "those portions of the United States territory lying south of the

The Wheeler expedition's greatest contribution were such O'Sullivan photographs as the stunning view of Grand Canyon shown at the right.

Wheeler's expedition crew with Mojave guides, 1871 (T. H. O'Sullivan photograph).

Central Pacific Railroad, embracing parts of Eastern Nevada and Arizona." With a thirty-man party that included a geologist, a reporter, and Timothy O'Sullivan, a Civil War photographer who had taken his cameras into the West after the war (he had previously served with the King Survey), Wheeler commenced his assignment by venturing into Death Valley in the middle of the summer; his timing was quixotic, to say the least, and nearly resulted in the death of two of his men in the valley's murderous 120-degree heat. Somehow they survived, and Wheeler readied them for the next—hardly less quixotic—adventure: a boating exploration up the Colorado.

Not even Powell's exposure of the river as being totally unsuited for general navigation beyond Black Canyon had convinced the Army; it needed a head of navigation far up into the Colorado canyons to supply its troops in the region, and it was determined to have it. So Lieutenant Wheeler was sent to find it. With three boats and one barge, an eighteen-man party (not including fourteen Indian guides and laborers) entered the river at Camp Mojave on September 16, 1871. Several days of strenuous, but not particularly dangerous rowing brought them to Black Canyon and the first of a series of rapids that would haunt the expedition to its conclusion. With

backbreaking effort, the boats were towed through one crushing torrent after another; two were swamped at Vernal Falls, resulting in injury to two men, and Wheeler nearly despaired. "Each rapid in turn," he wrote, "seems to be more powerful than the last." The climactic catastrophe of the trip occurred at Disaster Falls, when one of the boats was completely wrecked, together with all of Wheeler's notes. Finally, on October 20, the party reached Diamond Creek and an overland relief party.

EXCEPT FOR THE PHOTOGRAPHS of Timothy O'Sullivan, the first that had ever been taken in the river's lower canyons, the expedition was almost totally unproductive. It had duplicated the Ives journey of 1858, and while Wheeler managed to make it all the way to Diamond Creek by boat, as Ives had not, the achievement was of dubious value. A head of navigation, it goes without saying, had not been established in the Colorado's canyons. In 1872, Wheeler sent another expedition into the canyons, but again, the most valuable result was a collection of photographs, these taken by William Bell. Altogether, Wheeler's ambition to surpass the efforts of John Wesley Powell was a fruitless one.

If Wheeler's attempts to navigate the lower Colorado were quixotic, then the next major exploration of the

The last exploration: Members of the U.S. Geological Survey expedition of 1921.

river must be judged very nearly insane. On March 25, 1889, the Denver, Colorado Canyon, and Pacific Railroad Company was organized. Its president was Frank M. Brown, a Denver real estate promoter; its purpose was to build a railroad from the western slopes of the Rockies to the Pacific Coast—via the banks of the Colorado River.

Local financiers were not interested in putting money into the venture until they had some kind of guarantee that the impossible was possible. Brown, who believed utterly in what he was doing, set out to prove it could be done; he hired Robert B. Stanton as the railroad's chief engineer and organized the Denver, Colorado Canyon, and Pacific Railroad Survey to take the river's measure.

Late in March, 1889, the party started out from Grand Junction, Colorado. By the end of May, they had lost twelve hundred pounds of food to the river; by the middle of June all provisions had been lost and eight of the expedition's sixteen members had deserted. The remaining eight survived until they reached Lees Ferry, where fresh provisions were obtained, and once again they pushed off into the river. At Marble Canyon, President Brown's boat capsized, spilling him into a whirlpool; he was never seen alive again. Chief Engineer Stanton continued until there were only four stalwarts left (two, in-

cluding Brown, had drowned; one had been injured, and the rest had deserted). He then returned to Denver, organized a new party, continued the exploration to the Gulf of Mexico, and prepared a careful and detailed report of the whole venture. The railroad was never built, and like Wheeler's earlier expeditions, the most important contribution of the Denver, Colorado Canyon, and Pacific Railroad Survey was the more than two thousand photographs taken by the expedition's official photographer, Franklin A. Nims.

Exploration of the Colorado continued well into the twentieth century. In 1902, Francis Emile Matthes began work on a complete topographic map of the Grand Canyon for the United States Geological Survey. It took three years to finish just the Vishnu, Bright Angel, and Shinumo quadrangles; and while the map had to wait until 1923 for completion, Matthes' work is considered not only the most detailed rendering of the canyon in existence but one of the most beautiful examples of the map maker's art. The Survey extended its work to the whole river between 1921 and 1922, mounting full-scale river expeditions through all the canyons.

By then, however, other men were examining the river for other reasons. It was no longer enough to know the river—it must be used, and in the end, crippled.

PART TWO:

THE CONQUEST

INTRODUCTION

THE COLORADO'S ROLE as the embodiment of all the dark mysteries of an unknown country ended with the explorations of John Wesley Powell and those who followed him. By the end of the nineteenth century, its course was known from source to mouth; its tributaries had been charted, its canyons named, mapped, and measured; its geology had been catalogued, its history chronicled; romance and myth-making had given way to the spare precision of scientific prose and the lucid schemas of charts, tables, and diagrams. It is supremely paradoxical, then, that at this point in time the Colorado became hopelessly enmeshed in yet another manifestation of man's peculiar insistence that the realities of the natural world succumb to the demands of his imagination. Once again, the imperatives of myth and *must be* entered the river's story, this time with tremendous effect: for twentieth-century man had the power to do more than dream—he could translate his dreams into what he conceived of as reality. The three chapters that follow document the failure of one such dream, outlining the processes by which myth can alter reality—and conquer a river.

The particular myth that has plagued the Colorado in the twentieth century is an old one in the American narrative, older than the nation itself. It has been called by some the myth of the garden, a persistent belief that America's western lands comprised an enormous garden where a new society of independent freeholders would flourish and sustain American life. The creation and maintenance of such a class, Thomas Jefferson believed, was a requisite of true democracy: "Cultivators of the earth," he said, "are the most valuable citizens. They are the most vigorous, the most independent, the most virtuous, and they are tied to their country, and wedded to its liberty and interests, by the most lasting bonds."

The Westward Movement was seen as a continuing regeneration in which these "cultivators of the earth" would perpetuate their vigorous, independent, and virtuous society, enriching themselves, their regions, and their country. It was a compelling vision, as outlined by Henry Clay in 1832: "Pioneers . . . penetrate into the uninhabited regions of the West. They apply the axe to the forest, which falls before them, or the plough to the prairie, deeply sinking its share in the unbroken wild grasses in which it abounds. They build houses, plant orchards, enclose fields, cultivate the earth, and rear up families around them."

There was enough truth in the well-watered eastern third of America to strengthen the vision, and as the Westward Movement began to trickle across the Mississippi into the Great Plains, the idea found articulation in the Homestead Act of 1862, which guaranteed to the yeoman farmer 160 acres of the public domain on which to carve out his little corner of Eden. Unfortunately, Eden began to deteriorate the farther west one went; there was too much land and not enough water. Still, the myth would not die—irrigation was the answer, said the dreamers; irrigate, and all the billions of acres west of the Mississippi would blossom as the rose.

NOT SO, said John Wesley Powell in his *Report on the Lands of the Arid Regions of the United States* in 1878: "Within the Arid Region only a small portion of the country is irrigable." Moreover, he added, there was so little water for even the irrigable lands that monopolization of water—and therefore of land—was a profound danger that could destroy the possibility that the independent family farm would ever be a significant force in the arid West: "All the present and future agriculture of more than four-tenths of the area of the United States is dependent upon irrigation, and practically all values for agriculture inhere, not in the lands but in the water. . . . The question . . . is to devise some practical means by which water rights may be distributed among individual farmers and water monopolies prevented." Powell went on to outline his version of those "practical means," a plan that sought an intelligent way of uniting water to land, but few of the dreamers were listening.

Irrigation congresses began to convene, crying for nothing less than "a million forty-acre farms" in the West. Addressing one of these congresses in 1893, Powell again hammered away at his point: "I wish to make it clear to you, there is not enough water to irrigate all these lands; there is not sufficient water to irrigate all the lands which could be irrigated, and only a small portion can be irrigated. . . . I tell you, gentlemen, you are piling up a heritage of conflict . . . for there is not sufficient water to supply the land!" Still, they would not listen.

In 1902, the Newlands Act (largely inspired by, and in some respects patterned after, Powell's concepts of the initiation and control of western reclamation projects) was passed, creating the Reclamation Service. Among the Act's stipulations was that anyone receiving water from federally sponsored irrigation was limited to 160 acres of land irrigated by that water. This device, designed to prevent those water monopolies Powell had so feared, was from the beginning systematically ignored by large landholders and enforced only sporadically. The law never would be applied consistently, and so the myth of the great garden in the West filled with a million forty-acre farms, withered and died, replaced by factories in the fields and wandering armies of laborers who more accurately resembled the stifled working classes of the industrialized East than the vigorous, independent "cultivators of the earth" that Jefferson had eulogized.

THE MYTH DIED, but not before it had altered the Colorado River—for it was in the bleak deserts of the American Southwest that the dreamers had seen their most profound justification; the desert would be the greatest garden of them all, and the Colorado would be its fountain. The Salt River Valley Project on a major tributary of the Gila was begun only a year after the formation of the Reclamation Service. It was followed quickly by others, and soon a new element of demand entered the picture: the exploding, water-hungry urban areas of Southern California and central Arizona, each of which reached out to the Colorado to fill its needs. Dam after dam backed up the Colorado's water, which was siphoned off from the river in all directions and for all needs. Today, after a little more than sixty years of dam-building, the water experts tell us that the Colorado River is "over-committed." There is not enough water in the river to fulfill the demands made upon it. John Wesley Powell was right.

And so a final question presents itself: to what end have we sacrificed the Colorado River? The answer is not comforting: for the enrichment of those agri-industrialists who have been shrewd enough or lucky enough to have acquired the bulk of the desert's irrigable land and for the urban and industrial water needs of not more than two generations of Southwest residents. For this, and for only this, we have crippled a living river.

CHAPTER V

THE DESERT SHALL REJOICE, AND BLOSSOM AS THE ROSE

Ideal, Reality, and the Colorado as a Tool of Empire

Paul S. Taylor

TOO MUCH LAND, too little water, and water at the wrong places and at the wrong times. This was the western desert when John Wesley Powell descended the uncharted reaches of the Colorado River in 1869; and that is the desert today, in spite of nearly seventy years of water resource developments on the Colorado running into the billions of dollars. As men had once looked upon the river as the West's "natural thoroughfare" to the Pacific, they soon came to look upon it as something more: a natural resource whose life-giving waters would make the desert "blossom as the rose" enrich the arid lands of the Southwest, create farms where bleak wasteland existed, and bring unequalled prosperity to the region and all its people. Somewhere, the dream went wrong.

The chief problems in making the desert blossom have not been physical, for man has always found these easiest to master. Those that have plagued him most are financial and social; that is, human. First of these was how to finance the union of water to land—how to make the desert blossom. The second was how to unite people to land consistently with national ideals—how to make it blossom as the rose. On the Colorado River, both problems have created an enormous failure. In order to understand that failure, it is necessary to examine the concepts of water and land use in the West, for the history of the Colorado's misuse has its roots deep in a century-old struggle between ideal and reality.

EASTWARD, in the humid belt, the people of the United States were spared the problem of finance by the generosity of Nature. But from colonial days they had wrestled with the problem of how to achieve a proper union of people with land. In bitter political battles they had made decisions and stood by them. At the bloody cost of civil war, they had overthrown the southern system of large landholdings manned with slave laborers. In the midst of the same war, Congress seized upon the absence of the planters' spokesmen to reaffirm the Nation's faith in a society founded upon free laborers united, as owners, to the land they till. By passing the Homestead Act in 1862 Congress showed its intent to spread this kind of society, rather than the plantation type, across the nation to the Pacific.

As the era of development opened on the Great Plains and moved westward, a serious complication arose. Because water and land were separated, equitable distribution of land no longer achieved automatically the ideal of free laborers, independent upon their own land. Financing the union of water and land was beyond their capacity, whether as individuals or in groups. The intervention of either capitalists or Congress was necessary, therefore, to support settlement.

A generation was to pass after John Wesley Powell's descent of the Colorado before Congress gave carefully deliberated response to the vision of irrigating the West. But the thirty-three years between 1869 and 1902 were

147

Man, land, and machine—the ingredients of empire in Arizona's Salt River Valley, ca. 1931; all that is needed is water.

not years of indifference or idleness, for a spark had been ignited, men had glimpsed the possibilities of settlement, and tinder of advancing land values was lying about ready to take fire. They were years of land-grabbing, bureaucratic jockeying, engineering, surveying, congressional investigating, and legislative false starts.

Even before Powell could get his *Report on the Lands of the Arid Region* into print in 1879, Congress had passed the Desert Land Act of 1877, rushing it through both Houses and onto the desk of President Grant for signature, all within his last twenty-four hours in office. It was founded upon a false assumption: that the desert could be watered simply by giving 320 acres to anyone who would agree to irrigate it. The practical effect of the Act, as historian Fred Shannon has pointed out, was not to water the desert, but "to encourage monopolization while throwing dust in the public's eyes."

Against the visible failure of the Desert Land Act and its later modifications either to water dry land or to prevent monopoly, the alternatives began to take shape more clearly. Looking backward, Wallace Stegner has outlined these in *Beyond the Hundredth Meridian*. One alternative, he says, was that "the people themselves, by cooperative effort such as that of the Mormons, could organize and develop in unison what was impossible for anyone singly." The method had been "tested by New England barn raisings and corn huskings, and all the cooperative habits of country America, tested even more fully by the Mormon experience of thirty years and the New Mexican experience of ten generations." That method did indeed resolve the relation of people to land in the tradition of the Homestead Act, but aridity faced it with two challenges.

O N THE GREAT PLAINS, as Stegner has pointed out, one challenge came from "the men who were already beginning to ride like robber barons and kings over the public domain, and the corporations who were already, with Scottish and English and American capital, beginning to acquire those water-bearing half- and quarter-sections upon whose possession depended the control of range to support a cattle empire." Water went as the prize to those who grabbed its scattered sources first. On the more productive lands along the lower Colorado and other rivers, water less often was up for grabs. The high cost of financing huge dams and great canals ruled out cooperation among farmers, while it complicated the process of water acquisition by "robber barons and kings" and corporations. The grabbing was postponed until many decades later, when clusters of states would battle for short supplies of water and money in the congressional arena.

An alternative to cooperative development by farmers was development by private capital. Its danger—as shown by the results where tried—was the certainty of monopoly at the expense of working farmers.

A remaining alternative was development by government. Powell's choice between the alternatives was a clear reaffirmation of public responsibility for development under national policy as declared by Congress during the Civil War. "The question for legislators to solve," he wrote in his *Report on the Lands of the Arid Region*, "is to devise some practical means by which water rights may be distributed among individual farmers and water monopolies prevented."

The possibility of using the first alternative—cooperation among farmers to assure development and policy—faded fast. The long, slow course of history is still spelling out the prolonged grappling with development and policy under the second and third alternatives, using private capital and government.

Neither was initially eager to undertake the financing of large irrigation projects. Private capital was chary about investing heavily in face of the risks; these included fears that public regulation of private sale of water to farmers would reduce the returns to capital. Government likewise was not to be persuaded easily to abandon the hope underlying the Desert Land Act that private parties, given the land, could unite water to it and so spare the national treasury. The issue between the alternatives was deep, and was to remain unresolved into the early years of the twentieth century.

T HE 1890's were occupied with gropings for a means to spread irrigation. *Scribner's Magazine* carried a lead article on "Water Storage in the West" which surveyed the problems and prospects as they looked in January, 1890. Its author, Walter Gillette Bates, spoke enthusiastically of "the problem of the reclamation of an empire," then examined ways of solving it. No possible means was beyond his mental horizon. He considered even "increasing the rainfall," or how to "shift it...to the spring and summer months," but quickly dismissed this "simplest theoretical solution" because "no practical

People of the land, but deprived of its enrichment—a Negro laborers' camp in the Imperial Valley, 1935.

method of accomplishing this has yet been suggested." He reviewed the search by private companies, encouraged by rewards offered by territorial legislatures, for artesian wells to tap subterranean water sources; but he concluded that "these methods are unimportant compared with irrigation from such living streams as exist."

In many western states a common legal basis for large-scale private irrigation was the "rights of the first or 'prior appropriator' of water," and the common motivation to private action was to sell the appropriated water to settlers. "As the quick-witted Westerner stands by the side of one of the great rivers and looks over thousands of acres of desert land along its banks," wrote Bates, "he sees a fortune in the situation. Only get capital enough together, organize a great company, dig an immense canal which will 'appropriate' all the water in the river, and you command the whole valley. It is the position of the Western railroads repeated. Instead of waiting for settlers to come and dig little ditches . . . an immense capital digs one huge canal watering thousands of farms, and then draws settlers by advertisement and boom."

In attacking the problem on this scale, Bates reported that western enterprise had not waited for government aid; and private capital was already making the experiment: "The land belongs to the Government, and is taken up by individual settlers at merely nominal prices under the Desert Land Act. But the water belongs to the canal company, and it is this water that the settler really pays for." But even this bonanza from living streams was approaching its limit, and the "latest solution . . . is . . . water-storage," Bates said. He cited privately built storage dams near Merced; at Bear Valley, with seventy-five miles of canal; in San Bernardino County; on Sweetwater Creek near San Diego—all in California—and at Walnut Grove near Prescott, Arizona. "Private enterprise is eager to seize the golden opportunity before it is too late," wrote Bates, as he described greater projects "gravely put forward," including "diversion of a river as large as the Colorado [that] would seem the wildest folly to conservative Eastern men. . . . So all over the West, throughout Colorado, in central and southern California, in Montana and Idaho, on the Salt and Gila Rivers in southern Ari-

Mrs. Samuel Robinson, one of the Imperial Valley's earliest homesteaders; her husband would rise to become an assemblyman, his career founded on Colorado water.

zona, there are great companies, with capitals running into the millions, putting this idea into effect."

The remaining source of financing for development was government. Bates balanced pros and cons. He recited "obvious objections—the enormous outlay, [the] opportunity for jobbery, the danger that the work would be badly done." The latter hazards, he believed, could be overcome, for the "very magnitude and publicity of the undertaking would enforce more careful designing and sounder work." And he recognized persuasive arguments pointing to government construction: the government could afford to do what private enterprise could not; the government was not under pressure for quick dividends, nor under the requirement "that it should pay at all, in the strict commercial sense." The government, that is, could subsidize.

Furthermore, the government was in position to recapture incremental values created by its own investment.

Bates pointed out that "the United States owns the land, which private speculators do not. The latter must look for dividends from the rent of water, but the Government, if it owned the dams, could not only charge a yearly rental for the water, but could sell the land at greatly increased prices."

As his conclusion Bates wrote that forecasting the "growth of population, the filling up of all the countries which now welcome colonists, the consequent dearth of land, the impossibility of desert-reclamation by private capital, it is not altogether visionary to say that Governmental interference on the largest scale will be the inevitable result."

ACTION IN THE DIRECTION forecast by *Scribner's Magazine* came soon. In 1891 westerners took their first steps, bold and concerted, in search of government help to irrigate their region. A citizens' International Irrigation Congress convened in Salt Lake City, with delegates from a score of states and territories between the Great Plains and the Pacific Coast. In his preface to the proceedings, one "international" delegate, a Fellow of the Royal Geographical Society in Britain, reassured the "patriotic American" that he might find consolation for the western aridity "decreed by the laws of nature, [from a] study of the history of the world and the progress of mankind." After all, aridity had been "favorable to the highest development of the human race." Under like climatic conditions elsewhere, "art, science, poetry, statesmanship and war-like attitudes [have] flourished." Finally, the "Christian religion was founded in an arid region."

The delegates faced up to the two major issues of the day: How was irrigation to be financed? What policy was to govern the distribution of land and water? Delegate Francis G. Newlands, of Nevada, stated two major aspects of the problem of finance. The first was the financial inability of the West to proceed much further with water development on its own: "Irrigation has reached almost a stationary period. That is to say, we have throughout the arid region applied water to almost all the lands that are within easy reach of the rivers and streams. The field of individual effort seems to be almost exhausted, and the time now comes either for the action of the nation through Congress or the action of the various states. . . .'' The work, warned Newlands, "will require vast expenditures of money."

The second aspect of the financial hurdle was strongly political. Federal expenditures to irrigate the West, said Newlands (who eleven years later as congressman was to become co-author of the National Reclamation Bill), "will be met with opposition from the representatives from the east and from the middle west, who will claim that the United States has no right to expend large sums of money in the development of a particular section." Then, referring obviously to the Desert Land Act and its later modifications, he said that eastern representatives "will claim that the old and settled land policy (a policy well adapted to the middle west but totally unadapted to the arid west) should continue to prevail, viz., the gradual settlement of lands to pre-emption and homestead entries, and the sale of the lands at reasonable prices to settlers."

Gov. George C. Pardee of California supported Newlands' forecast of the necessity to overcome eastern opposition to national aid for western irrigation. "The people

from the East," he said, "would say that irrigation was a local affair and that there is enough land already in cultivation. They would say, 'We object to any further cultivation of the soil in the West, when the farms of New England are lying idle, when farm land can be bought for ten dollars an acre. . . .'. They feel jealous . . . that there are incentives in the great west that induce their young to leave the east."

The Irrigation Congress followed the analyses of Newlands and Governor Arthur L. Thomas, of Utah. It decided to ask Washington to grant all lands of the public domain, except mineral lands, "to the States and Territories needful of irrigation." In a gesture toward settlers on lands in the Great Plains who "had expended much time and labor upon the same; and paid into the United States Treasury . . . many millions of dollars, only to discover that irrigation . . . is necessary," a resolution pledged unwavered support to their "just demands" and asked the government to "donate at least a portion of the funds" paid by such settlers "toward the procurement of the means necessary for their irrigation."

The Irrigation Congress was both solidifying all-western political support behind a demand for national aid, and gingerly suggesting that the aid include cash as well as land.

The other issue to come before the congress was the question of what policy should govern the distribution of water and land. An amendment to the text of the prepared resolutions raised the question. Delegate Morris Estee, of California, asked from the floor that the trust to be created in the hands of states and territories from lands donated by the national government "shall be so conditioned as to secure the ownership of irrigable lands to actual settlers in suitable holdings, not in any case exceeding 320 acres."

It was not accidental that the resolution's proponent was a Californian, for the issue of land monopoly had rocked the politics of that state for a generation. A dozen years before, the California Convention of 1878–79, after extensive debate, had written into the state constitution a 320-acre limitation on state grants of land to settlers. This action was but the culmination of battles that had been reverberating through successive sessions of the legislature and on the hustings ever since statehood in 1850. Wrestling with the question of water monopoly in 1886, the state supreme court had awarded all the waters of the Kern River to the giant cattlemen, Miller and Lux.

The losers, forebears of the Kern County Land Company, stirred a storm of protest that began to sweep the state from end to end. To head off protest, Henry Miller suddenly gave back to those whom he had just defeated in court two-thirds of the water he had won. In exchange, the losers in court constructed a basin reservoir for his one-third. This tactic, so his biographer wrote, was the act of "a great statesman at the peace table." Public agitation promptly subsided. But these endless recurring battles over land and water monopoly in California had created many veterans deeply imbued with the hazards of monopoly. Morris Estee, author of the 1891 resolution against monopoly, had been a member of the Constitutional Convention and clearly was among them.

As debate on the 320-acre resolution proceeded, Newlands opposed it, not as wrong in principle but as untimely. Much of the talk by others, although ostensibly on the amendment, was irrelevant and diversionary, but demand from the floor for passage was strong. An unidentified delegate shouted, "Make it eighty."

DELEGATE JUDGE JAMES S. EMERGY, of Kansas, struck a note of deep outrage as he demanded passage of the Estee resolution. "Why these big farms?" he asked. "What did big land holdings do to the Roman Empire? It broke it up. Four weeks ago I rode across a farm in Texas twenty-eight miles long, and I was sick, although I sat upon the seat beside the proprietor of that land. Why, I would be sick in the stomach if I rode down that valley in California, over those long miles owned by one man. One man has no right to own that much land."

Delegate Mordecai, of California, helped further to bring the issue into sharp focus by declaring: "If you allow more than 320 acres of land to be taken up you open the door to a continuation of those great domains, which have been called to the attention of this Convention. Allow syndicates and corporations and private enterprises to absorb the territories which belong to the individuals thereof, and I, for one, gentlemen, am opposed to it. . . . We do not ask the Government to give us this great territory, to give away great blocks of ten, fifteen or twenty thousand acres, but we ask it, that we may continue as the government has done, to provide homes for the actual settlers in this great region which we inhabit."

Estee's 320-acre limitation resolution was finally "put and carried."

After two years the Irrigation Congress met again, this time in Los Angeles. As before, an aura of history and hope was cast over the convention, and the breadth of its purpose was given special emphasis. The National Executive Committee summarized its charge to the gathering in these words: "Irrigation—Applied to Agriculture, Applied to Horticulture. Its Far-reaching Ethical and Social Possibilities and Effects." Irrigation was more than economics and technology. In this catholic spirit and from the chair, Delegate William E. Smythe, of Utah, reminded the congress that the "greatest civilization of ancient times was built . . . [with] irrigation [as] the cornerstone of its economic system." Then he predicted that "during the twentieth century we shall see developed here the greatest civilization of modern times, and irrigation will serve as its foundation."

Breadth of purpose did not obscure immediate goals and tangible interests. The 600-member Los Angeles Chamber of Commerce took hold of arrangements for the congress with as much interest and enthusiasm as though it had been a purely local enterprise. As if in explanation, Gov. H. H. Markham of California reminded the delegates that "within twenty minutes' ride of this city, go in any direction you please, and you will find lands that, ten or fifteen years ago, were only worth 25 cents to $5 an acre, that today will pay a fair margin upon from $100 to $1000 per acre." Yet amid the phrases pointing to gains from irrigation in production of cattle and crops and land values, a representative of the Chamber of Commerce could speak of transforming "the desert into a garden of beauty." Did these mean the same thing? Were incremental values and beauty but two sides of the same coin? It might require a generation or two to yield up the answer.

JOHN WESLEY POWELL himself appeared before the Irrigation Congress to speak and be questioned. He spoke of physical limitations, of conflicting interests and purposes. "Not one acre of land should be granted to individuals for irrigation purposes," he said. "I want to say to you . . . the interests in these water rights will swiftly increase; . . . you are piling up a heritage of conflict and litigation over water rights, for there is not sufficient water to supply these lands. There is no water to put on half the lands now owned by the Government. There is not water enough in all the arid region to irrigate the lands which the Government has already disposed of. . . .

The burgeoning Salt River Valley in the 1930's, showing the fruit of corporate vigor and federal subsidy. Where are the people?

Cotton was the great money crop of agri-industry, nourished by reclamation water and harvested by stoop labor.

My prime interest is in such a system as will develop the greatest number of cottage homes for the people. I am more interested in the home and the cradle than I am in the bank counter."

The Second Irrigation Congress faced the same problems as its predecessor. First, was the problem of financing water development. Frederick H. Newell, in charge of hydrographic work for the U.S. Geological Survey, pointed out clearly that "men with small capital, or none at all, cannot divert the water, for streams which can be handled by them are no longer left unclaimed." The Desert Land Law, "under whose operations the public

land is passing away from the people," the Irrigation Congress declared officially, "is largely perverted from its original purpose. It offers the settler land upon terms with which he cannot ordinarily comply. The law becomes in its execution the instrument of corporations, who acquire land for $1.25 per acre, reclaim it on an average cost of $8.15 per acre, and sell it back again to the people upon profitable terms named only by themselves."

Col. R. J. Hinton, of New York and New Mexico, declared, "Water is the king of this country.... Capital is a kindly tool but a cruel master; and, in the arid region, you have already learned that lesson." He opposed granting public lands to the states. "I ask men to put aside speculative purposes and look at it as citizens. Would they like to see ... 40,000,000 acres made the football of a legislative body and the real estate influence that might gather around it?" The national government, "which owns these millions of acres, should, like other land-owners, pay for making him valuable" and expect its citizens to "return to the Treasury ... the price and cost thereof, and thereby save themselves the extravagant and overbearing prices which private corporations put upon them."

Gov. J. J. Gosper of Arizona shared Col. Hinton's views of government responsibility. Spelling out the foundation for appealing to the government for financial aid, he urged that "this Congress should have the courage and consistency to ask our great government to apportion from ten to forty acres of land.... with water enough to irrigate each piece, for a family to reside upon."

A California delegate introduced a resolution asking Congress to build the necessary reservoirs and canals to convey the water to the land, and to add the cost of such developments to the price of the land. Others thought this was further than the Second Irrigation Congress should go, and they prevailed. In the end, Congress was asked to care for and preserve forests and mountain watersheds, to appoint a nonpartisan national commission to investigate and recommend national legislation where state laws could not suffice, and to appropriate a portion of "money received from the sale of these [arid] lands to the practical investigation of means for their reclamation, from surface streams, storm waters or underground supplies." This would be "an act of simple justice" to settlers who had "suffered the severest hardships" because of lack of irrigation.

Where did these men come from, what land and what lives did they leave behind to sweat out existence in cotton-growing factories?

The question of policy, like that of finance, raised its head early. On the second day Dr. R. R. Blowers, a delegate from Lake County, California, in which Clear Lake is situated, demanded assurance of protection against water monopoly. "We wish the people . . . to own it," he declared, "instead of the millionaire companies, who have already made claim upon the water. The moment the President of the United States signs the appeal, tendering the different States of this Union the arid lands and the river waters, then that moment, Clear Lake and Cache Creek belong to a corporation composed of millionaires. That land is valued at from ten to a hundred million dollars. Do we propose to stand still and allow such rights to pass into the hands of those who have already too much?"

Blowers was the first delegate to the irrigation congresses to see beyond irrigation and declare against private monopolization of hydroelectric power as well. "We want to have the water . . . for power; we want to plow our land with electricity and heat. . . . I want the whole people, from now on—from generation to generation— to own that water—own that power."

Irrigation congresses were convened almost annually through the nineties, moving from city to city in the arid

155

Elated by the joy of a day's work done—or by the novelty of having their photographs taken—Mexican cantaloupe pickers in Imperial Valley, 1935, pause before being trucked back "home".

region. A core of the same delegates generally attended, and the problems debated remained the same—finance and policy. The conclusions too, were much the same. The West was being solidified behind a move to gain support for irrigation.

By NOW, the view of the congresses on policy was clearly delineated, and understood as a justification for national aid to the West. Actually solving the problem of financing water development was the remaining task. In 1900 the Irrigation Congress took a major step in that direction by holding the ninth congress in Chicago, close to the centers of national decision-making power.

The host city, metropolis of the Middle West, accepted the Irrigation Congress on its own terms. In welcoming the assemblage in the name of the mayor, City Attorney Howard S. Taylor said, "If the reclamation of the arid lands of the West shall be accomplished, as I understand is your purpose, your anticipation and desire, by the government of the United States, this end will be achieved: that the exploitation of these lands by private parties will be prevented, and the further dislocation of society and the erection of servitudes resting upon the necks of unborn generations will be prevented." The deliberations of the Chicago Irrigation Congress, as before, were filled with delegates' objections to monopoly.

Yet there were perceptible undertones of impatience

with this kind of talk. A fine line divided outright promoters bent upon obtaining government financing of irrigation from those who also wanted government financing but solely on the condition that private monopoly and speculation would be controlled. Delegate F. S. Goudy, of Colorado, a member of the resolutions committee at Chicago, sought to blunt the edge of an attack on corporations as canal builders and sellers of water by remarking humorously that "I am against all corporations—except my own." Then he proceeded to disparage "idealists" and "dreamers." "So far as the workings of the Desert Land Act is concerned," he said "I have no doubt that frauds have been committed on the government. . . . Fraud will continue, whatever legislation may be adopted in this country or any other country . . . men must dream sensible dreams . . . that are fitting to humanity and the conditions with which we are confronted as individuals and as human beings." Then he came to the real purpose as he saw it: "Let this Congress . . . agitate the question of obtaining money from the government for the construction of reservoirs . . . beyond the reach and possibility of inducing private capital or private enterprise to undertake . . . ."

So the Chicago recommendation to Congress omitted policy. The omission was protested from the floor, and a letter read from Gen. Nelson A. Miles, contending that private or corporate enterprise could not be trusted to control the improvement with "justice and equality for all concerned." But the protest was overridden when Delegate George H. Maxwell, who later won the accolade "Father of Reclamation," closed debate by giving his personal assurance that the omission was unimportant. "I doubt whether there is anybody else who has devoted as much time, or spoken publicly as much, or written as much as I have in behalf of the exact policy suggested in the letter of General Miles," he said. "It is the policy I believe in. I think the resolution is all right, and we are wasting time talking about it here." So the resolution passed.

Thus at Chicago in 1900 policy was left formally vague, in contrast to the Salt Lake City Irrigation Congress of 1891 where Delegate Estee's 320-acre limitation amendment from the floor was incorporated in the resolutions. Those in key positions at Chicago had their eyes fixed, above all, on persuading Congress to finance western reclamation as an extension of the "policy of internal improvements"—that is, an extension of the "pork barrel" without policy. Details, it appeared, could be worked out later.

THE UNITED STATES CONGRESS in 1902, however, was in no mood to vote money for irrigation while leaving details of policy to be worked out later. Its temper was as solidly for control of monopoly and speculation as that of the First Irrigation Congress in 1891. The development agency must be the government itself, not private interests. The House report on Congressman Newlands' reclamation bill of 1902 rejected the precedent, established with the railroads half a century earlier, of granting lands as an incentive for corporations to take over construction of costly public projects. The sacrifice of "our time-honored policy of encouraging small individual land holdings," the House Committee said, was too "stupendous a price." President Theodore Roosevelt, personally familiar with large cattlemen's holdings on the Great Plains, had insisted on strong controls over monopoly and speculation. The bill was explicit: government would finance and construct, but only on the condition that "no right to the use of water for land in private ownership shall be sold for a tract exceeding 160 acres to any one landowner."

Even so, many in Congress were convinced that the policy would be honored mainly in the breach. Congressman George W. Ray, of New York, leading spokesman against the bill, warned: "And so we find behind this scheme, egging it on, encouraging it, the great railroad interests of the West, who own millions of acres of these arid lands, now useless; and the very moment that we, at the public expense, establish or construct these irrigation works and reservoirs, you will find multiplied by 10, and in some instances by 20, the value of now worthless land owned by those railroad companies."

Westerners had to meet the attack of eastern skeptics. The Congressman in charge, Frank Mondell of Wyoming, assured the House that the bill was "a step in advance of any legislation we have ever had in guarding against the possibility of speculative landholdings . . . while it will also compel the division into small holdings of any large areas . . . in private ownership which may be irrigated under its terms." Senator W. A. Clark, of Wyoming, challenged anyone to draft a bill providing more effective protection against monopolization.

Apparently the congressional majorities were satisfied that public policy and public financing were inseparable

By the hundreds of thousands, dust-bowl refugees sought work in fields watered by the Colorado.

—in other words, that public financing and construction would indeed break up and compel the division of large, private landholdings. On June 17, 1902, the bill became the National Reclamation Act.

IN HARDLY ANY TIME at all after passage of the National Reclamation Act, the contest between public and private interests in irrigation moved from the halls of the irrigation and national congresses out onto the Colorado Desert. As much as two years earlier, enterprising men had begun to divert the waters of the lower Colorado River into Imperial Valley. There, on the California side, private enterprise made its biggest effort.

Physical factors favored quick results. The Colorado River bed was higher than the lands to be watered, which lay mostly below sea level. Diversion was simple; cutting an opening in the finely silted river bank was enough to start the flow. In form and principle the operation was a repeat of the primitive ditch dug by farmers with mules

and scrapers to divert flood waters from the river bank to cultivated fields below. But the Imperial Valley enterprise was on a much vaster scale and in the hands, not of benefiting farmers who divided water among themselves, but of promoters who sold water to them, with the California Development Company in charge.

Tensions and conflicts were not long in coming to the surface. Soon the incompatibility of private enterprise in water development on the Colorado Desert with planned development of the full flow of the river began to show, as Helen Hosmer outlines in detail in Chapter Seven of this book. The culmination of those conflicts and tensions—the raging floods of 1905, the collapse of the California Development Company and its acquisition by the Southern Pacific, and the emotional withdrawal of the Reclamation Service's efforts in the valley—altered much on the surface of things, but changed very little that was essential. The patterns of development remained precisely the same: large landholdings in the hands of the few, and the land's value tied inextricably to the availability of water from the Colorado River.

THE VALLEY, under private development, was not nourishing a community of landowning farmers as the Desert Land and Homestead acts intended. On the contrary, it filled steadily with seasonal and migratory landless laborers until, by the late twenties, about one-third of the population was of this class and of Mexican origin, residing mainly in "ghettos." Tenancy covered 168,000 acres, or more than 45 percent of the irrigated valley. Absentee corporations controlled the production of vegetable crops. Ninety-nine percent of the commercial melon crop was in the hands of 56 growers, averaging 667 acres each. Ninety percent of the lettuce crop was in the hands of 67 growers, averaging 336 acres each. The pattern of Imperial Valley society was plantation-like, industrialized and streamlined on the side of ownership and management. Towns withered.

Meanwhile, the danger of complete inundation of the valley from an uncontrolled Colorado River remained, even after the closure of the breach in 1907. The unsettling Mexican claims to Colorado River water also remained, thanks to the private enterprisers who cut the Mexican intake.

Facing these problems toward the end of the 1920's, Imperial Valley interests joined others in an appeal to Congress: solution of their problems admittedly was beyond the financial capability of private enterprise; they needed federal aid. Their appeal invited the help of the Reclamation Service—whose representative in 1905 had been ridden from the valley on a rail.

Prof. George Smith, of the University of Arizona, described the impending physical disaster which prompted the appeal. "The people of the Imperial Valley for 16 years have been fighting a defensive battle against the Colorado," he wrote, "sometimes gaining, sometimes losing, but in the main losing. They cannot hold out for many more years. At least once every year, in June, and sometimes at other seasons, the river threatens to change its course from the Gulf of California to the Imperial Valley, as it did in 1905. The only protection at present is the system of levees, called respectively, the first, second, and third lines of defense. Frequently the floods break through the first and second lines and reach the third line. Each year the river, through silt deposition, builds up that part of the alluvial fan in front of the levees, in some years as much as 4 feet, and each year the levees must be raised an equal amount. Over one quarter of a million dollars is expended each year by the farmers of Imperial Valley in this work. The limit will be reached soon. Levees 40 or 50 feet high can not be maintained."

Congressman Phil D. Swing, of California, with Senator Hiram Johnson, cosponsor of the Boulder Canyon Bill of 1928, maintained that construction of a high dam on the Colorado River would save "the lives of a half dozen communities and the property of 100,000 people."

Swing also addressed the second problem, that of Mexican claims to the Colorado River. He proposed construction of an intake on the United States' side of the boundary and an All-American Canal to be cut through drifting sand dunes. The purpose was to deliver water without physically touching Mexican soil, and so to forestall enlargement of the Mexican claims initiated by the California Development Company. "It is by the construction of a large dam and the All-American Canal," said Swing, "that the Government of the United States is given complete manual control over the river, so it could if necessary or desirable limit the water for Mexico."

Congress passed the Boulder Canyon Act in 1928, authorizing the damming of Boulder Canyon and construction of the All-American Canal, "as provided in reclamation law." Reclamation law includes the limitation on water service to 160 acres of land per individual. The question soon arose: Was public policy, as embodied in

Age was irrelevant, for of whatever age, the refugees must survive—and work was survival.

the 160-acre limitation on deliveries of public water to private landowners, to follow public financing and construction of Boulder [now Hoover] Dam and the All-American Canal? Private interests in Imperial Valley, ever on the alert, took early steps to assure that public policy would not follow public money.

When the contract between the United States and the Imperial Irrigation District was drawn, acreage limitation provisions were omitted. That was the first step. But, uneasy over the lack of legal foundation to support the omission, a spokesman for Imperial interests sought an official ruling that the 160-acre limitation was *inapplicable*. "He doesn't want any formal ruling, of course, if the Solicitor were to hold that the limitation applies," commented a legal officer of the government. One week before the Hoover Administration left office in 1933, Secretary of the Interior Ray Lyman Wilbur signed a letter stating that the 160-acre law "does not apply to lands now cultivated and having a present water right."

THE CONQUEST

THIRTEEN YEARS LATER, in 1945, Solicitor Fowler Harper questioned the legality of the 1933 exemption. After another nineteen years, in 1964, Solicitor Frank J. Barry overthrew it. The impact hit the large landowners of Imperial Valley first, and they promptly raised a war chest to oppose Barry's legal ruling in federal court. Then shock waves spread throughout the West. Many owners of excess lands had known for a long time that they were receiving public water, publicly financed, on suffrance only, and were uneasy that sometime a day of enforcement might arrive. Perhaps the Imperial Valley ruling foreshadowed an end to non-enforcement elsewhere, as well. Robert W. Long, vice president of the Irvine Company (owners of the 93,000-acre Irvine Ranch), warned an Imperial Valley gathering on July 1, 1965, that those who might think "this is a quite different situation than . . . in other parts of the State" should realize that "this is not so. It is exactly the same thing." The chief counsel of the Imperial Irrigation District corroborated this appraisal bluntly: "If the opinion of the solicitor Frank Barry is correct, it also applies to all areas receiving water from the Colorado River, including land in the Metropolitan Water District, which supplies water to some extremely large holdings on the coast." Among them was the Irvine Ranch.

Would the acreage limitation issue "stay put" even for Imperial Valley, where about eight hundred landowners hold acreage in excess of the 160 acres legally allowed them? Solicitor Frank Barry's 1964 ruling had taken the question away from administrators by placing it in the lap of the judiciary. Four years later the case still had not come to trial, and large landowners held hopes that a Republican victory in the 1968 national election might produce administrators who would reverse the Barry ruling and remove the issue from the judiciary. This consequence, in the words of the *California Farmer*, might let the whole issue "quietly die away without the courts ever being required to make a decision." Of course, this solution might not be final, for it "would leave the possibility open that in future years, landowners would be faced with a similar battle."

The *California Farmer* made no mention of farmers whose access to land in the valley is obstructed by this failure to observe the law. On the other side of the lower Colorado River, in Arizona, the Reclamation Service had completed its first great project in 1912—the Roosevelt Dam to irrigate the Salt River Valley. There the 160-acre controls over speculation and monopoly remained a shadowy gesture and no more. As in California, the large landholdings in Arizona shaped the patterns of society. Through the Cotton Growers Association, Arizona interests began soon after the dam was constructed to recruit seasonal workers from far and near, and to oppose restrictions on immigration from Mexico. Year by year a landless labor population was built-up, and the homestead pattern, spreading land ownership among the tillers of the soil, had even less chance in Arizona than in California.

Still the thirst grew in Arizona for more water for more desert land. A two-billion-dollar Central Arizona Project was proposed in 1949, the water to be brought by aqueduct from the Colorado River. The proposal stirred rivalry between states—never more than dormant—for the waters of the river. California helped kill the project in Congress, and one of its weapons was the historic failure of enforcement of the 160-acre law in Arizona. It was a bit like the pot calling the kettle black when Republican Congressman Donald L. Jackson, of California, recited the long record of circumvention of the law in Arizona. "True," he said, "the Bureau of Reclamation says that the 160-acre law will be enforced if the Arizona project is built. But we know that this law has never been enforced there. There is no reason to believe it will be enforced in the future. Rather, there is every reason to believe that it will not be enforced." Then Jackson described what he called the Arizona Bubble: "The most gigantic bubble ever to develop within the continental limits of the United States appears now to be taking shape here in the Congress in the form of the proposed Central Arizona Project. . . . In every financial transaction there is a beneficiary. . . . As 420 farms contain 55 percent of the irrigated land, it is therefore proposed to give them 55 percent of the irrigation benefits. Fifty-five percent of $420,019,000 amounts to $231,010,450. This is an average of about $550,000 for each of 420 farms. Just 420 individuals would receive this immense benefit. It would certainly appear to me, Mr. Speaker, that when it is proposed to spend more than half a million dollars of public money for each one of a favored few Arizona landowners, or speculators, Congress should step in and put an immediate halt to any discussion of any such proposal. If the Central Arizona project is . . . approved by the Congress . . . the idle land will immediately increase in value six to ten times. If he is not forced to sell all but 160 acres, and he chooses to farm the new acreage made available by the transportation of the Colorado River water, he can operate his additional land with the resultant increase of personal profits. It should be remembered that field crops are already subsidized. And 86 percent of the crops grown in the project are those common competitive field crops. So the Federal Government is being asked to pile these fantastic irrigation subsidies on top of, and in addition to, the present crop subsidies."

IN ARIZONA the drive for speculative gains was reaching a fresh crescendo in 1968. Bills before Congress proposed the building of larger reservoirs on the Colorado than the river could fill. Where would the waters to fill them come from—new processes for "milking" winter storms of their snow as they crossed the Upper Colorado? Perhaps the dream that Walter Bates in *Scribner's Magazine* discarded in 1890 could be revived, but spokesmen for Arizona were unwilling to wait to find out. What of nuclear-powered desalting of sea water? What of the waters of the Columbia or even the Yukon? Arizona's speculating landowners were unwilling to wait for answers. As a tactic they preferred to overbuild and underplan. They chose political planning in preference to rational planning for overall conservation and proper use of water and financial resources.

The driving force pushing project authorizations through Congress often is more concentrated than aspiration for broadly distributed benefits to mankind. The hope of speculative gains to large landholders, with unearned increment uncontrolled, is a powerful motive. Besides, there are contracts to be let and jobs to be had. In the jockeying among private interests for congressional approvals, "back-scratching" tends to replace rational planning, and policy shrivels.

In 1965, with a fresh Central Arizona Project proposal before Congress, the Grand Canyon Workshop of the Colorado Open Space Coordinating Council observed: "After fighting for twenty years to take Colorado River water from one another, Arizona, California, and other Colorado Basin states have agreed to share the river if they can take enough water from elsewhere to make argument unnecessary.... None of the Colorado Basin states has given up anything. Instead, they have agreed to cooperate in taking their water from the rest of the West and their financing from the entire country."

TWO YEARS LATER, with the Arizona Project again before Congress, the scramble for public water and public money returned to the forefront. Reporting opposition from Colorado's congressmen and water leaders as being the loudest and bitterest, the Phoenix, Arizona, *Gazette* noted that "arranging to put more water" into the over-committed Colorado River was the point at issue. Arizona, it said, wanted its aqueduct approved at once and augmentation of the supply of water in the river left for some indefinite future. "Colorado objectors to this type of gamble, and their colleagues in Utah, Wyoming, and California, want the in-put provided for at the same time the extra out-put is approved."

From Oregon, the Portland *Journal* reported that Chairman LaSelle Cole of the Oregon Water Resources Board didn't think it economically feasible to divert water from the Columbia River to the Southwest, adding that the Northwest has blocked a national study of the problem at present. "But we are not going to block it forever," Cole said, "because there is a lot of political muscle involved.... The West has to stay together and unify the programs."

From afar came a reminder that public policy and its enforcement, and the contribution of public money to western reclamation are considerations not to be overlooked. President Johnson had appointed a National Advisory Commission on Rural Poverty, which late in 1967 issued its report, *The People Left Behind*. Reclamation did not escape scrutiny and criticism. The commission found it "impossible to reconcile Federal expenditures for reclaiming and developing land with Federal expenditures for taking land out of production while surpluses of certain farm products mount." Then, turning directly to rural poverty, it observed that in the absence of substantial competitive crop production of lands reclaimed by the Bureau of Reclamation, "much of the South could have stronger agricultural and rural economies, with fewer poverty stricken people."

The Rural Poverty Commission made two specific recommendations for improvement: (1) that "no more public money be invested in developing privately owned farmland" until the nation needs more food and fiber, and (2) that "the Department of the Interior enforce the 160-acre limitation to give opportunity on the land to the many." This 1967 reassertion that policy and finance are tied together is reminiscent of California Delegate Morris Estee's 320-acre resolution adopted by the

*Colorado River empire: The desert of the Salt River Valley
blossoms in dark, rich rows—a dream come true.*

Irrigation Congress of 1891. Is the echo to be hollow or
resounding?

The Colorado Basin Act, authorizing an aqueduct
across the desert to Phoenix and beyond, became law
in 1968. Supporters did not deny the insufficiency of
water in the basin to meet project needs. Reclamation
Commissioner Floyd Dominy admitted there will be a
"gradual diminution of the amount of water available
to the central Arizona project, and, as a result of it, there
will be a gradual declining of the agricultural lands because the domestic and municipal uses are going to be
moving in the other direction."

Instead of accepting water shortage as a reason for
delaying the project until a solution is found, Congressman Morris K. Udall, of Arizona, employed it as a reason simultaneously to start both the project and the

search for a solution. In a 1967 address to a Los Angeles
audience, entitled "Countdown on the Colorado," he
said: "Recognizing that this new drain on the river
would bring shortages for all of us in twenty-five or thirty
years, we agreed to start right now on a big, solid, meaningful program of studies and actions to augment that
river so that, when the pinch of the 1990's comes, we will
have enough water to meet all the demands." He acknowl-
edged that augmentation "would require big, solid steps"
and "cost money—hundreds of millions of dollars."

Proponents and opponents understood each other.
Congressman James A. Haley, of Florida, like Congressman Udall, saw the Colorado Basin authorization bill
as one serving notice upon the nation of more big demands to come. When Commissioner Dominy agreed,
during questioning, that the Colorado River is short of

Colorado River empire: The human legacy of the misused river is etched in the face of a mother of seven; she is thirty-two years old.

water to meet demands of the pending project, Haley said: "You might as well face up to it; you have to go somewhere else to steal the water to meet the commitments down there."

Compromises held the Colorado Basin Bill together. Within the basin, areas seeking water were balanced one against the other and assigned priorities, some high, some low. To defenders of the Columbia River a ten-year moratorium was given upon an Interior Department study of importation of outside waters into the Colorado Basin, a bar upon surely the most solid, meaningful of the studies to which Congressman Udall had assigned so much importance.

No one in 1968 used the historic failure to enforce the anti-monopoly provisions of reclamation law in Arizona (as Congressman Donald Jackson of California had done

successfully in 1949) as a weapon to obstruct a shaky project—or, for that matter, even as leverage to achieve *observance* of reclamation law there.

The unflattering description of so-called "planning" for water development given by the Grand Canyon Workshop of the Open Space Coordinating Council is in process of fulfillment step by step on the Colorado. "They have agreed to cooperate in taking their water from the entire country."

Today, who besides the Commission on Rural Poverty remembers John Wesley Powell's counsel of 1879, that the task for legislators is "to devise some practical means by which water rights may be distributed . . . and water monopolies prevented"? Before the third quarter of the century has run its course, is reclamation on the Colorado going to leave behind both People and Nature?

CHAPTER VI

MAKING AN EMPIRE TO ORDER

Earth-Movers, Dam-Builders, and the End of a Free River

It would be difficult to imagine a more stunning example of the scope and ingenuity of twentieth-century technology than the dams of the Colorado River system. In a little over two generations, the wild Colorado has been harnessed by a series of dams strung like beads on a thread from the Gulf of California to the mountains of Wyoming. The living river that Powell knew has been sectioned off into placid desert lakes throughout much of its length, and the river's primordial task of carrying the *massif* of the Colorado Plateau to the sea, bit by grainy bit, has been interrupted, and will remain interrupted for the lifetimes of our children's children and beyond.

All in the name of empire, an empire of water—water for land, for people, for industry; water to power the generation of electricity to light all the dark corners of the American Southwest; water controlled and channeled, tamed so that it can no longer destroy.

The conquest of this river was the great technological adventure of its age. Listen to poet May Sarton, celebrating the joys of Boulder Dam in 1942:

Not built on terror like the empty pyramid,
Not built to conquer but illuminate a world:
It is the human answer to a human need,
Power in absolute control, freed as a gift,
A pure creative act, God when the world was born,
It proves that we have built for life and built for love
And when we are all dead, this dam will stand and
    give.

We have since learned—or it is to be hoped that we have learned—that this dream, like most technological dreams, had the power to diminish as well as enrich the quality of man's life. The conquest of the Colorado stands as an embodiment of what we are capable of destroying even as we create.

THE ADVENTURE began very badly. When in 1901 the California Development Company—owners, operators, and chief promoters of Imperial Valley, California—cut into the river near Pilot Knob Mesa, opposite Yuma, and diverted four hundred thousand acre-feet of water into the valley via the Imperial Canal, it began a chain of events that destroyed the company, nearly annihilated the valley, and created the 150-square-mile Salton Sea. During the spring floods of 1905, the river smashed through the inadequate restraints placed upon it and raged downhill into the valley, tearing up the land and ruining farm after farm; it would take two years of backbreaking effort and more than three million dollars to close the breach, an accomplishment in itself one of the engineering wonders of the day. (That struggle, as well as many other aspects of the Imperial Valley story, is narrated in detail by Helen Hosmer in Chapter Seven, following.) As poorly executed as it was, this primitive attempt to tap the waters of the Colorado was the first major effort on the part of modern man to turn the river to his own ends. It would not be the last.

One of the first irrigation ventures to be authorized under the aegis of the newly formed Reclamation Service was the Yuma Project of 1904, designed to deliver Colorado River water to some sixty-eight thousand cultivated

Boulder Dam, the key to empire.

THE CONQUEST

Effects of the flood of 1910 in Mexicali.

acres in the Yuma Valley. The Laguna Diversion Dam, the first dam on the river, was strung across the Colorado thirteen miles north of Yuma, with a complicated siphon system that transported water from the California side under the river to Arizona. Construction on the project began in 1905 and was completed in 1910, at a cost of nine million dollars. Shortly afterwards, the Reclamation Service's first large, multipurpose water resources project got underway on central Arizona's Salt River, a major tributary of the Gila 300 miles to the east. The original project, including Theodore Roosevelt Dam and Powerplant on the Salt River and Granite Reef Diversion Dam downstream, was completed in 1911 at a cost of ten million dollars. The Gila itself was presented with Coolidge Dam in 1928, constructed by the Bureau of Indian Affairs. The upper basin of the river system came into its share of early developments, too, including the Grand Valley Project on the Gunnison River in Colorado, the Uncompahgre Project, which brought water through a six-mile tunnel from the Gunnison to the Uncompahgre Valley, and the Strawberry Valley project in east-central Utah. The total cost of these Upper Basin projects exceeded eleven million dollars. By the end of the 1920's, then, tens of millions of dollars and twenty-five years had made a fair start on the piecemeal conquest of the Colorado. Already, however, there were men dreaming even

bigger things for the river; this was the most ambitious reclamation enterprise of its day—the Colorado River Project.

The history of the Colorado River Project is as complicated as a game of three-dimensional chess, involving a dozen bickering factions, convoluted political entanglements, quarreling states, complex financing, and questions of national, and even international, import. It began, once again, in the Imperial Valley.

The river had been turned back to its legitimate course in 1907 and partially blocked by the completion of Laguna Dam in 1910, but it had not been tamed. In 1910, it broke out of its old channel again and emptied into Volcano Lake, southeastward of the valley. Imperial farmers, with the aid of a million dollars in federal funds, constructed new levees to hold the river off. At its very next flood, the river wiped out the new levees.

THEN, following its superbly fickle nature, the river entered a period of drought. By the summer of 1915, it had fallen so low that the Imperial Irrigation District (I.I.D.—formed in 1911 and now owner and operator of the Imperial Canal and all its works) was forced to build a temporary rock-and-brush dam at the heading of the canal in order to divert the river's entire miniscule flow into the valley. That winter, however, a flash flood on the Gila dumped millions of gallons of water into the Colorado, which backed up behind the temporary dam for miles and ultimately inundated the Yuma Valley, including the town of Yuma. When the I.I.D. attempted to rebuild the dam during the summer of the following year, residents of the Yuma Valley threatened to dynamite it *and* its builders. A compromise was reached when the IID promised to destroy the dam every year before the Gila's flood season.

It was obvious, however, that there would be no compromising with the river itself. Each year, the river laid down a foot of alluvial silt; each year, the I.I.D. was forced to add another foot of height to its levees. The process could not go on forever, and the inhabitants of the valley went about the business of making money under the constant threat that all their investments could be wiped out at any moment.

Complicating an already complicated situation was the valley's uneasy relationship with the Mexican authorities across the border. Since much of the I.I.D.'s levee system extended south into Mexican territory, the company was

Celebrants boosting it up for the delights of Imperial Valley and the opening of Laguna Dam at Yuma's Pilot Knob Hotel—"3127 Miles West of Broadway."

The perils of the unpredictable Colorado, as well as the Gila, were made painfully apparent during the great Yuma flood.

Building brush levees on the banks of the Colorado.

at the mercy of Mexican officialdom whenever it became necessary to fight potential floods by sending a stream of men and materials across the border. Customs officers, displaying a finely honed vindictiveness for the thoroughly disliked *norteamericanos,* made things as difficult as possible, holding up men and supplies interminably—doubtless a reflection of the political situation, for in 1916 General "Black Jack" Pershing and his forces had invaded northern Mexico in pursuit of Pancho Villa, plunging Mexican-American relations to their lowest ebb since the war of 1846.

The position of the hapless valley farmers was not, in their view at least, noticeably improved by the fact that a generous portion of "their" water was being siphoned off to Mexican land. In 1904, since the Imperial Canal ran for most of its length through Mexican territory, the California Development Company had agreed that up to half the canal's diverted water would be reserved for use on the rich delta lands below the border. More than 830,000 acres of this land was in the ownership of a Los Angeles syndicate headed by Harry Chandler of the Los Angeles *Times*—a circumstance that would have measurable effect on Imperial Valley's plans for the future.

O NE OBVIOUS SOLUTION to the Mexican "problem" was another canal, this one to cut across only American territory and to be called, reasonably enough, the All-American Canal. In 1917, Phil Swing, a lawyer for the I.I.D. (and later a congressman serving the same interests), went to Washington to talk to the head of the Bureau of Reclamation, Arthur Powell Davis, a nephew of Major John Wesley Powell and a man with a long and understandable interest in the Colorado River. Swing persuaded Davis to investigate Imperial's water difficulties, and four years later the Bureau recommended the construction not only of the All-American Canal but also of a large dam on the Colorado for water storage, flood control, and power production. The site ultimately chosen was Boulder Canyon.

States in the river's upper basin, which included parts of New Mexico, Colorado, Utah, and Wyoming, set up an immediate howl, complaining that their needs for the river's water were not being adequately considered. As early as 1919, representatives from all seven states in the basin, including California, Nevada, and Arizona, had met in Salt Lake City to discuss the river's future and had formed the League of the Southwest as an or-

*Dredges were used continually to keep the Imperial Canal free
of the river's incredible load of silt; it was an almost hopeless job.*

ganizational basis for further discussions and agreements, if any. At that conference, the governor of Utah had succinctly described the upper basin's view: "The water should first be captured and used while it is young," he said, "for then it can be recaptured as it returns from the performance of its duties and thus be used over and over again." The lower basin states disagreed vehemently, and the haggling continued through two more conferences the following year, accompanied by periodic sniping in the *Times* from Harry Chandler, who was dead against *any* development on the river that might affect the water supply of his Mexican lands.

Finally, in November of 1922, seven state commissioners met with Secretary of Commerce Herbert Hoover in Santa Fe and, after fifteen days of bitterly contentious bargaining, hammered out the Colorado River Compact, dividing the river's annual average flow of 20,500,000 acre-feet* of water: 7,500,000 acre-feet would go to each basin yearly; the lower basin was given the right to an

*One acre-foot of water, it should be pointed out, is approximately enough to support five people living in an urban environment for a year.

additional 1,000,000 if needed. If any river water should be allocated to Mexico through international treaty, it would first come from the excess above the already apportioned 16,000,000 acre-feet; if this were not enough, each basin would donate an equal share from its allotment to make up the deficiency. Each of the commissioners and Hoover signed the compact, and from them it went to the legislatures of the respective states for ratification. One by one, the states ratified it, until only Arizona was left.

Arizona refused, knowing that ratification would smooth the way for the construction of the All-American Canal and Boulder Dam and the "thievery" of what Arizona considered her own natural resource—the electric power-producing potential of the Colorado's Arizona canyons. Moreover, Arizona wanted a dam at Bridge Canyon, some one hundred miles upriver from Boulder, so that she could construct a gravity canal to carry water to her parched midsection. Arizona, in her own view, was gaining nothing from the compact and giving away her right to use Colorado water for her own needs. "I'll be damned," said her governor, George W. P. Hunt, "if California ever will have any water from the Colorado

THE CONQUEST

River as long as I am governor of Arizona." Pragmatically, the remaining states rewrote the agreement and passed it through again as a *six*-state Colorado River Compact.

AT THIS TIME, another element entered the by now multi-leveled entanglements of the Colorado River Project. Los Angeles, already beginning to display the characteristics of the extruded metropolis she would become, needed water, and so did the rest of Southern California. In 1923, the head of the Los Angeles Water and Power District, William Mulholland (he had built the mammoth, two-hundred-mile Los Angeles Aqueduct between Owens Valley and the city ten years before) proposed the world's largest aqueduct—240 miles across deserts and mountains to the cities of Southern California—and laid the foundation the following year by putting in an early bid for more than one million acre-feet a year of the lower basin's water allotment.

While the Los Angeles Water and Power District laid its enormous plans, the proponents of the Boulder Dam and All-American Canal projects found their proposals strangling in a snake's nest of congressional antagonisms and vacillation. In 1923 Phil Swing, by now a congressman from the Imperial Valley district, introduced his version of the Boulder Dam bill to the House, and for the next four years saw it disappear again and again, smothered in committee. To the natural enemies of the project—led by Arizona—was added a lobbying association of private power companies, which waved the red flag of "socialism" and vehemently opposed government-owned power projects like Boulder Dam. Over in the Senate, California's Hiram Johnson found the going no easier, although he had a powerful ally in William Randolph Hearst's newspapers, which promoted the project quite as vigorously as Harry Chandler and the Los Angeles *Times* opposed it. On February 21, 1927, Johnson actually managed to manipulate his version of the bill to the floor of the Senate. There it met opposition in the form of a herculean three-day filibuster by Arizona's senators Henry Ashurst and Ralph Cameron, who managed to kill the possibility of a vote before the adjournment of Congress on March 4.

Swing reintroduced his own bill to the House when the next session of Congress opened in December. It had been much revised by then to satisfy as many of the dissident factions as possible, but again it languished in committee until May 15, 1928, when Swing persuaded the House Rules Committee to send it to the floor for a debate. Antagonists of the bill managed to postpone a vote until May 25, but it was their last effort. That day, the bill passed the House with a resounding majority. Johnson was less fortunate that year, however; again Senator Ashurst and Arizona's newest senator, Carl Hayden, put on a three-day filibuster in May, holding off a vote until their allies were able to put through a motion for adjournment, which passed on May 28.

WHEN CONGRESS REOPENED in December, however, Arizona's last-ditch efforts crumbled when a motion was made and passed to limit debate on the bill, thus smothering any possibility of filibuster. The bill came to a vote and passed the Senate on December 14. It provided for the construction of Boulder Dam, Imperial Dam on the lower reaches of the river, and the All-American Canal. It limited California's share of Colorado water to 4,400,000 acre-feet a year, plus a share in any surplus in any given year, and up to half the "extra" 1,000,000 acre-feet provided to the lower basin by the Colorado River Compact. It also gave Arizona and Nevada a royalty on the electric power produced at the dam, and undercut the objections of private power companies by providing that the government would not build the dam's generating stations, but would, in effect, sell nothing more than the power of falling water to outside companies.

The House expeditiously agreed to the various amendments introduced by the Senate, and on December 21, 1928, the Swing-Johnson bill was signed into law by President Calvin Coolidge. Arizona made one last effort by taking her case to the Supreme Court, but was ruled against in May of 1931.

The final step in the implementation of the Boulder Dam project itself was the sale of the dam's power-producing potential, so that the government would have assurance that the project could pay for itself within fifty years, as stipulated by the Boulder Canyon Act. After sifting through the twenty-seven applications for Boulder Dam power, the Department of the Interior finally signed firm contracts with the Metropolitan Water District (which received 36 percent of the power), the City of Los Angeles (19 percent), and the Southern California Edison Company (9 percent). Arizona and Nevada were each allocated 18 percent, but since neither could yet

Commemorating the signing of the Boulder Canyon Act, December 21, 1928. From left to right: Elwood Mead, commissioner of reclamation; Congressman Phil Swing; President Calvin Coolidge; Senator Hiram Johnson; Congressman Andrew Smith; William Mathews of the M.W.D.

find enough customers for the power, no contracts were signed, and the two states were simply given the right to exercise their claims within fifty years. After more than ten years of haggling, the All-American Canal and Boulder Dam were political, if not yet tangible, realities.

The third component of the three-part Colorado River Project, the Colorado River Aqueduct, took nearly as long to reach even political reality. Surveyors had laid out the route of the aqueduct shortly after the organization of the Metropolitan Water District in 1928; but before any work could be started, it was necessary first to formulate some kind of agreement between the various agricultural districts and the cities of Southern California who had joined the M.W.D. as to allotments of water, then to obtain government water contracts, and finally to manage the passage of a $220,000,000 bond issue for the construction of a diversion dam on the river and the 240-mile aqueduct itself.

The seven party agreement of August 18, 1931, took care of the first problem, and government water contracts followed immediately. After a six-week saturation campaign that took advantage of every means of communication then available (including messages on milk bottles and a sound movie entitled *Thirst*), the voters went to the polls and on September 29, 1931, passed the issue—one of the largest in the region's history and, for its time, an astounding sum.

All stages of the Colorado River Project were now assembled on paper: Boulder Dam, Parker Dam (to store water for Southern California), the Colorado River Aqueduct, Imperial Dam (to store and desilt water for the Imperial Valley), and the All-American Canal. The central factor in the whole project was Boulder Dam; its reservoir would store and regulate water delivered to Imperial Reservoir and to Lake Havasu behind Parker Dam; its bulk would give the users of the river their first workable protection from flood; and the power it produced would give the engineers of the Metropolitan

THE CONQUEST

Water District the energy they needed to lift water 1,600 feet from the river's bed over mountains and deserts to the Coastal Plain of Southern California. Boulder Dam was the key to empire.

THE HARD-HAT AMERICAN ENGINEER, with his khaki uniform, his pocketed slide rule, his tough determination to conquer any obstacle, great or small, was fully as romantic a figure in the 1930's as the American astronaut is today. He had built roads in the mountains of Peru, dams in Asia, and bridges all over the world. His expertise was in demand everywhere; he was considered one of the finest flowers of America's technological coming-of-age. The image was linked to another that captured the fancy of the era: the hard-nosed independent industrialist, whose foresight, integrity, school-of-hard-knocks experience, and gambler's instinct had transformed the face of America and given raw power to the concept of free enterprise. There was a great deal that was false in both images, but there was also enough truth to satisfy the demands of an age that could still look with missionary zeal upon the act of literally remaking the world.

In Boulder Dam the two images were commingled dramatically. It was the biggest dam in the world, an American dam through and through. Its design and construction was a monumental engineering accomplishment; the organization and logistics of the job, a stunning example of America's industrial know-how. The combination was irresistible to the public mind, and before the nation became comfortably smug with a surfeit of technological wonders, Boulder Dam stood as an embodiment of all the material virtues of America.

LONG BEFORE PASSAGE of the Swing-Johnson bill in 1928, the organization of the complex of construction industrialists that would become known as the Six Companies, Inc., creators of Boulder Dam, began slowly to coalesce. The heart of the organization was the Utah Construction Company, founded by a pair of Mormon brothers, E. O. Wattis and W. H. Wattis, in 1875. It was this company that built the seven-million-dollar Hetch Hetchy Dam in 1917, an experience that whetted the brothers' appetite for more such projects. In 1922, their near monopoly of the mountain states was challenged by Harry W. Morrison, of the Morrison-Knudsen Company of Idaho, and the Wattis brothers invited Morrison to join them in a dam-building partnership. "They took me in,"

E. O. Wattis of the Utah Construction Company, who died before the great dam was finished.

Morrison later claimed, perhaps accurately, "on the theory that when the competition gets tough and you can't beat 'em, then join 'em." Whatever the rationale behind it, the partnership was an effective one. It was strengthened immeasurably in 1925, when Frank T. Crowe came into the organization as an engineer to head up its dam-building projects.

After twenty years with the Bureau of Reclamation, Crowe had worked his way up to general superintendent. Tough, hard-driving, imaginative, and daring, he was the living image of the hard-hat field engineer. His life was dam-building, and the Wattis-Morrison combination gave him the opportunity to build dams; between 1925 and 1931, he built two of the biggest in the West—Guernsey Dam in Wyoming and the Deadwood Dam in Idaho. His big dream, however, was Boulder Dam. In 1919, while still with the Bureau of Reclamation, he had helped to make the first rough surveys of the damsite; and as the concept of such a dam slowly worked its way through the tangle of congressional debate, his eagerness increased. "I was wild to build this dam," he later recalled.

H. W. Morrison, *who set out to raise more than three million dollars.*

Charles A. Shea, *who operated out of a hotel room and understood men.*

"I had spent my life in the river bottoms, and Boulder meant a wonderful climax—the biggest dam ever built by anyone anywhere." His enthusiasm fired the Wattis brothers, and when the Boulder Canyon Act became law, they and Morrison began a campaign to get the construction contract from the government.

For the Wattis brothers, it was an astounding venture. Both were in their seventies and seriously ill (neither would live to see the completion of the dam). But the vision of building "the biggest dam ever built by anyone anywhere" was compelling, and they went after it with determination. Surety companies, who would have to underwrite the project, were expected to demand $8,000,000 as a cash guarantee before approval, but Wattis and Morrison were convinced that the figure could be haggled down to a firm $5,000,000. The Utah Construction Company put up $1,000,000; Morrison-Knudsen added $500,000; and then Morrison went out to get the remaining $3,500,000 needed, while Frank Crowe began the enormous task of designing the dam.

The first outside capital that Morrison approached was the J. F. Shea Company, Inc., of Los Angeles, tunnel and sewer-line specialists who had secured contracts for laying the water-supply lines of San Francisco, Oakland, and Berkeley. It was run by Charles Shea, a free-wheeling Irishman who operated the business from a room in the Palace Hotel in San Francisco and was reported to have once said, "I wouldn't think of going near a bank unless I owed them at least half a million dollars—you get respect then." Five hundred thousand dollars was what he contributed to the Boulder Dam project, and his long-standing alliance with the Pacific Bridge Company of Portland, Oregon, brought that organization in with another $500,000. Half of the money needed was now in hand, but W. H. Wattis was forced into a hospital bed with cancer of the hip. He knew he would die and was fearful that his death would leave his brother and the Utah Construction Company hopelessly committed to a speculation that might ruin them both. Harry Morrison's persuasive energies managed to allay the older man's misgivings, and Utah decided to stay.

The next company to add its expertise—and money—

Felix Kahn, who understood the complexities of finance and organization of great projects.

Alan MacDonald, who went through fifteen jobs before his partnership with Kahn.

to the project was MacDonald and Kahn, Inc., of San Francisco, an unlikely combination of Felix Kahn, a quiet Jew, and Alan MacDonald, an impetuous Scottish engineer who had managed to get himself fired from fifteen consecutive jobs in three years before teaming up with Kahn in 1908. Between them, the pair had put up more than seventy-five million dollars' worth of buildings on the West Coast, including San Francisco's Mark Hopkins Hotel. MacDonald and Kahn contributed one million dollars to the Boulder Dam fund.

While this five-way partnership was being assembled, an independent three-way combination was evolving out of the fervent, imaginative brain of Henry J. Kaiser, who was in Cuba in 1928 finishing up a twenty-million-dollar highway contract for the Cuban government and lying awake nights, scheming of some way to get in on the building of Boulder Dam. That scheming finally involved old-line California contractor W. A. ("Dad") Bechtel, who had worked with Kaiser on several projects. Initially, Bechtel was cautious. "Henry," he replied when Kaiser first proposed the idea, "it sounds a little ambitious." But

ambition was one of the driving forces of Kaiser's life-style, and he managed to persuade Bechtel to consult with John Dearborn, chairman of the board of the Boston construction firm of Warren Brothers, who had subcontracted the Cuban job to Kaiser. Dearborn was enthusiastic, and the three men finally entered the Boulder Dam combination as a unit, contributing the remaining $1,500,000 needed.

Eastern surety companies remained nervous, dubious whether any such loose organization of industrialists could hang together long enough to finish the job and skeptical, after examining the balance sheets of the companies (all were rich, but by eastern standards not resoundingly so), whether enough money could be raised; they became more respectful when the Utah Construction Company calmly produced a certified check for $1,000,000, and finally accepted the underwriting contract for the $5,000,000 the combination had raised. In February of 1931, the Six Companies, Inc., was incorporated in Delaware. The next step was the calculation of

Henry J. Kaiser, who lay awake in Cuba, dreaming of the Boulder Dam project.

W. A. ("Dad") Bechtel, who had his doubts: "Henry, it sounds a little ambitious."

costs and the submission of a bid to the Bureau of Reclamation, which had called for a deadline of March 4, 1931.

Frank Crowe had constructed a working model of the dam, and for successive days of deliberation it was wheeled into W. H. Wattis' hospital room in Denver as the Six Companies considered in detail every possible cost of the dam. The figure they finally came up with was nearly forty million dollars. An additional figure of 25 percent for contingencies and profit brought the final bid to $48,890,000—two days before the deadline. On March 3, Frank Crowe worked up the papers on the bid in his hotel room, and the following day it was submitted to the Bureau of Reclamation. In April the three bids finally submitted were opened in an empty store beneath the Bureau's Washington offices. The Six Companies had won. Their bid was $5,000,000 under one competitor, $10,000,000 under the other, and only $24,000 over the Bureau's own estimates. On April 20, they were given the contract.

The Six Companies had won the right to Boulder Dam; now all they had to do was build it.

"Our first hot argument," Frank Crowe recalled, "was over the organization chart. Kaiser thought the job should be run like an army, with a general in supreme charge. The idea got nowhere because no one, least of all Henry himself, wanted to be a private. . . . Kaiser and Morrison always thought of a job in terms of draglines and steam shovels. Kahn figured in terms of money and an organization chart. But Charlie Shea always thought in terms of men. He was the kind of man who'd ask you the time not because he wanted to know, but to see what kind of watch you carried. They were just about as different as any men could be."

It took three months to weld this disparate group of personalities into a working unit. Kahn wanted a board of directors to run the operation and deal with Crowe, superintendent of construction. Kaiser, of course, wanted a single director. The final compromise was a four-man executive committee: Charlie Shea was in charge of field construction; Felix Kahn looked after the money, legal affairs, and feeding and housing the construction crew; Steve Bechtel, "Dad" Bechtel's second son, was responsi-

Boulder City panorama—an instant city in the middle of the Nevada desert where summer temperatures could "fry a man's mind."

ble for purchasing, administration, and transportation; and Henry Kaiser, in recognition of his unique gift of making men work well together, was made chairman of the group. It was a superbly effective combination.

Six Companies laid out and built Boulder City, with all the refinements necessary for survival in the middle of the Nevada desert—including air conditioning—to house the swarms of depression-hungry laborers who flocked to the damsite for work. Roads for the movement of men and materials were cut through the desert, and the Interior Department authorized a branch line of the Union Pacific Railroad from Las Vegas, Nevada, to the bottom of Black Canyon, where machinery for the first stage of the work could be transferred to barges and carried up to Boulder Canyon.

The first stage was perhaps the most dramatic piece of

work in a series of steps whose drama matched that of the Colorado itself: the river had to be turned from its primordial bed and carried around the damsite. The incredible task involved four fifty-foot-diameter diversion tunnels driven through the face of the canyon's walls—two on each side, an inner and an outer tunnel. The outer tunnels would exceed four thousand feet in length, and each would ultimately be equipped with an enormous spillway for controlling the reservoir's level during flood times. The inner tunnels, the eventual basis for the penstock system that would deliver falling water to the hydropower plant at the foot of the dam, were more than three thousand feet in length. Blasting began on May 12, 1931, and eighteen months later—after three nearly disastrous floods, which Frank Crowe feared would "wash us right out of the canyon"—the tunnels were completed.

Perhaps the biggest problem of the dam-builders was the movement of men and materials. Above, a "monkey slide" elevator moves men.

On the evening of November 12, 1932, trucks began dumping rock into the river from a trestle bridge below the point where the river would have to be raised ten feet to flow through the tunnels. For fifteen hours, truckload after truckload—one every fifteen seconds—was dumped into the river, and slowly it began to back up against the barrier. By eleven-thirty the next morning, the river had been raised; a blast of dynamite opened the outer tunnel on the Arizona side, another opened the Nevada tunnel, and the river was turned.

Huge earth-fill coffer dams at each end of the damsite were constructed to wall off the river, and the exposed bed was pumped dry so that digging could commence down to bedrock, one hundred feet below. That point was reached in June of 1933, and the job of

raising a dam between the walls of Boulder Canyon began. By this time, the Six Companies had more than three thousand men scrambling around the bottom and walls of the canyon. "The problem," Frank Crowe said, "which was a problem in materials flow, was to set up the right sequence of jobs so they wouldn't kill each other off." The problem also was the sheer bulk of materials involved (including 3,250,000 cubic yards of cement, more than 3,000,000 board-feet of lumber, 662 miles of copper tubing, and an assorted tangle of wires, cables, pipes, and hoses), as well as the staggering complexity of the operation.

The dam was to be 726.4 feet high from its base, 1,244 feet long at the crest, 45 feet thick at the top, and 660 feet thick at the bottom. Had the dam been poured solid, it would have taken 125 years to dry, and the enormous

THE CONQUEST

Jackhammering at the rock of ages—a crew at work on the lower portal of diversion tunnel No. 1.

pressures exerted on it by its own bulk would have raised the internal temperatures of the concrete to heights capable of warping and cracking it. It had to be assembled piecemeal, like a gigantic game of children's blocks, with individual house-sized forms to take the concrete. There would be 200 such boxes eventually piled together, and each would have a network of copper tubes filled with refrigerant to maintain a steady temperature and consistent drying.

To fill the boxes, the largest concrete plant in the world had been erected on the Nevada side of Black Canyon, half a mile from the damsite. Seventy-eight feet by 118 feet in floor size and rising eight stories to the top of its tower, the plant could manufacture 6,600 yards of concrete every twenty-four hours—an amount equivalent to a stream twenty feet wide, one foot deep, and a mile in length. From the plant, railroad cars would carry sixteen-ton buckets to the damsite. There, overhead cables with skyhooks would pluck them from the cars and swing them out over the forms for pouring. On June 6, 1933, the first bucket skimmed down out of the sky and dumped its viscous load into a form, where waiting men immediately began tamping it down in preparation for the next bucket. For the next twenty-two months the buckets came swinging down to the dam, one almost every minute, as the boxes rose higher and higher in the canyon toward completion.

WHILE FRANK CROWE AND CHARLIE SHEA with their small army of workers watched the canyon walls fill, Henry Kaiser was proving his own worth to the project in a way that none of the partners had expected—as emissary to a sometimes difficult Washington. Early in the construction work, it became obvious that Congress, in its wisdom, had failed to appropriate enough money to keep the work going, so Kaiser journeyed to Washington and managed to lobby through a deficiency appropriation to take up the slack. Later he found himself facing the "terrible-tempered Harold L. Ickes," the New Deal's Secretary of the Interior, who charged the Six Companies with no less than seventy thousand individual violations of the eight-hour-day law. This law required government contractors not to resort to overtime except in emergencies, a device designed to spread the work around in a period of depression. Kaiser's contention that Boulder Dam was a "continuous emergency" was looked upon skeptically by Ickes, who fined the company $350,000. Kaiser was up to the challenge; he hired a press agent to put together a crisis-filled narrative entitled *So Boulder Dam Was Built* and mailed thousands of copies to congressmen and government officials; he went on the radio and invited newspaper interviews to relate how the project's immense obstacles had been overcome, painfully, one by one; he finally entered into active negotiations with the Department of the Interior, and when done had whittled the fine down to $100,000.

But Kaiser's most impressive coup, from the viewpoint of the Six Companies, was in persuading the government that the dam was finished when the Six Companies *said* it was finished. As Felix Kahn later explained: "It's one thing to build a great public work; it's something else to get a government bureau to admit it's finished. Unless you can saw the main job off at a reasonable point, they'll have you adding power equipment, transmission lines, roads, and other extras the rest of your life."

The last bucket of concrete was poured on March 23, 1935; following that, a pure cement mixture was pumped by force into the spaces remaining between the forms until every open crack and cranny of the dam was filled. Already, the diversion tunnels had been plugged to allow the river to start filling up behind the dam, and the diversion works were complete, including four 395-foot intake towers on either side of the river, the great penstocks that would deliver water from them to the powerhouse, and the two spillways and their tunnels on either side of the dam. By early fall, the U-shaped powerhouse (each of its wings as long as a city block and as tall as a twenty-story building) was finished, and although the generating machinery had not yet been installed, Crowe was ready to "saw the job off." On September 30, the dam was dedicated before twelve thousand spectators by President Franklin Delano Roosevelt. Five months later, Kaiser managed to convince the Department of the Interior that the obligation of the Six Companies was fulfilled, and the government took over operation of the dam and all its works.

Four of the principals involved in making Boulder Dam a reality were dead: Arthur Powell Davis, the former Bureau of Reclamation chief who had been instrumental in the dam's authorization, died in 1933; W. H. Wattis died six months after the Six Companies had won the contract; his brother, E. O. Wattis, died in 1934; and "Dad" Bechtel died in 1933 while on a trip to the Soviet Union. In addition, 110 of the thousands of men whose muscle and sweat had brought the dam to creation had died in the act, some by heat exhaustion and heart attacks, some by drowning, some by falls, and some, so rumor would have it, by being buried alive in the very body of the dam they had helped to build.

But the Six Companies had won a great prize: a profit of $10,400,000, prorated according to the capital contributions of the partners. Frank Crowe's share, besides a relatively modest salary for the five years' work, was

"There's something peculiarly satisfying about building a great dam," Frank Crowe remarked. *"You know that what you build will stand for centuries."*

President Franklin Delano Roosevelt delivering his Boulder Dam dedication address, September 30, 1935.

$300,000. The Six Companies held together for another six years, going on to build Parker Dam, Bonneville Dam and power plant on the Columbia River, Grand Coulee Dam on the same river, and the great piers for the San Francisco-Oakland Bay Bridge; and Frank Crowe himself would build Shasta Dam in California. But nothing, it is safe to say, would remain in their memories with the same fervency as the *massif* of Boulder Dam. "There's something peculiarly satisfying about building a great dam," Frank Crowe observed. "You know that what you build will stand for centuries." And Boulder Dam was not just a great dam—it was the greatest dam in history.

EVEN AS THE CONCRETE BLOCKS of Boulder Dam were climbing in the canyon of the Colorado, work on the second phase of the Colorado River Project—Parker Dam and the Colorado River Aqueduct—had begun; the first was hampered by political infighting that quickly took on the outlines of a gigantic farce, the second by a series of geographical obstacles that made its completion perhaps the most difficult in the long history of aqueduct-building.

Reclamation Bureau and Metropolitan Water District engineers arrived at the site of Parker Dam, about 150

miles south of Boulder Canyon, early in 1934 to begin drilling operations to determine the depth of bedrock. Arizona, still smarting over her rejection in Congress, announced that she would oppose—by force if necessary—any construction activity on her side of the river. Since Congress had not yet stipulated Parker Dam as a specific part of the Colorado River Project, Arizona's action had a certain legal standing, but the engineers ignored it; in order to hold drilling barges in the river, they anchored a cable on the banks of both sides of the river. Arizona's Governor, B. B. Moeur, then sent a contingent of militia to the area to "protect the rights of the State and report at once any encroachment on the Arizona side of the river." The military force injudiciously took to a pair of very antique ferryboats called the *Julia B.* and the *Nellie T.,* which were immediately dubbed "battleships" of the "Arizona Navy" by irreverent newspaper reporters covering the affair. After a most humiliating reconnaissance of the drilling operations—which culminated in one of the boats getting tangled in the cable and her crew being rescued by the enemy—the crestfallen members of the Arizona Navy retreated upstream. They later made their way to the damsite by overland transportation, and camped there throughout the miserable summer.

NOTHING FURTHER OCCURRED until November, when the reconnaissance party reported that the Six Companies, which had taken on the contract for the dam, was starting to build a trestle bridge toward the Arizona side. Governor Moeur declared the area under martial law and ordered the ejection of all trespassers and the repulsion of the "threatened invasion." Before an actual physical confrontation could occur, the battle was transferred to the courts, where an injunction by the Supreme Court, supported by congressional action specifically authorizing Parker Dam, finally took away Arizona's power to interfere.

Six companies immediately completed their trestle and, following the technique used in Boulder Canyon, drilled diversion tunnels; the river was then backed up by a rock-fill dam and forced around the damsite. If Boulder Dam was the world's tallest dam, then Parker Dam was the "deepest," for excavation crews had to dig down 233 feet before reaching bedrock. When completed in August of 1938, the dam was 320 feet high—but two-thirds of that height was below the river bed. Its reservoir, called Lake Havasu, impounded and desilted enough water to provide

Images of the Colorado: III

The Dam Builders

Boulder City . . .

"A bowl formed by barren, unsympathetic mountains had been selected for the site of the town," Theodore White reported in *Harper's* magazine. "It was a deadly, desert place." But the technology capable of building a Boulder Dam was equally capable of erecting a working city, complete with air conditioning, in the midst of sandstorms and brutalizing heat to house thousands of job-hungry refugees from the worst depression in American history. "The 'stiff' has never lived so well," White went on. "His comfort is greater than he can remember ever experiencing. . . ."

Man and the Colorado . . .

The immense scope of the Boulder Dam Project is suggested by the photograph above, right, a view of the river as it flowed free between the gargantuan walls of Black Canyon in 1922. The ultimate site of the dam is marked by the small point jutting into the river in the center of the picture. Conquering such an outsized example of time's handiwork required every tool that the ingenuity of man could provide — including hundreds of tons of dynamite to blast the walls of the canyon free of loose rock, to build roads where roads had no business existing, and to burrow tunnels into rock older than recorded time. Such enormous blasts as the one shown at the right, below, were planted by "cherry-pickers," one of whom is seen at the left. His rakish nonchalance was typical of men whose daily work included the possibility of a free fall through nearly a mile of sheer nothing.

Drilling Jumbos and Flash Floods . . .

The first task was to take hold of the river and turn it, so that work could be started on the dam itself. Diversion tunnels more than three thousand feet in length were rammed into the canyon walls; the portals of two of these are seen in the photograph above. To speed the operation, enormous "drilling jumbos" were devised (above right) to drill holes for the dynamite charges in the faces of the tunnels. Work in the tunnels was miserably hot; temperatures as high as 152 degrees were recorded, and heat prostration accounted for at least thirteen deaths. If that were not enough, there were periodic flash floods to contend with; on February 10, 1932, one of these broke through the levee protecting the tunnel portals and filled the excavations with three feet of water (below right).

Four Truckloads a Minute . . .

With the diversion tunnels complete, on the morning of November 12, 1932, the first of one hundred dump trucks rattled out onto the trestle bridge spanning the river and spewed its load of rock into the water — which was roaring past the bridge at 7,000 cubic feet a second. For the next fifteen hours, four truckloads of rock a minute were dumped into the river. When it had backed up behind the barrier to a height of ten feet, a dynamite blast opened the levees in front of diversion tunnel No. 4 and the stoppered river flowed into it. "She's taking it, boys!" a workman shouted. "She's taking it!" In less than a year, the river had been turned from a course it had laid down ten or twelve million years before.

Incessant, Monstrous Activity . . .

In *The Colorado,* Frank Waters described the scene as men and machines cut their way down to bedrock between the cofferdams that had sealed off the river: "The vast chasm seemed a slit through earth and time alike. The rank smell of Mesozoic ooze and primeval muck filled the air. . . . Down below grunted and growled prehistoric monsters. . . . They were steam shovels and cranes feeding on the muck, a ton at a gulp. . . . And all this incessant, monstrous activity took place in silence, in jungle heat. . . ." By June of 1933, bedrock had been reached and the first of the more than three million cubic yards of concrete that would go into the dam had been poured into a form and tamped down by encrusted workmen. "Two-thirds of the four thousand and more men employed on the dam . . . have at varying times and in different degrees been subjected to a college education," Theodore White wrote in *Harper's.* "This is a curious commentary on modern society. One is a little startled by the figures and feels that something is unaccountably wrong with a system that can utilize education to no better end than pushing concrete about a dam."

The Masonry of a Cyclops...

The complexity and megalithic bulk of the great dam would have rivaled the masonry of a cyclops. The scores of men scattered over the top and sides of the monster in the photograph at the left are rendered almost invisible by the sheer immensity of what they are building. Overhead, like a spider on a web, a bucket containing sixteen tons of concrete skims down toward one of the house-sized forms. On December 5, 1934, as the dam was shaping toward completion, the three millionth cubic yard of concrete was lowered to its top (below), and by March 23, 1935, the last bucket had been poured. In all the fervid rejoicing that followed the completion of "the greatest engineering structure of the twentieth century," the words of Theodore White alone carried a hint of reflection on the dam and its meaning to the men who had built it: "It is an extraordinary existence out there.... The men work with an enforced intensity and play with hilarious looseness. Their existence is a continual thrill, centered about the callous, cruel lump of concrete in the bottom of the canyon. And they love it. From designing engineer to lowest laborer, they are acutely aware of the immensity and importance of the dam. To them, it assumes a personality and they are devoted to it.... In each there is a feeling of ownership, but I think they have never paused to calculate the cost in terms of humanity."

COLORADO RIVER SYSTEM

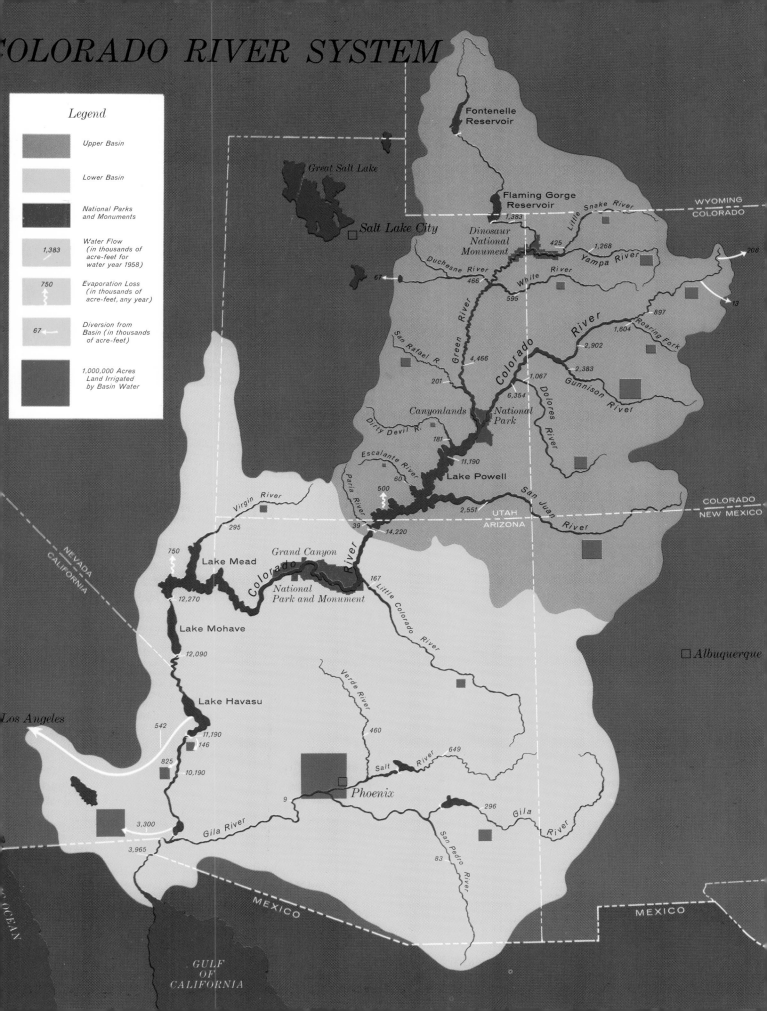

Legend

▨	Upper Basin
▨	Lower Basin
▨	National Parks and Monuments
1,383	Water Flow (in thousands of acre-feet for water year 1958)
750	Evaporation Loss (in thousands of acre-feet, any year)
67	Diversion from Basin (in thousands of acre-feet)
▨	1,000,000 Acres Land Irrigated by Basin Water

Fontenelle Reservoir

Great Salt Lake

Salt Lake City

Flaming Gorge Reservoir
1,383

Dinosaur National Monument

425

Little Snake River

1,268

WYOMING
COLORADO

208

Duchesne River
466

White River
595

Yampa River

Roaring Fork
897

13

San Rafael R.
Green River
4,466

Colorado River

1,604
2,902

2,383

207
1,067
6,354

Dolores River
Gunnison River

Dirty Devil R.
Canyonlands National Park

181

Escalante River
60
Parla River

11,190

Lake Powell

500

San Juan River

COLORADO
NEW MEXICO

2,551

UTAH
ARIZONA

Virgin River
295
39
14,220

750

Lake Mead
Grand Canyon
Colorado River

National Park and Monument

167
Little Colorado River

12,270

Lake Mohave

12,090

NEVADA
CALIFORNIA

Lake Havasu

□ Albuquerque

Verde River
460

Los Angeles

542
11,190
146
825
10,190

Salt River
649

Phoenix

3,300

9

Gila River

296
Gila River

3,965

San Pedro River
83

MEXICO

MEXICO

GULF OF CALIFORNIA

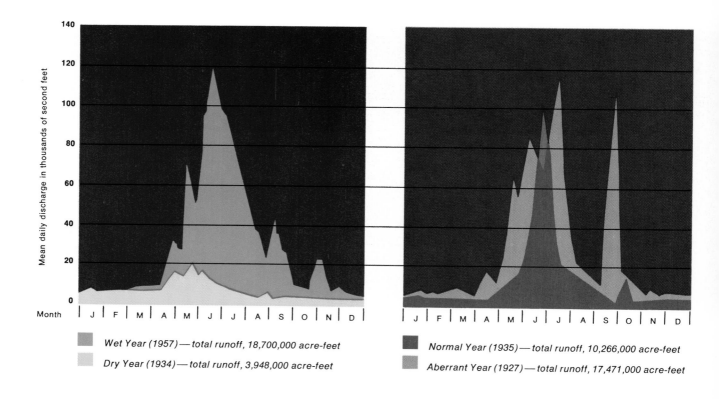

Wet Year (1957) — total runoff, 18,700,000 acre-feet	Normal Year (1935) — total runoff, 10,266,000 acre-feet
Dry Year (1934) — total runoff, 3,948,000 acre-feet	Aberrant Year (1927) — total runoff, 17,471,000 acre-feet

THE COLORADO AND THE LAW OF DIMINISHING RETURNS

At first glance, any map of the Colorado River system can easily deceive the viewer with the illusion of a water resource fully as voluminous as it is long and complicated. After all, it courses 1,700 miles from its source in the Rockies to its mouth in the Gulf of California, and is fed by a score of major tributaries and countless minor tributaries draining a region of more than 245,000 square miles, or 157,000,000 acres, one-twelfth the area of the continental United States. And to look upon a still-wild stretch of the Colorado during flood season, as the river plunges in a powerful brown tangle of water constricted between canyon walls, is to feel a momentary kinship with men who saw in this river the means by which the arid Southwest of America would be transformed into an enormous garden, who saw it as an inexhaustible tool of empire.

It was not—a fact that we are belatedly ready to admit. The 245,000 square miles that the Colorado drains has an annual average rainfall of only ten inches, only one-eighth of which ever survives to contribute to the volume of the river (the rest is lost through evaporation on the ground or by transpiration through the leaves of the basin's plants). What that one-eighth means to the volume of the river is illustrated by the tables above, and the map on the preceding page shows what happens to that volume before it is able to reach the Gulf of California. Aside from what is lost through evaporation from the surface of the system's man-made lakes (as much as 750,000 acre-feet in any given year from Lake Mead alone), great quantities of the river's flow are diverted to various reclamation projects within and without the basin, from the Gunnison Valley of Colorado to the Imperial Valley of California, and to such urban-use areas as Los Angeles. The effect of this evaporation and diversion varies from year-to-year, depending upon rainfall, but during a dry year the Colorado's flow at the mouth could be diminished to what one critic has called "an effluent trickle of brine."

This is what the Bureau of Reclamation means when it says that the Colorado River is "over-committed"; this is what it means to cripple a river.

The power of falling water was translated into energy and carried across the deserts to Southern California.

the 1,110,000 acre-feet that would ultimately be taken from the river by the Colorado River Aqueduct.

The aqueduct itself got underway on January 25, 1933, when the tunnel crews of Frank Weymouth, the Metropolitan Water District's chief engineer, broke ground on the first of the system's forty-two tunnels, which, when complete, would comprise the equivalent of a single tunnel ninety-two miles in length. Some mountains between the river and the Coastal Plain, however, could not be tunneled safely; to get the water across them 144 siphons were installed, many of them up to twelve feet in diameter. In other areas, the water had to be pumped over the mountains, 1,605 cubic feet a second being lifted as high as 441 feet at a time through five pumping stations scattered along the system's 241-mile length; each of these stations contained three great electric pumps, and together they required a great share of the Metropolitan Water District's Boulder Dam power allotment.

In addition to the tunnels, pump lines, and siphons, some sixty miles of open canal had to be gouged out of the desert sands. For this job, two immense, complicated machines that looked like relics of an antediluvian world were invented: the "canal-trimmer," a great welter of moving machinery which slowly ground its way across

A five-hundred-ton rotor is lowered into a dynamo casing in Boulder Dam's powerhouse.

Parker Dam, shortly after its completion.

the sand a foot at a time, cutting out the canal bed to precise dimensions; and its ugly cousin, the "canal-paver," which followed behind, laying down concrete and tamping it all in the same smooth operation. Like dinosaurs, the machines were unique to their time and place; when the job was done, they disappeared, done in by their own bulk and technological evolution—but for a time their crawling, clanking progress across the landscape provided one of the most eerie sights ever encountered on the American desert.

By use of such machines and nearly eleven thousand workers, the aqueduct was finished in 1939; water was delivered to Lake Mathews, the terminal reservoir 241

miles from Lake Havasu, in November, 1939, and from there to the cities of the Metropolitan Water District by the spring of 1941. The second phase of the largest integrated reclamation project in history was complete.

The final phase of the project, the All-American Canal and Imperial Dam, required one more power move on the part of the by now well-experienced Phil Swing before it could be prodded into being. Although the Boulder Canyon Act of 1928 had appropriated funds for the project, the government had put off beginning the work in the face of pressure from other states demanding funds for their own irrigation projects; by 1933, not a spade of earth had been turned, even while Boulder Dam itself was well underway. Swing carried his case to the Department of the Interior, and when they remained reluctant, to President Roosevelt himself, accompanied by an impressive array of supporters. The tactic was effective, and on October 24, 1933, the necessary money was released to start work on the canal.

The builders of the eighty-mile All-American Canal had obstacles of their own to overcome, particularly the shifting, unstable sands of the Walking Hills west of Pilot Knob, through which engineers would somehow have to force a concrete ditch faster than the moving sand could fill it in. The device utilized was another monster of a machine—a 650-ton dragline crane so large that it took twenty boxcars to carry its parts into the desert. Equipped with two flat mechanical feet to keep it from sinking of its own weight in the sand, the machine dug its way through the Walking Hills by "walking"—seven steps at a time. A shelf fifteen feet wide on either side was created and sprayed with oil or planted with vegetation to keep the sand from drifting into the finished canal.

In the meantime, in 1936, work began on Imperial Dam. Considerably less complicated and bulky than either Boulder or Parker dams—it was only twenty-five feet high—Imperial Dam was finished by 1938, complete with six sprawling desilting basins to clean the water of the particularly heavy deposits that the river then carried in its lower reaches, the accumulation from more than fifteen hundred miles of eroded territory. It supported two canals: the small Gila Gravity Main Canal, an awkwardly-named component on the east side of the river, and the mighty All-American Canal, which by the time of Imperial Dam's completion was nearing the final stages of its own construction.

On October 13, 1940, the first water from Imperial Dam reached the Imperial Valley via the All-American Canal, and by March of 1942 the valley had completely abandoned the old Imperial Canal of 1901. For years afterward its wandering, fifty-mile length stood as a kind of historical footnote—the remnant of a simpler culture whose little dreams of empire could not begin to match the sweeping vision of a society grown large and terribly efficient.

And so the great dream, the conquest of the Colorado, had finally come to pass, after men had schemed and planned for more than forty years to capture the river and make it their own. Never again would the river go on crushing rampages during its flood season; never again

would its thick, life-giving waters flow untapped to the sea while crops lay withering in the sun and men sweltered with thirst in the cities of the plain; never again would the river run free.

THE COMPLETION of the Colorado River Project was more than the fulfillment of forty years of dreams, however; it was, in many respects, the technological culmination of an epoch, that strange, badly focused, and vaguely confusing period we call the 1930's, a time of shrill hope and violent despair, of revolutionary political and social theories, and a time of vigorous and sometimes bloody confrontation between the haves and the have-nots; an age, in short, that could celebrate with a whole-souled gusto the spending of more than four hundred million dollars on the Colorado River in the middle of the most brutal depression in the history of America—and make heroes of the men who had spent it.

The age that followed it, neatly set off by the bloody convulsion of World War II and perhaps glutted by all the technological wonders of the war itself, could find little magic in dams, canals, reservoirs, and the like. The day of the earth-mover as one of the symbols and celebrations of the nation was diminished, if not gone forever. An ever-growing circle of opinion even held that the earth-mover was a fool, a destroyer, a villain stupidly tampering with the environment in a way that would bring ruin to it and to the legacy of future generations—surely a concept almost incomprehensible to men who had once gloried in the assurance that they were the great builders and makers of America.

Which is not to say that the conquest of the Colorado stopped with the completion of the Colorado River Project. It had hardly begun, for the Bureau of Reclamation was in the business of building dams, and the concepts of fifty years were not easily altered. World War II had just ended, in fact, when the next addition to the Colorado's dam complex was started. In 1944 the United States signed an international treaty with Mexico, guaranteeing that nation 1,500,000 acre-feet of Colorado River water a year. In 1946 the Bureau started construction of Davis Dam, about halfway between Parker and Boulder (by then Hoover) dams, to regulate the delivery of water to Mexico. It was completed in 1953, and was soon followed by Mexico's own Morelos Dam, below the border. Another dam was added to the lower river in 1957, when the Palo Verde Diversion Dam was com-

THE CONQUEST

Celebrating the opening of the All-American Canal, the last phase of the Colorado River Project.

pleted as a flood control and irrigation project, and still another when the Headgate Rock Diversion Dam was strung across the river a few miles below Parker Dam.

The upper stem of the Colorado got its first major project with the completion of the seven-hundred-foot Glen Canyon Dam in 1965—a dam that surely matched the scope and drama of Boulder Dam itself, but which somehow failed to capture the public imagination and support that the earlier, pioneering effort had enjoyed. The Green River—the Colorado's left arm—had received Flaming Gorge Dam earlier, and above it, the Fontanelle Dam. The Bureau of Reclamation has from time to time proposed additional damsites on the main stem of the Colorado-Green, although so far the agency has been blocked in its efforts on several fronts.

BY NOW the Colorado River Project has swollen to become the Colorado River *Basin* Project, taking under its supervisory wing an area one-twelfth the size of the forty-eight states—245,000 square miles, or 157,000,000

acres. The Bureau's reclamation proposals for this immense territory were contained in its Pacific Southwest Water Plan of 1964, which formed the basis of its forthcoming requests for legislative authorization of a number of projects whose total cost exceeded $1,250,000,000—more than three times the cost of the Colorado River Project of the 1930's. In addition to the fourteen dams already in operation on the Colorado and its tributaries, the Basin Project calls for another twelve (two of which are already under construction), together with numerous major and minor diversion and irrigation works. Two of the largest projects proposed were a dam at Marble Gorge and the Central Arizona Project. Marble Gorge Dam, in the words of the Bureau of Reclamation, "would be the initial cash register unit for the project. The revenue from the sale of power produced at its power plant would help pay for the construction of all facilities proposed." Responding to various public pressures, the Bureau has decided to "defer" this particular project to some indefinite future, which by no means implies that

Imperial Dam, whose narrow concrete bulk was a monument to the enterprise and persistence of Imperial Valley investors.

it has been abandoned. The Central Arizona Project, which includes a three hundred-mile open canal to divert 1,200,000 acre-feet of Colorado River water from Parker Dam to central and south-central Arizona and four multipurpose dams on the Gila River system, was authorized by Congress in 1968.

Even while it makes its proposals on such a grand scale, the Bureau has long since recognized (with Major John Wesley Powell, who came to the same conclusion in 1893), that there simply is not enough water in the Colorado River to support them: "Demands for water may very well exceed the remaining uncommitted supplies within the next 25 or 35 years." An obvious solution to the problem, in the Bureau's view, is to go to another source to supplement nature's lack of foresight, and the source instantly mentioned has always been the Columbia River. The Pacific Northwest has let it be known in no uncertain terms that it rejects the whole idea, but the Bureau is confident that the area's reactionary stand can be overcome diplomatically. As Regional Director Robert

J. Pafford, Jr., put it in a 1966 speech before the Southwest Regional Water Resources Symposium, "We can see no reason why an import aqueduct should not serve both regions with multipurpose water benefits. Our entire western water program has been built on statesmanship. We feel confident that this same statesmanship will prevail and that the water 'haves' can share with the water 'have-nots' with both of them reaping multiple dividends."

In less than seventy years, then, the wildest, freest river in the West has already been transformed into one of the greatest plumbing systems in the history of the world, and future developments seem destined to convert the entire river system into an enormous pipeline. Surely this will be one of the most admirably expansive engineering marvels of the century, and yet...

We are allowed to wonder whether the Bureau of Reclamation has ever heard of the Red Queen's admonition to Alice: "Continue until you get to the end, then stop." We are also allowed to wonder if there is anyone left who will ever again want to write a poem to a dam.

CHAPTER VII

TRIUMPH AND FAILURE IN THE IMPERIAL VALLEY

A Case History in the Misuse of a River

Helen Hosmer

The Imperial Valley of California is one of the richest farming areas in the world. Once a part of the Colorado Desert, this man-made garden spot is a monument to the individual vision and enterprise, the public policy and energy that have converted millions of acres of the arid West to productive use. At the same time, Imperial Valley is something less than this dream of realized fruitfulness implies; it is at once the realization of a dream and its denial; it is a land of bitter contrasts, a place where a confrontation of public policy and private power calls into question the entire purpose of western reclamation.

The issue which faces Imperial Valley—and the American people—is simply whether or not public reclamation efforts are for the development of what we think of as "family farms" or for the benefit of what Californians have come to call "agri-industrialists." Imperial Valley, as its farm economy exists today, is dependent upon the Colorado River dams and canals built by the government. At the same time, these rich lands—acre by acre more productive and profitable than the most avaricious dreams of the homesteaders who settled the trans-Mississippi West—are held or worked by people more accurately described as industrialists than as dirt farmers. "A man cannot make it on less than a thousand acres around here" is a statement that drops lightly from agricultural experts and ranchers in Imperial Valley.

At the present time, the Department of the Interior has challenged not only the assumption that an Imperial Valley farmer needs a thousand acres to get by, but also the right of any landowner to receive water for more than the 160 acres specified by the reclamation law as the maximum holding that publicly subsidized water may irrigate. This concept is very simple and not at all new. But the application of it is far from simple, for Imperial Valley is not ordinary and is not new. The beneficiaries of Hoover Dam and its subsidiary works, the owners and operators of Imperial Valley, may with good color of reason maintain that they are the legitimate inheritors of this empire; that they, or their predecessors, created this garden out of nothing, and that they, with their efficiency, their energy, their willingness to experiment, to improve, and to develop, are entitled to what they have.

What they have—these men who pour a quarter of the Colorado River across their parched fields—is not what public land or reclamation policy ostensibly was created to foster. Nor were these lands developed by means which were in accord with the spirit of the laws for the disposition of the public domain. In the present there lies a question of important public policy. But the question is not newly risen; rather it is a heritage of the past, of the history of the development of Imperial Valley.

ON VISITING IMPERIAL VALLEY one may get the impression of the American Dream suddenly gone wrong: The giant farms are getting bigger; migrant laborers form the labor force for the absentee agri-industrialists; young Americans are leaving the valley for want of jobs; the towns—in a period of unparalleled prosperity—seem to be withering away. Industry avoids the valley. A 992-acre farm (nearly what a man needs "to make it") nets $580,000 on one year's subsidized cotton crop, while grocery clerks and truck drivers get less than half the gen-

Hop-picking in the Imperial Valley, Mt. Signal in the background (Dorothea Lange photograph, 1935).

eral California scale. Yet there is nothing *suddenly* gone wrong. Imperial Valley never was a place built by the kind of effort and the kind of people we associate with the notion of the farming frontier.

"Misbegotten at the outset," Carey McWilliams has said, striking to the heart of the matter:

Misbegotten at the outset, Imperial Valley has always had the character of an aborted community: a half-formed, twisted, ill-conceived mongrel. The social affairs of the valley have always been as badly snarled as its financial affairs. Indeed, the tangle of social relations reflects the original cross-purposes which came of the fateful attempts to undertake for private profit a development which was essentially public in character.

Imperial Valley is an offspring of the Colorado River. Once a part of the Gulf of California, the valley was cut off by the deltaic deposits of the river. The river itself built the barrier which stretches from the neighborhood of Yuma to the Baja California shore, separating the below-sea-level valley from the gulf.

In modern times, since the first sixteenth-century Spanish explorers, the river has flowed into the gulf. But time and again before this, through millennia rather than centuries, the river has switched its course, now to the gulf, now to the inland sink. The most direct route to the gulf carries the river along the southeastern side of its delta. The shortest channel to the sink of the Colorado Desert would employ the Alamo Barranca, on the northwest side of the delta. Between these two channels is a meandering system of overflow channels, mostly tending toward Volcano Lake, situated on the crest of the hump formed by the delta silt. Waters that found their way to Volcano Lake during flood periods flowed both to the south through Hardy's Colorado, and to the north, through the New River.

In the long past the untamed Colorado was a river of wild extremes. Though one of the major rivers of the continent, it carried very little water at its lowest stages. (For example, in November of 1775, Anza, who had previously crossed the river on rafts, was able to wade across the stream.) But each June when the melted snows of the Rockies reached Yuma, the river would be a grand torrent, carrying fifty, a hundred, even a hundred fifty thousand cubic feet of water past a given point each second. Each cubic foot of water might contain as much as a quarter-pound of silt—more silt to build a delta already as deep as a thousand feet, a delta made up of the entire original contents of the Grand Canyon and much more.

IMPERIAL VALLEY is composed of the rich alluvial soil laid down by the Colorado River. To irrigate this potentially fertile desert, it was necessary only to turn a part of the Colorado; for with the river riding higher than the valley, with already established channels coursing through the desert, the water would run from the river to the valley of its own accord. The idea was so startlingly simple that someone thought of it almost immediately after California and the Colorado River were acquired by the United States.

Dr. Oliver Meredith Wozencraft took the credit for thinking up the grand scheme, and it is simple justice to accord him the title, "Father of Imperial Valley." For Wozencraft not only perceived the notion of irrigating the valley, but he also built a far greater scheme, a plan whereby he might gather to himself all of the benefits of that development.

Wozencraft, born in Ohio, educated in medicine in Kentucky, first came to the Colorado Desert by way of Yuma on his way to the California placers in 1849. In the desert crossing several of his party nearly collapsed, and Wozencraft set off on his mule to search for water. He must have been standing on the banks of the Alamo Barranca where it crossed the boundary from Baja California to swing north toward the sink when he got his great idea. "It was then and there that I first conceived the idea of the reclamation of the desert," he later wrote. What he must have seen was that the northward-tending Alamo could with a little improvement be made to carry river water across hundreds, thousands, of square miles of the downward-sloping desert.

A man of many interests, Wozencraft became a member of the California Constitutional Convention, a commissioner of Indian Affairs, and in 1856 a lobbyist for the Atlantic-Pacific railroad project. In this latter role he found himself advocating the central route ("Let the great national heart send forth its mighty pulsations through the central artery, transmitting and diffusing life and culture to all members of the confederate body") and damning the proposed southern route across the Colorado Desert, pointing to "the great absurdity of locating a road over a desert, a country in which even a coyote could not get an honest living."

If Wozencraft was still developing his vision of watering the desert, one must assume that he just did not want any land-grant railroads going through his potential pasture. Indeed, he suggested the desirability of "private enterprise" constructing a southern route. And in another place he put forward a theory that has a sinister ring to it in light of his later project—that, slavery being unprofitable in the South, freedmen might well thrive in desert areas unfit for white habitation. "I deem it necessary... that a proper field should be opened for our superfluous black population," he said.

In 1859, just three years after he had told a San Francisco audience that "God in His wisdom had placed His permanent seal of desolation on the [Colorado] desert," Oliver Wozencraft asked the California legislators to give it all (and more) to *him*—six thousand square miles of it! *And they did,* "in one of those grand gestures which the young west made so beautifully towards its pioneers." They gave—but it was not quite theirs to give; essentially their gift was a petition to the federal Congress, an endorsement by California of the excellent motives in his avarice, a guarantee that the California delegation would assist him in sequestering the public domain.

Dr. Wozencraft went to Washington. He had gathered every bit of available data about the desert, and he approached Congress with an impressive display of whatever information was favorable. The negative report of John Russell Bartlett of the 1852 boundary commission he dismissed as the narrow vision of a narrow man; he embraced and circulated instead the words of Professor Blake of the Pacific Railway survey:

The Colorado River is like the Nile.... If a supply of water could be obtained for irrigation, it is probable that the greater part of the desert could be made to yield crops of almost any kind. By deepening the channel of New River... a constant supply could be furnished to the interior portions of the desert.

Bᴜᴛ ʙʟᴀᴋᴇ ᴜɴᴅᴇʀsᴛᴏᴏᴅ ᴄʟᴇᴀʀʟʏ the mechanics of the Colorado delta and he added the prophetic words (which Wozencraft ignored), "It is indeed a serious question, whether a canal would not cause the overflow once more of a vast surface, and refill, to a certain extent, the dry valley of the ancient lake."

Blake reasoned that over the ages the river changed its course many times—first flowing to the desert sink through the Alamo and New River channels until the sink became a deep inland lake, and then to the sea, leaving the lake stranded until, in the burning desert heat, it evaporated.

He could see clearly the shoreline of the "ancient lake" (which he named "Cahuilla" after an Indian tribe) forty feet above sea level. But more significantly, he could also see that the "warping-up" of land near the river and along its inundation channels suggested that the river was fast approaching the point that it might swing back to an inland course once more. He could see that the river had overtopped its banks at high stages near Pilot Knob, from which the flood flow was westerly along the course of the Alamo Barranca. The jungle-like growth of the mesquite, screwbean, willow, wild hemp, and carriso that matted the low banks and clogged the barranca stopped the flow from cutting its main channel into the Alamo—for the descent from Pilot Knob to the bottom of the sink was much steeper and shorter than the channel to the sea.

By May 1862 Wozencraft had convinced the Public Lands Committee of the House of Representatives that it suited the interests of God, the National Spirit, and Progress to turn over the Colorado Desert to private enterprise. It was no secret that Wozencraft was to be the beneficiary. One may well wonder at the sense of timing involved in attempting a land grab of such proportions *one week* after the passage of the Homestead Act. Congress, less pliable than the California legislature, refused Wozencraft, yet he kept trying through the summer of 1862. He seems to have felt that his failures were the result of a congressional preoccupation with the Civil War. And he did not stop trying: at the age of seventy-three (in 1887), he was back in Washington again offering a Colorado reclamation bill. While it was being crucified behind closed doors in committee, the great dreamer died.

The men who brought the first farmers into the Colorado Desert in 1901 were more sophisticated than Wozencraft. Charles Robinson Rockwood and C. N. Perry were construction engineers for the Southern Pacific Railroad, familiar with handling men, money, and materials. Anthony Heber and Sam Fergusson were land agents of the Kern County Land Company. They knew the art of coaxing settlers to western farmlands. It had been their daily bread. All four men had seen the railroad in action long enough to feel that the big money was easy money if one could seize the moment.

Their plan for developing the desert was simple and appealing. They staked a claim to twenty thousand acre-feet of Colorado River water, posting a notice near the salt cedars where the river flowed, and filed for a canal right-of-way from the federal government. They let it be

Calexico in 1904. Already, the nourishment of Colorado River water has caused the desert to blossom.

known that they were about to bring river water to the rich delta lands, which anybody could buy from the government for $1.25 an acre—up to 160 acres under Homestead Law or 320 acres under Desert Land Law. They incorporated (in New Jersey) as the California Development Company with $1,500,000 in capital stock and then started their long and desperate scramble for actual cash. Along the way they picked up a Yuma promoter named Blaisdell and an army surgeon named Heffernan, both of whom knew their way around the desert and had some financial backing.

Events in California played into their hands. By 1900 Southern California was sweetly scented with orange blossoms and wetted with irrigation ditch water; land prices were soaring. At the same time the famous irrigation engineer George Chaffey, promoter of the successful Ontario and Etiwanda projects in California and more recently the unsuccessful Mildura project in Australia, was not only available but burning to recoup his losses from the Australian fiasco. The moment was ripe. On April 3, 1900, Chaffey signed a contract with the California Development Company to bring the Colorado River

to the desert.

Chaffey planned to build his headgate at Pilot Knob, just north of the Mexican border; bypass the barrier of the sand dunes (the "walking hills") by cutting his canal parallel with the river for four miles; connect with the ancient overflow barranca called the Alamo in Mexico; improve its channel for the next fifty-two miles westward; and install another control works on Hall Hanlon's land, where the Alamo River entered the United States. The Mexican lands through which the canal must pass belonged to General Guillermo Andrade, who had long sought to tap the Colorado River and establish an agricultural empire on the Mexican half of the Colorado delta.

BEFORE THE FIRST WATER came through the system, the settlers were on their way. They had seen the brochures: government land at $1.25 an acre, to be watered at a cost of fifty cents an acre-foot! They arrived to do battle with sandstorms and scorpions . . . with coyotes that came right up to their flapping tents or ramadas . . . with water—half mud, half rusty-red grit—scooped up into basins and settling pans . . . blistering, eye-searing, skin-

Looking east to the town of Imperial, 1904—a discouraging scene of shacks, brush ramadas, and tents in the middle of a wasteland; yet people saw what they wanted to see.

scorching heat . . . desert winds blowing sand through the cracks of flour barrels, tearing down the tents, scattering pots and pans . . . the delta always on the move ("What? You ain't seen the country yet? Look out the door and you'll see a hundred miles of it go by in five minutes!"). Candles for light, butter kept in gallon bottles and sold by the pint, cut lengths of mesquite brought from Flowing Well and priced at ten dollars a ton . . . the March sun setting the mud like stone, the steady heat baking it, seaming it with cracks and gullies . . . the little greasewood bushes clinging to the silt like iron shafts sunk in concrete, to be pulled up one at a time by a team of horses dragging chains ("a quarter-section takes a man four, five weeks just to clear").

The first three families were Bill Van Horn, his wife, and six children; Frank Gilette, his wife, and seven children; and Lawrence Van Horn, four children, and no wife—all in a caravan from the Salt River Valley, bringing two Fresno scrapers, ten crates of chickens, five cows, and a bull. They arrived in January, 1901, before Chaffey's ditches were carved out. The three men started digging. The two women tried to keep the seventeen children from getting lost to the sandstorms or the rattlers.

George Chaffey's biographer, J. A. Alexander, builds a story ending in the betrayal of his hero at the hands of the California Development Company. Alexander says Chaffey had not seen the company's books (he was told they were in Jersey City) and had his sleeves rolled up before he learned he had signed with a bankrupt company. Confronting Heber, Rockwood, Ferguson, and others, he tore up the contract in their faces; created the subsidiary Delta Investment Company (wherein he placed all the assets of the project purchased at fifty cents on the dollar; changed the name Colorado Desert to Imperial Valley; demoted Rockwood to "assistant engineer"; ousted Fergusson as advertiser; organized a second subsidiary known as the Imperial Land Company to promote settlement; and, with a Riverside publicist in charge of promotion, set up his own system of mutual water companies to operate through a tricky device called tri-party agreements. He hired engineer Perry to gather a crew and make a survey; bought the Mexican land from Andrade; gave Hanlon $20,000 for his worthless piece of swampland; paid the delinquent tax bill in Jersey City, made himself

An overflow of Calexico in 1900—building and selling and dreaming of empire in the Colorado Desert.

president of the California Development Company *and* the Delta Investment Company, raised capital among his friends in Los Angeles, and began digging a canal on Thanksgiving Day, 1900. Six months later a trickle of red, muddy river water came through the boundary ditch at the new town of Calexico, and the wooden headgates at Hanlon's Heading were completed on May 14, 1901.

Chaffey had dug an unlined, wavering canal and built a wooden, temporary headgate to coax a wild, silt-heavy river riding from twenty-five to two hundred feet above sea level along the very rim of the valley toward down-sloping desert land. Had that been his only contribution, the $300,000 with which the original promoters bought him out, in a quick squeeze play guised as the "Rockwood Syndicate," would have been a high price indeed. But Chaffey had given them more than a crude canal and a wooden headgate. He had perfected a magic formula for debasing the intent of the Homestead and Desert Land acts. He had designed a mechanism for turning water appropriation into land appropriation.

THE CALIFORNIA DEVELOPMENT COMPANY took water out of the Colorado. It "sold" the water to its dummy Mexican corporation—the *Sociedad y Terrenos y Irri-*gación de la Baja California—which conveyed the water to Calexico. "Mutual water companies" (whose membership was composed of the farmers who were going to use the water) in turn bought it for fifty cents an acre-foot, delivering it to the individual users at that cost, plus a small annual per-acre charge for the construction and operation of the necessary local ditches. The mutual companies, in consideration of a contract to provide all the required water at this modest cost, gave the CDC all their "water stock."

The water stock was the key to the operation. Water would be delivered only to the holders of water stock. The stock was issued at one share to the acre. It represented no tangible asset; it was a "right" to get water, and, as such, water stock was often referred to as "water rights." Under the rules set up by the CDC, a parcel of land had to be completely "covered" by water stock before *any* water would be delivered. Thus, the farmer who filed on 160 acres had to buy 160 shares of water stock. The "retail" price of water stock was about $25 a share.

To this point it would appear that the CDC, which owned or had owned all of the water stock represented in hundreds of thousands of acres laid out on paper by the eight mutual companies (all of which, needless to

Downtown Brawley in 1905, before water had yet had a chance to enrich the town as it was enriching the land around it.

say, had been organized and officered by the CDC inner circle), was doing no more than selling at an exorbitant price bits of that appropriation notice tacked up near Pilot Knob. But the system had better possibilities. The CDC had responsibilities; it had to maintain its works. It had to *deliver* as much as four acre-feet of water a year for each share of water stock, and do it fairly cheaply, too. Hence the formation of the Imperial Land Company. The Imperial Land Company did not originally have a large amount of land to sell; the CDC–Imperial Land Company promoters had bought up school sections, filed on parcels as individuals, and picked up some Indian reservation land scrip, but the basis of the successful operation of the Imperial Land Company lay in its ability to purchase huge blocks of water stock from the CDC at low prices.

A PROSPECTIVE FARMER (or speculator) bought his water stock from the Imperial Land Company, which also helped him file his claim to government land. If a prospect wanted to file on a full 320 acres under the Desert Land Act, the Imperial Land Company would discount the $7900 worth of water stock 10 percent for a cash sale, or (as was more usual) hold the water stock against a

6 percent note. This note in effect was a mortgage on the land, for without the water stock the land was worthless. Under the Desert Land Act the farmer could get a patent on his land as soon as he "proved up" his water and paid the nominal $1.25 per acre—which in practice meant that within a few weeks or months of the time that a farmer made his deal with the Imperial Land Company the land was technically his. If he defaulted in his water-stock payments, it was inevitable that the land would come into the possession of the Imperial Land Company. Water stock was land.

More direct methods of taking possession of land were exposed in the U.S. District Court 1908, when several directors of the Imperial Land Company were convicted of a conspiracy to defraud the government. They had been unable to resist the temptation of hiring people to file on desert land for them. At 320 acres per filing, with water to be "proved up" almost instantly and at little cost, section after section of the public domain fell into their hands, often to be resold quickly in large parcels. Testifying at their Los Angeles trial, the accused directors, pleading guilty to the charges, all declared that their sole intent had been "to encourage settlement . . . and dispose of water stock acquired in the course of work done for the promotion and extension of the water system in the district."

Thus the Imperial Land Company soon had many thousands of acres to sell, as did its insiders and associates. They owned the towns. Special trains kept the big tent in Imperial City filled with buyers on auction days. Town lots captured the speculative spirit of even penny-ante plungers. And townsite boundaries expanded in easy accommodation to the sound of paper rustling in the hot offices of the Imperial Land Company, as discounted water stock was exchanged for money. The manipulation of water stock explains the empty treasuries of the CDC and the mutual water companies, and the bursting coffers of their rich brother, the Imperial Land Company. Discounted water stock explains the ten thousand acres purchased by the Hammers in 1904. Water stock explains the government's desperate move to rescue its dwindling public domain by challenging the land survey, thereby holding up many final grants until the illegal manipulation could be halted. Water stock gave W. L. Holt (the hero of Harold Bell Wright's popular novel, *The Winning of Barbara Worth*) the townsite which became Holtville and the farming district organized under Mutual Water Company # 7. Holt acquired eighteen thousand shares of water stock for $50,000; stock was land, mortgages, banks.

Water stock *was* land, but in the peculiar, once-removed sense that already was appropriate to Imperial Valley. In a way water stock, millions of dollars' worth of it, represented nothing but a cheap headgate on the Colorado and some indifferently scraped-out overflow channels—two or three hundred thousand dollars' worth of work at the most generous estimate. Technically, the water stock was not even that; it represented only the right to buy water delivered through these works, or to take over the works in case water was not delivered. On this rock Imperial Valley was founded.

I N 1904 THERE WERE seven thousand settlers in the valley. One hundred thousand acres had been taken up, though not all of it was watered: there was not enough money in the mutual water companies to build the needed canals and ditches. The Southern Pacific Railroad had extended its line through Calexico, and a party of Los Angeles bankers arrived to be feted at the ranch of the California-Mexican Land and Cattle Company—one thousand acres of lush crops around Calexico, managed by Walter Bowker for Harrison Gray Otis of the

Los Angeles *Times,* and his partner, General M. H. Sherman. Below the border, C & M held another 876,000 acres, with 15,000 acres of it watered by the Colorado River through the CDC's waterworks, which also watered Charles Rockwood's 9,000 acres and the acres of other CDC directors scattered within the boundaries of the fifty-two miles of the "Mexican Company." By 1904 the lands below the border were drinking up seven times as much river water as the lands in Imperial Valley, all without benefit of water stock.

In 1904 dairy yields in the valley were $100,000; barley, $150,000; hay, $125,000; cattle feed, $75,000; and other crops—honey, vegetables, fruits, turkeys—$700,000. It appeared that melons were going to create a new market, and cotton samples had aroused enthusiastic reactions in the East. There were around ten thousand head of cattle, several thousand horses and mules, and many thousands of hogs. Holt's brother Leroy announced a gain of 26 percent at his bank. The Western Union opened offices in the valley; a horse racetrack was being graded; the first cement curb and sidewalk was laid in front of the new brick Hotel Imperial, built by the Imperial Land Company; ten Pullman cars and a diner arrived with two hundred people to attend a sale of town lots; the auctioneers sold $50,000 worth of land in one day; Miss Charlotte Preston bought 101 books for Imperial School with money she had raised entirely herself; the Women's Christian Temperance Union held temperance meetings and offered a gold medal on the best essay; and Holt urged greater church attendance to combat the sin and evil creeping north from Mexicali.

I N 1904 ROCKWOOD AND HEBER were locked in mortal combat for control of the CDC. No two men were better suited to kill the goose that had laid their golden egg; no two men could have been less endowed with the qualities of strong, honest, dedicated leadership that were needed for the solid and logical development of the prematurely blooming valley.

Heber—small, slick, dapper, wearing pince-nez glasses and a thin, knowing smile, quick to anger, well versed in both hard and soft sell—was entirely ignorant of, and even more indifferent to, the subtle, precarious balance of the Colorado's channel. Rockwell—large, heavy jowled, bearlike, carrying a deep, slow-burning resentment (frustration and anger at the unpredictable, unmanageable river, fury at the slick manipulators who

were forever doing him out of the fruits of *his* idea)—
was so preoccupied with CDC politics that in the spring
he left the problem of getting water to the farmers' crops
to his assistant and went to Los Angeles to round up
support to oust Heber.

Early in March, 1904, the new spring crops were
planted, and the main canal was silted up solid for four
miles, Rockwood's dredge utterly inadequate to the task
of clearing the channel. The farmers watched their
parched crops, their dry ditches, muttered about law
suits, talked about the government's new Reclamation
Service, about its plan for the Laguna Dam at Yuma
and about cheap water on 160-acre farms and no interest
charges. William E. Smythe, the famous Irrigation Congress pamphleteer, came to the valley to tell the farmers
how to formulate a water users' association and to talk to
them about the Reclamation Service. Heber had already
tangled with the Reclamation Service.

I N AUGUST, 1903, the service had filed on eleven thousand acre-feet of unappropriated waters of the Colorado and announced a grandiose plan for harnessing the
lower basin of the river with four dams and reservoirs,
hydroelectric plants for each, plus canals to irrigate
1,200,000 acres. This was a direct challenge to the CDC
monopoly. Anthony Heber met this challenge with a
boast that was to touch off an immediate controversy
and lead to regrettable consequences. In February, 1904,
Heber told J. B. Lippincott, chief engineer of reclamation
in the Southwest, that the original twenty thousand acre-
feet claimed by the CDC (a small portion of the Colorado's annual flow) was sufficient to give the company
practical control of the whole river forever! Lippincott
asked Heber if he would mind repeating that to his colleague, Frederick H. Newell. Heber obliged. The newspapers broadcast the story. When the Reclamation
Service, in reaction to Heber's grotesque boast, declared
that the Colorado was a navigable stream in theory, in
historic use, and by treaty with Mexico, and that nobody
had any absolute right to remove water from a federal
stream, a wave of apprehension swept the valley.

The counterthreat of the Reclamation Service was
political hay for Imperial promoters. With their whole
empire reared on fraud or near-fraud, they were understandably disturbed. *Somebody*—if not everybody—must
be out to "get" them. It was the government! First there
had been the infamous U.S. Department of Agriculture

soil report of 1902, which had said that 35 percent of the
delta, including much of the lands slated for irrigation,
was too alkali-laden to be reclaimable. "Alka-LIE-
Report!" the valley press jeered—nervously. Then there
had been the resurvey questioning ownership of the land
itself. And now this!

Heber had provoked a showdown and had no recourse
but to press it to its logical conclusion. As Smythe said
later, "You have aroused a sleeping lion, Mr. Heber!"
Senator Perkins and Representative Daniels were induced
to sponsor a bill declaring the Colorado River to be more
useful for irrigation than navigation. The hearings on the
bill started in Washington on March 21, 1904.

At the hearings, the chief protagonists were Heber and
Smythe—Department of the Interior officials stayed away.
Bit by bit Smythe exposed the inner workings of the CDC,
its chicanery, basic corruption, its 400 percent yearly
profits garnered from the settlers, and its water giveaway
to the Los Angeles syndicate in Mexico. "These gentlemen", said Smythe, "have gone in there and claimed the
melting snows of the Rocky Mountains as their property
. . . should the Congress remove the government's only
claim to the river by declaring it to be no longer a Navigable Stream, they would be giving it away forever to
the California Development Company."

H IGHLIGHT OF THE HEARING was a query by a Mr.
Hitchcock, a committee member: "Then you think
there should not be any limit to the profits a private corporation should be permitted to earn while taking the
public waters of the river and irrigating and controlling
largely the public lands?"

"I am opposed", Heber answered, "to the government
interfering in every instance with the private property
and . . . profits of any private corporation."

In the end Heber was so discredited that even Daniels,
sponsor of the bill, voted with the committee to kill it
after a memo from the Department of the Interior ad-
vised that international treaties with Mexico forbade
congressional redefinition. Heber, nearly hysterical before it was all over, made a threat: "It is my earnest
desire to worship at our own altar and to receive the
blessing from the shrine of our own government, but if
such permission is not granted, of necessity I will be compelled to worship elsewhere." And he went on to translate his oratory by announcing that he had in fact already
initiated talks with Mexico whereby a new intake would

*Given time enough and water enough, the soil carried down from
the Colorado Plateau would sprout anything that would grow.*

be cut below the border, placing the valley's use of Colorado River water entirely outside the jurisdiction of the United States.

On June 10, Heber signed a contract with Mexico for a Mexican intake and appropriate headworks.

The summer floods brought some water and much silt to the valley. Reclamation Service men, accompanied by Smythe and Paul Van Dimas, came to the valley at the request of the settlers and helped them organize their water users' association. Heber, playing the game with a disarming show of sincerity (while furthering plans for the Mexican cut) offered to sell the CDC for $5,000,000; the settlers countered with $1,250,000. Through the efforts of W. L. Holt, the price was compromised at $3,000,000. Holt and C. S. Lombard went to Washington to persuade President Roosevelt to buy.

While Heber stalled for time by dickering to sell the CDC to the government for $3,000,000, Rockwood was busily dickering in San Francisco to sell the CDC to the Southern Pacific Railroad for $200,000. Mr. E. H. Harriman's Southern Pacific men, Epes Randolph and W. J. Doran, were not slow to see what the CDC had to offer beyond an underdeveloped waterworks, an empty treasury, and serious responsibilities. The CDC had an extremely valuable asset in its Mexican subsidiary, which held one hundred thousand acres of irrigable delta lands below the border. The new Mexican intake, which would

solve the silting problem, defeat the Reclamation Service, and remove the irrigation of both Imperial Valley and the Mexican lands forever from the meddling authority of the United States, would cost about $200,000, Rockwood said. Randolph agreed to the proposal, subject to Harriman's approval; Rockwood promised to deliver CDC board approval. The contract would take the appearance of a loan, the $200,000 "to be used by it [the CDC] in paying off certain of its floating indebtedness and in completing and perfecting its canal system." In return for this "loan," the CDC would turn over majority control to the Southern Pacific, which would take entirely to itself any proceeds from the sale of the Mexican lands. Heber would be out, and Rockwood would remain on the board of directors and continue as chief engineer.

Making good his threat, Heber had anticipated Rockwood in ordering a cut to the CDC canal from the Mexican part of the Colorado. Rockwood, whatever he may have felt about the advisability of making a cut before there was money to build an adequate protective headgate, accepted the decision and pressed the work forward, either from motives of political policy, or the need of the farmers for more water, or both. By the end of September, 1904, the 3,300-foot cut from the river to the canal was complete. The river was now ready to change its course from the Gulf of California to Imperial Valley. The channel that it sought had been dug for it; there was

*Colorado Country: From beauty, utility, as the incipient agri-
industrialists of Imperial Valley cut into the river's flow
(Escalante River, near Lake Powell).*

An Imperial Valley farmer of 1904 digs a few spadefuls of earth from the
banks of a ditch, and the desert is made to pay off the mortgage.

no gate to close it off once it started its run for its ancient lake bottom, the Salton Sink.

AMONG THE FARMERS of the valley there was thought only of melons and alfalfa, of the need for *plenty* of water. In September the Brawley *News* reported:

"There is fully three times [as large an] opening just below Pilot Knob [as] there was last year. A few miles down the river the company seems to have dug another opening which will empty into the main canal where it is badly filled up. Thus we feel confident there will be all the water that will be needed to irrigate every acre that can possibly be put to crop this fall!'

Holt and Lombard were still in Washington. They sent a wire to Heber at the end of September saying negotiations for the sale of the CDC to the United States looked hopeful. Heber decided that the time had come for a mass meeting.

Heber and Van Dimas (representing the Reclamation Service) shared honors on the platform of the crowded meeting hall at Brawley in the first week of October. Heber, wearing his enigmatic smile, stood up and dropped his bombshell: he was withdrawing his offer to sell; the water was now being taken from Mexico—the government could not own and operate concessions in Mexican territory. Van Dimas tried to speak. Heber shouted to the settlers that, if they signed with the government, every

foot of canal would be closed down, the spigot would be turned off. He whipped them, and himself, into a fury. Van Dimas, he brayed, had led them on with false promises in order to put them out of business.

Van Dimas had no chance. The valley psyche, aroused by the anxieties of the complicated issues, the overwhelming need for water *now,* found in Van Dimas the object of its passion. The farmers grabbed him, dragged him outside to the waiting barrel of tar and bag of chicken feathers. Afterward they rode him south on a rail, gathering support on the way, traveling the eight miles south to Imperial, then down through Cameron Lake and Calexico to the border, where they tossed their wretched object to the Mexican police. They went back after that to what had been described as "the fattest, longest barbecue and the most expensive fireworks display in the history of the Colorado Desert," courtesy of Anthony Heber and his associates.

Heber had won. In January, 1905, the Department of the Interior, while affirming the navigability of the Colorado and the freedom from preemption of its waters, recognized the claims of Imperial Valley and declined to interfere—if it had ever had any such intention—with the passage of water through existing canals. But as for the purchase of the CDC, its tangled affairs, the poor condition of its canals, headgates, and ditches, the uncertainty of the soil resulting from alkali, and the million or

Colorado Country: Not even a determined speculator like Anthony Heber could have transformed country like this into a real estate promotion—but he might have tried (Utah Maze, from Maze Overlook).

The spreading, uncontrolled river washes out the tracks of the Southern Pacific, 1905.

so dollars in debts of the company, as well as the lack of law whereby the government could deal with the problem of water taken through the Mexican intake, made purchase appear "unjustifiable at that time."

The Mexican intake was nothing less than a breach in the riverbank which the Colorado had been seeking to break through—sometimes with partial success—for decades. The disaster which followed on the heels of the Mexican cut was the result of many things that might not have happened, but did; yet it was not just an unfortunate accident but rather a fitting, and almost inevitable, result of the political preoccupation and financial irresponsibility of the CDC. Of the millions of dollars' worth of paper assets that had passed through its hands, of the hundreds of thousands that at one time or another must have lain in its coffers for a few days, there was not enough at hand to build even a temporary headgate to control the flow of water into the new cut. (Rockwood's deal with the Southern Pacific had, of course, to await board approval and the board would not meet until June.)

The first small winter flood came down the river in February of 1905, bringing silt that clogged the new intake. Dredges were set to work deepening the channel. A few weeks later came another flood, in March a third. Rockwood grew nervous, threw a dam across the intake.

A fourth flood in April swept the dam away. Still, any anxiety seems to have been confined to Rockwood and his assistant, Perry. In the valley there was only praise for the flow of water, except at the New Liverpool Salt Works, at the bottom of the sink, which was being gradually submerged by the overflow. The melon crop excited everybody; freight-car loadings were at a new peak. Rockwood and Heber went to Jersey City for the directors' meeting: Rockwood won. The Southern Pacific was in and Heber was out. Heber returned to organize support in the valley, but his days of glory, tar, and feathers were over. He went to Goldfield, Nevada, a fair prospect for a jobless promoter. There he died in a hotel fire, never having laid eyes on his greatest monument, the Salton Sea.

In August, 1905, the river took charge in earnest, rapidly caving in the banks of the intake, deepening and widening its new channel. Southern Pacific engineers sought to check it with a dam of pilings and brush mattresses, but on November 30 the Gila River flooded and was swallowed by the Colorado, which in a single angry, red torrent smashed the dam and widened the breach to six hundred feet. The sink was already a vast lake, the New Liverpool Salt Works buried under sixty feet of water which had risen seven inches daily, spreading out until it was over four hundred square miles—an inland sea in the heart of the desert.

THE WHOLE COLORADO RIVER was pouring into Imperial Valley. Its force washed out the silt of the New and the Alamo rivers as though it were sugar melting. Rapids formed. The rapids grew into cataracts. The cataracts became falls, falls that cut back, upstream toward the river, at the rate of hundreds, even thousands, of feet a day. Widening the barrancas as it deepened them, the river in the space of a few months carried down to the Salton Sea four times as much silt as was excavated in building the Panama Canal. But it was the "cutting back"—not the filling of the sink nor the damage to the farms and towns along the widening, crumbling barrancas—that caused the greatest dismay: if the barrancas were cut too deep they would become useless for irrigation and drainage; if the river cut back to Yuma, it would not only destroy the government's new Laguna Dam then under construction, but it might well dredge itself a channel *below* sea level, making it all but impossible to return it to its original channel toward the gulf.

As the intake became wider, Southern Pacific's engineers built a $60,000 barrier dam. When the November flash flood came down the Gila and the swollen Colorado discharged 2,300,000 acre-feet of water, the barrier dam was smashed like a broken toy. And now the Salton Sea was lapping against the sixty miles of main Southern Pacific tracks. Five times the track was moved to higher ground.

There were two problems: to turn the river back, or not to turn it back entirely. There was a flood to check, but there would be shriveled crops surrounding an inland sea and thousands of people as well as crops dying of thirst if the river were turned back completely.

On April 19, 1906, Rockwood was relieved of his duties, and engineer H. T. Cory, aided by Hind and Clarke, took over. In June the crevasse was a half-mile wide and the river, spread out over an eight- to ten-mile width, collected in separate streams as it ran down the slope of the basin discharging into the Salton Sea. Thousands of acres were inundated, and thousands more eroded and furrowed, useless forever. Calexico and Mexicali were partially destroyed. Thirty thousand acres of cultivated land in the western part of the valley were cut off from water, became dry, barren and uninhabitable when the wooden flumes carrying irrigating water were swept down into the Salton Sea.

After six tries, the break was closed on February 10, 1907, all the water again going down the old channel

In an attempt to close the breach in the river's west bank, piles were driven for a brush dam.

toward the gulf. It had taken 2,057 carloads of rock, 321 carloads of gravel, and 203 carloads of clay, all dumped into those swirling waters, to turn the river back. It had taken a labor force of six Indian tribes: Pima, Papago, Maricopa, and Yuma from Arizona, Cocopah and Diegueño from Mexico—four hundred men and their women and children (two thousand in all), set up in camps and policed by *rurales*. And the Southern Pacific Railroad footed the bill. E. H. Harriman was the hero of the hour: he had saved the valley.

VERY FEW SETTLERS were aware of the fact that Harriman had had no choice. As President Theodore Roosevelt pointed out in a fascinating exchange of telegrams with Harriman, the CDC belonged to the Southern Pacific. As parent to the delinquent child, it was up to the Southern Pacific to put Humpty Dumpty back together again. Harriman's denial that the CDC was a Southern Pacific enterprise had a hollow ring. On the President's desk were masses of documentation concerning the CDC and its labyrinthian crosshatch of deals, contracts, lawsuits, and interlocks including, of course, the contract with Southern Pacific which had given the CDC to them for $200,000.

In the long run, Southern Pacific had little to complain about, for being heroes of the flood had paid off hand-

Four times the runaway river broke through restraints before the break was finally closed in 1907. Above, an S.P. train inches its way over inundated rails.

somely. It had cost them more than a million dollars to put the river back into its old channel. They had collected $700,000 from the government for their trouble. The $200,000 they had "loaned" the CDC was nearly covered by the $171,523.37 worth of notes and mortgages they held. They had sued Rockwood, Heber, Heffernan, Mrs. Rockwood, and Blaisdell, and had collected some $270,000 more in capital stock. They had a lawsuit pending against George Chaffey for $900,000. They had repaired and greatly strengthened their tracks and extended them into Mexico. When they sold the decrepit waterworks back to the farmers of Imperial Valley in 1912, they asked for and received $3,000,000, a sum which did not include the assets of the mutual water companies nor the valuable Mexican lands. For the canal system, drainage system, and equipment, the people paid $7,500,000 more. It was only the beginning of the bond issues needed to keep the water of the Colorado River flowing toward the irrigated farms of Imperial Valley. Was it any wonder that the farmers swallowed their pride, forgot their hostility, and began the long courtship of government which brought about Hoover Dam, Imperial Dam, the All-

American Canal, and the hydroelectric plant at Pilot Knob? They had paid and paid for a faulty, malfunctioning waterworks and for battles with a river which they could not control. They would pay no more—at least very little more.

THE DEVELOPMENT OF IMPERIAL VALLEY can be seen from different points of view. It has generally been seen as a struggle against nature, a fight in which the champions of American progress, whatever their occasional personal defects, wrested a new land from the bleak Colorado Desert. Another way that the story might be told, one that has not been done, would be to tell of the "grass roots" development of the valley, the story of the Desert Land Act farmers who themselves built the farm economy of the valley, who cleared the land, planted crops, and turned the water onto the land. These points of view are legitimate enough—but one may ask, Are they the central, the peculiar, factors in the development of the valley?

The answer must be no. For the men who organized the California Investment Company, the Delta Invest-

*Waterpower: Haystacks in Imperial Valley give mute refutation to Oliver Wozencraft's dictum that
"God in His wisdom . . . placed His permanent seal of desolation on the . . . desert."*

ment Company, the Imperial Land Company, the mutual water companies, two separate Mexican companies, and many special-purpose companies related to these were not essentially interested in bringing water to the settlers of the desert. They were interested, rather, in making money on the appreciation of desert lands. Their means of bringing water to the desert were so incidental to their purposes that the raw power of the Colorado River was affronted, and in the disastrous floods of 1904-6 is seen the fitting climax of their work.

As for the hardy farmers who settled the valley—who were they? For the most part, they appear to be energetic speculators, more eager for a quick cash turnover than for a homestead to bequeath their heirs. The very nature of the Southern California economic climate and the pitch of the Imperial Land Company promotion tended to draw people who looked for a swift killing, farmers who saw a short and lively future in turning 320 acres of desert into green fields that would bring a hundred dollars an acre. This is why the proposals of the Reclamation Service, proposals which would have brought long-term benefits of the greatest magnitude to the small

farmer in the valley, could be defeated by the farmers themselves. To be sure, not all farmers were so short-sighted; to be sure, the more powerful interests in the valley exploited specious arguments against the Reclamation Service; but it is absurd to assume that so many people were dupes where their own closest interests were involved. The majority, at least the majority in terms of influence and energy, were on the side of the quick-buck promoters, "Why can't you leave us alone?" was their response to the Reclamation Service in 1904.

The heritage of Imperial Valley's misbegetting is an economic and social climate that is almost the complete reverse of the Jeffersonian ideal imbedded in the Homestead Act, the Desert Lands Act, and the Reclamation Act—even in the promotional literature that brought settlers to the valley. The events in the history of the valley have imposed an ownership pattern and a social view which demand that the most powerful interests in the valley must fight tooth and nail against the federal government's effort to impose acre limitations on the use of Colorado River water delivered from Hoover Dam. Again the cry is raised, "Why can't they leave us alone?"

221

PART THREE:

THE LEGACY

223

INTRODUCTION

PERHAPS THE MOST compelling aspect in the story of man and the Colorado is the fact that this river is one of the most used rivers in America and that its utilization has been particularly exploitive and damaging. The traditional uses of rivers for commerce and communication, for the establishment of centers of civilization, and as integral units of regional and national life have been exploitive, certainly, but these uses have depended upon the preservation of living rivers for their purposes. The Colorado has not—indeed, could not—be so used. Unnavigable except for a small portion of its lower reaches and situated in an environment uncommonly resistant to the civilizing influences of man, the Colorado could never have become what many wanted it to become— the "great natural thoroughfare" of the West. No great cities clustered on the river's banks; no bustling port for the commerce of the world sprouted at its mouth.

Yet the river did have something to offer man: water. And driven by the conviction that the Colorado was pre-destined to be the great fountain of the American Southwest, man proceeded to exploit it. The futility of that dream has been demonstrated. The Colorado was no more capable of watering all the desert wastes of the Southwest than it was of floating coal barges from the Rocky Mountains to the Gulf of California. We refused

to acknowledge this fact, however, until we had already plunged great concrete wedges into the river through the greater part of its length and altered its existence for the sake of our own. This legacy we have given to the generations that will follow us is an exercise in misapplied expediency; its monolithic crudity and pointlessness are thrown into embarrassing relief when compared to the legacy that the river itself has created. For the river and its canyons have a value that transcends the shortsighted purposes to which man and his eager technology have put them. They are a part—perhaps the greatest single part—of what Wallace Stegner has called "the geography of hope", and as such surpass in lasting usefulness all the dams the ingenuity of man could ever contrive.

America has developed the most astounding technology on the face of the earth. This is no small achievement, nor is it something we should lament. Technology has been the genius of America and an integral part of our culture; to insist that our dependence upon it is in some way a distortion of America's meaning is to deny history. There are few today who would willingly abandon the creature comforts that technology has provided; indeed, there are some who probably could not survive without them. What must be lamented, then, is not technology itself—which is precisely as "good" or as "bad" as the men who control it—or even America's inevitable love affair with it; rather, it is the misapplication of that technology, for it is that which is threatening one day to create a society in which it will be quite impossible to live. We can no longer quietly endure our own stupidities. The concept of a mass man, with which most social critics were infatuated not so many years ago, takes on chilling overtones when it is realized that what we are facing is not some rarefied theory concerning intellectual "class" but the very real existence of *masses of men* sweltering in their own frustrations, trapped in an environment that provides fewer and fewer guarantees of spiritual or even physical survival. Within such a society, every technological mistake, every misapplication of our own genius, is a potentially deadly threat to the quality of our future existence—or to existence itself.

This is not a particularly new concept, nor has it been stated here in a particularly fresh way. Yet it is one that needs to be emphasized within the context of this book, for while the Colorado has been one of the most thoroughly damaged victims of technological miscalculation, it also has created one of the most spectacular of those wilderness landscapes whose very existence is a kind of spiritual salve for the agonies of civilization. Aside from the opportunity wilderness provides for the standard recreational delights of fresh air, exercise, and escape into serenity—it also offers a man new measures of his meaning. The games people play to impress one another and themselves lose their point when confronted with such landscapes. A phenomenon like the Grand Canyon may make a man feel small or it may make him feel large—it does not matter which. The point is that it compels him to feel *something,* to respond to his own existence with a force of recognition that the society in which he normally functions cannot inspire. For a man standing on the bank of the Colorado and gazing up at the Canyon's rim—or for one standing on the rim and gazing down at the river—the term "self-realization" may acquire meaning, perhaps for the first time. That is a spiritual dividend whose value a world beginning to strangle in its own inadequacies cannot afford to underestimate, for if a man somehow can acquire true measure of himself—a satisfaction, even a celebration, in himself—there is hope that he will have the strength not only to survive the pressures of a society grown large and all but incomprehensible, but to help change and even reduce them.

That is the final, most important "use" of the Colorado River. That is its legacy. That is why this book was written.

CHAPTER VIII

PILGRIMS, POETS, AND RIVER-RUNNERS

The Grand Canyon as a National Experience

THE PILGRIMS

"Leave it as it is," Theodore Roosevelt said in the spring of 1903, while standing at the edge of Grand Canyon. "The ages have been at work upon it, and man can only mar it. What you can do is to keep it for your children, your children's children, and for all who come after you, as one of the great sights which every American if he can travel at all should see."

Americans have rarely paid much heed to the admonitions of their presidents, particularly those that could not be enforced, but in the case of Grand Canyon they have followed Roosevelt's instructions with a cheerful enthusiasm. Grand Canyon is preserved throughout most of its length as a national park and through the rest of its length as a national monument, and while we have not left it precisely as it was in Roosevelt's day, neither have we marred it to any appreciable degree. The closest threat was the Bureau of Reclamation's Bridge Canyon Dam proposal of 1964, which would have backed water up into the National Monument, but such a chorus of outrage greeted the idea that the Bureau ultimately gave up the plan—at least temporarily.

Moreover, Americans have paid almost religious obeisance to Roosevelt's doctrine that the Grand Canyon was something "which every American if he can travel at all should see." No one, so far as is known, has ever taken a poll to determine how many Americans have visited Grand Canyon, but the percentage must be astounding; of those living who have not visited it, most are probably planning to do so in the near future; the rest may be just too poor to consider it. Every year, millions of "pilgrims," including the lame, the halt, and the blind, gather at the North or South Rims of the Canyon to soak in its wonders. For most, it is their first trip, but for others it is the fifth, sixth, or tenth—for Grand Canyon fever, like malaria, can strike its victims with periodic regularity.

Even to those who have not seen it, and will never see it, the Grand Canyon is quite "real," visually, through seventy years of propaganda, including movie travelogues, television specials, photographs, postcards, paintings, drawings, calendars, brochures, pamphlets, pocket manuals, poems, magazine articles, newspaper stories, Sunday supplement vignettes, and books.

In brief, the Grand Canyon has become a national pride, a national heritage, a national experience.

The history of this phenomenon is a short one, for the Grand Canyon remained relatively unvisited during the first great age of the western tourist—the 1870's. While curiosity-seekers and communers-with-nature had discovered and broadcast the delights of Yosemite Valley, the Garden of the Gods, the Big Trees, and the parks of the Rocky Mountains—and had inspired the creation of Yellowstone National Park in 1872—it was not until the late 1880's that a significant trickle of tourists began to cross over the tableland country between Flagstaff and

This dapper, superbly nonchalant tourist spoke for a generation of Grand Canyon pilgrims. The purpose of the blue ribbon is a mystery; perhaps he stood closer to the edge than anyone else.

THE LEGACY

Captain John Hance, trail guide, hotelkeeper, and the Grand Canyon's "official prevaricator."

the South Rim to take in the Grand Canyon. It was a hot, rough, two-day trip over primitive roads via stagecoach, and once arrived there was not much to do but look at the canyon, look at it some more, and go back—unless one wanted to listen to the wondrous lies of Captain John Hance or pay a dollar to risk a broken neck by clambering down his handmade trail to the canyon floor.

THIS DOUGHTY INDIVIDUAL had come to the area in 1881 as an itinerant prospector in search of whatever he might turn his hand to. He found instead the Grand Canyon, and although he did discover a small asbestos mine in the bottom of the canyon, it was never more to him than an excuse to remain. He simply fell in love with the biggest hole in the world, and remained infatuated until the day of his death nearly forty years later. "Oh, he believed in God, I guess," a friend once said of him. "But mostly he believed in the canyon." He planted a cabin in a wooded area near the eastern edge of Grand View Point, raised a few cattle, carved out a trail six thousand feet to the bottom of the canyon, picked desultorily at his asbestos mine, and spent most of his time wandering the canyon bottom and rims. When a heavy rain washed out his original trail, he found an old Indian trail, refurbished it, and characteristically named it "Hance's Trail." When the tourists began to drift in, Hance became the Canyon's first Chief Guide and Tour Director, and by the mid-1880's he was advertising in the Flagstaff newspaper:

> Being thoroughly conversant with all the trails leading to the Grand Canyon of the Colorado, I am prepared to conduct parties thereto at any time. I have a fine spring of water near my house on the rim of the Canyon, and can furnish accommodations [sic.] for tourists and their animals.

Hance was an accomplished liar, a teller of tall tales who could have held his own with a Jim Bridger, a James P. Beckwourth, or any one of the other mountain men who had raised the outlandish fib to the level of a minor art. Two of his tales have become classics, of a kind. In one, Hance has been chased by a hungry bear and, in his haste to climb a handy tree, has dropped his gun. For a while, the bear does nothing more than throw a few rocks at him, but he soon notices the gun, picks it up, looks it over, throws it to his shoulder and gets off three wild shots at the cringing Hance. "I do believe," the Captain's next line always went, "that if there'd been another cartridge in that gun he'd 'a got me, sure." This would be followed by silence, at which point some innocent straight man in the audience was sure to ask, "What happened then?" "Oh, by-and-by he got tired and ambled off," the Captain would reply. If things went right, the straight man would again speak up: "Did he take the gun?" The Captain would smile, slowly. "Well, no, he didn't. You see, there was *some* honor in him." The second story was reserved for those times when the canyon was packed from brim to floor with fog, the top of which he would then claim to have crossed on foot, equipped with a pair of snow shoes: "You know that blasted fog pretty ner fooled me. It was good and thick goin' over but when I come back it was so thin that I sagged with every step. Once I thought I was goin' to hit bottom. Just like walkin' on a featherbed, only worse. Plumb wore me out gettin' back."

CAPTAIN HANCE's string-line tourist operation received competition in 1892, when Pete Berry, another miner smitten by the magic of the Grand Canyon and far more intrigued by it than by the copper mine he had discovered in its bottom, built a small log-cabin hotel at Grand View Point, about two miles east of Hance's "ranch." Like Hance, Berry had carved his own trail in

*Peter Berry's Grand View Hotel, the Canyon's most sumptuous
hostelry in the years before the Sante Fe and Fred Harvey.*

the canyon walls, and until the opening of the safer Bright
Angel trail in 1903, the Grand View Trail and Hance's
Trail were the two principal tourist routes in and out of
the canyon from the South Rim. In 1895, the Grand Canyon Copper Company, Berry's operation, erected the
more ambitious Grand View Hotel and went into the
tourist business in as big a way as the limited clientele
could provide. In 1896, a tent-and-shack affair called
the Bright Angel Hotel, erected near the site of the future
Grand Canyon Village, was added to the slowly expanding complex of tourist facilities on the South Rim.

ONE OF THE EARLIEST professional tourists to visit the
Grand Canyon in these years was Burton Holmes,
World Traveler and Lecturer, who came to the South
Rim in the summer of 1898 with a group of men and
women fellow-travelers. His record of the trip was pub-
lished as part of a ten-volume set entitled *The Burton
Holmes Lectures* (1905), complete with Photographs by
the Author; it is a treasure, in more ways than one.

The group boarded the Santa Fe for the trip across
the plains and deserts to Flagstaff, Arizona, a town barely
removed from a frontier condition. "The arrival of our
party with cameras and chronomatographs, with almost a
mile of film, and rather more than two hundred weight
of plates," Holmes reported, "causes the citizens to smile
and murmur to themselves, 'Here comes another group

of sanguine photographers, doomed to disaster and
defeat.'"

Leaving murmurous Flagstaff behind, the Holmes
group boarded a two-coach stage line for the forty-eight
hour trip to the South Rim. "When there are so many
passengers that one coach would be overcrowded,"
Holmes reported, "a second coach, or 'trailer', is attached.
. . . Unhappy are the mortals who become inmates of
that trailer; they assiduously collect all the dust, their
view is cut off by the forward coach, and they see little
else. When crossing the broad stretch of desert . . . deep
wheel-ruts in the yellow soil cause the first coach to
act like an over-laden schooner in a heavy sea: a nerve-
shaking inclination to starboard is followed by a sudden
reeling lurch to port, accompanied by suppressed excla-
mations and frantic clutchings at the stanchions. These
antics of our flag-ship are seen by those in the trailer
through a cloud of dust, and serve as prophecies and
warnings. . . ."

After another day of lurchings and inclinations, the
party broke out of the aspen groves of the San Francisco
Forest and a little later caught a glimpse of paradise:
"Late in the afternoon we glance toward the northeast
and see revealed, but oh, so faintly, in far-off regions,
whether of sky or earth we cannot yet be sure, a vision of
rosy glory, a suggestion of the infinite, a something that
takes hold on the attention and will not let it go; a some-

229

thing that in spite of all its vagueness, remoteness, and unearthliness, causes our pulses to beat faster, for we know that yonder pinkish line is an emanation of the glory of the cañon, brooding on the distant further shore of the great gulf that we have come so far to see."

Like most people attempting to describe the Canyon, Holmes frequently became unhinged; we will encounter more of his lambent convolutions later in this chapter, but for the moment, let us move on to the more pedestrian —and comprehensible—details of their arrival at Hance's tent-hotel in the woods near the rim of the canyon: "The ladies are assigned to single tents, of which a score are scattered about. The men, all hungry as wild beasts, are led into a canvas caravansary big as a circus tent, where canvas cages for each one of us have been provided. We write our names in the register of this unique hotel, and then pick up and curiously peruse another volume of handwriting, marked, *John Hance's Visitor's Book*. To begin with our attention is focused on the, as yet unknown, personality of Captain John Hance, the owner of the book, by this entry: 'John Hance is one half—the Cañon is the other half.' This instantly inspired a desire to meet the cañon's other half and when a moment later that desire is fulfilled, we gaze with awe and call to mind a second statement found in the Canon Bible: 'God made the Canon. John Hance made the trails. Without the other, neither would be complete.'"

After eating, and gazing with awe upon the lanky spade-bearded figure of the old Captain, the party then went to stare with even greater awe at the canyon itself: "One day spent on the rim satisfies some minds. We are inclined to tell ourselves that we have seen all that it is possible to see; and many, feeling thus, depart the next morning after their arrival. But those who stay are rewarded as no travelers have ever been rewarded elsewhere. . . ."

The reward was a mule trip down Hance's Trail. "Like Dante, we begin our wanderings in a obscure savage wood," said Holmes, who found it difficult to resist classical allusions, "but unlike Dante we are mounted—not on the winged horses of the Muses, but—on the mules and the burros of good old Captain Hance, who in our case replaces Virgil as guide. . . . The only lady in our little band of bold adventurers must bow to the strict rules of Captain Hance and don divided skirts, for the old guide will have no ladies in his train who will not ride astride. The reason for this rule will soon be manifest. . . .

"With a tremor born of surprise and dizziness, we launch our animals into the abyss. The path down which we have turned appears impossible. . . . The pitch for the first mile is frightful . . . and to our dismayed, unaccustomed minds the inclination apparently increases, as if the cañon wall were slowly toppling inwards, and we anticipate the horror of the moment when the animals will not be able to retain a footing. . . .

"There may be men who can ride unconcernedly down Hance's Trail, but I confess that I am not one of them. My object in descending made it essential that I should live to tell the tale, and therefore, emboldened by the thought of a duty I owed to prospective auditors, I mustered up sufficient moral courage to dismount and scramble down the steepest and most awful sections of the path on foot. . . . 'On foot,' however, does not express it, but on heels and toes, on hands and knees, and sometimes in the posture assumed by children when they come bumping down the stairs; thus did I glissade around 'Cape Horn,' and past a dozen other places, where neither the mocking laughter of the men nor the more bitter words of sympathy from the brave Amazon could tempt me to forget that my supremest duty was to live to give a lecture on the cañon."

Holmes survived to the bottom, and spent the day wandering the rocky banks of the coffee-colored river and listening to a number of Hance's tales. After an overnight stay in the bottom, the group returned to the rim, Holmes remaining in the saddle, and finally left the Canyon at the end of June.

They returned in August, and this time encountered Pete Berry and the Grand View Hotel, which received the full weight of the Holmesian prose: "I cannot say enough in praise of our kind host and of the comforts offered by this log hotel. Here, even in the colder seasons, a long sojourn would be a not uncomfortable experience. There is a cheeriness about the interior, an aspect of solidity and warmth in the stout log walls, and a white-aproned, white-capped European personage, quite worthy of the title 'chef' presiding over the cuisine. For one of those wandering Continental culinary artists had drifted to this distant end of earth in the course of his restless world pilgrimage, and while he lingered near the cañon, all visitors to the Grand View Hotel enjoyed the luxury of Continental cooking—a luxury that here appears to be ridiculously out of place." As for Berry himself: "Unlike Mr. Hance, Berry is a man of few words, but those few

The rigors of trail-riding are documented in this stunning view of about 1904. Count the pilgrims. . . .

words are always to the point. There is nothing of romance in the soul of Peter Berry; when he meets a bear, it is not the bear that does the shooting."

After a trip down and up the Grand View Trail, which Holmes considered an improvement over that of Hance, he left the Canyon once again, with a parting word to his readers: "It had been wiser, perhaps, for me to nurse with selfish pleasure my memory of the Grand Cañon rather than to try to make you see in mere words the biggest beautiful thing in all the world, the most entrancing scene that ever dawned upon the eye of man. For such it is, and such it will in future be proclaimed by all who look upon it. If I excite your curiosity to see and know, I shall have done enough."

Someone DID ENOUGH; BY THE TURN of the century there were enough customers visiting the Grand Canyon for the Santa Fe to extend its line from Flagstaff to the Bright Angel Hotel. President Theodore Roosevelt's visit in the spring of 1903, when he gave his famous admonition to leave the Canyon "as it is," doubtless gave a tremendous boost to business, and in 1904 the Fred Harvey Company, which knew a good thing when it saw it, opened the El Tovar Hotel near the terminus of the railroad, and bought up the Bright Angel Hotel, lock, stock, and tent. This was soon too much for John Hance and his unambitious little tent-hotel business, and he took to hanging around the Grand View Hotel and the El Tovar, telling his stories, soliciting customers for his trail, and generally exercising his position as unofficial greeter and Canyon clown. He became so much a part of the Grand Canyon scene that in his later years the Fred Harvey Company provided the old man free board and room.

Pete Berry, in the meantime, had sold out his interests in the Grand Canyon Copper Company, including the Grand View Trail and Hotel, to a group of speculating eastern financiers. When the copper market collapsed in 1907, these worthies then sold out to William Randolph Hearst, who, like the Fred Harvey Company, had his eye on the tourist game; it was a good investment, particularly after 1908, the year that Theodore Roosevelt, implementing his own advice, proclaimed the Grand Canyon a national monument. During the next few years, Hearst attempted to pull customers away from the Tl Tovar, and while the effort was not entirely successful, by the time the National Park Service took over the facilities of the South Rim in 1919, the year that Grand Canyon National Park

was created, Hearst had more than made back his investment. To his everlasting sorrow, however, the park's remunerative concessionaire's lease had gone to the Fred Harvey Company.

The lease was a valuable prize; by 1919 the Grand Canyon had entered its first golden age of tourism; it had become a "must" on the itinerary of any sightseer worthy of the name, and every summer thousands paid homage to what had become to America, as it had always been to John Hance, a shrine. One of the men who would have welcomed credit for this was George Horace Lorimer, editor of *The Saturday Evening Post*. He had taken over the moribund magazine in 1898 and, through the exercise of astounding energy, absolute devotion, and an unerring instinct for delineating the virtues of mainstream America, had raised the *Post* to a level of a family magazine with an influence that exceeded even that of Edward Bok's *Ladies' Home Journal*.

LORIMER DISCOVERED THE GRAND CANYON shortly after the turn of the century and, as with all his hobbies (among other things, he was a devotee of the summer automobile excursion), it occupied his mind to the point of obsession. A single sunset in the Grand Canyon, he was known to maintain, exceeded the beauty and wonder of any painting ever created by the hand of man—a judgment that included the *Post*'s own covers, which is an indication of the depth of his feeling. Lorimer utilized the columns of the *Post* with great frequency to broadcast the wonders of the Grand Canyon in everything from editorials to short stories, and his incessant campaign to have it made into a national park, his biographer has claimed, was a major factor in the passage of the bill signed by President Woodrow Wilson on February 26, 1919 that gave it national park status.

In the fall of 1912, Lorimer persuaded one of the *Post*'s regulars, humorist Irvin S. Cobb, to make a grand tour of the Far West and write a series of articles about it for the magazine. Inevitably, Cobb's first stop was at the Grand Canyon.

Things had changed considerably since the days of Burton Holmes. Not only was it possible to arrive by train, instead of the lurching, two-day stagecoach ride from Flagstaff, but there were three first-rate hotels to choose from, the best of which was the $250,000 El Tovar, with its private dining rooms, enormous fireplaces, Music Room, Art Room, Ladies Lounging Room, Barber Shop,

Images of
the Colorado: IV

The Photographer and the River

The wonder of the canyons of the Colorado has been expressed to three generations through the medium of photography. Millions may have visited the river and its canyons, but hundreds of millions of Americans and Europeans have "known" them primarily as pictures printed in a book or magazine, seen in a motion-picture travelogue, or glimpsed in 3-D through a stereoscope.

The seeming objectivity of the camera has lent an air of authority to the presentation of such awesome landscapes, so far removed in scale and character from scenes most persons know. But if the camera is comparatively objective, it is not impartial. The photographers of exploration have told us one thing, those of the early days of tourism something else, and those of our own wilderness-starved era are giving us yet another image of the supposedly changeless.

The first scientific exploration into the Big Canyon of the Colorado, the Ives expedition of 1857-58, produced a report elegantly illustrated by two skillful artists. The resulting impressions of the river and its canyons—more often romantic than realistic—have been documented earlier in this book. Major Powell, in his 1869 voyage through the length of the Green and Colorado river canyons, neglected to bring a photographer, but no less than four were associated with his later expeditions in 1871 and 1872: E. O. Beaman, a professional photographer from New York; Clem Powell, nephew of "The Major" and assistant to Beaman; James Fennemore, a professional from Salt Lake City, hired when Beaman left; and John K. Hillers, a German immigrant employed as a general handyman for the party. It was Hillers who finally best mastered the difficult trade of making successful wet-plate negatives by the hundred when "home base" was a soggy little boat or a forlorn, overnight campsite. On the opposite page is a shot of Hillers at work in just such a site. Below is half of a stereo he made sometime in the summer of 1872, showing "The Major" himself in one of the expedition boats in the Canyon of Lodore.

As the second Powell expedition did not go below Lees Ferry until 1872, Timothy H. O'Sullivan would seem to have been the first photographer to have reached the Grand Canyon itself. O'Sullivan, fresh from three years with Clarence King's "40th Parallel Survey," was chosen by Lt. George M. Wheeler to accompany his "Surveys West of

the 100th Meridian." In September and October of 1871, Wheeler's party proceeded upstream from Fort Mojave through Black Canyon, to Diamond Creek in the lower Grand Canyon. The value of the difficult expedition up the river was dubious, as it covered the same ground that Ives had been over more than ten years earlier, but O'Sullivan made some magnificent photographs. Above is a stereo made at Grotto Spring; in the shadow of the rocks at the lower left is a little black tent—O'Sullivan's portable darkroom. Unfortunately, the greater part of O'Sullivan's scores of Colorado River plates were lost—not in the rapids of the river, but somewhere in transit between Yuma and San Francisco.

In 1872, William Bell served as official photographer for Wheeler. On the previous two pages are a remarkable pair of Bell photographs: a big view at the mouth of Kanab Creek and a stereo showing the photographer making the very picture. Such river-level scenes dominate the photographs of the Colorado and its canyons left by the explorers; for not only was the wet-plate equipment of the day hard to lug about, but these men necessarily had the explorer's eye view. The running river was the central fact in their day-to-day experience. Bell experimented with dry-plate photography on the 1872 expedition but with unconvincing success. In time, however, the dry negative would give greater mobility to the cameraman by relieving him of the need to operate a complete darkroom service in the wilds.

The view at the left was made by Timothy O'Sullivan just above Mirror Bar in Black Canyon. His portable darkroom is, in this case, set up in the bow of his flatboat, *The Picture.* At the right is a moment in Marble Gorge, captured by modern photographer Philip Hyde in 1964.

Hyde has written about the problems of documenting the canyons, and in some places his thoughts are what might have been set down by any one of the photographers of exploration: "I don't know when I've had to work under more difficult—and exhilarating—conditions. There was never enough time, and if working with a view camera demands anything, it is time to look hard, to set up, to take down. There was some resentment on my part towards the river because it was really dominating, and there is always the illusion held by photographers that they should somehow dominate a situation. For twenty days the illusion faithfully remained an illusion. The clouds, rain, and threatening skies harassed me. I was frustrated two-thirds of the time because we were always behind schedule. Our 'extra' days evaporated while we dried out by driftwood fires or spent hours laboring out portages...."

Henry G. Peabody, coming to the Grand Canyon country around 1900, worked with the dry-plate negative that would have permitted the photographers of exploration to enlarge their vision of the possibilities of photography and to capture more of the diversity of the river and canyons. But a new age had dawned—the age of the casual tourist. Peabody rode his equipment-laden pony up and down the rims of the canyons, translating onto glass the view that millions came to see in person. His spectacular photographs from the rims appear frequently throughout this book.

Overleaf is a recent photograph by Philip Hyde, a winter scene from the head of the Kaibab Trail on the Grand Canyon's South Rim.

241

In a 1904 article for the *Overland Monthly,* an aspiring cameraman asked a leading question: "What amateur photographer is there, who, having viewed Peabody's photographs of the Grand Canyon of the Colorado, does not wish to go, see, and experiment for himself?" Two who translated wish into action were Ellsworth and Emery Kolb, amateurs who became professionals under the demanding tutelage of the river and its canyons. In 1904, they erected a studio (seen at the left) near the tollgate at the head of Bright Angel Trail and made a living photographing agitated tourists who were about to descend the trail and wanted the moment recorded for history.

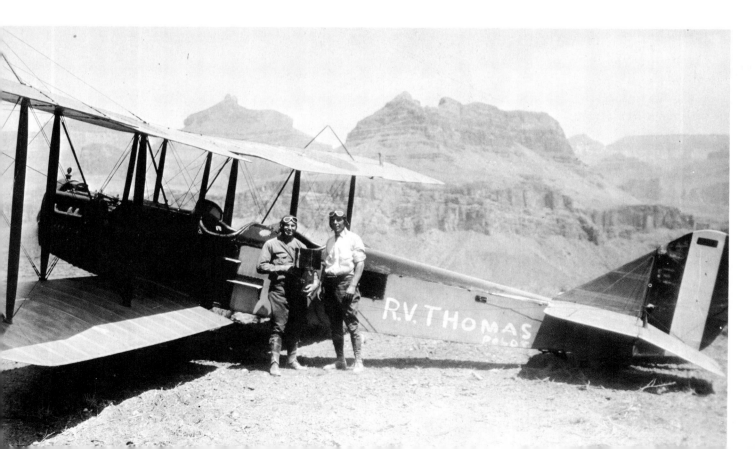

The Kolb brothers made the Grand Canyon and the Colorado their life work, accumulating thousands of photographs of tourists, views from the rims, and river-level scenes. The one shown on the top of the opposite page was taken during a winter storm in 1911—one of the photographs resulting from the brothers' classic river trip of that year recorded in *Through the Grand Canyon from Wyoming to Mexico*. Their dedication was total, and among the many "firsts" they achieved was the moment documented below, when with pilot R. V. Thomas they landed the first (and, to this date, only) airplane on the Tonto Plateau in August, 1920.

Emery Kolb, seen here at the right holding the Pathé camera the brothers used to make the first motion pictures on the Colorado River during their 1911 river journey, still operates a studio on the South Rim of the Grand Canyon. His career, which began not long after the last age of exploration, has spanned nearly the whole twentieth-century history of Grand Canyon photography, from the bulky glass-plate era of Peabody to the age of the Polaroid and the four-color artistry of such men as Philip Hyde.

Today, we again begin to see the river that Ives and Powell and Wheeler saw. Philip Hyde says, "Too many people experience the canyons in reverse—from the rim, looking down into the abyss. You cannot grasp the scope of the Grand Canyon from the rim, however you try. A canyon must be known from its bottom as well as its top to truly comprehend its scale, and certainly you cannot really know the Grand Canyon unless you know its maker, the river. And the river, for all its awesome power, is also the agent that creates the living space for man. It is at the meeting of the river and the rock that those little things happen that make the landscape have meaning and sympathetic scale."

At the left, a river-raft party tests the scale of Marble Canyon in a Hyde photograph. On the following page, a lone member of the Powell 1871 expedition is measured against the scale of the Canyon of Lodore in a photograph by E. O. Beaman.

The splendiferous El Tovar, seen shortly after its opening in 1904.

Amusement Room, Club Room, Solarium, Grotto, and Roof Garden. Other additions included an Indian museum called the Hopi House, two more canyon trails—Bright Angel and Hermit—and an embryonic village, complete with post office and grammar school, to house the employees of the hotels and the railroad.

Some things had not changed, however, including the heart-stopping rigors of trail-riding, and Cobb's recollection of his first descent into the canyon via the Bright Angel Trail is easily the best part of his account of the stay at Grand Canyon: "At the start there is always a lot of nervous chatter—airy persiflage flies to and fro and much laughing is indulged in. But it has a forced, strained sound, that laughter has; it does not come from the heart, the heart being otherwise engaged for the moment. Down a winding footpath moves the procession, with the guide in front, and behind him in single file his string of pilgrims—all as nervous as cats and some holding to their saddle-pommels with death-grips. . . .

"The parade moves on. All at once you notice that the person immediately ahead of you has apparently ridden right over the wall of the cañon. A moment ago his arched back loomed before you; now he is utterly gone. It is at this point that some tourists tender their resignations—to take effect immediately. . . .

"You reflect that thousands of persons have already

done this thing; that thousands of others—men, women, and children—are going to do it, and that no serious accident has yet occurred—which is some comfort, but not much. The thought comes to you that, after all, it is a very bright and beautiful world you are leaving behind. You turn your head to give it a long, lingering farewell, and you try to put your mind on something cheerful—such as your life insurance. . . .

"As you emerge on the lower side you forget all about your life-insurance papers and freeze to your pommel with both hands . . . and all your vital organs come up in your throat, where you can taste them. If anybody had shot me through the middle just about then he would have inflicted only a flesh wound. You have come out on a place where the trail clings to the sheer side of the dizziest, deepest chasm in the known world. . . .

"My mule had one very disconcerting way about her. . . . When she came to a particularly scary spot, which was every minute or so, she would stop dead still. I concurred in that part heartily. But then she would face outward and crane her neck over the fathomless void of that bottomless pit, and for a space of moments would gaze steadily downward, with a despondent droop of her fiddle-shaped head and a suicidal gleam in her mournful eyes. . . . But either the time was not ripe for the rash act or else she abhorred the thought of being found dead in the

Very Important Pilgrims, I: President William Howard Taft in 1911; he appears unimpressed.

Very Important Pilgrims, II: William Jennings Bryan in 1904; he appears ready to give a speech.

company of a mere tourist, so she did not leap off into space, but restrained herself; and I was very grateful to her for it. It made a bond of sympathy between us. . . .

"By the Bright Angel Trail it is three hours on a mule to the plateau . . . and it is an hour or so more to the river-bed, down at the very bottom. When you finally arrive there and look up you do not see how you ever got down, for the trail has magically disappeared. . . . Under these circumstances it is not so strange that some travelers who have been game enough until now suddenly weaken. Their nerves capsize and the grit runs out of them like sand out of an overturned pail. . . .

"Coming back up out of the Grand Cañon is an even more inspiring and amazing performance than going down. But by now . . . you are beginning to get used to the sensation of skirting along the raw and ragged verge of nothing. Narrow turns where, going down, your hair pushed your hat off, no longer affright you; you take them jauntily—almost debonairly. You feel that you are now an old mountain-scaler, and your soul begins to crave for a trip with a few more thrills to the square inch in it."

IF THE ESSENCE of canyon-climbing had not altered noticeably by 1912, neither had Captain John Hance, whom Cobb characterized as "the official prevaricator of

the Grand Cañon. It is probably the only salaried job of the sort in the world—his competitors in the same line of business mainly work for the love of it." Everyone who knows them has his own favorite among Hance's stories, but the one that Cobb encountered shortly before leaving may well be the best of the lot, and certainly it provides a fittingly irreverent climax to Cobb's Grand Canyon narrative: "It concerns the fate of one Total Loss Watkins, an old and devoted friend of the captain. As a preliminary he leads a group of wide-eared, doe-eyed victims to the rim of the Cañon. 'Right here,' he says sorrowfully, 'was where poor old Total slipped off one day. It's two thousand feet to the first ledge and we thought he was a gone fawnskin, sure! But he had on rubber boots, and he had the presence of mind to light standin' up. He bounced up and down for two days and nights without stoppin', and then we had to get a wingshot to kill him in order to keep him from starvin' to death!'"

The South Rim obviously has changed even more in the years since Cobb's visit than it did between 1898 and 1912. It is now possible to get to the Canyon by automobile or bus over a major highway from Flagstaff in a little over an hour, and while the train (diesel-powered now) still comes in daily from the main line, airline service is provided at an airport just eight miles south of the park.

Very Important Pilgrims, III: Theodore Roosevelt in 1911; he appears prepared for something strenuous.

The El Tovar is still there, as is an expanded Bright Angel Lodge, but these are now abetted by the modernistic Yavapai Lodge, together with motel cabins, a trailer court, and two expansive campgrounds. Grand Canyon Village has become a bustling little sub-sub-metropolis with its own high school. The South Rim has difficulty these days in even beginning to take care of all the people who come to the Grand Canyon.

BUT NOTHING ESSENTIAL has changed, for those who come are still pilgrims seeking the almost transcendental experience of the Canyon. Through the efforts of such men as George Horace Lorimer, Theodore Roosevelt, John Muir, and even Burton Holmes and Irvin S. Cobb, together with those thousands of books, pamphlets, calendars, photographs, *et alia* mentioned earlier—the Grand Canyon has been lifted from relative obscurity to become a crown jewel among the hundreds of stunningly beautiful natural wonders that Americans have come to view as perhaps the richest portion of their national heritage. Wherever the spirit of John Hance may be—and surely he hovers rakishly on one rim or another, thinking up spectral lies—it is to be hoped that he finds the transformation satisfactory; for he was the first and greatest pilgrim of them all.

Chapter VIII:

THE POETS

"Those who write about the Canyon," Joseph Wood Krutch once remarked, "generally begin by saying that it is indescribable; then they undertake to describe it." The truth of his statement is amply reinforced by the briefest sampling of the works produced by three generations of Grand Canyon-describers, for of the scores—perhaps hundreds—of writers who have come to the Grand Canyon few have been able to resist the challenge of articulating what they have seen. The Grand Canyon, with an immensity and variety beyond human scope, has the qualities of an abstraction, and like attempts to give literary form to other abstractions, efforts to describe the Grand Canyon have been wildly inconsistent. In their quest for the sufficiently expansive metaphor, the cosmic simile, or the precise detail, Grand Canyon-describers have stretched their imaginations to—and sometimes past—the breaking point, producing a body of literature that ranges in quality from the sublime to the ridiculous.

Clarence E. Dutton, in his *Tertiary History of the Grand Canyon* in 1882, understood the enormity of the task as well as anyone has, for he perceived it as a problem of providing order for apparent chaos—a chaos outside the human experience: "The Grand Canyon of the Colorado is a great innovation in modern ideas of scenery, and in our conceptions of the grandeur, beauty, and power of nature. As with all great innovations it is not to be comprehended in a day or a week, nor even in a month. It must be dwelt upon and studied, and the study must comprise the slow acquisition of the meaning and spirit of that marvelous scenery which characterizes the Plateau Country, and of which the great chasm is the superlative manifestation. . . . Great innovations, whether in art or literature, in science or in nature, seldom take the world by storm. They must be understood before they can be estimated, and must be cultivated before they can be understood." Dutton spent a great deal of time "cultivating" the Grand Canyon, and his resultant descriptions have a force of understanding that transcends even the baroque literary conventions of his time, as illustrated by an excerpt from his rendering of the panorama from Point Sublime: "In all the vast space beneath and around us there is very little upon which the mind can linger restfully. It is completely filled with objects of gigantic size and amazing form, and as the mind wanders over them it is hopelessly bewildered and lost. . . . Everything is superlative, transcending the power of the intelligence to comprehend it. There is no central point or object around which the other elements are grouped and to which they are tributary. The grandest objects are merged in a congregation of others equally grand. Hundreds of these mighty structures, miles in length, and thousands of feet in height, rear their majestic heads out of the abyss, displaying their richly-molded plinths and friezes, thrusting out their gables, wing-walls, buttresses and pilasters, and recessed with alcoves and panels. If any one of these stupendous creations had been planted upon the plains of central Europe it would have influenced modern art as profoundly as Fujiyama has influenced the decorative art of Japan. Yet here they are all swallowed up in the confusion of multitude."

Few writers in this first age of the Grand Canyon-describer possessed Dutton's ability to combine wonder, understanding, and scientific detachment into a workable literary mosaic. Most, presented with a spectacle that far surpassed their frequently mundane talents, capitulated by falling back upon the outworn classicisms and wretched excesses that characterized the romantic tradition in its last, most convoluted phase. One of the worst offenders in this regard was none other than the professional travel lecturer, Burton Holmes. Even Holmes knew that it was impossible to do justice to the Canyon, (which was quite an admission from someone who could compare himself to Dante and Captain Hance to Virgil): "A soul returned from Paradise would scarcely be at a greater loss for words or similes than one who strives to give the message of the Colorado Cañon to an expectant audience." Needless to say, the admission did not stop him: "And yet it must be done, no matter how ill. Let me then beg your sympathy and pray your pardon while I slowly draw the veil, and with reverential gesture reveal at first a mere glimpse, and then another until at last the mind and eye be prepared to take and hold impressions born of wider vistas, which in themselves are but puny fractions of a mighty entirety that cannot be revealed. Within a half a hundred yards of our forest-ridden tents yawns this unworldly chasm; great rocks stand about trembling on the brink, old pine-trees shed their cones into these hazy depths that are not fathomable to the eye. And we, unless we are of sterner stuff than the insensate rocks, must tremble too as we stand here listening to the most appalling silence that ever smote the ear of man, an awful silence that seems to tell the endless story of eternity and death."

Better writers than Holmes (and there were a great many) frequently were jolted into the same kind of excess. At times, it seemed as if writers were dredging up the most antiquated literary usages they could remember in an effort to match the antiquity of the Canyon itself. Listen to Charles F. Lummis, surely one of the best regional writers of his time, first, as he describes *other* people's reactions to the Canyon: "I have seen people rave over it; better people struck dumb with it; even strong men who cried over it; but, have never yet seen the man or woman that expected it." It would be hard to top that as a gently moving bit of phrasing. Now, hear him on the Canyon itself: "Come—and penitent—ye of the United States, to marvel, upon this chiefest miracle of our own land."

JOHN MUIR, whose description of the Sierra Nevada as the "range of light" has never been equalled, surpassed even "chiefest miracle" in his own tortured rhetoric: "Wilderness so Godful, cosmic primeval, bestows a new sense of earth's beauty and size. But the colors, the living, rejoicing colors, chanting, morning and evening, in chorus to heaven."

One of the principal problems confronting any Grand Canyon-describer, of course, is the search for the appropriate metaphor. Unfortunately, the most outsized metaphor that a man is likely to come up with has a tendency to appear pedestrian when put against the stunning reality of the Canyon. Most, like Dutton, have fallen back on the device of comparing the Canyon's geological structures with those of man, as did Frank Waters in *The Colorado*: "For one thing, it contains every shape known to man. Lofty peaks, whole mountains rise out of its depths. There are vast plateaus, flat-topped mesas, high buttes and monoliths. And all these are carved in the semblance of pyramids, temples, castles; of pinnacles, spires, fluted columns and towers; porticoes and abutments, bridges and arches, terraces, balconies, balustrades. They are solid and fragile, bare and covered with latticework and delicate carving. It is a stage that seems expressly built to contain in perpetuity appropriate sets for every dynasty, every religion, every legend and myth-drama that man has known—a vast universal depository, as it were, of mankind's structural and architectural heritage."

WHEN THE STANDARD STRUCTURAL METAPHOR was abandoned for something more imaginative, the results could be grotesque. Henry Van Dyke, who was capable of producing competent, if not inspired, poesy, essayed a 141-line poem in 1909 entitled "Daybreak in the Grand Canyon of Arizona," and the particularly flavorful portion that follows illustrates the desperation to which any writer could be driven:

> Be still, my heart! Now Nature holds her breath
> To see the vital flood of radiance leap
> Across the chasm; and crest the farthest rim
> Of alabaster with a glistening white
> Rampart of pearl; and flowing down by walls
> Of changeful opal, deepen into gold
> Of topaz, rosy gold of tourmaline,
> Crimson of garnet, green and gray of jade,
> Purple of amethyst, and ruby red,
> Beryl and sard, and royal porphyry;
> Until the cataract of color breaks
> Upon the blackness of the granite floor.

Irving S. Cobb was driven to unconscious humor in his own effort. After issuing the standard disclaimer—"Nearly everybody, on taking a first look at the Grand Canyon, comes right out and admits its wonders are absolutely indescribable, and then proceeds to write anywhere from two thousand to fifty thousand words, giving the full details"—he went on to devote a mere 650 words in giving the full details and climaxed it with what must certainly stand as the most inelegant metaphor ever applied to the Canyon: "Imagine, if you can, a monster of a hollow approximately some hundreds of miles long and a mile deep, and anywhere from ten to sixteen miles wide, with a mountain range—the most wonderful mountain range in the world—planted in it; so that, viewing the spectacle from above, you get the illusion of being in a stationary airship, anchored up among the clouds; imagine those mountain peaks—hundreds upon hundreds of them—rising one behind the other, stretching away in endless, serried rank until the eye swims and the mind staggers at the task of trying to count them. . . . Imagine other ravines opening from the main one, all muzzling their mouths in her flanks like so many sucking pigs; for there are hundreds of these lesser cañons, and any one of them would be a marvel were they not dwarfed into relative puniness by the mother of the litter. . . ."

The trouble with words and the Grand Canyon, of course, is not just that it is indescribable, but that it *defies* description. Few have been able to resist the challenge;

one who did so was the British writer, J. B. Priestley, who visited the Canyon in the mid-thirties, and his carefully understated words are at least as effective as the most orotund flights of curlicued prose: "There is of course no sense at all in trying to describe the Grand Canyon. Those who have not seen it will not believe any possible description. Those who have seen it know that it cannot be described. . . . In fact, the Grand Canyon is a sort of landscape Day of Judgement. It is not a show place, a beauty spot, but a revelation. The Colorado River made it; but you feel when you are there that God gave the Colorado River its instructions."

Understatement may, in fact, be the key to any attempted articulation of the Grand Canyon, for it denotes a certain seemly humility, a sense that what is involved, as Dutton suggested, is understanding—an understanding that can only come, if it comes at all, with time. The girl who at the turn of the century put down her impression of the Canyon in John Hance's *Visitor's Book* (now reposing in the National Park Museum at the South Rim) obviously was fully aware of the impossibility of doing the Canyon justice, and her words consequently say as much as and probably more than the more ambitious prosody we have seen here: "I think that it is very deep and grand and that it must have taken a very long time to make it."

The Grand Canyon, after all, is an experience, not a simple visual phenomenon easily translatable into words—a spectacle that resists words, distorts them, gives them a touch of the surreal quality of the Canyon itself. It also explains why every attempt, by no matter how careful a craftsman, is susceptible to any number of wretched excesses. It would be better, all things considered, not to try at all—a contention corroborated by a reading of Edwin Corle's *Listen, Bright Angel,* perhaps the best single history of the river and its canyons. It was published nearly twenty-five years ago, and among approximately one hundred thousand words of text there is not a single attempt to give the Canyon visual form—no reference to battlements, latticework, pyramids, temples, upside-down mountain chains, imaginative varieties of color, or even piglets. Yet the Canyon is there—its geology, ecology, prehistory and history—in stark and wondrous detail. The book ends with an admonition that stems, like the book itself, from a deep appreciation of the Canyon's essential quality, which words can only distort, and his advice is something that every writer, would-be writer, or mediocre poet should heed respectfully before ventur-

THE LEGACY

ing to describe the indescribable: "So let the Grand Canyon speak to you; *listen* with an open mind, long and attentively. Apart from what it yields of history, geology, ethnology, archaeology, paleontology, anthropology, and any and all other 'ologies' representing divisions of the classified knowledge of man, the *Grand Canyon* has something to say—to *you*."

Emphasis supplied.

THE RIVER-RUNNERS

For most of the pilgrims who have come to the Colorado and its canyons during the past century, the experience has been a limited one, though even in its limitations enough to jar the sensibilities into disbelief, as Dutton suggested. To stand on the rim, north or south, is for most people in itself the outside dimension of experience; others take to the trails to enlarge even that boundary, but this is as far as most of the pilgrims go. There are some, however, who feel a need to cross the boundary itself, to enter an older, deeper experience by stepping from the world of human time to the geologic time of the still canyons and the river that made them.

These are the river-runners, a stalwart and fast-growing breed of men and women—and children—who make their own kind of pilgrimage throughout each summer to Lees Ferry on the Colorado, where they enter Galloway boats, Nevills boats, custom-designed wooden, aluminum, and fiberglass boats, neoprene rafts, canoes, and kayaks for the often violent, sometimes dangerous and to most of them utterly beautiful ten-day, 300-mile run through the Grand Canyon to Lake Mead. In the summer of 1968, 3,609 river enthusiasts tumbled down this still-wild stretch of the Colorado, reliving, for a time, the lonely pioneering explorations of John Wesley Powell and exulting in an intimacy with the river, the Canyon, and all the profound forces they represent—experiencing a "oneness with the Canyon," as one of them has decribed it.

R IVER-RUNNING on the Colorado, like the more sedate forms of Grand Canyon–watching, is a comparatively recent recreational development. For John Wesley Powell and those who came after him for more than a generation, the tumbling journey down the Colorado was a necessity—and while it cannot be denied that such men sought and found adventure in it, few of them would have cared to describe the trip as a form of recreation. As the Grand Canyon began to fall into the ken of the tourist, however, there were some who took to the river for nothing more practical than the sheer adventure of it —a challenge, delight, and beauty of a kind that most people would never know.

The first purely recreational trip down the river was undertaken in September of 1909 by Ohio manufacturer Julius F. Stone. Accompanied by Nathaniel Galloway, a trapper who had run much of the river in search of pelts, and equipped with Galloway's specially-designed "cockpit" boats, Stone left Green River City, Wyoming (Powell's starting point), on September 12 and arrived at Needles, California, on November 19. The pair made it through without a single upset, an accomplishment rarely matched and one that may be attributable to Galloway's innovation in river-running: instead of taking rapids bow first, as Powell had done, Galloway ran them stern first, so that he could see where he was going. The method was adopted by nearly all who followed him.

I N THE WINTER OF 1911, one of the most renowned of all the river trips was undertaken by a pair of brothers with a hunger for challenges and an instinct for publicity. Ellsworth and Emery Kolb arrived at the Grand Canyon in 1902, bought a small photographic studio in Williams, Arizona, and moved it to the head of the Bright Angel Trail. There they made a transient living by photographing people about to descend the trail to the canyon floor, an event that most visitors understandably felt should be immortalized. The brothers went after immortality themselves when they decided to run the Colorado from Green River City, Wyoming, to Needles, California, and record the trip on motion-picture film for the first time. They left Green River City on September 8, 1911, equipped with Galloway boats and thousands of feet of film. After a month-long rest during November at their Grand Canyon home, they arrived at Needles on January 18, 1912.

They had not been so fortunate as Stone and Galloway. They had upset several times, once losing a great deal of photographic equipment, and more than once had been forced to make extensive repairs on the boats. Moreover, Emery took ill during part of the trip, which increased Ellsworth's work load to grueling proportions. For all its problems, however, the journey was a resounding success, for the brothers had let nothing stop them from taking movies and still photographs of everything they could document—the running of rapids, the scenery, the repairing of boats, and camp life—compiling one of the

Emery Kolb shoots some of the footage of the first motion pictures
ever made on the Colorado, while brother Ellsworth shoots a rapid.

most complete photographic records of the river system ever produced. Emery took the films and photographs on a profitable lecture tour of the East, while Ellsworth, after making a quick trip from Needles to the Gulf of California in 1913 to round out the journey, sat down and wrote *Through the Grand Canyon from Wyoming to Mexico,* which—even though inaccurately titled—has since become a classic among river-running enthusiasts. Ten years later, Emery went through the Canyon again as chief boatman of the United States Geological Survey's exploration expedition.

Perhaps the most deliberately unnecessary and faintly ludicrous of all the early river trips was that organized and conducted by Clyde Eddy in the spring of 1927. Eddy, a member of the Explorer's Club of New York, had offered in newspaper advertisements "A fine opportunity for geology students, or young members of teaching faculties, to do field work in virgin territory," and received more than one hundred applications. From these, he selected eleven—eight college boys, one camera-

man, one member of the American Museum of Natural History, and one identified simply as Parley Galloway of southeastern Utah, presumably a relative of Nathaniel Galloway. All but Galloway were totally inexperienced in river-running, and all were motivated by what moved Eddy himself—the *idea* of running a river. A thirteenth member, a tramp that Eddy picked up at Green River, Utah, joined them before departure; his motivations have been lost to history. To reinforce the curious logic of the expedition, Eddy brought along a bear cub and a dog as mascots, companions, or whatever. On June 27, 1927, the three boats—the *Powell,* the *Dellenbaugh,* and the *Coronado*—pushed off into the Green River.

The ambitious expedition soon learned that it was no light matter to run the Colorado River. By the time the group had fought its way to Lees Ferry, four men—the tramp, the cameraman, and two college boys—had had enough. Somehow, the remaining nine, as well as the bear cub and the dog, made it through to Needles after six cruel weeks. Eddy, following in the footsteps of the Kolb brothers, promptly set down the adventure in a

THE LEGACY

The stagecoach trip from Flagstaff to Grand Canyon was one of dust, lurchings, and inclinations.

book: *Down the World's Most Dangerous River,* which sold well enough to justify a British printing.

Surely the saddest of all the river trips in the years before it became a yearly pastime for thousands was the honeymoon journey of Mr. and Mrs. Glen R. Hyde in the fall of 1928. Why they decided to do such a thing on their honeymoon is beyond imagination, but the two of them set off from Green River, Utah, in October, carried in a scow of Hyde's own design, featuring sweep oars at each end. The odd boat served them well for the first part of the trip, and less than a month after their departure they arrived at Bright Angel Creek. There, they debarked and climbed up to the South Rim to ask Emery Kolb about the river below Bright Angel Creek. Kolb tried to talk them into using life preservers for the rest of the trip, but Hyde waved off the possibility of trouble. Mrs. Hyde, however, might have had her doubts, for Kolb reported that shortly before their departure she looked down at her muddy, water-soaked boots and remarked,

"I wonder if I shall ever wear pretty shoes again."

They were never seen again. When it became obvious that their long silence signified something more than normal delays, search for them began. All that was ever found was the boat, partially swamped but otherwise undamaged. Kolb speculated that Mrs. Hyde had been swept into a rapid while holding the boat's line, and that Hyde had drowned attempting to save her.

The monolith of Boulder Dam put an end to the possibility of river journeys from the Green to the lower Colorado, but it did not appreciably detract from this aspect of the river's wild appeal. All during the 1930's adventurers of one kind or another ran both the upper and lower reaches of the river. By 1939, it was even possible to buy a ticket for a trip down the Colorado, for by then Norman D. Nevills had organized Mexican Hat Expeditions, Inc., the first commercial river-running operation on the Colorado. Until his death in 1949, Nevills led annual trips down the river in an improved, wider version of the boat

A pair of motorized pilgrims view Marble Canyon at the mouth of Soap Creek, 1921.

designed by Nathaniel Galloway at the turn of the century. His business was purchased by James P. Rigg, Jr., John B. Rigg, and J. Frank Wright, and by 1950 it had several competitors, including the "Woman of the River," Mrs. Georgia White, whose neoprene raft trips down the Colorado surely have made her one of the most unusual career women in history.

BY THE MID-1960's, several hundred people a year were riding the river. By then, of course, the trip was a short one, since Flaming Gorge Dam, Glen Canyon Dam, and all the dams strung along the lower river reduced the length of wild water to a mere 279 miles between Lees Ferry and Lake Mead. Even this water was not truly wild, for, as one river-runner complained gently, "the river's level is no longer controlled by the snow melt in the Rockies, but by the Bureau of Reclamation. This introduced an element of uncertainty: we could never be sure that we would not wake up one morning and find insufficient water to float our boats. . . ."

Still, the trip is a magic one, for the canyons of the river remain a genuine challenge, and their beauty a constant delight. In 1969, more than five thousand adventurers will course down the river. For those who might wonder why they do it, the answer can only be a paraphrase of the reason given by mountain-climbers: because the river and the canyons are there. Listen to one of them, Haldane Holstrom, writing finish to his solo journey of 1937, for nothing he says has changed: "I find I have already had my reward, in the doing of the thing. The stars, the cliffs and canyons, the roar of the rapids, the moon, the uncertainty and worry, the relief when through each one . . . the campfires at night . . . the real respect and friendship of rivermen I met. . . .

"This may be my last camp where the roar of the rapids is echoed from the cliffs around and I can look at the stars and moon only through a narrow slit in the earth.

"The river and the canyons have been kind to me. . . ."

257

CHAPTER IX

CONSERVATION AND THE COLORADO

Conservation Comes of Age in Twentieth-Century Controversies

Roderick Nash

The American conservation movement, like the Colorado River, began with faint stirrings—trickles of ideas in a few far-seeing minds. The river patiently grooved canyons into massive plateaus. Conservation had an equally obdurate adversary in the exploitative relationship of the pioneer to the natural world. One erosive process required some ten million years; the other began in earnest less than a century ago. Inevitably, their paths crossed; the result was change, for both the river and the movement.

From his beginnings in the early Pleistocene Age until only yesterday, geologically speaking, man traditionally directed his energies to conquering, not conserving, the environment. In the first place, natural resources seemed inexhaustible. The problem was too many rather than too few trees. Moreover, the Judeo-Christian tradition taught that as the result of a gift from God the natural world belonged to man for his exploitation. Genesis 1:28 commanded the first couple to "be fruitful, and multiply, and replenish the earth, and subdue it: and have dominion over the fish of the sea, and over the fowl of the air, and over every living thing that moveth upon the earth."

The first white Americans stood squarely in this tradition. A massive assault was directed at the New World environment in the name of progress, civilization, and Christianity. Men slashed at the earth in pursuit of raw materials. The strength of individualism and competitiveness in the American value system supported the pioneer's insistence that the land he owned could be used as he willed. The interest of society, present and future, made little difference. Considerations of immediate profit dictated attitudes toward the land.

In this unpromising context, such early prophets of enlightened environmental management as Henry David Thoreau, George Perkins Marsh, and John Wesley Powell attempted to gain an audience. They challenged the prevailing conception of the land's purpose, exposed inexhaustibility as a myth, and even made so bold as to question the dogma of free enterprise when land health was concerned. Time was on the side of such men as these.

Several developments around the turn of the century help explain conservation's coming of age. Mounting evidence that the nation could exhaust—and, in fact, was exhausting—many of its vital resources proved highly important. Another precondition for conservation was an increasing public apprehension over the effects of concentrated wealth that came to a head in the era of Progressivism, a political philosophy that held that the federal government should take an active, positive role in American economic life.

Finally, the early American conservation movement benefitted enormously from the growth of widespread uneasiness over the psychological and physical consequences of the passing of the frontier. For two and a half centuries the frontier had been almost synonymous with abundance and opportunity in the New World. As a consequence, few could regard the 1890 Census' announcement of the end of the frontier without regret. Suddenly, the nation seemed middle aged, and conservation acquired new appeal. In a sense, conservation would *be* the new frontier. It would keep the nation prosperous, vigorous, demo-

Conservation's battleground: A view of Grand Canyon from Moran Point (Henry G. Peabody photograph, ca. 1900).

John Wesley Powell, the pioneer philosopher of natural resources development.

Gifford Pinchot, champion of utilitarian conservation.

cratic, and beautiful. For a civilization, in short, that had begun to notice its first gray hairs, conservation was a welcome tonic.

The conviction that natural resources could be scientifically managed in the long-term interest of the general public provided the mainspring of Progressive conservation, which envisioned, as Gifford Pinchot put it, "the complete and orderly development of all our resources for the benefit of all the people." The means to this end was efficient planning, devised by scientists, implemented by engineers, and guided by an understanding of the interrelationship of resources. Progressives expected the returns of conservation to be nothing less than the perpetuation of national greatness. W J (he insisted on this punctuation) McGee, a disciple of Powell and colleague of Pinchot, regarded the conservation movement as the capstone to the crusade for human rights that began with the American Revolution. Little wonder President Theodore Roosevelt opened the famous White House Conservation Conference of May, 1908, with an allusion to conservation as "the chief material question that confronts us."

America's rivers were well suited to the kind of comprehensive, multiple-purpose planning Progressive conservationists advocated. Indeed western water development, along with western forestry, formed the heart of

the early movement. John Wesley Powell broke the paths. His 1878 *Report on the Lands of the Arid Region of the United States* broached the reclamation idea: with federal financial and technical support, land normally too arid for agriculture could be fructified by irrigation. Having run much of the rampaging Colorado by boat, however, he knew well that water in rivers was unique among natural resources; what happened at one place on a river could affect areas hundreds of miles downstream, possibly an entire watershed. In the Colorado's case, this drainage area amounted to over 240,000 square miles or one-twelfth of continental United States. Consequently, Powell thought of conservation in regional, rather than local, terms. This marked a breakthrough of major importance in American conservation history and heralded the concept of regional planning.

Powell succeeded in igniting the enthusiasm of several young colleagues in the Geological Survey who would help bring his ideals to realization. W J McGee, the champion of multiple-purpose river development, was one, but more important for reclamation was Frederick H. Newell. A Pennsylvania-born engineer who trained at the Massachusetts Institute of Technology, Newell joined the Geological Survey in 1888 and immediately began a national water resources inventory. Hydrologists measured the flow of the Colorado in 1894 and 1895. At the same time,

Newell joined forces with Representative Francis G. Newlands of Nevada and George H. Maxwell, a California
lawyer, in a campaign to publicize the advantages of
federally financed irrigation. The campaign culminated
in the Reclamation (or Newlands) Act of June 17, 1902,
which established a mechanism for applying the proceeds
from the sale of public lands in the West to federal reclamation projects, and created the Reclamation Service
(now the Bureau of Reclamation). Powell died the same
year, but his ideas now had official sanction.

AFTER THE EPOCH-MAKING RECLAMATION ACT OF 1902,
conservationists pressed on their campaign to control and develop the nation's water resources. The "Conquest of Water," W J McGee grandly declared, was as
crucial to human progress as the "Conquest over Fire,
Knife, Spring, and Wheel" and, indeed, "the single step
remaining to be taken before Man becomes master over
Nature." Before his untimely death from cancer in 1912,
McGee labored ceaselessly for comprehensive river development. For Gifford Pinchot, Chief Forester and the con-
fidant of President Theodore Roosevelt, the single most
important aspect of water conservation was the preven-
tion of prime damsites from falling into the hands of
private developers. Multiple-purpose management would
be precluded, and the lucky entrepreneurs, Pinchot feared,
could quickly extend their control from hydropower to all
of industry. Eventually civil liberty itself might be threatened. Consequently Pinchot believed that if permission to
build dams was granted to private parties at all, it should
be in the form of a revocable lease and that the power
to regulate the operation of the facility should reside with
the government.

Despite the force of these arguments and the example
of Ontario's successful operation of a publicly controlled
hydropower system, legislation was slow in appearing. Private interests crying "Socialism!" and a Congress partially
disenchanted with Rooseveltian conservation resisted waterway regulation. Finally, in 1920 the Federal Water
Power Act forbade the granting of damsites in fee simple
and established the Federal Power Commission to super-
vise the leasing arrangements. Control over rates, rental
fees, and recapture procedures was much weaker than
many Progressive conservationists had hoped, and the
Federal Power Commission, they feared, would prove
little more than a rubber stamp for the private utility companies. Still, the Federal Water Power Act established the

principle of public ownership of water resources if not
strict management over them. Unquestionably the act
advanced the possibility of public development of the
Colorado.

ALONG WITH PRIVATE DEVELOPERS, state rivalries posed
an obstacle to regional water conservation. Water,
obviously, was a limited commodity: what one state removed from a river another could not use. The Colorado
is a case in point. Its annual flow is relatively small (about
one-twenty-fourth that of the Mississippi, for example),
and as soon as reclamation became a subject of discussion,
states in the Colorado Basin began to eye each other suspiciously. In 1919 the Upper Basin states, fearful of the
growing demand for water of the Lower Basin, principally from Southern California, began negotiations for an
equitable division of Colorado River water. Secretary of
Commerce Herbert Hoover joined the deliberations in
1921, and the Colorado River Compact was executed the
following year. A milestone in conservation history, it
assessed the average flow of the river at Lees Ferry at
15,000,000 acre-feet a year and split it equally between the
Upper and Lower Basins. This cleared the way for the beginning of the nation's first multiple-purpose project on a
major river, culminating in Hoover ("Boulder" until the
name was changed in 1947) Dam at Boulder Canyon on
the Colorado River.

The completion of Hoover Dam in 1935 marked the
realization of Progressive conservationists' dreams with
regard to America's rivers. Nature had been subdued to
man's will on an unprecedented scale; the federal government had taken the lead in a multiple-purpose project;
the welfare of the people in a vast region stood to be
advanced. On the Colorado, not the Tennessee as is com-
monly supposed, comprehensive river development began.
The Tennessee Valley Authority, to be sure, deserves its
reputation for effective regional water conservation, but
Hoover Dam was the pioneer.

WHILE THE UTILITARIAN CONCEPT of American conservation forged ahead to achieve Hoover Dam, the
"preservation" side also gathered momentum. To preservationists, conservation meant scenery, parks, wilderness,
and recreation rather than dams, hydropower, and reclamation. Although overshadowed in the Progressive era by
utilitarian conservation, the preservationists had already
tasted success. Between 1864 and 1885 California's Yosem-

THE LEGACY

ite Valley, New York's Adirondack Mountains, and the Yellowstone region in Wyoming all received some degree of protection in their natural condition.

As Gifford Pinchot had been the catalyst of utilitarian conservation, a wiry Scot named John Muir unified the preservationists. A self-styled "poetico-trampo-geologist-bot. and ornith-natural, etc!-!-!-!," Muir believed that nature, especially in its wilder forms, reflected God and refreshed man. Combining this transcendentalism with glowing descriptions of California's Sierra Nevada, Muir gained a nationwide reputation as a nature writer. In 1892 he took the lead in founding the Sierra Club, which would come to play a crucial role in the history of conservation and the Colorado.

John Muir recognized the potential of the Grand Canyon of the Colorado as a wilderness preserve before the turn of the century. His 1898 descriptive article in *Atlantic Monthly* concluded with a plea that the Canyon be designated a national park. At first his idea got no further than the 1882 attempts of Senator Benjamin Harrison to make the region a public park. But while the government would do nothing more than vaguely categorize Grand Canyon a "forest reserve" in 1893, the public came to regard it a wonder of the West on a par with Yellowstone and Yosemite. Thanks to the Santa Fe's 1901 spur railroad to the South Rim, tourism increased to the point that construction of the famous El Tovar Hotel was appropriate. In May, 1903, President Theodore Roosevelt included the Canyon on his tour of Western parks and delivered his oft-quoted "leave-it-as-it-is" advice. On a camping trip in the Sierra with John Muir later that summer, Roosevelt heard more arguments in favor of protecting the Grand Canyon. Action was not forthcoming, however, until January 11, 1908, when Roosevelt signed an executive order creating the Grand Canyon National Monument. True national park status followed on February 26, 1919, and the Canyon became part of the recreational empire of the effective first director of the National Park Service, Stephen T. Mather.

IN HOOVER DAM and Grand Canyon National Park, the Colorado River experienced both the utilitarian and the preservationist concepts of conservation. For a time the river was big enough for both. Yet the latent conflict between these two theories could not be surpressed for long. A portent of what would come had been given by the Hetch Hetchy controversy in California years earlier.

John Muir, founder of the Sierra Club and "poetico-trampo-geologist-bot. and ornith-natural, etc!!!"

San Francisco needed a municipal water supply; in the Sierra 150 miles away was the Hetch Hetchy Valley, an excellent potential reservoir and damsite. Hetch Hetchy, however, was also part of Yosemite National Park. Preservationists, led by John Muir and the Sierra Club, fought plans for its development. But Gifford Pinchot, who had sparred with Muir for more than a decade over the meaning of conservation, defended San Francisco's proposal as a perfect example of the "wise use" of a natural resource. Even Theodore Roosevelt, with his deep personal commitment to wilderness preservation, could not easily gainsay the material demands of a growing city; he eventually sided with Pinchot.

As the Hetch Hetchy controversy broadened into a national issue after 1908, the schism in American conservation widened. Did "conservation" mean planned development or the preservation of nature? Was it primarily economic or aesthetic? The answer that it meant both (the "multiple-use" formula, as it is now called) might work in a regional plan but was meaningless for a small area. Hetch Hetchy Valley could be either wilderness *or* a reservoir—not both.

The upshot of the Hetch Hetchy battle was a 1913 congressional decision in favor of the dam—and a determination on the part of preservationists to permit no further encroachments on the National Park System. The next

Sweeping Back the Flood

The Hetch-Hetchy dam provided the first open conflict between utilitarians and preservationists.

great test of that determination involved the Colorado.

In 1915 President Woodrow Wilson designated eighty acres near the confluence of the Green and Yampa Rivers in Utah as a national monument for the purpose of protecting a deposit of dinosaur bones imbedded in a sandstone ledge. With the exception of a few paleontologists, hardly anyone noticed the isolated reservation for several decades. Then in 1938 President Franklin D. Roosevelt enlarged Dinosaur National Monument to over two hundred thousand acres. Its deep canyons and sagebrush benchland attracted the attention of wilderness enthusiasts. The Bureau of Reclamation was also interested. Beginning in 1940, its engineers surveyed the upper Colorado River Basin with an eye to constructing dams and storage reservoirs. The Upper Colorado River Compact of 1948, allocating water among the Upper Basin states, cleared the way for the Bureau's recommendation of a ten-dam, $1,500,000,000 Colorado River Storage Project. One of the five dams recommended for initial construction was at Echo Park, almost exactly in the center of Dinosaur National Monument. The resulting reservoir would, at capacity, back water forty-four miles up the Yampa and sixty-three miles up the Green.

On learning that Dinosaur National Monument was threatened with inundation, preservationists became alarmed. Here was another Hetch Hetchy—an attack on the integrity of national parks and monuments that could well presage the collapse of the entire system under the pressure of utilitarian conservation. Preservationists sensed that the Echo Park controversy would be a showdown. "Let's open this to its ultimate and inevitable extent," one declared in 1950, "and let's settle . . . once and for all time . . . whether we may have . . . wilderness areas . . . in these United States."

The conservationists who squared off over Dinosaur National Monument in the 1950's bore little resemblance to those who had contested Hetch Hetchy forty years before. The preservation crusade had grown strikingly in sophistication and effectiveness. Persuasive exponents of the importance of wild country in modern America extended the early intellectual explorations of Henry David Thoreau and John Muir. The ecologist and wildlife manager, Aldo Leopold, argued in the 1930's that modern man's power to shape his environment should entail a sense of responsibility for the other life-forms sharing the planet. This was not a matter of economics or even aesthetics, Leopold insisted, but of simple ethics. It followed that conservation should not mean development of nature so much as maintaining its balance. In these terms wild places like Dinosaur National Monument had significance as land in ecological harmony against which man could measure the effects of his violence and hopefully, "learn an intelligent humility toward [his] place in nature." Other twentieth-century champions of preservation, men such as Robert Marshall and Sigurd Olson, stressed the psychological importance of unmodified nature. Some men found wilderness essential, they pointed out, either as an alternative to the drabness of civilization or as a means of regaining serenity and perspective. Still others linked the continued existence of wild country to the maintainence of the sanctity of the individual in a mass society. "If we ever let the remaining wilderness be destroyed," Wallace Stegner warned, "we are committed . . . to a headlong drive into our technological termite-life, the Brave New World of a completely man-controlled environment."

THE PRESERVATION MOVEMENT had also grown in size. When John Muir led the Hetch Hetchy protest, he could have called on only seven national and two regional conservation organizations. Fifty years later the figures had jumped to 78 and 236. The political effectiveness of private conservation efforts likewise had increased enormously. The Hetch Hetchy controversy revealed the disadvantage of not having professional lobbyists in Washington to conduct the infighting that could translate public opinion into political decision. After 1918 the National Parks Association helped remedy this defect, and in 1935 Robert Marshall organized the Wilderness Society. With headquarters in Washington, it defined its purpose as "fighting off the invasion of wilderness and . . . stimulating . . . an appreciation of its multiform emotional, intellectual, and scientific values." The Isaak Walton League and the National Wildlife Federation also became towers of preservation strength on a national level.

Unquestionably, the most important asset of the preservationists on the eve of the Echo Park controversy was the support of a large and growing number of Americans. As the amount of wilderness in the country shrank, desire for protecting what remained increased. It was the familiar story of not appreciating something until threatened with its deprivation. Publicizers like Stephen T. Mather of the National Park Service labored to make Americans aware of the irreplaceable value of their parks. Serving as a sort of chamber of commerce for wilderness, Mather and his colleagues produced an astonishing volume of illustrated publicity and stimulated periodicals to carry articles on the nation's natural wonders. Over two million persons saw Emerson Hough's 1922 plea in *The Saturday Evening Post* for the preservation of the Kaibab Plateau, including the North Rim of the Grand Canyon, as a "typical portion of the American wilderness." If such a place was to be saved in its natural condition, Hough maintained, future generations could learn "what the old America once was, how beautiful, how splendid." The railroads' "See America First" campaign also attracted public attention to places like the Colorado's canyons, by pointing out that they were unmatched in Europe. And, ironically, the availability and vogue of the automobile, the nemesis of preservationists today, was highly important to the growth of the wilderness movement. With a car or two in every garage, the national parks and monuments were not merely names on pictures but realistic targets for the family planning a vacation. This possibility of personal contact did much to broaden the social base on which the preservation movement rested.

The status of reclamation, and utilitarian conservation generally, also changed in the half century between Hetch Hetchy and Echo Park. Technological breakthroughs eased the fears about resource exhaustion which had impelled early conservation. In addition, many Americans came to realize that an environment conducive to survival was not enough. The land had to do more than just keep people alive; it must bring them joy! This was the basis for the emphasis in American conservation since World War II on *quality* of the environment. Beauty and recreational opportunity, rather than productivity, became the new yardstick for measuring the success of land management. Utilitarianism was partially eclipsed. Reclamation, in particular, seemed to many to have passed its zenith. The choice sites had been developed; those that remained were more difficult to build, more expensive, and at greater distances from the areas their water and power might serve. Bananas, some critics of reclamation contended, *could* be grown on the top of Pike's Peak if the nation were willing to commit the necessary dollars and effort. Even without considering expense, others noted, the development of *new* cropland through irrigation made little sense when that already under cultivation produced more than the economy could absorb.

In this context of rising support of wilderness preservation and rising criticism of multiple-purpose river development, the battle over Dinosaur National Monument began. Since 1940 it had simmered within the Department of the Interior as the Bureau of Reclamation and the National Park Service attempted to ascertain each other's intentions. Late in 1949 it became clear that the reclamationists were indeed planning a dam at Echo Park and that National Park officials opposed the proposal. By this time, too, several private preservation groups had got wind of the dam and raised a general alarm.

Faced with an interagency conflict in his department and growing public unrest over Echo Park Dam, Secretary of the Interior Oscar Chapman decided to hold a public hearing in April, 1950, to ascertain the position of the contending schools of conservation thought. The testimony revealed the depth of the schism. While acknowledging the importance of natural beauty, reclamationists and political leaders in the affected states made clear that they believed the highest use of Dinosaur was as a storage reservoir. Their opponents at the hearing argued that the upper Colorado should be developed — but without impairing existing national parks and monuments. Water development or wilderness preservation: it was a case of one "good" versus another.

Late in June, 1950, Secretary Chapman directed a memorandum to the Bureau of Reclamation and the National Park Service stating that "in the interest of the greatest public good" he was approving Echo Park Dam. The decision silenced National Park Service opposition, and private preservationists realized that their only hope for saving Dinosaur lay in carrying their case before Congress and the public. The Colorado River Storage Project required legislative authorization, and Echo Park Dam could still be deleted. On Dinosaur's behalf a number of the larger preservation organizations pooled their strength in several lobbying agencies and raised money. "Perhaps the stage is set," one preservationist remarked late in 1950, "for a full dress performance by all those . . . who are protecting the West's recreational and wilderness values."

David R. Brower, executive director of the Sierra Club, and Howard C. Zahniser, who served the Wilderness Society in a similar capacity, led the crusade for Dinosaur. With unprecedented vigor and skill, they launched a national campaign against the dam. Hard-hitting illustrated pamphlets, prepared for mass distribution, asked the public: *"Will you DAM the Scenic Wild Canyons of Our National Park System?"* and *"What is Your Stake in Dinosaur?"* A professional motion picture, in color, received hundreds of showings throughout the country. Wallace Stegner edited a book-length collection of essays and photographs showing the importance of keeping Dinosaur wild. Conservation periodicals featured numerous articles on the monument. More important from the standpoint of national opinion was the extensive coverage the controversy received in *Life, Collier's, Newsweek,* and the *Reader's Digest,* as well as in newspapers all over the country.

SPOKESMEN FOR DINOSAUR brought the fruit of a century of American thought on the meaning and value of wilderness to bear on the issue. General Ulysses S. Grant III, grandson of the President, defended Dinosaur because "our industrial civilization is creating an ever greater need for the average man . . . to reestablish contact with nature . . . and to be diverted from the whirling wheels of machinery and chance." It would be tragic, he added, to sacrifice the canyons for "a few acre-feet of water and a few kilowatt hours." George W. Kelley of the Colorado Forestry and Horticultural Association pointed out that "wilderness areas have become to us a spiritual necessity, an antidote to the strains of modern living." Wallace Stegner agreed that the importance of places like Dinosaur was not only as a sanctuary for rare wildlife but for "our own species" hard-pressed by "twentieth-century

strains and smells and noises."

Aldo Leopold suffered a fatal heart attack on April 21, 1948, while fighting a brush fire, but his ideas about the ecological significance of wilderness figured prominently in the defense of Dinosaur. Bernard DeVoto first applied them to the controversy in an influential article in *The Saturday Evening Post.* The monument was important, he declared, "as wilderness that is preserved intact . . . for the field study of . . . the balances of Nature, the web of life, the interrelationships of species . . . presently it will not be possible to study such matters anywhere else." Leopold's "land ethic" concept was reiterated by Charles C. Bradley, who estimated that the amount of paved land in the United States equalled the amount of wilderness. For him this dramatized the danger of Americans losing their sense of the "man-earth relationship." Quoting Leopold, Bradley pleaded for the retention of Dinosaur in an unaltered condition as a gesture of human respect for the biotic community. Howard Zahniser added that "to know wilderness is to know profound humility, to recognize one's littleness, to sense dependence and interdependence, indebtedness and responsibility."

Beginning with the House and Senate hearings on the Colorado River Storage Project in 1954, preservationists carried the defense of Dinosaur into politics. Using the example of Hetch Hetchy Valley to give substance to their arguments, the nation's foremost spokesmen for wilderness delivered thoughtful statements to the legislators. When the committees, dominated by western congressmen, reported favorably on Echo Park Dam, the preservationists worked feverishly with direct mailings, flyers, editorials, and articles in an effort to arouse a storm of protest at the grass roots level. Their success was evident in the mail that poured into the House in the spring of 1954—the ratio of those who wanted Dinosaur wild to those favoring the dam was eighty to one. As a result, Congress postponed consideration of the entire Colorado River Storage Project. "Controversy over the proposed Echo Park Dam," said Speaker of the House Joseph Martin, "has killed any chance for . . . approval this year."

IN PREPARATION for the renewal of the Echo Park controversy in the Eighty-fourth Congress in 1955, friends of the wilderness made it clear to their opponents that, while they sympathized with the Southwest's need for water, they were prepared to use their public support to block the passage of the whole project unless the dam was

THE LEGACY

David Brower, former director of the Sierra Club, utilized that organization's considerable influence in a continuing fight to save Grand Canyon.

eliminated. Reclamation and hydropower interests, in other words, were confronted with a choice between development that respected wilderness values or no development at all.

At the second set of congressional hearings beginning in March, 1955, the wilderness bloc made bold to challenge the Bureau of Reclamation on its own terms. David Brower used simple arithmetic to show that the Bureau had erred in its calculation of the water that would be lost by evaporation from a reservoir in Dinosaur. Taking the reclamationists' own figures, Brower showed that the lake would actually lose far more water than advertised and that alternate damsites, outside wilderness areas, were preferable with respect to evaporation. In the face of the embarrassed engineers' angry cross examination, Brower defended his allegations successfully enough to raise questions about the economics of the entire Colorado River Storage Project. After Brower's testimony, the suspicion that the Bureau of Reclamation was more interested in perpetuating its own empire than in wisely using the land lingered in many quarters.

As the bill went through the legislative process in the

spring of 1955, exchanges were heated. Supporting Echo Park Dam were western interests: congressmen, governors, civic clubs, chambers of commerce, utility companies, water-users associations, and the Bureau of Reclamation. On the other side were Southern California water users (who bitterly resented any Upper Basin development that might diminish the Colorado's flow), some eastern congressmen, many educational institutions, conservation and "nature" organizations, and a mounting tide of public opinion. Sensing that support of the dam was regional and opposition national in scope, Senator Richard L. Neuberger of Oregon afforded his colleagues an amendment deleting it. Several came to his support when the bill reached the floor in April. "Certainly, Mr. President," Paul H. Douglas of Illinois argued, "we should keep some wild places" to "benefit the human spirit." Echo Park Dam, Douglas continued, would contribute its share to transforming the nation "into a placid, tepid place, greatly unlike the wild and stirring America which we love and from which we draw inspiration." After senators favoring the dam replied that it would actually beautify Dinosaur, Hubert H. Humphrey of Minnesota pointed out that "where once there was the beautiful Hetch Hetchy Valley . . . there is now the stark, drab reservoir of O'Shaughnessy Dam." Senator Arthur V. Watkins of Utah gained the floor and demanded that the discussion "get back to fundamentals." Then for half an hour he reiterated the advantages of the Echo Park damsite from the standpoint of irrigation, hydropower, and cost. Calling for a vote at the conclusion of his speech, Watkins had the satisfaction of seeing the Neuberger amendment defeated. All but three western senators cast negative votes.

In the House, however, the pressure of public sentiment proved harder to resist. On July 8, 1955, the Committee on Interior and Insular Affairs reported a Colorado River Storage Project bill *without* the controversial dam at Echo Park. "We hated to lose it," Representative William A. Dawson of Utah explained, but "the opposition from conservation organizations has been such as to convince us . . . that authorizing legislation could not be passed unless this dam was taken out."

IN SPITE OF THEIR SUCCESS in the House, many wilderness supporters feared the restoration of the dam to the project. In confirmation of their uneasiness, congressmen and governors of the Upper Basin met in Denver on November 1, 1955, to plot strategy. Learning of the planned meeting, Howard Zahniser rushed a full-page open letter into the Denver *Post* of the day before. It made clear that unless Echo Park Dam were permanently deleted, the wilderness lobby would use every legal means to block the entire project. The open letter hastened to add, however, that the preservationists "are *not* anti-reclamationists, and are NOT fighting the principle of water use in the west." Thus put in the awkward position of defeating their own interests if they continued to insist on a dam at Echo Park, the Denver strategists promised to drop it from the project: "No dam or reservoir constructed under the authorization of the Act," the revised bill read, "shall be within any National Park or Monument." This satisfied the preservationists, and the developers, grateful to secure even a modified Colorado River Storage Project, quickly pushed the new bill into law. It authorized four major dams: Flaming Gorge on the Green well above Dinosaur National Monument, Curecanti on the Gunnison, Navajo on the San Juan, and Glen Canyon on the main Colorado just above Lees Ferry.

In the Echo Park controversy American conservation turned a significant corner. For the first time preservation had prevailed over utilitarian conservation in a major confrontation. The Echo Park affair revealed that henceforth the private, citizen-action group with a talent for arousing public opinion would be a strong candidate for the leadership of American conservation. The legacy of the conflict was widespread suspicion of the government's purposes with regard to the environment. Finally, the showdown at Echo Park left little doubt that in the future partisan conflict would be the mechanism for environmental decision-making. The deletion of the dam was literally *bludgeoned* from the reclamationists; their minds remained unconvinced. Even after the 1956 settlement, rumors of a reactivated Echo Park Dam persisted, and preservationists remained on guard.

O N OCTOBER 15, 1956, dynamiting began for Glen Canyon Dam, the first undertaken with the authorization of the Colorado River Storage Project Act. Its reservoir, named Lake Powell, would at capacity have a length of 186 miles, a shoreline of 1,800, and would be, according to the Reclamation Service, a "Jewel of the Colorado," opening this section of the wild river to boating, fishing, water-skiing, and camping. Preservationists remained skeptical. After rejoicing in the Echo Park victory, they suddenly awoke to the fact that Glen Canyon,

although not in the national park system, was a region of incredible beauty and inspiring wildness. That realization was manifested in 1963 with the publication of a new volume in the Sierra Club's lavish Exhibit Format Series, *The Place No One Knew: Glen Canyon on the Colorado*. Eliot Porter's photographs and David Brower's editing drove home its moral: a needless reservoir was inundating one of the wonders of the New World simply because Americans had not known of its beauties and had not protested soon enough. Dinosaur was saved by vigilance and stubbornness; Glen Canyon was lost through apathy. Moreover, the preservationists charged, the reclamationists had acted in bad faith in regard to Rainbow Bridge. Arching an unbelievable 309 feet over Bridge Creek, about five miles from the Colorado, Rainbow is the largest known natural stone bridge in the world. Not until 1909 was it first seen by a white man. In 1910 it was designated a national monument and thus, according to the provisions of the Colorado River Storage Project Act, was exempted from alteration by a dam or reservoir. Indeed, the act specifically instructed the Bureau of Reclamation to take "adequate protective measures to preclude impairment of Rainbow Bridge National Monument." But when filled to capacity Lake Powell would back up water in Bridge Creek to and *through* Rainbow Bridge. Some geologists even suggested that the unnatural amount of water at the foot of the arch would eventually seep into the porous sandstone and cause the bridge to collapse. Reclamationists discounted this possibility and, just as they had with Hetch Hetchy and Echo Park, stressed the way Lake Powell would "open" Rainbow Bridge to thousands of visitors. The issue became academic on January 21, 1963, when the gates of the new Glen Canyon Dam closed and the lake started to fill. Park and wilderness advocates sorrowfully anticipated the violation of the principle they had won with so much effort in the Echo Park controversy.

Preservationists became doubly-determined to win the next battle for wilderness along the Colorado River. And this one could not but be climactic, for the Grand Canyon itself was at stake.

T HE IDEA OF BUILDING DAMS in the Grand Canyon was not new with the 1960's. Two sites in particular had long attracted the attention of engineers: Bridge and Marble canyons. A bill authorizing the construction of a dam at Bridge Canyon had actually passed the Senate in 1950 only to be summarily defeated in the House. Hydrologists had also long discussed an elaborate plan to bring water from a reservoir in Marble Canyon through a forty-mile tunnel under the Kaibab Plateau to hydropower facilities in Kanab Creek. Ninety-one percent of the Colorado's water would have been diverted from its normal course through the Grand Canyon.

According to the seminal National Park Service Act of 1916, the alteration of natural conditions by hydropower projects in Grand Canyon National Park or Grand Canyon National Monument, immediately downstream, was clearly illegal. The legislation stated that "the fundamental purpose of the . . . parks . . . is to conserve the scenery and natural and historic objects and the wildlife therein, and to provide for the enjoyment of the same in such manner and by such means as will leave them unimpaired for the enjoyment of future generations." But reclamationists took heart from a provision in the act of February 26, 1919, establishing Grand Canyon National Park. "Whenever consistent with the primary purposes of said park," it declared, "the Secretary of the Interior is authorized to permit the utilization of areas therein which may be necessary for the development and maintenance of government reclamation projects." This obvious inconsistency left the way open for widely varying interpretations of the legality of Grand Canyon dams.

The Grand Canyon controversy began to gather momentum in 1963 when the Bureau of Reclamation made public its multi-billion-dollar Pacific Southwest Water Plan. To solve the growing Southwest's water shortage, engineers proposed diverting water from the Columbia River and transporting it in a series of tunnels, ducts, and canals into the Colorado. The increased flow would be utilized with the aid of a series of dams and diversion facilities. One of them, the Central Arizona Project, called for hydropower dams at Marble and Bridge canyons. The sale of the electricity they produced would be used to pay for transporting water from Lake Havasu on the lower Colorado to the Phoenix-Tucson area.

The Bureau of Reclamation anticipated preservationist opposition: Marble Canyon Dam would flood fifty-three miles of Redwall Gorge, considered equal to the now inundated Glen Canyon. The proposed high dam at Bridge Canyon would back water up into a portion of Grand Canyon National Monument. In preparation for the inevitable protests, Commissioner of Reclamation Floyd Dominy ordered the construction of a scale model of the Grand Canyon and used it to argue that the dams and

reservoirs he proposed would not damage scenic values. Indeed the lakes would permit millions to enjoy the little-seen beauties of the inner canyon with unprecedented safety. On this basis Secretary of the Interior Stewart Udall initially supported the dams and ordered the National Park Service to cease its opposition in the interests of department unity. Such official backing and the tenor of congressional hearings in 1965 and 1966 led many to expect that the dams would be approved by the Eighty-ninth Congress. But on June 9, 1966, a now-famous advertisement appeared on full pages of the *New York Times* and the Washington *Post.* "Now Only You Can Save Grand Canyon From Being Flooded—For Profit," its headline blared. The ad cost the Sierra Club $15,000, but it paid remarkable dividends, as mail deploring the dams poured into key Washington offices. The greatest success of the ad was unexpected: on June 10 the Internal Revenue Service warned the Sierra Club that henceforth any donations it received might be ruled non-deductible under a ruling forbidding organizations in its tax status from engaging "substantially" in efforts to influence legislation. If the warning was designed to help the cause of the dam builders, it was a backfire of colossal proportions, for it appeared that the Sierra Club was being punished for altruistic efforts on behalf of Grand Canyon. The charge of the Internal Revenue Service became front page news all over the country, multiplying the effect of the ad many times. People who didn't care in the slightest about wilderness now rose on behalf of the Sierra Club in the name of civil liberties. Could bureaucracies intimidate citizen protest? Were only the well-heeled lobbies to be tolerated? (The Sierra Club continued its attack and, true to its warning, the Internal Revenue Service rescinded the club's tax-exempt status—shortly before Christmas.)

The simple plea to "SAVE GRAND CANYON" (as bumper stickers proclaimed) headed preservationist arguments. If we can't protect the Grand Canyon, they asked Americans, what *can* we save? In answer to Commissioner Dominy's contention that the dams would not alter much of the canyon and their reservoirs would not even be visible from most places on the rims, the preservaitonists replied that it was important on emotional grounds to *know* that the free-flowing, living river that had cut the chasm was cutting it still, even if it couldn't be seen. Dams, furthermore, would eliminate the possibility of a supreme adventure: running the Colorado by boat through Grand Canyon.

Supporting these points were charges that the dams served no purpose other than to make money to finance other parts of the Central Arizona Project. Was the nation so poor it had to use the Grand Canyon as a "cash register," preservationists wondered? Then they pointed out that coal-fired thermal plants or nuclear generators could perform the dams' functions equally well and at less cost to the taxpayer. Another criticism stemmed from the preservationists' belief that the dams would actually *waste* the Colorado's limited water supply through evaporation and seepage into the reservoir walls. In this way the dams were represented as working against the very purpose of the Pacific Southwest Water Plan and the Central Arizona Project.

AGAINST THIS BARRAGE, as well as against that emanating from California water users who resisted any upstream development of the Colorado, the dam builders had one trump—Columbia River water. But even this slipped away in the summer of 1966: the Pacific Northwest wanted no part of the idea.

As a result of the previous summer's furor over the Grand Canyon dams, reclamationists brought revised proposals to the opening of the Ninetieth Congress in January, 1967. They would abandon Marble Canyon Dam entirely and extend Grand Canyon National Park sixty miles upstream as added protection for this part of the Colorado. Downstream from the park, however, the new plan called for the abolition of Grand Canyon National Monument so that Hualapai Dam (as Bridge Canyon Dam had been renamed) would not inundate any area in the national park system. Preservationists remained adamant. One bullet in the heart, they maintained, was just as deadly as two. And changing names on a map did not alter the fact that there would no longer be a live river in Grand Canyon.

On February 1, 1967, the dam builders' hopes plunged when Secretary Udall announced that he had changed his mind about the Grand Canyon dams. Speaking on behalf of the Johnson administration, he declared that all support for Marble Canyon Dam had been withdrawn and that Hualapai, or Bridge Canyon, Dam should receive further study. For the time being, Udall suggested, the Central Arizona Project should plan to receive its money and power from a thermal plant. In response to continuing pressure, the Senate Interior and Insular Affairs Committee voted in June to authorize the Central Ari-

The controversy over the Grand Canyon dams inspired editorial comment the nation over (Los Angeles Times).

zona Project without either of the controversial dams. The committeemen also acted to reserve the Bridge Canyon site for future determination by Congress, thereby precluding the possibility of Arizona's obtaining permission from the Federal Power Commission to build the dam itself. On August 8 the Senate passed a damless Central Arizona Project.

In the House the issue remained unresolved during 1967, but in 1968 the Colorado Basin Act provided for an aqueduct—and no dams. While the fate of the river is still vague, the chances of the dam-builders seem slim. Insistence on a dam, it appears, will only delay the time when Colorado water will reach central Arizona. This realization even brought from reclamationists the grudging concession that the Grand Canyon dams were really not essential for providing water to the Southwest—they only paid the bills. Whether the situation will change appreciably under the administration of Richard Nixon and the new Secretary of the Interior, Walter J. Hickel, remains to be seen, but at this point it seems that preservationists have finally ended the era of utilitarian conservation on the Colorado. More precisely, reclamation has reached its own natural limits. Further development can

The ad that caused the fuss . . .

SHOULD WE ALSO FLOOD THE SISTINE CHAPEL SO TOURISTS CAN GET NEARER THE CEILING?

EARTH began four billion years ago and Man two million. The Age of Technology, on the other hand, is hardly a hundred years old, and on our time chart we have been generous to give it even the little line we have.

It seems to us hasty, therefore, during this blip of time, for Man to think of directing his fascinating new tools toward altering irrevocably the forces which made him. Nonetheless, in these few brief years among three billion, wilderness has all but disappeared. And now these:

1) There is a bill in Congress to "improve" Grand Canyon. Two dams will back up artificial lakes into 148 miles of canyon gorge. This will benefit tourists in power boats, it is argued, who will enjoy viewing the canyon wall more closely. (See headline). Submerged underneath the tourists will be part of the most revealing single page of earth's history. The lakes will be as deep as 600 feet (deeper for example, than all but a handful of New York buildings are high) but in a century, silting will have replaced the water with that much mud, wall to wall.

There is no part of the wild Colorado River, the Grand Canyon's sculptor, that will not be maimed.

Tourist recreation, as a reason for the dams, is in fact an afterthought. The Bureau of Reclamation, which backs them, prefers to call the dams "cash registers." They are expected to make money by sale of commercial power. *They will not provide anyone with water.*

2) In Northern California, four lumber companies are about to complete logging the private virgin redwood forests, an operation which to give you an idea of its size, has taken fifty years.

Soon, where nature's tallest living things have stood silently since the age of the dinosaurs, the extent of the cutting will make creation of a redwood national park absurd.

The companies have said tourists want only enough roadside trees for the snapping of photos. They offer to spare trees for this purpose, and not much more. The result will remind you of the places on your face you missed while you were shaving.

3) And up the Hudson, there are plans for a power complex—a plant, transmission lines, and a reservoir on top of Storm King Mountain—destroying one of the last wild and high and beautiful spots near New York City.

4) A proposal to flood a region in Alaska as large as Lake Erie would eliminate at once the breeding grounds of more wildlife than conservationists have preserved in history.

5) In San Francisco, real estate developers are day by day filling a bay that made the city famous, putting tract houses over the fill; and now there's a new idea—still more fill, enough for an air cargo terminal as big as Manhattan.

There exists today a mentality which can conceive such destruction, giving commerce as ample reason. For 74 years, the 40,000 member Sierra Club has opposed that mentality. But now, when even Grand Canyon can be threatened, we are at a critical moment in time.

This generation will decide if something untrammelled and free remains, as testimony we had love for those who follow.

We have been taking ads, therefore, asking people to write their Congressmen and Senators; Secretary of the Interior Stewart Udall; The President; and to send us funds to continue the battle. Thousands *have* written, but meanwhile, the Grand Canyon legislation has advanced out of committee and is at a crucial stage in Congress. More letters are needed and more money, to help fight a mentality that may decide Man no longer needs nature.*

David Brower, Executive Director
Sierra Club
Mills Tower, San Francisco

☐ Please send me more details on how I may help.
☐ Here is a donation of $_____ to continue your effort to keep the public informed.
☐ Send me "Time and the River Flowing," famous four color book which tells the complete story of Grand Canyon, and why T. Roosevelt said, "leave it as it is." ($25.00)
☐ Send me "The Last Redwoods" which tells the complete story of the opportunity as well as the destruction in the redwoods. ($17.50)
☐ I would like to be a member of the Sierra Club. Enclosed is $14.00 for entrance and first year's dues.

Name_____

Address_____

City_____State_____Zip____

---

*The previous ads, urging that readers exercise a constitutional right of petition, to save Grand Canyon, produced an unprecedented reaction by the Internal Revenue Service threatening our tax deductible status. IRS says the ads may be a "substantial" effort to "influence legislation." Undefined, these terms leave organizations like ours at the mercy of administrative whim. (The question has not been raised with any organizations that favor Grand Canyon dams.) So we cannot now promise that contributions you send us are deductible—pending results of what may be a long legal battle.

The Sierra Club, founded in 1892 by John Muir, is nonprofit, supported by people who, like Thoreau, believe "In wildness is the preservation of the world." The club's program is nationwide, includes wilderness trips, books and films—as well as such efforts as this to protect the remnant of wilderness in the Americas. There are now twenty chapters, branch offices in New York (Biltmore Hotel), Washington (Dupont Circle Building), Los Angeles (Auditorium Building), Albuquerque, Seattle, and main office in San Francisco.

proceed only in defiance of knowledge about the amount of water actually available and of benefit-cost economics. The Colorado, in other words, has been stretched to its limits in the service of man's body. Yet it still retains the capacity to satisfy his spirit. In this standoff, perhaps, is the final lesson of conservation's civil war over the river: both development and preservation can exist on one waterway, and both are necessary.

The fight to save Grand Canyon diverted the attention of park and wilderness enthusiasts from an unexpected new problem: the increase of their own numbers. In the past preservationists labored to persuade Americans to visit places of scenic beauty like Grand Canyon or Dinosaur National Monument. Their success in this endeavor now, ironically, seems the source of the next major threat to wilderness. Crowding can impair the value of a natural scene just as surely as economic development. Grand Canyon National Park is already feeling the strains of popularity. Attendance in 1967 was 1.8 million, up a million since the late 1950's. The meaning of this growth is evident in the park superintendent's confession in regard to the South Rim during peak vacation periods: "If campers don't get here before noon . . . the rangers at the entrances tell them they have to leave before night." Existing hotel and motel accommodations in the park fill up even faster, and the National Park Service balks at building more for fear of turning the rim into a major city. Daytime traffic is also a problem. When cars have to circle a parking lot at an overlook seeking a space, or double-park, something is lost when the view finally appears. But keeping people and cars out of the park violates the democratic implications of its purpose. Preserving natural conditions for civilized people is a trying business.

THERE ARE, to be sure, parts of Grand Canyon National Park where a man can be alone in the wilderness, but park administrators have found most visitors either loath to make the effort to reach them or are physically incapable. Yet others feel the cost is too great when they read the superintendent's statement that "we've . . . got to consider a tramway down to the floor of the canyon, and possibly mini-trains or mini-buses for tours along the rim." How much, many are wondering, should the national parks' purpose to keep scenery unimpaired be sacrificed to their purpose to make that scenery available for public enjoyment?

The recent and rapidly growing vogue of boat tripping

"Back—just a little farther back!" was the caption for this Los Angeles Times *cartoon.*

down the Colorado through Grand Canyon is producing its own set of people problems. In the mid-1950's only about 150 persons had *ever* run the canyon. Last year alone three thousand made the trip. A dozen outfitters conduct scheduled two-week runs, and the popular campsites are in use night after night during the summer. Deterioration of the quality of the experience of the inner gorge is sure to result unless limits are placed on travel. But in this case what happens to the principle of a public park and the freedom that should be associated with wilderness?

Wilderness, like water, is a finite commodity. The Colorado once had ample stores of both. But demands for both increased to the point where the allocation of the river to one or the other became a matter of intense competition. The development of Colorado water seems to have reached its practical maximum. The American appetite for wilderness, on the contrary, shows no signs of declining. Conservation's new frontier will be recreational engineering, the protection of natural beauty from its lovers. And, as in the past, we can expect that what is learned on the Colorado will be both inspiration and warning to conservationists everywhere.

At left is one of the newspaper advertisements that inspired the Internal Revenue Service to cancel the Sierra Club's tax-exempt status, shortly before Christmas, 1966.

CHAPTER X

THE PARKLANDS OF THE COLORADO

The Colorado River's "Geography of Hope."

William E. Brown, Jr.

In a way the Colorado has ceased to be the mighty thing it was. The once empty landscapes through which it courses are empty no more—except in a few places. On drawing boards and charts, in thick reports, are plans for this river. Men thousands of miles away, who may never have seen the river, want to turn it to their purposes. And some of them have the power to do this. They would alter its course, confine it, divert it, consume it. And all the while the river—now a minor stream relative to the demands upon it—flows with interruptions from the Rockies to the sea.

Where will it end? Will this lord of plateaus and deserts be tapped until it is dry? The functional uses to which the river can be put are infinite in the schemes of men. But the river itself is finite in the water it can give.

There is yet another dimension of demand and supply —one dealing with aesthetic qualities, not material quantities. For not all the pressures upon the river relate to functional uses. More people than ever before come to the Colorado to experience its natural wonders, and to sport upon its man-made lakes.

These diverse pressures have produced a spectrum of views on how to manage the river—a spectrum originating in the different policies that serve the interests of conservation, agriculture, aesthetics, recreation, economic development, and so forth. At the extremes of the spectrum are opposing viewpoints. One of these sees the river as a means only, a servant of man. The other sees it as both end and means, an entity in its own right, and a source of inspiration and re-creation for man. Those holding the first view would continue to bend the river to

man's functional purposes. The others want remaining natural sections of the river retained—because this would be a substantive good, and because a great river can bend men toward appreciation of the aesthetic-spiritual values to be derived from nature.

These partisans have clashed before. They will clash again. Meanwhile, the river flows its interrupted course to the sea. And whatever the outcome of the argument, the decisions of men will determine the fate of the river— at least for a short geologic while. . . .

FROM SHINING MOUNTAINS to steaming delta the Colorado River flows some fourteen hundred miles. Most of its course cuts athwart great plateaus composed of layered sediments—sandstones of ancient deserts, limestones of ancient seas, shales of ancient lakes and streams. In the bottom of Grand Canyon the combination of rising land and rolling river has laid bare the roots of the earth— granites and schists two billion years old. All is chaos and jumble at this deepest level, which records the mighty birth pangs of the globe.

But the mile-thick sediments above are remarkably unaltered. Across hundreds of miles they lie flat, in the uniform sequence of their deposition. So the Colorado Plateau Province, viewed in the large, is a horizontal structure, made of different sediments laid on like blankets on a bed. Each of these blankets has it own character, best defined by color and composition. Navajo Sandstone is the same basic stuff in Utah as in Arizona or New Mexico, and, across most of its great extent, it will rest on the Kayenta, and the Kayenta will rest on the

273

The Turks Head on the Green River, Canyonlands National Park, Utah (Philip Hyde photograph).

THE LEGACY

Wingate, and so on. Wherever erosion has exposed these rocks, they can be recognized and hailed as old friends, or avoided if one dislikes them. Certainly the sheer red cliffs of the Wingate are more attractive than the muddy-looking slump of the Moenkupi. The best rock exposures, the most dramatic, are those engineered by streams. And the best of all these make up the canyon walls of the Colorado and its right arm, the 700-mile-long Green River.

The plateaus and canyons are not all, for the Colorado-Green system extends beyond them at its upper and lower ends. Both rivers begin in the high Rockies where massive earth movements have tangled older landscapes. And in the Lower Basin, below Grand Canyon, the Colorado flows sluggishly through deserts flanked by barren mountains. Still, the heartland of the drainage basin is the maze of canyons from Flaming Gorge to Lake Mead. Except along that defiant part of the Green's course that crosses the Uinta Mountains, these canyons have been carved from elevated plains and plateaus. Slashing downward through these horizontal structures, the rivers and the rains have created a vertical canyon world, from whose depths the sky sometimes appears but a blue slit framed by nearly overarching cliffs.

I T ALL BEGINS in the perpetual snows of the Front and Wind River ranges of the Rockies. On a summer's day one can climb up through the spruce and fir forests to the high open world of tundra and granite peaks and glacial snow. Relatively few people get this high, to the very ridge piece of the continent. Here a million snows have gutted the peaks, and in their hollow shells lie green tarns fed by dripping snowbanks. From the tarns the trickling waters descend and unite with one another to form creeks, then rivers, than *the* river.

To see these beginnings, go high in the Neversummer Mountains of Rocky Mountain National Park. This is a pure world, and most people who come here respect it. They find here the wonderful constancy of the natural world at work. A single drop of water lingers, catching sunlight, then drops from the frayed edge of retreating snow—itself the remnant of an ocean-born storm. The drop blends with its fellows and seeps across a rocky apron into the tarn. There its parts disperse and mingle still more. Eventually these bits of water—barring evaporation or diversion en route—will flow across the delta, 1,400 miles away. They will carry into the blue sea microscopic

burdens of silt, and drop them there. In this process is the story of the rivers, and of the landscapes they cross.

A T THE SOUTHWEST CORNER of Rocky Mountain National Park, within fifteen air miles of its source, the Colorado enters its first man-made entrapment, one of a long series of dam, reservoir, and diversion complexes that support concentrations of human population in the arid lands within and bordering the drainage basin. The Colorado–Big Thompson Reclamation Project undercuts the Continental Divide. It gathers surplus waters from the west side of the Front Range and transports them by the thirteen-mile Adams Tunnel to the dry east side, there to irrigate the farms of the South Platte Valley. The tunnel is an exceptional example of man's ingenuity in altering the course of nature. For the Front Range is the last rampart between moisture-bearing westerly winds off the Pacific Ocean and the High Plains of eastern Colorado. Its peaks wring the clouds nearly dry on the west side before letting them pass over the crest. This is the phenomenon that produces a rain shadow—an area of relative dryness on the lee side of a topographic barrier. In terms of water distribution, the Colorado—Big Thompson Reclamation Project sawed off the Front Range by watering the dry lands in the rain shadow.

By-products of the reclamation project are hydroelectric power and creation of two large reservoirs—Lake Granby and Shadow Mountain Lake. Linked by channel to one another and to Grand Lake, Colorado's largest natural body of water, these are the Great Lakes of Colorado. At an elevation of more than eight thousand feet, the lakes are surrounded by forest-mantled hills and mountains. Their waters and shores make up the Shadow Mountain National Recreation Area—a scenic playground for boaters, fishermen, and campers that complements the majestic beauty of the bordering park.

Once past Lake Granby, the Colorado resumes its course. It crosses the Park Range through 2,000-foot-deep Gore Canyon, then breaches the westernmost outriders of the Rockies to reach the plateau country. Here the skyline changes. Flat-topped mesas replace jagged alpine peaks. And the long lines of cliffs begin to close in.

Below Grand Junction, where the Gunnison River disgorges its load, the Colorado flows through Grand Valley between two great escarpments, the Book Cliffs to the north and the frayed edge of the Uncompahgre Plateau to the south. This plateau, a giant upwarp of the earth's crust, is a core of hard crystalline rock covered by softer sediments. At its edge, where the uplift created a fault line, erosion has eaten into the rock, carving fjord-like canyons that meander back from the scarp into the body of the plateau. Thin mesas separate these canyons. Rising from their floors are towering monoliths and spires, some of them capped by balanced rocks. These are remnants of the plateau, isolated by erosion from the cliff walls.

COLORADO NATIONAL MONUMENT preserves the finest, most tortured section of the Uncompahgre scarp, where the cliffs rise 1,000 to 1,500 feet above the canyon floors. Far on the eastern margin of the Colorado Plateau Province, the monument is in a region of wide river valleys. The topography is not typical of the main-line canyons farther downstream, where the Colorado itself is deeply incised thousands of feet below the plateau surface, but here is the beginning, and a harbinger of the canyon country to come.

Crossing the Utah line, the Colorado rushes to its junction with the Green—which, meanwhile, has pursued a perverse course across the Uinta Mountains to get there. Descending from its headwaters in the Wind River Range, the Green crosses sandy deserts and weirdly carved badlands. Then it butts into the foothills of the Uintas. Before construction of Flaming Gorge Dam, the river picked up force from streams draining off the north slope of the oddly oriented east-west Uinta range, then plunged through Flaming Gorge and on to the Canyon of Lodore. Its tributary from the east, the Yampa River, also follows a remarkably contrary course, using the axis of the Uintas for its bed. Nowhere else in the United States are streams so out of harmony with mountains. Here they refuse to follow the lowlands but seem to attack the highlands instead. Out of this stubbornness were born the magnificent deep canyons of Flaming Gorge Recreation Area and Dinosaur National Monument.

More than ninety miles long, Flaming Gorge Lake is flanked by the walls of Red and Horseshoe canyons in the south, and by rolling hills and buttes to the north. The shoreline ranges from low flats to cliffs more than fifteen hundred feet high. In the wide, shallow valleys north of the canyons are many campsites. Launching ramps give boaters access to the cliff-bound parts of the lake. Below the dam, which rises 502 feet above the bedrock of Red Canyon, river runners take float trips through the scenic canyon country within Ashley National Forest. The recre-

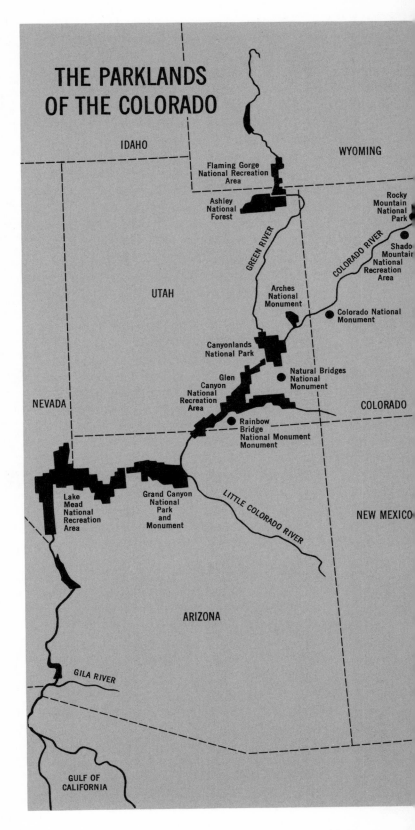

THE PARKLANDS OF THE COLORADO

IDAHO

WYOMING

Flaming Gorge National Recreation Area

Rocky Mountain National Park

Ashley National Forest

GREEN RIVER

COLORADO RIVER

Shado Mountain National Recreation Area

UTAH

Arches National Monument

Colorado National Monument

Canyonlands National Park

Natural Bridges National Monument

Glen Canyon National Recreation Area

NEVADA

COLORADO

Rainbow Bridge National Monument Monument

LITTLE COLORADO RIVER

NEW MEXICO

Lake Mead National Recreation Area

Grand Canyon National Park and Monument

ARIZONA

GILA RIVER

GULF OF CALIFORNIA

Echo Park from Harper's Corner, Dinosaur National Monument, Colorado-Utah (Philip Hyde photograph).

ation area encompasses two distinct geological zones. In Wyoming, the land is mainly flat, composed of horizontal layers of sediment. In Utah, colorful rocks that once lay flat were bent upward and forced into grotesque positions by the great earth movements that built the Uintas. The best place to read these ancient geologic happenings is at the entrance to Flaming Gorge proper. Here the Green River knifed through steeply tilted formations to produce the brilliant red portals that fascinated Major Powell.

Dinosaur national monument is superimposed on the junction of the Green and Yampa Rivers—which are themselves superimposed on a mountain range. The lower Yampa's meandering canyon and Lodore, Whirlpool, and Split Mountain canyons on the Green hint of

the ancient sedimentary plain that once covered the east end of the Uinta Mountains. The streams became well established on this plain. When the buried mountains heaved upward in great crustal movements, the streams maintained their winding courses—cutting through the soft sediments and on into the hard rock of the rising mountains. It is this kind of superimposed, inherited stream course that often explains the anomaly of streams "attacking" mountains instead of going around them.

These same geological processes of uplift and degradation stripped away the 5,000 feet of sediments that once covered Dinosaur Quarry, discovered in 1909 by Earl Douglass of the Carnegie Museum. The quarry was once a sandbar in a stream bed. Here, it is theorized, the bodies of dinosaurs accumulated in floodtime. Buried quickly by sediments, their bones changed to mineralized fossils. After 140-million years the same agent that buried the bones—running water—uncovered them. That this exhumation happened when men were around to discover it is purest chance, for a few seconds of geologic time either way, and the world's greatest known deposit of Jurassic dinosaurs would have been lost to science. As it is, hundreds of specimens have been recovered and many of them are on display in the nation's museums. Today the quarry is an in-place exhibit, enclosed by the monument visitor center. Here visitors can watch scientists at work as they probe the fossil-bearing rock. Originally, Dinosaur National Monument included only the quarry site. Today, greatly enlarged, it straddles the Utah-Colorado border to include spectacular canyons through the Yampa Plateau and the folded mass of the Uinta Mountains.

The Green and Yampa are rough, turbulent rivers, but hundreds of people run them yearly. Tucked into the canyon depths are wood-fringed meadows on the stream floodplain, like Echo Park and Rainbow Park, where boaters rest after rough runs through the gorges at places called Disaster Falls and Hells Half Mile. The monument hinterlands include an extensive outback of plateaus and mountains, interspersed by the jutting headlands of side canyons descending to the main streams. From some such high point Major Powell looked 2,000 feet downward to the Green and saw canyon walls "buttressed on a grand scale, with deep alcoves intervening; columned crags crown the cliffs, and the river is rolling below."

Below Dinosaur and Ouray, the Green slides through Desolation Canyon, Gray Canyon, and Labyrinth Canyon on its way to rendezvous with the Colorado in Canyonlands National Park. This nearly continuous stretch of canyons breaks between the East and West Tavaputs plateaus, then entrenches in a wide basin and plateau country whose horizon is marked by the sweeping scarps of the Roan and Book cliffs. South of these cliffs, in the peninsula between the converging rivers, lies Arches National Monument. Here red-rock Entrada Sandstone has weathered to form natural stone spans, some of them hundreds of feet across. Arches is high, hot desert country looming above the Colorado, which borders it on the southeast. Intricate drainage patterns lace the weirdly eroded land. These are the dry washes carved by runoff from summer showers beating on huge expanses of slickrock. With no place to go, except away, the rains rush into the waiting

channels and thunder together into the Colorado, carrying with them the tools of rock and sand that give the river its abrasive power. Along the higher reaches of these washes are springs and seeps. Some of them, in shaded alcoves under the cliffs, form pools that support a profusion of aquatic plants and animals. It is a pleasant shock to stumble upon these hidden oases after the heat and dehydration of the windswept plateaus.

Arches and its sister national monument to the south, Natural Bridges, exemplify the high plateau lands bordering the Colorado River. Both are notable for great natural spans of rock fashioned from fractured and jointed sandstone that has been subjected to weathering extremes— for extremes of heat and cold and wind and drought and water are the norm here. At Arches the combined agents of degradation have first produced vertical fins of high-standing sandstone, then quarried out their centers to make scores of windows and arches. At Natural Bridges entrenched streams first cut intricate meanders whose walls were also finlike, then straightened their tortuous courses by boring through the obstructing walls.

IN TERMS OF GEOLOGIC TIME, both places illustrate the almost furious pace and dynamism of erosion in the Colorado Plateau Province, where all the conditions of material plasticity and active forces of degradation are present in proper combination. A close observer sees and may even hear and touch constant evidence of erosion— the churning power of a flash flood, the white scar and piled debris of a fresh rockfall, the splintering crack of expanding ice in a crevice, the crumbling surface of rocks under subtle chemical attack. Here are remorseless forces constantly at work leveling the land, destroying all illusions of permanence. Here one begins to understand, however dimly, what a few million years can mean to a landscape. And such understanding is good preparation for the quintessential heartland of the Colorado—Canyonlands National Park.

Canyonlands—with endless variations and from innumerable intermediate levels—is two experiences: from above and from below. Here, at the junction of Green and Colorado, the earth has been disemboweled. From above, one looks deep into the thirty-mile-wide gash. From below, expanding horizons step upward and outward to the sky. The overview allows a seeming comprehension. But below, the intricacies of the earth's wracked body are too many and too diverse for comprehension.

THE LEGACY

From Island in the Sky—uttermost point of the plateau-peninsula between the convergent rivers—the vast erosion basin can be seen in the large. The horizon line is formed by the rims of the high plateau out of which the basin was carved. Above the horizon float three mountain ranges—the La Sals, the Abajos, and the Henrys. Altogether it is a stunning sight. The falling off of the land—from the Island to the White Rim nearly two thousand feet below, and then another thousand to the rivers—is breathtaking. On this narrow point, almost surrounded by the abyss, one does get the sense of clinging to an island, suspended in a sea of space—space, moreover, that is not resting securely, but seems itself temporarily suspended and about to collapse into the void. If, as sometimes happens, a raven sails over this void and folds its wings and falls 500 feet, all the elements of sheer height and trembling space come together as a wrenching blow in the observer's viscera.

THE SHIFT from overview to involvement in Canyonlands can be made in many ways: through the rivers' gorges into the wild waters of Cataract Canyon; by a cliff-hugging road down Shafer Canyon to the White Rim; by foot trail into the jumbled chasm of Upheaval Dome, then on down to the bottoms along the Green; by jeep trail from Squaw Flat into the wonders of the Needles, or up the lush drainage of Salt Creek. Almost inaccessible across the Colorado are the Maze and Land of Standing Rocks. Each of these great sectors of the park would deserve to be a park in its own right. Each is an infinitude of eroded splendor, divided and subdivided again and again into individual basins, crevices, and monoliths. Men who have spent their lives wandering through this tortuous land keep finding new places.

From the river only the inner canyon walls can be seen. Up the next step, atop the rims of the inner canyon, the erosion basin's wilderness of towers, buttes, spires, and pinnacles comes into view. On the White Rim, one can look down through Monument Basin to the river, or upward at the grand 2,000-foot terrace of the Orange Cliffs. Back on top of the Island, at Grandview Point, the whole scene comes together again—that scene described by Frederick S. Dellenbaugh in 1908 as a "marvelous mighty desert of bare rock, chiseled by the ages out of the foundations of the globe; fantastic, extraordinary, antediluvian, labyrinthian, and slashed in all directions by crevices."

But in all this grandeur and overwhelming scale there are particular elements that one can attach to and become intimate with. Angel Arch in Salt Creek Canyon is one of these. The quiet beauty of Chesler Park, ringed by a bristling forest of 300-foot needles, is another. And in innumerable places one can find small mazes within the larger ones—places where the standing rocks and the convoluted passages between them form playgrounds for exploring children. On the sandy floors of these shaded crevices are imprinted the tracks of the creatures that live here. In a cave may be found the refuse and graffiti of an old cowboy line camp. Or an overhang may shield a smooth wall brightened by the colors of older graffiti—the unfaded pictographs of prehistoric Indians.

EXCEPTING THE CONTROVERSY over dams in Grand Canyon, possibly nowhere else have conservation-preservation values been so polarized as in Glen Canyon. For 200 miles, from the Dirty Devil River to Lees Ferry, Glen Canyon winds through the red-rock plateaus of southern Utah and northern Arizona. Over the ages scores of tributary streams and flash-flood channels carved side canyons that claw back into the plateaus toward bordering highlands. It was these side canyons—narrow and twisting, with deep pools, clear streams, and beautiful vegetation—that inspired Powell to the name Glen Canyon. And for those few who have known these cool grottoes and hidden glens, their progressive flooding by the rising waters of Lake Powell is a tragedy. Only in the farthest reaches of the larger tributaries will some of these exquisite places survive.

Glen Canyon Dam has resolved the issue, and, in creating the lake for power and reclamation purposes, has opened up a magnificent, heretofore almost inaccessible, region for thousands, ultimately millions of boaters. But the poignancy of the choice between conservation and preservation still remains. Much has been lost; much has been gained. As a people, and on this very river, we will face such choices again. Will we have the wisdom to properly order our values to assure that the highest value is served by the choice that is made? This is not a question of good or evil. For each proponent has his own hierarchy of values, and for him the value at the top of hierarchy is by definition highest. Nor can some cosmic arbiter impose a given system of values in a changing world. Obviously such choices will always be difficult. But at the very least, we must as a people be aware that there *are* choices; that there is validity also in the remote, the exquisite, the rare. Without such awareness, and some choices guided by it, our national environment will lose the charm of variety. And more: without the restraint that such choices presuppose, our environment may be used up.

Still, Glen Canyon National Recreation Area is a great place as it is. The soaring dam and the lacework bridge just below it are thrills in themselves. Nearby, the National Park Service, in cooperation with the Bureau of Reclamation, operates a visitor center and guided tours through the dam. From Wahweap, a major developed area with overnight and day-use facilities, it is fifty miles by water to the trail in Bridge Canyon that leads to Rainbow Bridge. This, the largest known natural stone span, is but one of many bridges and arches along the shores of Lake Powell. Looming over the lake and its associated canyons, buttes, and mesas are high-standing plateaus, like the Kaiparowits and the Aquarius, and intrusive mountains, like the Henrys and the massif of Navajo Mountain. Off their slopes come the streams and cloudburst floods that have dissected this land into the intricate patterns occupied by the lake waters.

BELOW THE DAM is the recreation area's riverine district—fifteen miles of clear, cold, free-flowing water where the big lunkers give trout fishermen fits. These few miles of swift but rapidless river are all that remain of the Glen Canyon of old. The pristine beauty of the larger canyon that so few knew can be known here. With good boat access at Lees Ferry, thousands take the upstream trip. The cliffs rise nearly two thousand feet along this stretch. Alternations of sunlight and shadow make art forms of their stained and fractured walls. The return by moonlight, just floating with the current, is an indescribably moving experience.

At Lees Ferry, where Powell rested and resupplied, the Paria River marks the lower end of Glen Canyon and the beginning of Marble Gorge. It is one of the few places where the cliffs break away from the Colorado, allowing ancient and modern men to cross the canyon system. So it became a crossroads for Mormon immigrants, miners, Indian traders, and missionaries. Today a stone fort, dugway roads, and scattered mining tools recall those days of passage and wilderness enterprise—days that ended only yesterday with the construction of Navajo Bridge in 1929. The role of Lees Ferry as a point of river access hasn't ended yet. For to this place—the only break in the canyons between Glen Canyon Dam and the lower end of Grand Canyon—still come the river-runners who float

and boat through Grand Canyon. This trip has become big business. Thousands of people in recent years have shared the trepidation that Powell felt when he heard the roar of white waters beyond the bend, that "unknown danger, heavier than immediate peril."

So many people have written about Grand Canyon. It is too well known through these writings, through art, photographs, and films, and through the firsthand experience of millions to attempt superfluous description. It is enough to say that Grand Canyon National Park and Monument, North Rim or South Rim—from the rim, from the river, from any point between on any trail—will reward a hundred times over all efforts to get there by anyone who can look and see, hear, and understand—anyone whose sensibilities respond to what is, indeed, grand.

Rather than description, then, let a kind of meditation be offered. The tallest, proudest man can stand silent and abashed on the rim of Grand Canyon—without shame, without apology. For all men are crushed under the weight of the ages that wrought the work below; all men are small on this stage. Mankind, in this perspective, somehow ceases to be the end-all and be-all of the universe. Where was man a million years ago, and where will he be a million years hence? What will this canyon system look like then? What will have happened to the dams man built, and to the very canyon walls that anchor them today? Will the river still flow, having erased the obstacles that slowed it for awhile? Probably so.

It is this perspective, of time and the remorseless dynamic of working waters, that lies at the heart of the Colorado's deepest inspirational quality. One might wonder if these reflections touch human values. Is it good to put man down this way? Man evolved from primordial slime. He fought against all manner of indifferent forces and malignant enemies. He lives today by the grace of finely balanced natural powers, any one of which could mindlessly come unhinged and destroy him. Man, then, has striven mightily. His continued existence is largely a matter of chance. What can be the human value of reminding him of his transience as a species and his mortality as an individual—as this river, entrenching itself ever deeper into the foundations of the earth, must remind him?

Man has become arrogant. The power he wields seems greater than it is. His self-confidence, bred of shortened

THE LEGACY

view, blinds him to the tenuousness of his existence, to the frailty and narrow bounds of the sphere of life he must inhabit. In pursuit of an object, he carelessly blasts those things that stand between him and attainment. In time, if unchecked, his own power—strong enough to destroy him, too weak to save him—may be his nemesis.

SALVATION, if there is to be salvation, will come when man realizes the limits of his power, when he sees his true stature in the universe. When man acknowledges that he, too, like every other species, is subject to, not exempt from, the abiding rules of life, maybe he will stop destroying the earth's limited bounty; stop corrupting its flickering life. Maybe then he will stop tempting the forces that would destroy him.

But Grand Canyon offers other, less somber, sorts of inspiration. This very morning someone anticipates the dawn at an isolated rim point, there to watch the sun's first rays probe gloomy depths. Form and color emerge slowly. Light touches a pinnacle here, a spire there. Rhythm and momentum build as the void takes shape. Each dawn is like Genesis lived over.

The sense of beginnings strikes at many points in Grand Canyon. Nowhere does it strike deeper than in the Inner Gorge—that slot of a canyon within the canyon where river and rocks meet. Here all the larger canyon's distractions of color and form and softening vegetation are left behind. Only turbid water and black rock remain in stark confrontation.

Beyond Grand Canyon National Park the Colorado flows through the primitive area of Grand Canyon National Monument, where volcanos poured lava over the North Rim to dam the river. Geologically speaking, this happened only yesterday. Impounded for awhile, the river overflowed the lava dam, then ground it down. The abutments of the dam and the rough water over Lava Falls recall this brief encounter. Except for river-runners, the monument is little known. Relatively few people have taken the unimproved North Rim road to Toroweap Point. Here the canyon rims are less than a mile apart and the river is 3,000 feet straight down. At no other point on the Colorado is the gorge so deep and narrow.

Downstream from the national monument the Colorado keeps to its canyons prison for another ninety-three miles, finally breaking out through the cliffs of Grand Wash Fault. Here the great plateaus drop behind, replaced by a desert of basins and mountain ranges. Lake Mead National Recreation Area occupies the entire 240-mile river course from Grand Canyon National Monument to Parker Dam. This huge area includes some of Grand Canyon's loveliest spots: the vast lakes, Mead and Mohave; and the dams, Hoover and Parker.

In the years since towering Hoover Dam was completed in 1935, millions of people have enjoyed the area's combination of desert and water recreation, and the tour of Hoover Dam, an engineering wonder whose whirring turbines symbolize the dependence of a region on a river. The expanse of the lakes, their varied and remote shorelines, their extensive hinterlands—with canyons, mountains, and many desert types—offer outback experiences for the adventurous. For the weekenders from the Southwest's crowded cities, the developed sites provide the full range of lodging, camping, and water-sport facilities.

Within the bounds of Lake Mead National Recreation Area, it is possible to see all four faces of the Colorado—natural entity, natural resource, recreational resource, inspirational resource. The experience is baffling, for man's management of the environment produces many effects. These effects are judged good or bad—depending on viewpoint, which is subjective; or on factual knowledge of natural limitations, which is objective only to the degree that knowledge is valid and full. How to synthesize subjective and objective factors of judgment, to the end of wise, necessary, and humane action—or inaction, as the case may be?

Given the accelerating pressures from a growing and ever more demanding population upon the natural fabric we inhabit, this question will continue to plague us on the Colorado—which is but a microcosm of our larger environment. Under such pressures it is easy to dismiss the subjective in favor of the objective. Mainly, this has been our habit. Value judgments, aesthetics, qualities derived from the affective parts of our natures, are fuzzy and hard to handle. They get in the way of common-sence solutions.

But the affective part of man is a very big part of him. It's the part that has found and created beauty and inspiration in his life. It's the part that relieves the gloomy catalogue of folly and slaughter that fills most of the volumes devoted to man's history. It would be a shame if our descendants were to find in the world they inherit from us nothing to stimulate their affective parts; that is, nothing to give them joy. That is why it is important what happens to the Colorado. Perhaps this is the only criterion upon which we can unite.

Images of
the Colorado: V

Lava Creek, South Rim, Grand Cañyon National Park

The Accessible Wilderness

Vermilion Cliffs from the road to Page, Arizona

It is a lovely and terrible wilderness, such a wilderness as Christ and the prophets went out into; harshly and beautifully colored, broken and worn until its bones are

exposed, its great sky without a smudge or taint from Technocracy, and in hidden
corners and pockets under its cliffs the sudden poetry of springs....
—Wallace Stegner

Light. Space. Light and space without time, I think, for this is a country with only the slightest traces of human history. In the doctrine of the geologists with their scheme of ages, eons, and epochs all is flux, as Heraclitus taught, but from the mortally human point of view the landscape of the Colorado is like a section of eternity—timeless....

The Needles from Devil's Pocket, Canyonlands National Park

Under the desert sun, in that dogmatic clarity, the fables of theology and the myths of classical philosophy dissolve like mist. The air is clean, the rock cuts cruelly into flesh; shatter the rock and the odor of flint rises to your nostrils, bitter and sharp. Whirlwinds dance across the salt flats, a pillar of dust by day; the thornbush breaks into flame at night. What does it mean? It means nothing. It is as it is and has no need for meaning.
—Edward Abbey

284

Pinyon trees in foreground, Chester Park, Utah

View southeast from Grandview Point, Canyonlands National Park

Hendrik van Loon once remarked—I have not checked his figures—that the entire human population of the earth could be packed in a box only a mile wide, deep, and high. He then went on to add that if such a box were dropped into the middle of Grand Canyon, it would just about reach the rim but be not much more conspicuous than many of the mesas which here and there rise almost as high. Only a confirmed misanthropist will feel that the experiment would be worth making, but the visitor is soon struck by a more benign demonstration. This is that men—even hordes of men—cannot fill the Canyon sufficiently to detract from the sense of vast emptiness....

—Joseph Wood Krutch

(Overleaf) This place exerts a magnetic spell. The sky is there above it, but not of it. Its being is apart; its climate; its light; its own. The beams of the sun come into it like visitors. Its own winds blow through it, not those of outside, where we live. The River streams down its mysterious reaches, hurrying ceaselessly; sometimes a smooth sliding lap, sometimes a falling, broken wilderness of billows and whirlpools. Above stand its walls, rising through space upon space of silence. They glow, they gloom, they shine. Bend after bend they reveal themselves, endlessly new in endlessly changing veils of color.... Bend after bend this trance of beauty and awe goes on, terrible as the Day of Judgment, sublime as the Psalms of David. Five thousand feet below the opens and barrens of Arizona, this canyon seems like an avenue conducting to the secret of the universe and the presence of the gods....

—Owen Wister

Toroweap Overlook, Grand Cañyon National Park   *Cathedral in the Desert, Glen Canyon National Recreation Area (overleaf)*

In the hot stillness, punctuated now and then by the cascading scale of the canyon wren's song, we gradually became aware of a new sound. Little by little, it grew louder as we drifted along, and when we reached the bend where Soap Creek comes in from the right and the Colorado veers left, it exploded in a sudden, mighty crescendo. This was the voice of a major rapid, a constant, pulsing growl of such mesmeric power that the sound seemed to possess a substance of its own.... On either side of, and below, the tongue—that V of smooth water that projects downstream from the mirror-slick stretch at the head of the rapid—all was madness. Ten-foot waves leaped up and curved back on themselves in perpetual violence....

Once on the tongue, I faced downstream and braced myself, as my boat gathered speed with every yard. Then with a great hiss the first wave was upon us. The boat reared skyward, perched on top for an instant like the cap on a mushroom, then plunged into the trough beyond. Up, down, up, down, we hurtled. Jets of spray stung our faces; the roar of the rapid drowned out our voices. I strained at the oars to keep the boat headed into the waves and avert a broach which could lead to an upset. Gradually, I pulled to the right, out of the main current; and at last, my lungs heaving from the effort and my arm muscles knotting with cramps, I reached the eddy and rowed triumphantly to the beach. Between hitting the tongue and hitting the beach, perhaps a minute had elapsed....

—François Leydet

So long as Americans continue to value both the useful and the beautiful qualities of the landscape, so long as they cherish both fields and wilderness, so long as they are beset by both nostalgia and wanderlust, for so long will the problems of conflicting demands arise.

In such dilemmas, we usually speak of compromise. The compromises are never true ones, for beauty does all the compromising. Splitting the difference between utility and beauty again and again ultimately will leave nature next to nothing; half of a half of a half of a half is a sixteenth.

Suppose someone were to counter a suggestion to compromise on the Colorado dams by saying, "Certainly. Two dams block the river today, Hoover and Glen Canyon. You may keep Hoover, if you will remove Glen Canyon Dam and let Glen Canyon begin its return to the world of beauty.

"Ridiculous!" is the only possible reaction. And for so long as such a statement is ridiculous, the cause of the American landscape is a losing battle, to be fought from barricade to barricade, but always backward.

When will the tide turn?
——Daniel B. Luten

293

Middle Granite Gorge at Granite Falls

There may be some ... who believe without question that any and all forms of construction and development are intrinsic goods, in the national parks as well as anywhere else. ... There are some who frankly and boldly advocate the eradication of the last remnants of wilderness and the complete subjugation of nature to the requirements of—not man—but industry. This is a courageous view, admirable in its simplicity and power, and with the weight of all modern history behind it. It is also quite insane. ...

—Edward Abbey

The power of wonder and the unknown are intangibles we must cherish if we are to comprehend our problems. In them was the wellspring of our dawning culture, and from it the first significant expressions of man's mind. ...

If wonder is one of man's great potentials, playing a major role in the progression of his thinking and knowledge, and unspoiled nature a means of invoking it, here is reason enough for preservation. The stature of man has increased because of beauty, harmony, and the challenge of mystery, not through ugliness, warped and twisted psychosis, and divorcement from the natural scene. While wildness may be only one facet of the entire complex it can never be forgotten in surveying man's relationship to the universe. ... Should the time ever come when we allow our engrossment with comfort and technological progress to erase our longings to the point where we no longer dream of an unspoiled world, then I fear for America. ...

—Sigurd Olson

Druid Arch, Canyonlands National Park

The wilderness and the idea of the wilderness is one of the permanent homes of the human spirit. Here, as many realized, had been miraculously preserved until the time when civilization could appreciate it, the richness and variety of a natural world which had disappeared unnoticed and little by little from Europe. America was a dream of something long past which had suddenly become a reality.

That most of it is no longer a wilderness is no cause for regret. But it is a cause for congratulation that the four centuries and more which have passed since Columbus set sail have not been long enough to permit men to take over the whole continent as completely as they long ago took over Europe. And that fact is responsible for an important part of the difference which still exists, spiritually as well as physically, between the Old World and the New. The frontier, so long an important influence on the temper of the American, no longer exists. But ... the continent can still boast a spaciousness, a grandeur, a richness and a variety which a European can hardly imagine until he has seen it.

These are things which other nations can never recover. Should we lose them, we could not recover them either. The generation now living may very well be that which will make the irrevocable decision whether or not America will continue to be for centuries to come the one great nation which had the foresight to preserve an important part of its heritage. If we do not preserve it, then we shall have diminished by just that much the unique privilege of being an American. . . .

—Joseph Wood Krutch

The Colorado River at Granite Falls, Grand Cañyon National Park

THE CHARACTER AND GEOLOGIC HISTORY OF THE GRAND CANYON DISTRICT

CLARENCE E. DUTTON

Abridged from Clarence E. Dutton's Tertiary History of the Grand Canyon District,* *the first geological study of the canyons of the Colorado and still recognized as a classic. Footnotes have been added by the present editor.*

I: *The Plateau Province*

In numerous works upon western geology those features which give the Plateau Province its distinct character have been the subjects of extended description. . . . The province is capable of subdivision into component districts, each of which, while preserving the plateau features, has peculiarities of its own. . . . The interest in this remarkable province no doubt culminates in that portion of it which drains into the Grand Cañon of the Colorado. This is the westernmost—perhaps we may say the southwesternmost—portion of the Plateau country. North of it rise the High Plateaus of Utah; to the eastward are the central regions of the Plateau Province; and to the southward and westward is a sierra country. . . . Upon the west the district terminates abruptly upon the brink of a great wall . . . along the great escarpment which overlooks the rugged sierras and desert. From the very foot of that wall the calm repose of the strata with horizontal surfaces changes at once to the turmoil of flexed beds and jagged mountain crests. It is a portion of that trenchant boundary line which separates the topography of the Plateaus from that of the Great Basin and of the region south of the Great Basin so sharply that we may almost hurl a stone from one region to the other. It is not so obvious where the eastern limit should be drawn. The Grand Cañon receives from the north the drainage of four distinct plateaus: the Sheavwits, Uinkaret, Kanab, and Kaibab. East of these lies a fifth, the Paria Plateau, which drains into the Marble Cañon, and the Marble Cañon is but the prelude to the Grand Cañon. Structurally the Paria Plateau is quite similar to the others; it has shared in their history and evolution, and its topography is substantially the same in many respects, though not in all. It differs from the rest mainly in lying at a lower level and in the fact that the greater portion of its surface is covered with Triassic rocks, while the others present an almost unbroken expanse of Carboniferous beds. These two facts run off into consequences which are very interesting in themselves, but which often mar the simplicity which is presented to the mind in the study of the Grand Cañon district, as limited to the other four plateaus. . . .

If we were content to discuss merely the existing topography, the northern boundary would soon be chosen at the base of the Vermilion Cliffs, where the splendid succession of terraces ends and the broad expanse of the desert begins. But the geologist, looking beyond the visible present into the past, seeks for history and the process of evolution. The history of the Grand Cañon district is a remarkable one, and its few remaining records are in great part disclosed to us in the terraces which lead up to the High Plateaus. These terraces may be regarded as the appanage of either district—as the common ground where the threads of their respective histories are interwoven. . . .

The southern boundary of the district is a continuation of the western boundary. The grand escarpment which overlooks the sierra country to the west stretches southward across the Colorado, preserving identical features as far as . . . thirty or forty miles south of the river. . . . The great mural termination of the Carboniferous platform which constitutes the surface of the district slowly changes its trend south of the river and at length follows an east-southeasterly course through eastern Arizona. There, as at the Grand Wash, the surface of the country descends at once from the horizontal platform into a lower country, apparently identical in its topographic and geologic features with the Great Basin and with the terrible desert along the lower courses of the Colorado. . . .

The four plateaus thus far named, all lie upon the northern side of the Colorado. They are for the most part divided by distinct lines and only here and there shade into each other. The westernmost is the Sheavwits Plateau. Its western boundary is a gigantic escarpment, overlooking the Grand Wash, a broad and deep valley descending from the north to the Colorado, and reaching the river at the mouth of the Grand Cañon. This "wash" carries the drainage from a considerable area lying to the northwestward, and also from the western wall of the plateau. No river runs there, but only occasional deluges of mud, whenever the storms from the southeast are flung against the lofty battlements and break in torrents of winter rain. The plateau wall had its origin in a great fault along the course of which the country east of it has been hoisted several thousand feet above the country on

Monographs of the United States Geological Survey, Government Printing Office, Washington, 1882.

the west. . . . From the crest of the escarpment the plateau has a very gentle slope towards the east and northeast, for a distance of about thirty miles. . . . The eastern limit of the Sheavwits is at the foot of the Hurricane Ledge, one of the most striking of the strong geological and topographical features of the region. The profile of the country, which has gradually declined from the western verge of the Sheavwits, suddenly leaps upward 1,600 to 1,800 feet. Here begins the Uinkaret Plateau.

It is the narrowest of the four but is strongly marked in its features. Its southern portion has been the scene of basaltic eruptions of considerable magnitude, though far inferior in extent and mass to those of other districts around the borders of the Plateau Province. But they are very interesting in consequence of their connection with other features of the plateau and with their history. The cones and *coulées* are in an excellent state of preservation, and some of them have a singular freshness and an aspect of great recency. The positions of many of the basaltic masses, amid the stupendous scenery of the great chasm and its tributary valleys, are highly impressive and suggestive. . . . The western boundary of the Uinkaret is the Hurricane Ledge, which preserves its features throughout the entire length of the plateau and continues far beyond it with increasing emphasis to the northward. The eastern boundary is not so persistent. It consists in part of the Toroweap fault, which is a strong feature in the vicinity of the Grand Cañon, but diminishes northward and finally dies out about eighteen miles from the chasm. North of this there is no structural and no resulting topographical feature separating the Uinkaret from the next subdivision.

The Kanab Plateau is the broadest of the four and the least pronounced in its features. It is a simple monotonous expanse, without a salient point to fix the attention, save one. This is a magnificent side cañon, cutting through its central portion and opening into the heart of the Grand Cañon. . . .

Next in order, east of the Kanab Plateau, rises the Kaibab. It is typical in its form, being nearly flat upon its summit and terminating in lofty battlements upon its eastern and western sides. It is much higher than the other three plateaus and has an elevation of 7,500 to 9,300 feet. Its broad surface is clothed with magnificent forest, opening in grassy parks, which during the summer are gay with flowers of rare beauty and luxuriance. It is a paradise to the explorer, who, weary of the desert, wanders with delight among its giant pines and spruces, and through its verdant but streamless valleys. This plateau is an uplift between two great displacements, throwing in opposite directions. Towards the north these converge, and near the little village of Paria, at the base of the Vermilion Cliffs, the western fault merges into the eastern and the plateau ends there in a cusp. The western fault in its southern portion splits into three, which die out upon the brink of the Grand Cañon or hard by it. The eastern displacement is a monocline of huge proportions, and about mid-length it divides into two parallel monoclines, which die out upon the southern side of the Colorado. The total length of the Kaibab from the Vermilion Cliffs to the Grand Cañon is about 90 miles, and its width at a maximum about 35 miles.

East of this plateau the surface drops quickly across the great monocline, nearly four thousand feet, upon the region draining into the Marble Cañon. This region is divisible into two parts, a northern and a southern. The former, named the Paria Plateau, is a terrace of Triassic strata, scored with a labyrinth of cañons but otherwise featureless so far as its summit is concerned. It terminates abruptly towards the south by a line of cliffs, describing a semicircle convex southward. They are an extension of the Vermilion Cliffs, and their position, projecting far in advance of the main line, is very instructive when viewed in connection with the grand erosion of this part of the Plateau Province. Their profiles drop upon a lower platform which extends far to the southward, hot, dreary, and barren to an extreme degree. Diagon-

ally across this lower platform lies the course of the Marble Cañon, which in depth and grandeur is surpassed only by the Grand Cañon.

Still eastward, and more to the northward, is another large plateau, the Kaiparowits, nearly equal to the Kaibab, both in area and altitude. It reaches out from the southern cape of the Aquarius, extending to the Glen Cañon of the Colorado. . . .

Thus far the description has been confined to regions lying north of the Colorado. Upon the southern side is an expanse of plateau land equally extensive. Those well-marked boundaries which subdivide the district north of the Grand Cañon into individual plateaus do not appear upon the southern side, or else appear in such changed relations that they cannot serve the same purpose. The country which drains from the south into the cañon really has no subdivisions but is a single indivisible expanse, to which the name of Colorado Plateau has been given. Its strata are very nearly horizontal, and with the exception of Cataract Cañon and some of its tributaries, it is not deeply scored. Low mesas, gently rolling and usually clad with an ample growth of pine, piñon, and cedar; broad and shallow valleys, yellow with sand or gray with sage, repeat themselves over the entire area. The altitude is greater than the plateaus north of the chasm except the Kaibab, being on an average not far from 7,000 to 7,500 feet. . . .

Fifty or sixty miles south of the river rise the San Francisco Mountains. They are all volcanoes, and four of them are of large dimensions. The largest, San Francisco Mountain, nearly thirteen thousand feet high, might be classed among the largest volcanic piles of the West. Around these four masses are scattered many cones, and the lavas which emanated from them have sheeted over a large area. . . .

II: *The Geological History*

We may now attempt the somewhat difficult task of extracting the history of the Grand Cañon district. . . . Of the earlier Paleozoic[1] conditions prevailing in the Plateau Province we know as yet but little. Already many perplexing problems have arisen which will require much study to solve, and their solutions promise to be extremely difficult. Within the boundaries of the province exposures of rocks older than the middle Carboniferous are very few and far between. Those which have received attention hitherto are confined to the Uinta Mountains and the lowest depths of the Grand Cañon. Limiting our attention to the latter region, we find beneath that system of strata which we have thus far treated as Carboniferous[2] a great variety of beds which range in age from the Archæan[3] to the Devonian.[4] Throughout the Kaibab and Sheavwits divisions we find the so-called Carboniferous resting sometimes upon highly metamorphic schists of undoubted Archæan age, sometimes upon the eroded edges of strata which have yielded . . . Silurian[5] fossils. . . . In general, the rocks classed as Carboniferous rest upon the Archæan, while the older Paleozoic beds come in only at intervals. The contact is always unconformable and usually in a high degree. The horizontal Car-

[1]*215,000,000 to 550,000,000 years ago. During this period, the great middle portion of North America was an enormous basin, part of the time lowlands and part of the time almost completely submerged by inland seas. In its earlier phase, this Paleozoic basin (which included most of the American Southwest) was covered by a series of sedimentary deposits to a thickness of several thousand feet; in the region of the Grand Canyon District, these were principally fine limestones.*

[2]*Deposited during the latter half of the Paleozoic era, when areas of swampland were buried under layers of clay.*

[3]*The period of earliest known life, 1,600,000,000 to 2,000,000,000 years ago.*

[4]*The middle period of the Paleozoic era, 350,000,000 years ago.*

[5]*390,000,000 years ago.*

boniferous beds appear to have been laid down upon the surface
of a country which had been enormously eroded and afterwards
submerged. In the Grand Cañon this single fact is indicated to
us throughout the length of a long, narrow, and tortuous cut
thousands of feet in depth. . . . With the Carboniferous began that
long era of deposition which extended without any real break
into Tertiary[6] time. The record of each period seems to be complete in the strata, and the deposition was apparently continuous
over the area of the Plateau Province taken as a whole, though
here and there we may detect evidence of a brief interruption in
some small areas. There are some general facts connected with
this process of accumulation of strata which merit special notice.

(1) The strata of each and every age were remarkably uniform
over very large areas and were deposited very nearly horizontally.
In the interior spaces of the province we never find rapid incre-
ments or decrements of the strata. They do indeed vary in thickness, but they vary in the most gradual manner. Around the old
shore lines, however, which form the present borders of the Plateau country, we find the volumes of the strata much larger than
elsewhere. But as we depart from them towards the heart of the
province, we observe, in the course of two or three leagues, a considerable diminution in their thickness, and thenceforward the
attenuation is so slow that we discover it only by comparing cor-
relative sections many leagues apart. Very analogous is the constancy of lithological characters. As we trace the individual beds
from place to place, we find their composition to be as persistent
as their thickness. The sandstone of a given horizon is always and
everywhere a sandstone, the limestone a limestone, the shale a
shale. Even the minuter structure of the beds is similarly maintained, and features which are almost abnormal are equally constant. The Jurassic and Triassic sandstones[7] are everywhere cross-
bedded after their own marvelous fashion. The singular cherty
limestones at the summit of the Carboniferous are quite alike on
the brink of the Grand Cañon, at the junction of the Grand and
Green rivers, and in the borders of the great Black Mesa at the
south. The curious Shinarump conglomerate is the same in the
Pine Valley Mountains, in the terrace at Kanab, at the base of
the Echo Cliffs, and in the Land of the Standing Rocks. The
lower Triassic shales and upper Permian[8] shales, with their gorgeous belts of richest colors and beautiful ripple marks, and with
their silicified forests, have hardly varied a band or a tint from
the brink of the Sheavwits to the pagoda buttes of western Colorado. . . .

All of these strata seem to have been deposited horizontally.
Even the base of the Carboniferous has a contact with unconformable rocks beneath, which was but slightly roughened by hills
and ridges. In the Kaibab division of the Grand Cañon, while the
great body of Carboniferous strata was horizontal, we may ob-

serve near the brink of the inner gorge a few bosses of Silurian
strata rising higher than the hard quartzitic sandstone which
forms the base of the Carboniferous. These are Paleozoic hills,
which were buried by the growing mass of sediment. But they are
of insignificant mass, rarely exceeding two or three hundred feet
in height, and do not appear to have ruffled the parallelism of
the sandstones and limestones of the massive Red Wall group
above them.

(2) Another consideration is as follows: as we pass verti-
cally from one formation to another in the geological series, we
observe the same diversity of lithological characters as is found
in other regions. The limestones occur chiefly in the lower Carboniferous, and in very great force. At the summit of the Carboniferous also are seven to eight hundred feet of calcareous strata.
But in the Mesozoic system[9] limestones are rare, and constitute
but a very small portion of the volume. By far the greater part
of the entire stratigraphic column is sandstone, and the various
members of this class show great diversity of texture and composition. Some are excessively hard adamantine quartzites; very
many are common sandstones in massy beds. By small gradations
these pass into sandy shales, containing more or less argillite,
and such shales form a large proportion of the bulk of the Permian and Trias. These shales in turn pass into marly beds, which
have vast thickness in the Cretaceous[10] and form a considerable
portion of the Eocene.[11] Beds of gypsum are also frequent, forming thin separating layers in the shaly divisions, and sulphate of
lime is a very important ingredient of the arenaceous strata from
the base of the Carboniferous to the summit of the Jurassic. . . .

Thus it will be noted that while the strata are remarkably
homogeneous in their horizontal extensions, they are very hetero-
geneous in vertical range. And this heterogeneity is found not
only in the chemical constituents, but also in the texture and in
the mechanical properties of hardness, compactness, and solu-
bility. This consideration is an important one, since upon it
depends the result which is obtained by the attack of the eroding
elements—the architecture of the cliffs and profiles.

(3) Another general fact of importance is that during the
Mesozoic ages the surface of deposition was maintained very
nearly at sea-level throughout the entire province. With regard
to the Carboniferous strata it does not yet appear that the same
was true. . . . The lower Carboniferous strata (Red Wall group)
consist chiefly of limestones, and the overlying lower Aubrey
group corresponding to the coal measures is a series of sandstones of exceedingly fine texture and often gypsiferous. There is
a notable absence in these beds of signs of very shallow water,
such as ripple marks, cross-bedding, coarse clastic material,
and littoral remains, organic or otherwise. . . . On the other
hand, there is no reason to suppose that the depth was at all

[6]*7,000,000 to 55,000,000 years ago.*

[7]*Deposited 165,000,000 to 190,000,000 years ago.*

[8]*The last period of the Paleozoic era, 215,000,000 years ago.*

[9]*The era extending from 60,000,000 to 190,000,000 years ago.*

[10]*95,000,000 years ago.*

[11]*55,000,000 years ago.*

SHEAVWITS PLATEAU.   Hurricane Fault.   UINKARET PLATEAU.   Mt Trumbull   Toroweap   KANAB PLATEAU.

profound. It is rather by contrasting the total absence of the signs of very shallow water with the presence of decisive signs of it in the Mesozoic and Permian that we are drawn to the inference of somewhat greater marine depths in the early and middle Carboniferous.

In the upper Aubrey series we come upon some indications of shallow water, and from the base of the Permian upwards these are ever present. In the Permian, Trias, and Jura we find instances of those peculiar unconformities by erosion without any unconformity of dip in the beds. Perhaps the most widely spread occurrence of this kind is the contact of the summit of the Permian with the Shinarump conglomerate which forms the base of the Trias. Wherever this horizon is exposed this unconformity is generally manifest. Between the base of the Permian and the summit of the Carboniferous a similar relation has been observed in numerous localities, and there is a similar instance in the lower Trias. . . .

These occurrences and others point decisively to the inference that during the great era of accumulation, lasting from the closing stages of the Carboniferous to the Eocene, the surface of deposition never varied far from sea-level, and now and then the waters retreated from it, but only for very brief periods. On the whole the deposition proceeded almost continuously. It necessarily follows that in the long run the underlying beds sank deeper and deeper as the newer ones were piled upon them. . . .

When we reach the Cretaceous age we find that a little more light may be thrown upon the physical condition of the province. . . . So large are the areas where this series is the surface of the country, and so readily does the mind restore it to the places from which it has been denuded, that we feel almost as if we saw this great formation in its entirety. Wherever we turn in the Plateau Province, the Cretaceous tells us the same story. All over its extent it is a lignitic and coal-bearing formation. We find coal or carbonaceous shales from the base of the series to the summit. Very abundant also are the remains of land plants in recognizable fossils, and these fossils occur not only in the carbonaceous layers but in the sand-rock and marls as mere casts or impressions of wood and leaves. Intercalating with these are many calcareous layers which yield marine mollusca in the lower and middle Cretaceous, and brackish water mollusca in the upper Cretaceous. . . .

At the close of the Cretaceous[12] important vertical movements were inaugurated, which finally revolutionized the physical condition of the region. Around the borders of the Plateau Province some important flexures were generated at this epoch, and portions were uplifted sufficiently to undergo a large amount of denudation. Perhaps the most striking instance of this is the one described in the work on the High Plateaus extending from the eastern and southern flanks of the Aquarius southward to the Colorado. This area consists of Jura-Trias strata, from which the

[12]*Which occurred about 94,000,000 years ago.*

Cretaceous had been eroded before the deposition of the Tertiary. Beneath the lava-cap of the Aquarius, the lower Eocene may be observed resting upon the Jurassic sandstone, and a little further westward it lies across the basset edges of the Cretaceous. Southeastward from the Aquarius and along the course of the Escalante River, the same relation is inferred to have existed, but the great erosion has swept everything bare down to the Jura-Trias, and the evidence of the extension of the Eocene here is mainly indirect. But the two monoclines are in full view, between which the Escalante platform was hoisted, and their age is unquestionably pre-Tertiary and post-Cretaceous. These relations are repeated in many other localities, and they indicate to us very decidedly that the Cretaceous closed amid important disturbances.

Still the deposition of strata was not yet ended. It went forward with seemingly undiminished rapidity, but under circumstances somewhat different from those hitherto prevailing. Soon after the advent of the Eocene, the waters became fresh and remained so until they disappeared altogether. . . .

The Plateau Country formed one continuous lake south of the Uinta Mountains. The vertical movements which followed the close of Cretaceous time shut it off from access to the sea. If we are at liberty to go on as we have done and to draw broad inferences from the drainage channels concerning the mode of evolution, we can very quickly frame a theory of the distribution of those vertical movements. Thus we know that during Cretaceous time the Plateau area was wide open to the ocean towards the southeast, or towards the Gulf of Mexico. For the Cretaceous system stretches from the heart of the province clear across New Mexico and into Texas, with no other interruptions than some short mountain ranges (themselves largely composed of Cretaceous strata) and such gaps as have very plainly been produced by Tertiary erosion. Let us assume that at the beginning of the Eocene, or very soon thereafter, the western and northwestern part of New Mexico was uplifted slightly more than regions either east or west of it, the axis of elevation trending nearly north and south. The effect would have been to make an almost, if not completely, closed basin of the Plateau Country.

It should seem that the passage from the brackish water to the fresh water condition was quite sudden, and as the same is true of widely extended areas outside of this region, we are apparently obliged to assume that the movement of which this was a result affected the entire western portion of the continent, and that it was one of elevation. A considerable number of large lakes being formed, the next process was the desiccation of these lakes and the evolution of river systems. So long as the region occupied a low altitude, this process . . . would be very protracted. Before a large lake can be drained, its outlet must be cut down. But several causes in the present instance would combine to render this action very slow and feeble. The elevation being small, the declivity and consequent corrasive power at the outlet must be correspondingly small. Moreover, the waters issuing

West Kaibab Fault   No I   East Kaibab Minocline   KAIBAB   Devonian Silurian and Archæan, unconformable   PLATEAU.   Sea Level

from a large lake contain little or no sediment; and sediments — sand, grit, etc. — are the tools with which rivers chiefly work in corrading their beds. Corrasion by clear water is an exceedingly slow process.

It is not surprising, therefore, to find that the lakes produced by the first action of the elevating forces persisted for a very long time. This persistence is a general feature of the Eocene lakes of the West. The Plateau lake seems to have been one of the largest and most enduring, for it did not wholly vanish until the close of the Eocene. The volume of sediment accumulated upon its bottom was very large, ranging from 1,200 to more than 5,000 feet in thickness, and these deposits represent Eocene time exclusively. Here we are confronted by the same paradoxes as those we encountered in viewing the Cretaceous condition of the region: a tract which is rising yet sinking; a basin which is shallow, which receives great thickness of deposits, and yet is never full.

At length we detect evidence of the gradual cessation of deposit and of the progressive upheaval of the country. . . . The final desiccation of the lake began in its southern or southwestern portions, and . . . the lake shrank away very slowly towards the north, finally disappearing at the base of the Uintas at the close of Eocene time. . . . Upon the floor of this basin, as it emerged, a drainage system was laid out. Such a drainage system would necessarily conform to the slopes of the country then existing. Taking the supposition already made, that the uplift was somewhat greater upon the eastern than upon the western side of the province, the configuration of the principal drainage channels would be very much like that now existing. The trunk channel would flow southwestward and westward, while the tributaries would enter it on either hand very much as the larger and older tributaries now do. The affluents on the south side are the San Juan, the Little Colorado and Cataract Creek, which seem to be due to just such an original surface. On the north side of the Colorado, the arrangement of the tributaries also seems to conform to the assumption. . . . The argument here adopted concerning the origin of the drainage system affords little scope for discussion. Rivers originated somehow. It seems almost a truism to say that they originated with the land itself, and that their courses were, in the first instance, determined by the slopes of the newly emerged land surface. . . .

With this period began the great erosion, which has never ceased to operate down to the present time. Concerning the details of that process we know but little, and we can only guess at its general character during the earlier stages. Erosion is here associated with a large amount of uplifting, and we may conjecture that as the uplifting went on, the inequalities produced by erosion became greater and greater, the valleys grew deeper, and the intervening mesas stood in higher relief. This is merely an application of the general law that the higher the country, the more deeply is it engraved by erosion and the greater are its sculptured reliefs. . . .

During the latter part of Eocene time, the degrading forces no doubt made great progress in destroying and removing the Mesozoic deposits, which I have shown originally covered the region. We cannot, however, in this district find any epoch separating the later Eocene from the Miocene. To all intents and purposes they formed here a single age. From the time when

the great erosion was begun until it reached a certain stage . . . not a single detail can be pointed to beyond the principal facts of elevation and erosion. We are, so to speak, passing a long interval of time in the dark. We must, therefore, stride at once from the middle Eocene to an epoch which may be provisionally fixed at the close of the Miocene. . . .

At the close of the Miocene, or thereabout, the greater part of the denudation of the Mesozoic should have been accomplished. . . . The whole region had, during the long interval of Eocene and Miocene time, undergone a great amount of uplifting, and this progressive movement itself constitutes a condition highly favorable to corrasion; for the higher the country rises, the greater become the declivities of the streams, and of those factors which determine a stream to corrrade, the most potent by far is declivity. While the country rises, therefore, the streams are making the reliefs greater — are creating larger surfaces of edgewise exposure and longer and steeper slopes. Thus, every advantage is given the agents of erosion.[13]

The area thus exposed to rapid denudation was a very large one, and the corrasion of streams apparently went on over its entire expanse, without any very great local variations of amount, except perhaps near the borders of the watershed. While the normal method of decay is expressed in the recession of cliffs, we must not suppose that single and comparatively straight lines of cliffs stretched across the whole region and slowly wasted backwards. We should rather conceive of the platforms as being cut by a labyrinth of drainage channels, ramifying over their entire expanse, and as being attacked within and without and all around — as a great conflagration spreads through every square, street, and alley of a city. . . .

At the epoch when the cutting of the present Grand Cañon began, no doubt the district at large presented a very different aspect from the modern one. While the greater part of the denudation of the Mesozoic had been accomplished, there were some important remnants still left which have been nearly or quite demolished in still more recent times. The basalts of the Uinkaret and Sheavwits have preserved some extensive Permian outliers, and even these must have shrunken greatly by the waste of erosion during the long period occupied in the excavation of the Grand Cañon. Although the basalts which cap Mounts Logan and Trumbull are certainly very ancient and are older than the faults — or at least older than a great part of the faulting movements — there is no assurance that they are as old as the origin of the present cañon. Still I do not doubt that they go back nearly as far, and they are certainly much more ancient than the inner gorge at the Toroweap. At the time of their outpour large masses of Permian strata overspread the region. These are not limited to the few remnants described on the Uinkaret, but we find the summit of the Permian similarly protected by basalt in many widely separated localities. . . . Thus there is a general accord of testimony that at the period of the older basaltic eruptions very large bodies of Permian strata lay upon the Carboniferous platform. In truth, it seems as if the summit of

[13]*This helps to explain the nature of the river system today, for the Colorado and its tributaries were superimposed upon a rising land; strong or weak, they maintained their original courses — which today have no relation to the structures which they cross.*

Echo Cliffs.

MARBLE CAÑON PLATFORM.

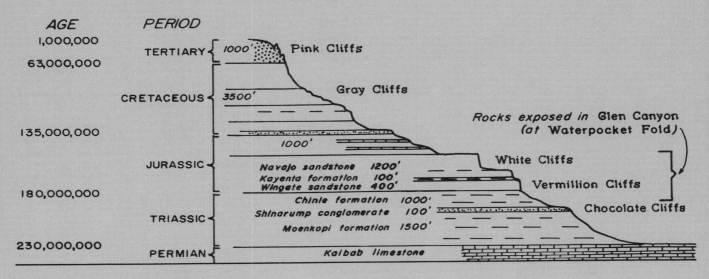

AGE	PERIOD		
1,000,000	TERTIARY	1000'	Pink Cliffs
63,000,000			
	CRETACEOUS	3500'	Gray Cliffs
135,000,000		1000'	*Rocks exposed in Glen Canyon (at Waterpocket Fold)*
	JURASSIC	Navajo sandstone 1200'	White Cliffs
180,000,000		Kayenta formation 100' / Wingate sandstone 400'	Vermillion Cliffs
	TRIASSIC	Chinle formation 1000' / Shinarump conglomerate 100'	Chocolate Cliffs
230,000,000		Moenkopi formation 1500'	
	PERMIAN	Kaibab limestone	

Rock sequence in southern Utah

the Permian then constituted the surface of the country, just as the summit of the Carboniferous does now. The fact that the older basalts, wherever found, rest upon the same geological horizon, viz. the summit of the Permian, suggests to us the further inference that the region near the river was then flat and destitute of deep cañons and valleys such as now exist there and, therefore, destitute of great hills, buttes, or mesas. The meaning of this is a base-level of erosion. The rivers could not corrade, because they had reached for the time being their limiting depth in the strata. . . .

We may then conjecture the reason for the somewhat remarkable fact that the same stratum or geological horizon is almost everywhere the surface of the interior platform of the Grand Cañon district. Before the last upheaval we may conceive of the region occupying the situation of a base-level in which the inequalities which may have existed were obliterated. . . . The amount of upheaval which took place at the epoch in question may be roughly estimated. It varies from two to three thousand feet. The uplifting forces then suspended operations for a time, and the drainage system sought a new base-level. During this paroxysm of upheaval the outer chasm of the Grand Cañon was cut, the river corrading down to the level of the esplanade in the Kanab and Uinkaret divisions, but below that horizon in the Kaibab. The corrasion was probably done as rapidly as the country rose, or very nearly so. At first we may presume that only a narrow gorge was cut—like the upper portion of the Marble Cañon. But the river found its base-level after the uplifting ceased, and the cañon slowly widened by the recession of the cliffs. . . .

We come now to the final upheaval, which has brought the region to its present condition. The Colorado River, after re-

maining without corrasion at the level of the esplanade of the Cañon during the greater part of Pliocene time, at length resumed the operation of sinking its channel. A new paroxysm of upheaval set in; the faults increased their displacement; the volcanic vents reopened. This time the upheaval was greater than before, amounting probably from three to four thousand feet. The narrow, inner gorge at the Toroweap was swiftly cut, and it is in this respect a type of the lower deeps of the entire cañon. Everywhere the rapid corrasion of the deeper gorges is revealed. The epoch at which this latest upheaval took place is no doubt a very recent one in the geological calendar. It began most probably near the close of the Pliocene. . . .

No doubt the question will often be asked, how long has been the time occupied in the excavation of the Grand Cañon? Unfortunately there is no mystery more inscrutable than the duration of geological time. On this point geologists have obtained no satisfactory results in any part of the world. Whatever periods may have been assigned to the antiquity of past events have been assigned provisionally only, and the inferences are almost purely hypothetical. In the Plateau country Nature has, in some respects, been more communicative than in other regions and has answered many questions far more fully and graciously. But here, as elsewhere, whenever we interrogate her about time other than relative, her lips are sternly closed, and her face becomes as the face of the Sphinx.[14]

[14]*While geologists have refined techniques considerably since Dutton's day, the matter of geologic time is still subject to uncertainty. Scientists today estimate that Grand Canyon's beginnings occurred somewhere between 12,000,000 and 7,000,000 years ago. All agree on one fact, however: the Canyon is still being formed.*

ACKNOWLEDGEMENTS

The author wishes to thank the following individuals and organizations for their help, without which it would have been quite impossible to have created this book: Gale B. Johnson, who assisted in much of the basic research; Helen Hosmer, who opened her own extensive files for my use; John Barr Tompkins, of the Bancroft Library, University of California; Robert A. Weinstein, whose photographic research assistance was indispensable and who provided many rare items from his own collection; Robert M. Utley, historian for the National Park Service; Merrill D. Beal, chief park naturalist at Grand Canyon National Park; John A. Hussey, western regional historian for the National Park Service; Emery C. Kolb, of the Kolb Brothers Studio, Grand Canyon; Dr. Edwin H. Carpenter, of the Huntington Library, San Marino, California; Ruth I. Mahood, of the History Division of the Los Angeles County Museum of Natural History; Dr. Carl S. Dentzel, director of the Southwest Museum, Los Angeles; Mrs. Alys Frese, of the Western Collection of the Denver Public Library; Josephine Cobb and Joe D. Thomas of the National Archives, Washington, D.C.; Jim Hart and William J. Williams, regional information officers for Regions 2 and 3, respectively, of the Bureau of Reclamation; and Patricia Hoar, of the Henry J. Kaiser Memorial Library, Oakland, California.

Most of all, thanks to Wallace Stegner, whose encouragement, faith, ready advice, and assistance are, the author hopes, adequately reflected in the book. If *The Grand Colorado* is "for" any one person, it is for him.

NOTES ON THE AUTHOR AND CONTRIBUTORS

T. H. Watkins, general author and editor of *The Grand Colorado*, is currently editor of *The American West* magazine. His articles on history and conservation in the West have appeared in *The American West*, the Sierra Club *Bulletin*, and *Cry California*, and he is the author of three additional books: *San Francisco in Color* (1968), which initiated the "Profiles of America" series by Hastings House; *Here Today: San Francisco's Architectural Heritage* (with Roger Olmsted, 1968); and *California in Color*, another entry in the "Profiles of America" series, which will be issued in the spring of 1970. A recent article in *Cry California*, "Infernal Machines on the Public Lands," has become a major force among federal agencies for a revision of policy in regard to the recreational use made of public and National Park lands in the West.

Wallace Stegner has for most of his writing life been deeply concerned with varying aspects of the West—its history, its exploitation, its beauty, and its influence on the nature and quality of man's life—a concern that has led him to translate the western experience into literature in numerous short stories and many novels, including *The Big Rock Candy Mountain* (1943), one of his earliest and best works. His conservation writings, a representative sampling of which is currently available in *The Sound of Mountain Water* (1969), long ago became an important articulation of the American conservation movement, and his historical books have placed him with the handful of western historians who have enlarged an understanding of the importance of the West to the whole of the American narrative. Among his historical studies is *Beyond the Hundredth Meridian* (1954), a biography of John Wesley Powell, portions of which have been reproduced in *The Grand Colorado*.

Robert C. Euler is chairman of the Center for Anthropological Studies at Arizona's Prescott College and formerly chairman of the Department of Anthropology at the University of Utah. He has published a great many articles and scientific papers in archeology, ethnology, ethno-history, and cultural change, and is the author (with Henry F. Dobyns) of *The Ghost Dance of 1889 among the Pai Indians of Northwestern Arizona* (1967). He also is anthropological consultant to the Hualapai Tribe of Arizona. "The Canyon Dwellers" first appeared as an article in the May, 1967, issue of *The American West*, and much of the expeditionary research for the article was financed by the Arizona Power Authority, Dr. and Mrs. F. E. Bumgarner, the National Science Foundation, and Prescott College.

Paul S. Taylor, professor emeritus of economics at the University of California, Berkeley, is an economist, agrarian historian, and nationally recognized authority on reclamation law, farm labor history, and the uses of irrigation in the West. His background includes service as a consultant to the secretary of the interior and the Bureau of Reclamation between 1943 and 1952, and his more recent consulting service for the federal government has taken him to such diverse regions as Viet Nam and Peru. He is the author of numerous articles on the use and misuse of water in the West, including "Water, Land, and People in the Great Valley" (*The American West*, March, 1968); and was author (with photographer Dorothea Lange) of *American Exodus: A Study in Human Erosion* (1943), a text-and-photograph examination of the dust bowl years in the West that some have compared to John Steinbeck's *The Grapes of Wrath*. *American Exodus* will be republished soon in a revised edition by the Yale University Press and the Oakland Museum.

Helen Hosmer came by her knowledge of the gap between dream and reality on California's farms directly; after graduation from the University of California at Berkeley in 1929, she spent several years working in the field for the Farm Security Administration, aiding in the establishment of migrant workers' camps in the Great Valley. The conditions she encountered led her to found *The Rural Observer*, a newspaper devoted to improving the living and working conditions of the labor force that made possible the profound wealth of California's agri-industry. Among those she worked with in this enterprise were John Steinbeck, Dorothea Lange, Paul S. Taylor, and Carey McWilliams, Jr. In later years, she served as an editor, free-lance radio writer, historian, radio news commentator, and editorial assistant for *The American West*. "Triumph and Failure in the Colorado Desert" first appeared as an article in the winter, 1966, issue of *The American West*.

Robert A. Weinstein, graphics editor of *The American West* and an authority on the history of photography in the United States, is a research associate in western history for the Los Angeles County Museum of Natural History and special consultant on photographic archives and history to the Special Collections Department of the library of the University of California at Los Angeles. He is also a graphics designer and artist whose illustrations appeared in a two-volume edition of Richard Henry Dana's *Two Years Before the Mast* (1964), and the author (with Russel E. Belous) of the more recent *Will Soule: Indian Photographer at Fort Sill, Oklahoma, 1869–74* (1969). "The Photographer and the River" was adapted from "Image Makers of the Colorado Canyons," an article written with Roger Olmsted that appeared in the May, 1967, issue of *The American West*.

Roger Olmsted, a former curator of the San Francisco Maritime Museum, served as editor of *The American West* from 1966 to 1969, and is now an associate editor of the magazine and curator of the History Division of the new Oakland Museum. In addition to many articles on maritime history and the history of photography in the West (including "Image Makers of the Colorado Canyons"—see above), he is the author of *Scenes of Wonder and Curiosity* (1962), an edited selection of excerpts from Hutchings' *California Magazine, 1856–1861*, and *Here Today: San Francisco's Architectural Heritage* (with T. H. Watkins; 1968), as well as articles for the conservationist quarterly, *Cry California*.

Roderick Nash is assistant professor of history at the University of California at Santa Barbara and a scholar who has devoted much of his study to the history of the conservation movement in America and the influence the wilderness has had on the formation of American character, an interest best revealed in his much-acclaimed *Wilderness and the American Mind* (1967). He is a river-runner of considerable experience, and his many trips down the Colorado River have inspired in him a deep concern over the river's fate that is reflected in his contribution.

William E. Brown, Jr., is eminently qualified to discuss the quality of the parklands of the West. He has been with the National Park Service for more than twelve years and for six of those twelve was an editor and writer for the service's public information programs. He later became regional historian for the southwest region—an area that encompasses many of the parks described in "The Parklands of the Colorado"—and for the past year has been a special assistant in environmental affairs to the director of the southwest region.

PICTURE CREDITS

Inside front cover, inside back cover: U. S. Geological Survey.

PART ONE
Pages 14, 15: Henry G. Peabody photograph; courtesy of Robert A. Weinstein.

Chapter One: Page 18: Library of Congress. Page 19: Robert C. Euler. Pages 22, 23: Huntington Library, San Marino, California. Pages 25, 26: Robert C. Euler.

Chapter Two: Page 28: History Division, Los Angeles County Museum of Natural History. Pages 30, 31: Bancroft Library, University of California, Berkeley. Page 33: Frans Halsmuseum, Haarlem, The Netherlands; courtesy of *American Heritage*. Pages 36, 37: Museum of the American Indian, Heye Foundation. Pages 42, 43: The British Museum Manuscript Collections, London, England. Pages 44-47: Library of Congress. Pages 48, 49: Bancroft Library. Pages 50, 51 Library of Congress. Page 52: Bancroft Library. Pages 54, 55: The British Museum Manuscript Collections; courtesy of *American Heritage*. Page 56: Bancroft Library.

Chapter Three: Page 60: Henry G. Peabody photograph; courtesy of Robert A. Weinstein. Page 67: Bancroft Library. Page 71: History Division, Los Angeles County Museum of Natural History.

Chapter Four: History Division, Los Angeles County Museum of Natural History, Pages 90–104: U. S. Geological Survey. Pages 114–123: Earth Sciences Library, University of California, Berkeley. Pages 127, 132: Los Angeles County Museum. Pages 138–141: Huntington Library.

PART TWO
Pages 142, 143: U. S. Geological Survey.

Chapter Five: Pages 146, 149: Dorothea Lange photographs; courtesy of Paul S. Taylor. Page 150: Title Insurance and Trust Company, San Diego, California. Pages 152–163: Dorothea Lange photographs; courtesy of Paul S. Taylor.

Chapter Six: Page 164: U. S. Bureau of Reclamation. Page 166: Imperial Valley District Association; Leo Hetzel, photographer.

Page 167, top: History Division, Los Angeles County Museum of Natural History; bottom, Bancroft Library. Pages 168, 169: Bancroft Library. Page 171: U. S. Bureau of Reclamation. Pages 172–175: Henry J. Kaiser Memorial Library, Oakland, California. Pages 176: U. S. Bureau of Reclamation. Page 177: Bancroft Library. Pages 178–180: U. S. Bureau of Reclamation. Page 182, top: U. S. Bureau of Reclamation; bottom: Henry J. Kaiser Memorial Library. Page 183: Henry J. Kaiser Memorial Library. Page 184: U. S. Bureau of Reclamation. Page 185, top: U. S. Bureau of Reclamation; bottom: Henry J. Kaiser Memorial Library. Pages 186–191: Henry J. Kaiser Memorial Library. Page 192: U. S. Bureau of Reclamation. Page 193: Henry J. Kaiser Memorial Library. Pages 194–196: U. S. Bureau of Reclamation. Page 197: Map by John Beyer, drawn after a map by A. Morgan. Page 198: Charts by James Stockton. Pages 199–203: U. S. Bureau of Reclamation.

Chapter Seven: Page 204: Paul S. Taylor. Page 208: History Division, Los Angeles County Museum of Natural History. Page 209: Title Insurance and Trust Company, San Diego, California. Page 210: Los Angeles County Museum, Page 211: Title Insurance and Trust Company. Pages 214, 217, 218: Los Angeles County Museum. Page 219: Imperial Valley District Association photograph; Leo Hetzel, photographer. Page 220: Southern Pacific Company. Page 221: Imperial Valley District Association.

PART THREE
Pages 222, 223: Henry G. Peabody photograph; courtesy of Robert A. Weinstein.

Chapter Eight: Pages 226–230: Maude Collection, History Division, Los Angeles County Museum of Natural History. Page 233: Henry G. Peabody photograph; courtesy of Robert A. Weinstein. Page 234: Huntington Library. Pages 235–237: Los Angeles County Museum. Page 238: Huntington Library. Pages 240, 241: Robert A. Weinstein. Pages 244, 245: Emery C. Kolb, Grand Canyon, Arizona. Page 248: Huntington Library. Page 249: Maude Collection, Los Angeles County Museum. Page 250, left: National Park Service, Grand Canyon, Arizona; right, Emery C. Kolb. Pages 251, 255: Emery C. Kolb. Page 256: National Park Service. Page 257: Maude Collection, Los Angeles County Museum.

Chapter Nine: Page 258: Robert A. Weinstein. Page 260, left: National Park Service, Grand Canyon, Arizona; right, Sierra Club, San Francisco. Page 262: Bancroft Library. Pages 263–271: Sierra Club.

Chapter Ten: Page 275: Map by Owen Welsh.

Appendix: Page 303: Chart by James Stockton.

INDEX